McGraw-Hill Series in Political Science

Joseph P. Harris, *Consulting Editor*

THE UNITED NATIONS
Background, Organization, Functions, Activities

McGraw-Hill Series in Political Science

JOSEPH P. HARRIS, *Consulting Editor*

THE UNITED NATIONS
Background, Organization, Functions, Activities

AMRY VANDENBOSCH

Professor of Political Science
University of Kentucky
Lexington, Kentucky

WILLARD N. HOGAN

Professor of Political Science
State University Teachers College
New Paltz, New York

FIRST EDITION

1952

McGRAW-HILL BOOK COMPANY, INC.
New York   Toronto   London

THE UNITED NATIONS
Background, Organization, Functions, Activities

Library of Congress Catalog Card Number: 52-6006

To SERGEANT ROBERT LESLIE JONES, JR.
and his comrades
of many nations

INTRODUCTION

In this book Professors Vandenbosch and Hogan have presented a lucid picture of the complex factors involved in the processes and practices of international organization. Their approach to the multiple facets of this activity appears to be quite objective and sufficiently comprehensive to furnish an over-all evaluation of the progress already achieved.

It is almost impossible, indeed, for any author dealing with the dynamic problems of international relations ever to give a completely up-to-date report. Events flow swiftly, and frequently a decision on mere procedure does affect basically the course of action on a fundamental substantive matter. Professors Vandenbosch and Hogan have come close to that desirable goal and do not fail to indicate where students can find follow-up information concerning items of particular interest.

The literature on the United Nations and the Specialized Agencies already embraces hundreds of titles, outside the publications of the intergovernmental bodies themselves; yet, not all phases of their evolution have been fully surveyed nor submitted to the fire of critical appraisal.

One point that this book brings forth with particular emphasis is that all activities of the United Nations system are part of an indivisible aim: collective security. This collective security, as the authors point out, is the hope of all men, and the human being thus again becomes the principal subject of international action.

Opinions may differ as to the actual degree of world community achieved from the political standpoint, but there seems to be a general agreement on the geophysical and geodemographic unity of the world emphasized and made more evident by scientific and technological progress.

There may also be different evaluations of the prospects of building supranational as distinguished from international bodies through which the world can strive for higher forms of organization.

But there can be no controversy over the fact that all peoples, whatever may be their individual philosophy, even those now under the temporary sway of nationalism, wish to be a part in the broader picture of the world as their best insurance against being by-passed by the process of advancement towards a better and more peaceful life.

And, as the authors show, they are all playing a role, through the development of national foreign policies, based upon the expressions of public opinion and their contributions to a worldwide supranational public opinion.

Public opinion always acts reasonably when well informed. This book of Professors Vandenbosch and Hogan will contribute to its enlightenment.

B. COHEN
Assistant Secretary-General
for Public Information
The United Nations

NEW YORK, N.Y.
March, 1952

PREFACE

The purpose of this book is to give an explanation of the United Nations—its background, organization, functions, and activities. This volume has been prepared primarily for introductory college classes studying the United Nations system or contemporary international organization. It is hoped, however, that the book will also be useful in connection with discussion groups and as a source of information for those who wish to go beyond the daily paper or the weekly news digest.

The United Nations is as broad in scope as the whole field of international relations, and it is involved in a tremendous variety of important activities. The Charter provides for an extensive organization, which has become more ramified in the course of the few years of the institution's development. The authors have attempted to present a systematic treatment of both the complex structure and the varied activities in a single, convenient volume. This is no small task, and we shall be gratified if the performance is moderately successful.

Footnotes have been kept to the minimum, in the feeling that they are more bothersome than helpful to the less advanced student as well as to the general reader. Neither have we considered it wise, for two reasons, to include a comprehensive bibliography. First, a complete list of all the documents and other publications by and about the United Nations would by itself fill a small volume. Second, such a bibliography is unnecessary for our purposes. A student or reader who wishes to engage in further pursuit of any particular point may consult the bibliographic note on page 331. The sources indicated there will give him additional information, and many of them include bibliographies which can be used for still further investigation.

Many of the chapters were used in preliminary form in classes at the University of Kentucky, Berea College, and the State University Teachers College at New Paltz. The comments and questions of our students were very helpful, and we are grateful for this opportunity of a "trial run." We wish to express our thanks to William Agar, Acting Director, Special Services Division, U.N. Department of Public Information, who was always willing to answer questions and to assist us in locating materials concerning the United Nations. Mrs. Glennalou Ryan provided an invaluable service in typing, checking details, and helping with preparation of the manuscript. There is strong reason for us to include the conventional recognition of the encouragement and assistance of our wives, Mary Belle Vandenbosch and Hildur C. Hogan. All statements, interpretations, and possible errors, however, are the responsibility of the authors alone.

The period covered by this book runs to September 1, 1951. It has been possible to consider developments after that date to only a slight degree.

AMRY VANDENBOSCH
WILLARD N. HOGAN

LEXINGTON, KY.
NEW PALTZ, N.Y.
April, 1952

CONTENTS

LIST OF TABLES

PART I
BACKGROUND

Chapter 1

WORLD COMMUNITY

When Wendell Willkie made his famous flight around the world in 1942, he returned with the conviction that "our thinking in the future must be world-wide." [1] The experience of traveling 31,000 miles in forty-nine days impressed Mr. Willkie with the fact that moving from one continent to another had become quick and easy. In terms of travel time there are no longer any distant points in the world. The peoples of the Far East are as close to America as California is to New York by the fastest trains. The establishment of close contacts among the peoples of the world means that their activities affect one another and that their problems have become matters of mutual concern.

Human society has been revolutionized by modern technology, especially in the fields of transportation and communication. At the beginning of the nineteenth century it took eight to ten days for a passenger to go by stage from New York City to Boston, a distance of about 250 miles. When the American federal government was being established in 1789 it took two weeks to notify George Washington that he had been elected President and to bring him from Mount Vernon to New York. Today the same trip could be made in four hours by train or in one hour by airplane. The difficulties of travel to the southern and western parts of the United States were even greater, and at some seasons of the year communication practically ceased over large parts of the country. When the colonial settlers first came to North America a perilous ocean voyage of weeks or months was involved. Now overnight flights to Europe are a matter of routine.

Less than 150 years ago, inventors who attempted to build steam railways were considered to be demented. A school board in Ohio probably reflected the popular attitude when it refused the use of its schoolhouse for a discussion of railroads in these words: [2]

You are welcome to use the schoolhouse to debate all proper questions in, but such things as railroads are impossibilities and rank infidelity. There is nothing in the

[1] Wendell Willkie, *One World,* Simon and Schuster, New York, 1943, p. 2.
[2] Quoted in Avery Craven and Walter Johnson, *The United States: Experiment in Democracy,* Ginn, Boston, 1947, p. 339.

word of God about them.   If God had designed that His intelligent creatures should travel at the frightful speed of fifteen miles an hour, by steam, He would have clearly foretold it through His holy prophets.   It is a device of Satan to lead Immortal souls down to Hell.

Henry Clay, in his speech [3] attacking President Andrew Jackson for vetoing the bill to improve the Maysville (Kentucky) road, said that it took his family four days to reach Lexington from Maysville in April, 1829.   This is a distance of about 68 miles, and the trip now takes about an hour and a half by automobile.

There has been a tremendous acceleration in the speed of contacts between peoples living at distances from each other.   In the span of two lifetimes the attitude toward speed of travel has changed from considering 15 miles an hour a frightful speed, to debates over whether a human being could travel 60 miles an hour and live, to nonchalant acceptance of a jet airplane pilot's report that he "loafed along" at 500 miles an hour.

Communication developed even more rapidly in terms of speed.   Before the telegraph, telephone, radio, and television, messages could be transmitted over long distances only as fast as the most rapid form of transportation.[4] Now messages travel around the world at about 186,000 miles a second, the speed of light.   A man making a speech in a large auditorium can be heard thousands of miles away before the sound waves of his voice reach the rear rows of the audience before him.   The famous case of the Battle of New Orleans has often been cited to illustrate the differences in human affairs occasioned by the rate of communication.   That battle was fought on January 8, 1815, when the War of 1812 had been over for fifteen days.   The Treaty of Ghent ending the war had been signed on December 24, 1814.   It was not until February 19, six weeks after the battle and almost two months after the war was over, that General Jackson heard the news!   In contrast, the Security Council of the United Nations passed its first resolution in the Korean case less than twenty-four hours after the outbreak of the fighting.   Without the modern technology of communication, the war might have been over before the Security Council learned that it had started.

Rapid transportation and instantaneous communication have made possible a network of world-wide contacts and interests.   The most distant parts of the globe are no longer the personal concern merely of an occasional traveler. Millions of people, including the fictional but all-important "average citizen," find woven into their daily lives the consequences of modern technology, which has shrunk the barriers of time and distance to a small fraction of their former significance.   There is quick, easy, and frequent contact by large numbers of people between countries and continents.   The news from all over the world

[3] This was Clay's speech on the American System given at Cincinnati, Ohio, Aug. 3, 1830.
[4] Except for a few localized exceptions like smoke signals, flashing lights, etc.

can be known everywhere the same day it happens. The social pattern of small, isolated communities has given way to a large and complicated system, no part of which can be insulated from the impact of events vital to distant parts of the world.

Development of the new pattern of human society has been accompanied by a fundamental change in the impact and implications of warfare. It is no longer possible to restrict the fighting to the actual battle area and to make a sharp distinction between combatants and noncombatants. Modern war is industrialized war. The worker in a munitions factory is as important as the soldier at the front. The transportation system and the food supply become the object of enemy attacks. The purpose is to break the resistance of the enemy by destroying his capacity for waging war. Any technique that tends to destroy or undermine the ability to resist is brought into use. Air power, high explosives, atomic bombs, guided missiles, and other devices make it possible to strike the enemy far behind the lines. This means "total war," involving mass destruction of lives and property and threatening the very survival of civilization. Under these circumstances a resort to war anywhere is of concern everywhere, simply because the forces inherent in modern technology create a situation in which no country can hope to remain immune from the spreading effects of war. The most powerful country cannot, by itself, assure its own security. Protection from the ravages of war can be found only in cooperative action for the prevention of war. Recognition of this fact lies at the heart of the belief that "our thinking in the future must be world-wide."

Modern society is also characterized by a condition of economic interdependence. Because of the uneven distribution of important mineral resources, the differences in climate, and the diversity of soils, no one country can produce all the commodities which are necessary for its economic life. Moreover, the advantages of geographic specialization make it profitable for countries to exchange products rather than try to be self-sufficient. This situation naturally affects some countries more than others. Great Britain, for example, is dependent upon imports for a large part of its food supply, and half its people would starve if they were cut off from the rest of the world. The vital importance of this fact may be appreciated by recalling that at the beginning of World War II the British government boasted of an increase in food stocks which would make it possible to hold out against blockade for four months.

The United States and the Soviet Union, because of their large size and varied resources, are not as economically dependent as smaller countries. Yet they, too, are highly dependent upon other countries. The United States consumes about 50 per cent of the world's output of tin, but that important metal is not mined in this country. The United States produces practically no nickel, while Canada alone accounts for about 90 per cent of total world production. The United States is the greatest consumer of rubber; until recently, most of the supply was imported, but the dependence on overseas areas in this respect has been reduced by the ability to produce synthetic rubber. The "American standard of living" owes much to American resources and productivity, but without imports it would lack coffee, tea, bananas, cola drinks, chocolate, spices, high-quality steel, telephones, most cosmetics and pharmaceuticals, and many other familiar products. Vastly inferior and more expensive substitutes would have to be found for materials which now go into the making of automobiles, newspapers, electrical appliances, soap, paint, insulation materials, machinery of all types, and large numbers of other articles. It is somewhat ironical that a country as powerful as the United States is deficient in some thirty materials which are essential to the prosecution of war.

The condition of economic interdependence also applies to exports. Much of the industrial and agricultural production of the United States is tied to the availability of export markets. Even before World War II, the United States sold abroad about 10 per cent of its annual production. In the case of certain staple industries this ran as high as 20 or even 50 per cent. The foreign market is important to many industries, such as automobile and machinery manufacturers. This situation also applies to agriculture, since the United States exports great quantities of wheat, tobacco, hog products, and cotton. When measures to combat the depression were being considered by Franklin D. Roosevelt's first administration, Secretary of Agriculture Wallace pointed out [5] that a self-contained United States

must be prepared to make permanent the retirement of from 40 to 100 million acres of crop-land. Forty million if we take out good land; 100 million if we take out the worst. Furthermore, if we continue year after year with only 25 or 30 million acres of cotton in the South instead of 40 or 45 million acres, it may be necessary after a time to shift part of the southern population, and there is a question as to just what kind of activity these southern farm laborers should engage in. We will find exactly the same dilemma, although not on quite such a great scale, in the corn and wheat belts.

It has been estimated that in 1937 some 2,400,000 Americans made their living by producing industrial and agricultural goods for export, not counting transport workers and others whose jobs depended indirectly on the export trade.[6]

The great importance of world trade for the domestic prosperity was well stated by Secretary of State Cordell Hull in a speech before the American section of the International Chamber of Commerce on May 2, 1933, in these words: [7]

[5] H. A. Wallace, *America Must Choose*, World Affairs Pamphlets, No. 3, Boston, 1934.

[6] Horace Taylor and Harold Barger, *The American Economy in Operation*, Harcourt, Brace, New York, 1949, p. 679.

[7] U.S. Department of State, *Press Releases*, May 6, 1933, p. 315.

The far-reaching effect of international trade is further understood when we recall that South American countries must export and sell abroad from 30 to 50 percent of their total production; England must sell 25 percent; New Zealand, 40 percent; and Japan 45 to 60 percent. America must look mainly to those countries to purchase her surplus foodstuffs, raw materials and finished manufactures. A slump on the international market, from any cause, with a serious drop of export prices and values, can cause a breakdown of the entire economic and financial life of these large exporting countries, and this in turn paralyzes our own foreign trade and, as has been demonstrated during this panic, cuts in half our production and trade among ourselves here at home, and throws millions of wage-earners out of employment. . . . The view is eternally sound that our home market must be supplemented by a growing foreign trade for the purpose of stable and desirable domestic prosperity.

The technological and economic factors are by no means the only ones which involve a substantial degree of interdependence among the peoples of the world. All aspects of human culture transcend national boundaries and reflect cosmopolitan tendencies in human activities, interests, and loyalties. There is a common heritage of law, philosophy, literature, art, religion, and ethical ideas throughout Western civilization. Latin America has a common heritage from Latin Europe. If any American is tempted to think of a self-sufficient United States, let him reflect that the very language in which he expresses himself is a borrowed product. If any Soviet citizen is similarly tempted, let him remember that Karl Marx was a German who worked in England. The truth is that the culture of every country is strongly, if not predominantly, affected by conditions and movements in other parts of the world. Furthermore, such influences are not limited to the fact of historical derivation. Each country is a part of the world. Hermit kingdoms and iron curtains may distort that fact, but they cannot eliminate it.

The great religions of the world claim adherents in many lands. Christianity, Judaism, Mohammedanism, Hinduism, Confucianism, and the others have a world-wide influence. They represent forces which must be taken into account by the policies of national governments. Roman Catholics in Eastern Europe and Zionists in the United States are only two examples of this fact. Science also is international in its scope and outlook. It has produced its wonders by a process of cross-fertilization between the ideas and work of men and women from many countries. To wrap science in the trappings of nationalism is to suffocate it.

Every important social and economic group is to some extent opposed to another group within the same country and sympathetic to a similar group in other countries. Employers' associations share with labor unions the tendency to organize across national frontiers. A scientist, a chess player, or a vegetarian may have more in common with fellow enthusiasts in distant lands than he does with many people in his own home town. The ideological conflict of the modern world is in itself evidence of the fact that social groups and interests are not organized exclusively along national lines. The idea of completely independent, self-sufficient, and homogeneous countries is a legal fiction which receives some psychological encouragement from the abstractions of maps with their boundaries and separate blocks of color. The legal fiction and the map, however, do not encompass the whole of the social reality.

Recognition of contemporary technological, economic, and cultural conditions and forces leads to the question, "Is there a world community?" It is not easy to give a simple and definitive answer to this question. If "community" is taken in the biological sense of a population in a habitat, the earth can be viewed as one habitat and the human race is certainly one species. If, on the other hand, one considers the idea of locality and relative smallness of area as the test, the world as a matter of definition could not be one community. If communication is the essential factor, as it would seem to be by etymology, then the existence of modern technology means that there is a world community. However, the psychological or subjective criterion, that a community exists when its members feel that they "belong together," is not satisfied. Nor can a world community be said to exist if emphasis is placed on the idea of group likeness and homogeneity in contrast to other groups which show greater cultural divergencies.

The question, "Is there a world community?" is partly one of fact and partly one of terminology. There is a substantial degree of interdependence, and the processes of social interaction operate on a world-wide scale. Quick and easy communication has linked many countries, and its universal extension is technically feasible.

The sense of world community exists, but only in an embryonic stage since it is the dominant loyalty of a very small fraction of the world's population. Narrow nationalism remains a powerful force, and attitudes based on feelings of antagonism are prevalent and ominous. In this situation, the best answer to the question posed above is to consider community as a matter of degree,[8] and to say that a world community does exist. It is, however, much more advanced in its technological phases than in its psychological and governmental aspects. Man's capacity to organize the developing world community lags behind the forces which are creating that community. It becomes necessary, therefore, to consider the problem of world political organization in terms of the state system and the development of international cooperation.

[8] This is consistent with the historical development of the term in the social sciences. See the article on "Community" in the *Encyclopedia of the Social Sciences*, Vol. 4, Macmillan, New York, 1931.

Chapter 2

THE STATE SYSTEM

The state is the basic unit of international society. There have been several different kinds of states in the course of history, and the one most commonly prevailing today is the nation-state. There is a strong tendency to assume that the peoples of the world have always grouped themselves together in nation-states, but nothing could be further from the truth. Indeed, the present state system is hardly three centuries old. The state, it must be remembered, is not an end in itself, but an instrument in meeting man's social needs. Thus the form and character of the state have changed with man's shifting economic conditions and social needs.

ANCIENT STATE SYSTEMS

Two forms of the state were found in ancient times: the city-state and the empire. The first was found in a very high degree of development among the ancient Greeks.[1] The modern city is a trading, manufacturing, and residential community, and its political boundaries do not extend beyond this community. It is highly dependent economically and does not enjoy political autonomy. The Greek city-state, however, was not exclusively an urban or trading center; it also included within its political boundaries a considerable area of the surrounding territory. From the point of view of this discussion the most important characteristic of the city-state was its political independence. The Greek city-states, large and small, were regarded as independent sovereign bodies, each the equal of the other. They were to a large degree economically self-sufficient. An important characteristic of the Greek city-state was the amazing vigor of its political life. The whole of the individual's life was identified with the city; he was bound to it by religious, cultural, and economic as well as political ties. This many-sided intimate relationship of the citizen to his city produced an intense patriotism for his small but independent political community.

A number of independent political units living in such proximity must in-

[1] City-states were also found in Italy in antiquity and in Italy and northwestern Europe in the Middle Ages.

9

evitably develop some form of interstate relations.   In fact, the Greek city-states developed an incipient interstate order not unlike that of our modern international system.   They were united by a large network of treaties regulating their commercial and other relations.   Diplomatic representatives were exchanged, and the principles and practices governing such exchange reached a high degree of development.   Certain practices, like the immunity granted to diplomatic agents, were remarkably like those found in modern international law.   There were laws regulating the rights of aliens, the right of asylum was recognized, and on occasion aliens were naturalized.

Two important fundamental ideas in the field of international relations have come down to us from the Greek city-states, namely, those of arbitration and of confederation.   While often resorting to arbitration as a means of settling disputes with one another, they failed to utilize this method in times of great crisis.   The devastating Peloponnesian War, which left both parties exhausted and Greece an easy prey to the foreign conqueror, might not have been fought had Sparta accepted the offer of Pericles to submit the dispute to arbitration.   The numerous leagues and confederations of Greek history indicate that the Greeks also had the idea of confederation on the basis of equality. The Greeks were apparently the first in the history of Europe to establish an interstate council.   The amphictyonic council, though primarily a religious body, is of great significance in the history of international relations, for it attempted to limit the cruelties of war by laying down certain rules of warfare. Among the measures prohibited under the rules were the cutting off of a city's water supply and the annihilation of populations.

Another striking similarity between the ancient and medieval city-state and the modern national state is the strong tendency toward imperialism exhibited by both.   Like the modern national state the Greek city-state sought to attain a high degree of economic self-sufficiency.   But with the increase of population, resulting from the growth of commerce and industry, self-sufficiency became steadily more difficult, if not impossible, of attainment. Large quantities of necessities had to be imported.   This economic condition soon reflected itself in the foreign policy of the city-states, as indicated by the desire to open foreign markets, the efforts to establish fortified trading posts in foreign lands, the multiplication of colonies, the attempt to levy tribute on foreign cities, and the frequent reduction of leagues to empires.   Athens under Pericles was reproached for having changed the Delian Confederation into a despotic empire, "enslaving her cities contrary to treaty." [2]

In spite of the fact that the Greeks were united by the bonds of race, religion, language, and customs, they failed to solve the problem of their inter-city relations.   Though they made truly remarkable progress in the rudimentary development of an international law and organization, they failed to impress their interstate system with unity and stability.   In this respect they forecast

[2] F. Melian Stawell, *Growth of International Thought*, Holt, New York, 1930, p. 22.

the same fatal inability of the nation-states centuries later. They failed to develop their interstate institutions far enough. The separate political entities were unwilling to subordinate their particular interests to the larger interests of all Greece. They exhausted themselves fighting each other and in the end were overcome by foreign foes.

The second form of political organization known to the ancient world was the empire, which had its origin in the conquest of a large number of principalities, small kingdoms, and city-states. While a few of the empires developed rather elaborate systems of imperial administration, most of them rested upon military despotism and quickly suffered disintegration. The Babylonian, the Persian, the Assyrian, the Egyptian, and the Macedonian were among the larger of the empires of the ancient Near East. Even among these states, whose underlying principle was dominance and not the free association of equals, some forms of interstate relations were present. Treaty relations were not uncommon among the units of the empire and between them and lesser states.

With Rome we have the development of a city-state into an empire that covered nearly all the Mediterranean region and extended its rule even as far as England. During the period of the empire, Rome dealt with other peoples on the basis not of equality but of subordination. The Roman Empire impressed order upon the world but at the expense of the liberty of the peoples it conquered. But even Rome made a contribution to the modern system of international law and organization. The development of international law in its formative period was greatly influenced by the Roman institution of the *jus gentium*. Since the traditional Roman law was applicable only to Romans, aliens were at first tried under their own laws. But when the magistrate had to apply laws to cases between Romans and non-Romans, or when there was no Roman law applicable in cases involving Roman citizens, he would seek a rule already common in the practice of most nations. This law, *jus gentium*, came to be understood as "the law which all men everywhere obey." At this stage it dealt with subject matter now known as private international law, or conflict of laws. Later *jus gentium* came to be identified with natural law, and later still, in the early Middle Ages, its use as a term became limited to that part of natural law which deals with *jus inter gentes*, that is, the law governing the relations between peoples, or international law. Aside from this the contribution of the Romans to international law and relations was slight.

THE RISE OF THE NATIONAL STATE

The fall of the Roman Empire was not immediately followed by the rise of the modern state. There was a long transition period of nearly a thousand years, during which the "state" actually disappeared from Western Europe. When the nomadic hordes from the north and northeast swarmed over the

Roman Empire a period of rapid disintegration set in. The state had once more to be built up within a primitive society. This long historical process can be only briefly described here.

Though the political unity of the Western world had been shattered, the spell of the former political universalism long continued to sway the medieval mind. The theory had ultimately, however, to yield before the facts. In the welter of barbarian disorder the primary need of the people was for protection, and to obtain it they turned to the strong man of the immediate neighborhood rather than to a distant shadow emperor. The strong man became the lord of the district. Imperial unity disappeared, and in its place came a hierarchy of knights, barons, counts, marquises, dukes, and kings. Each received his lands from the one next above him in the hierarchy, and in return was required to render military service and economic dues. At the base was the peasant, bound to the soil in serfdom. The distinction between public office and private property was lost; political power became identified with land ownership. The general result was the fragmentation of political power. Though the king was generally able to exact tribute, he was unable to enforce order in every district of his dominions. The local lords carried on war and diplomacy very much as if they were the sovereigns of independent states.

While Europe thus underwent a long period of economic and political disintegration, a strong cultural unifying agency remained in the Church. Christianity had been for a long time proscribed, but Rome finally had been compelled to come to terms with the new religion. Although the state had earlier been hostile to Christianity, it now gave it a favored position. The changed position of the Church had far-reaching effects on its character. Its rapid growth and preferred position soon enabled it to contest with the empire itself for supremacy. Since the people of the Middle Ages regarded themselves as Christians first, under the spiritual authority of the Papacy, they felt only a secondary loyalty to the temporal princes. As long as that attitude prevailed the Church had a powerful advantage over the secular authorities, for no ruler could long remain in power after he had been excommunicated by the Pope and his people enjoined from obeying him. Through the acquisition of vast areas of land the Church also enjoyed a large measure of temporal power. An institution of such universal influence necessarily exerted a strong cohesive force in an age of disintegration. It is not surprising therefore that the medieval Church rendered valuable services in the interest of internationalism. It sought to restrict the ravages of incessant warfare. By its declaration of the "truce of God" the Church forbade fighting on certain days of the week and in certain seasons of the year, and it endeavored constantly to extend the number of days of truce. Moreover, the Church forbade fighting in the vicinity of church buildings and against certain classes of the population, such as clerics, pilgrims, merchants, women, and peasants. The Church thus tried to abate the rigors of war and to alter its character, changing it from a private to a pub-

lic affair.   The Papacy also encouraged arbitration by serving as an arbitrator
in the settlement of several important disputes.   For example, the Pope acted
as arbitrator in the famous dispute between Portugal and Spain concerning
the boundaries of the areas in the New World which they claimed on the
grounds of discovery.

From the chaos of feudal society the nation-state of modern times gradually
emerged.   The thousands of loosely associated petty lordships of which feudal
society was composed were finally consolidated under the king to make the
monarchical, national state.   To this movement of unification the growth
of commerce and the consequent development of towns gave a tremendous
impetus.   The towns with their compact populations, their vigor and greater
economic and political strength became more than a match for the feudal
barons.   The chief interest of the burghers was in extending trade over a
constantly wider area, but the fragmentation of political power and the incessant warfare which accompanied it obstructed and depressed trade.   The
townsmen, therefore, joined forces with the king to break the political power
of the barons.   At this stage of historical evolution the new middle class
was the ally of the king in establishing the absolute monarchy, for a strong
central government able to keep law and order over the whole country was
clearly in its interest.   At a later date it led the movement for a limited,
constitutional monarchy.   Centralized control having been established, it demanded such share in political power as its steadily mounting economic power
seemed to justify.

The passing of feudalism and the emergence of the modern state is vividly
reflected in the writings of Machiavelli, an Italian statesman and diplomat
who lived from 1469 to 1527.   Machiavelli marks the close of one epoch and
the beginning of another.   The idea of a united Europe under an imperial
ruler did not interest him, and he was frankly and thoroughly nonreligious or
secular in his outlook.   He was passionately interested in the national unification of his native Italy.   He saw other countries unified under strong kings,
and since he believed that Italy could be unified only under a strong mon-
arch, he wished to advise the Italian prince on how to maintain and extend
his authority.   Machiavelli was a man of the world and based his advice on
observation and experience.   The prince who would be successful, he concluded, must stop at nothing.   He must be prepared to use not only physical
force and craft but, if the circumstances demanded it, even fraud and treachery.
The state was an end in itself and was not bound by the rules which govern
private morality.

The term "national state" has been used to describe the separate independent states which emerged from feudal society.   But what is the national state,
as contrasted with other forms of the state?   It is the union of nationality, or
nation, with the state.   What is the nation and how did it develop?   The
Middle Ages gave birth to the great peoples of Europe as we now know them

—the French, the Germans, the Italians, the Spanish, and the English. Some centuries later, as a continuation of this movement, nationalities developed in the remainder of Europe, the Americas, and more recently in Asia and limited parts of Africa. Each of these peoples emerged with a common language and a fairly definite national culture and became identified with certain geographic areas. In the course of time a very strong feeling of community interests developed. Just what the common qualities or definite interests are which produce this strong feeling of unity it is difficult to say. One may point to certain common elements, such as language, religion, territory, custom, race, and the tradition of a common political life, but no one of these is inseparable from nationality. The Swiss, Belgians, and Canadians have no common language, the Jews until recently had no common territory, the Indians have separated into two states, and it is highly doubtful whether there are any nations with a racial stock of a high degree of purity. In the last analysis a people are a nation if they believe that they constitute a nation, and that belief is the most important element in the situation or movement.

Though nationalism may be difficult to define or explain, there can be no doubt of the tremendous influence it exerts in the life of the modern world. Carlton J. H. Hayes, a leading American historian and student of the movement, calls it the "most significant factor in public life today." [3] The force of nationalism is illustrated first of all in the irresistible drive toward making state lines coincide with those of nationality, of establishing nationalities as political units. When a state is based upon nationality it is called a "national state." The movement to make the nation and the state one was of long duration, and the forces behind the movement are not yet spent. Two of the great nations of Europe, the German and the Italian, did not achieve political unification until the latter half of the nineteenth century. The present force of the movement can be seen in South Asia, where peoples are vigorously striving to achieve national unity. Nearly all the young nations of that region have since World War II won the struggle for political independence.

The movement did not, however, operate everywhere to enlarge the state. In multinational states, like those of Austria-Hungary, Turkey, and the British Empire, it operated to break up the larger units. When the movement tends to dissolve larger states into numerous small states, it is clearly operating counter to the economic forces and the technological developments of modern society, which are integrating constantly larger areas.

More significant even than the historical process set in motion by nationalism is the state of mind that generally accompanies it. The nationalist mentality exalts loyalty to the nation or the national state, making it superior to every other loyalty. In the Middle Ages, men were primarily loyal to their religion and their spiritual authorities; later, everything yielded before loyalty to the national state. A powerful American metropolitan daily journal for a

[3] *Essay on Nationalism,* Macmillan, New York, 1926, p. 1.

long time carried as its slogan at the top of the editorial column the words of
the American patriot, Stephen Decatur, "Our country, in her intercourse with
nations may she be right, but our country right or wrong." Men have been
filled with a holy zeal for furthering their country's "sacred mission" or realiz-
ing her "manifest destiny" and have unquestioningly and cheerfully laid down
their lives for their country. Because of these characteristics nationalism has
been compared to religion.[4]

THE NATIONAL STATE AND IMPERIALISM

The national state had hardly emerged before it set out on a policy of colonial
expansion. Commerce was instrumental in the formation of the nation-state;
thereafter, it strongly influenced, if it did not dominate, its policies. The
Dutch were still fighting for their independence when their government
chartered the East India Company to stake out a vast trade area in the
Far East. The movement of expansion which began in the early modern
period has continued intermittently, reaching its climax in the period just
preceding World War I. As a result of this movement nearly one-half of the
world's area came into a relationship of political subordination to a small group
of advanced powers. It becomes necessary briefly to examine the economic
and political forces behind this extraordinary movement.

With the growth of commerce a money economy arose and with it a scarcity
of gold and silver. Moreover, the rising national kings were rapidly increasing their expenditures, both in maintaining costly courts and in carrying on
wars or preparing for future ones. Under these conditions it was easy for the
king and his ministers to be misled into believing that the precious metals constituted a form of wealth more desirable than other forms. They, therefore,
bent every effort toward building up a large supply of gold in the national
treasury. One way of acquiring gold and silver was by mining it, either at
home or by the discovery and the exploitation of rich new mines in distant
lands. Spain became rich through the latter method. Most of the other
rising European national states had to content themselves with the indirect
method, the method of acquiring the precious metals through a large, profitable foreign trade. By stimulating exports and depressing imports a large
surplus trade balance was built up, which so-called "favorable" balance of international trade could be paid in gold and silver. This policy of stimulating
exports and depressing imports and of forcing the balance to be paid in gold
is called "mercantilism." In practice, it led to the application of the principle of monopoly to all phases of colonial trade. Only the nationals of the
mother country were permitted to sell in the market of the colony or to purchase raw materials or commercial luxuries there, and the carrying trade
between the mother country and the colony was likewise reserved for them.

[4] *Ibid.*, Chap. 4, "Nationalism as a Religion."

This monopoly of trade and shipping was enforced by very severe penalties —the confiscation of cargo and vessel, and sometimes even death.

In the beginning, the governments and the chartered trading companies had no desire for political control over the backward areas. They desired only trading monopolies, but they discovered that they could not safeguard these monopolies and obtain a lucrative trade unless they also governed, and so against their wishes even the trading companies became rulers over vast areas. The shift from a commercial to a territorial and political basis did not solve all the problems of the profit-minded companies. The more important ones steadily declined or got into difficulties, and in the end their governments had to take over their interests, assuming both liabilities and assets. Thus the powers of the Dutch East India Company were transferred to the Dutch government in 1798, while the British East India Company continued sixty years more before being taken over by the Crown.

Following the Napoleonic Wars there was a period of about a century during which the general interest in colonies declined. This waning interest was the result of several influences. France had lost an enormous colonial empire to Great Britain, and the latter in turn had lost her richest colonies by revolution. Spain likewise had lost almost a whole continent through independence movements. Of what profit were colonies if they could be retained only by costly wars and if their ultimate destiny was independence anyway? The free-trade doctrines of Adam Smith had gained wide popularity, and under their influence governments were steadily relaxing the restrictions on their colonial trade. With the growth of the industrial revolution domestic markets expanded enormously and the relative importance of colonial trade declined correspondingly. The French Revolution had also popularized certain liberal and humanitarian ideas which had a bearing on colonialism. All these forces had a share in producing a strong anticolonial movement from 1815 to about 1875.

A combination of forces caused imperialism to break out with renewed force in the third quarter of the nineteenth century. The industrial revolution led to a steady acceleration of production, with the result that the home market of most of the industrial countries seemed to have become saturated. The less advanced industrial countries began to raise their tariff walls to save the home market for their own less developed industries. As a result, pressure was brought to bear upon the governments of industrial countries to find an outlet for the ever-increasing volume of machine products. Improved means of transportation had lowered shipping costs so that goods could successfully be shipped over long distances. New inventions and the production of new goods led to an increased demand for tropical products such as cotton, rubber, and copra, while higher standards of living brought about a demand for other products like sugar, coffee, cocoa, tea, and bananas. Markets and raw products did not exhaust the needs of the industrialized countries. Machine production under a system of *laissez faire* led to great accumulations of capital which could no longer find a sufficiently profitable outlet at home to satisfy the hunger of the investors for dividends. Undeveloped countries offered higher returns on investments, but the owners of surplus capital were loath to invest their money in backward areas unless their investments were safeguarded by the existence of political control, preferably by the home government but at any rate by one of the advanced powers. Thus the chief economic forces operating almost unbridled in the industrial and capitalist society of the day pushed the governments in the direction of imperialism.

There were still other forces impelling toward imperialism. The new medical science, improved methods of sanitation, and hygiene steadily cut down the death rate. Though increased productivity of the machine enabled a given territory to support a larger population than before, there nevertheless developed an anxiety about the future. This fear of population pressure reinforced the economic forces making for imperialism. Psychological factors likewise played a part. While imperialism netted the average citizen nothing but an increased tax burden, he was nevertheless an ardent supporter of the aggressive imperialist policies of his government. Often the humbler the citizen the more eagerly he grasped at the expansion of his ego through the exploits and enhanced prestige of the state of which he was a citizen. As a result of these various forces, governments had the support of nearly every class in the state for their imperialist policies.

During this last recrudescence of imperialism, Africa, the islands in the Pacific Ocean, and large parts of Asia fell under some form of Western political control. Imperialism did not everywhere take the same outward form. Here it resulted in outright annexation, as in the case of the Philippines, Korea, and large areas of Africa; there, in the establishment of protectorates, as in the case of Egypt; elsewhere, in unequal treaties and extraterritorial rights, as in China; and still elsewhere, in temporary occupations and the control of customs, as in the Caribbean and Central America. Sometimes it took such vague and indefinite forms as spheres of influence and interests. Frequently there was a progression, a ripening of one form into another until the stage of complete annexation was reached.

The peak of colonial expansion was reached at about the first decade of this century. At that time nearly half the earth's surface and over a third of its population were under colonial rule. In terms of population Great Britain had the largest empire, followed by France, the Netherlands, Japan, Germany, the United States, Portugal, Belgium, Italy, and Spain.

The imperialism of the last years was self-destructive; it sowed the seeds of its own disintegration. The earlier imperialism sought primarily trade in the backward areas; the chief economic characteristic of the latter imperialism was the export of capital to these regions and the introduction there of the capitalistic system of production. This involved the construction of good roads and railroads, the development of rapid means of communication, and the introduction of a money economy where only barter within numerous small areas had existed before.   Western standards of administration were introduced at the behest of the new enterprises and education at the demand of the middle-class liberals in the mother country.   In brief, the introduction of the capitalistic system of production led to the growth of towns and an indigenous middle class, and brought about the same economic, social, intellectual, and political transformation which was the basic cause underlying the development of nationalism in the West.[5]

The penetration of Western influences developed a cultural defense reaction in the colony.   Since World War I the colonial world has been rocked from end to end by movements for national independence.   Because the movement in India was under the leadership of an unusual personality employing startling methods, the nationalist movement in that country for years engrossed world attention, but similar movements of varying intensity developed in Burma, Indochina, China, Korea, the Philippines, and Indonesia and is now developing in Africa.   The result has been a period of decolonization, beginning about the time of World War I.   The British Dominions first became equal partners of the Commonwealth with the United Kingdom; shortly after World War II, India, Burma, Ceylon, the Philippines, and Indonesia became independent.

The conclusion of World War I also saw the establishment of international supervision of the administration of former enemy territories.   This was a recognition of the principle that the government of undeveloped areas was a matter of international concern requiring some sort of international regulation, in so far as certain peoples were not yet ready for self-government.   The mandates system, as this arrangement was called, was converted into the trusteeship system under the United Nations.   In addition all members of the United Nations have, in ratifying the Charter, accepted very comprehensive obligations with respect to their dependencies.   They undertake to ensure the political, economic, social, and educational advancement of the people in their dependent areas and to prepare them for self-government.

CHARACTERISTICS OF THE MODERN STATE SYSTEM

We have seen how the political fragmentation of the Middle Ages finally yielded to a political reintegration, resulting in the formation of a new political unit, the country-state, which was to develop a century or two later into the nation-state.   After a century or more of struggle the king had acquired mastery over the cities and barons within his territory and freedom from Pope and emperor externally.   The king did not have long to wait for a justification and rationalization of the new state of affairs by a learned jurist.   In 1576

---

[5] N. J. Spykman, "The Social Background of Asiatic Nationalism," *American Journal of Sociology*, Vol. 32, pp. 396–411.

there appeared a book [6] by a French writer, Jean Bodin, in which the legal theory of the new state was expounded. This theory is noteworthy for the exposition of the doctrine of sovereignty. Bodin defined sovereignty as the "supreme power over citizens and subjects, unrestrained by the laws." The chief function of sovereignty is law-making, and since the sovereign is the source of law, he is not bound by it. While the sovereign is thus above the law he is not free from moral restraint; he is limited by obligations arising from natural and divine law. Moreover, the sovereign is morally bound to observe treaties with other sovereigns and contracts with his own subjects. While Bodin favored an absolute monarchy, he distinguished carefully between the state and the government or ruler and held that the possession of sovereignty was the characteristic of the state, regardless of the form of government.

The new states existed for a considerable time before they were actually recognized in a formal document. In the Treaty of Westphalia of 1648 the new states were for the first time recognized as the component units of the world's political organization. This treaty in effect gave the new society of national states a fundamental law. In this fundamental law the individual states were recognized as having certain characteristics, the two most important of which were sovereignty and equality.

Since Bodin the doctrine of national sovereignty has been restated and elaborated innumerable times. The doctrine received classic formulation in a much-quoted passage in one of Chief Justice Marshall's opinions.[7]

The jurisdiction of the nation within its own territory is necessarily exclusive and absolute. It is susceptible of no limitation not imposed by itself. Any restriction upon it, deriving validity from an external source, would imply a diminution of its sovereignty to the extent of the restriction, and an investment of that sovereignty to the same extent in that power which could impose such restriction. All exceptions, therefore, to the full and complete power of a nation within its own territories, must be traced up to the consent of the nation itself. They can flow from no other legitimate source.

It would be quite impossible to build a system of international law on the basis of a doctrine of sovereignty like that outlined above. Only chaos can obtain in a world of states each without responsibility to the other and none recognizing a higher law than that flowing from its own consent. Indeed, the first fruits of the doctrine of a world of separate states "unrestrained by law" was a long period of savage warfare and chaos. A brilliant Dutch jurist, Huig de Groot, who later became known as the father of international law, was shocked at the licentious conduct of the new states. "Throughout Christendom," he wrote, "I saw a license of which savages would be ashamed. Men rushed to arms on the most frivolous pretexts, and once war was declared there

---

[6] *The Republic.*
[7] *The Schooner Exchange v. M'Fadden,* 7 Cranch 116, 136 (1812).

was no respect for the laws of God or men, nothing but a riot of fury as though authorization had been given for every sort of crime."

Horrified by the license of the period, Grotius, the Latinized name by which de Groot is generally known, set out to prove "that there does exist a common law between nations," binding alike in war and peace. His great book, *The Law of War and Peace* [8] appeared in 1625, while Europe was being ravaged by the Thirty Years' War. Grotius insisted that there exists a universal standard of justice applicable to states as well as individuals, and he appealed to the statesmen of his day to make state practices conform to this higher law. The need of some restraint upon the licentious conduct of states was so generally felt that Grotius's appeal at once met with a vigorous response. Thus, before the new system of separate and sovereign states had been recognized in an international treaty, the forces for a new legal integration of the world had been set in motion.

The second characteristic of the modern state system is the equality of all its members. "No principle of general law is more universally acknowledged," said Chief Justice Marshall in an opinion over a hundred years ago, "than the perfect equality of nations. Russia and Geneva have equal rights." States are not, however, equal in population, area, economic strength, or any other of a number of practical tests that may be applied. In population they vary from a few hundred thousands to several hundred millions; in area the Soviet Union with a territory of more than eight million square miles stands out in sharp contrast to Luxembourg with about a thousand square miles. A system which ignored such actual inequalities by giving all states equal rights would not long endure. As a matter of fact, the modern state system does not accord all states equal rights. Reference may be made to two of the most outstanding examples of legal inequalities in international constitutional law. Under the Covenant of the League of Nations the large powers were granted permanent seats on the Council, while the small states had to be content with elective, rotating seats. The same system has been continued in the Charter of the United Nations. The International Labor Organization Convention likewise gives a favored position to the large powers. The exigencies of world politics naturally give the large powers a much greater influence in world politics than the smaller ones can hope to exercise. The only sense in which states can be said to be equal is in the protection of such rights as international law gives to all states. The weakest state is entitled to have its rights respected by the strongest.

The most striking characteristic of the modern state system is just this great inequality of states in practical world politics. This is so universally recognized that states are spoken of as first-, second-, or third-, and even fourth-class powers. A state's rank in world politics is dependent upon a combination of factors, among which population, geographical position, area, natural resources,

---

[8] The book was written in Latin under the title of *De jure belli ac pacis.*

economic development, social cohesion, tradition, and military strength may be listed. The cynic may say that it is only the last which counts in this rating of states, but it must be remembered that military strength is largely determined by the other factors named. The United States and the Soviet Union are today the two strongest states. They are frequently called superstates, while Great Britain and France are regarded as Great Powers. China was granted a Great Power position in the United Nations primarily because of its enormous population and its strategic position in Eastern Asia, especially in World War II. China has the area and population of a Great Power, but it is undeveloped industrially and lacks social cohesion and political unity. India now probably has a better claim to a Great Power position than China. Italy and Japan, both weak in natural resources, held a position among the Great Powers because of their population, geographical position, and military prestige. Their military expenditures, however, placed a terrific strain on their economic systems, and their position among the Great Powers was therefore a bit precarious.

The task of naming the states which rank as second-class powers becomes even more difficult, and to fix the rank of lesser states is practically impossible. Australia, Brazil, Canada, Poland, Spain, Rumania, Mexico, Czechoslovakia, Yugoslavia, Turkey, Argentina, Sweden, Belgium, and the Netherlands are among the states which may be listed as of secondary rank. Belgium and the Netherlands, though both small in area and population, are both very productive. Belgium administers a large and important colonial territory, and the Netherlands did so until recently.

The role which states play in international politics varies from time to time. Changes in technology, the exhaustion of certain key resources, a disastrous war, the loss of colonial empire, and political unification movements may affect the ranking of states in world politics. The unification of Germany and of Italy; the westernization of Japan in the last half of the nineteenth century; the defeat of Germany and the dissolution of the Austro-Hungarian Empire in World War I; the defeat of Italy, Germany, and Japan in World War II—all these brought about marked shifts in the power relationships of the states. Such shifts are always accompanied by a strain in world politics, as it destroys such balance of forces as exists at the moment.

The number of sovereign or independent states in the world at present is about seventy. There are a few small states, like San Marino, Liechtenstein, Andorra, and the Vatican City, whose position in the family of nations is so anomalous that they can hardly be included in the number of fully sovereign states. Liechtenstein, for example, was, in 1920, denied membership in the League of Nations on the ground that it was not in a position to meet all the international obligations which would rest upon it by virtue of the Covenant. Likewise difficult to classify are the trust areas under the United Nations. At present they play an important though passive role in world politics.

It should not be forgotten that nationalism is not the only force which sweeps across world politics.   Panracial movements, such as Pan-Germanism, Pan-Slavism, Pan-Latinism, Pan-Hispanism, Pan-Africanism, and the Pan-Asiatic movement have upon occasion exerted a considerable influence in world politics. Again, other movements, such as Pan-Islamism, have sought concerted action not upon the basis of nationality or race but upon the basis of a common religion.   At times Pan-Islamic movements have caused France, Great Britain, and the Netherlands, which had large Mohammedan populations in the colonial territories, much concern.   Mohammedans, however, are divided religiously. Moreover, their first loyalty is to the nationalist movements of the countries in which they live rather than to Pan-Islamism.   The Soviet Union, and Communists throughout the world, would like to force the reorganization of the world upon a horizontal rather than a vertical basis.   They emphasize class interests and differences rather than national ones.

Chapter 3

THE DEVELOPMENT OF INTERNATIONAL COOPERATION

Consideration of world community and the state system reveals that modern life is inextricably international and interdependent, but that its political organization is based fundamentally upon the conception of separate and independent nation-states. Therefore, the area of effective government action does not conform to the conditions and requirements of the time. International organization, which may be defined as the agencies and methods of international cooperation,[1] has been developed in answer to this situation and in an attempt to meet this need. It has to do with the structure and procedure of cooperative relations between or among the nation-states of the world. International organization would not exist if the entire world were organized as one superstate. Nor would there be a place for it if the various nation-states were completely self-contained and separate from each other. International organization presupposes a situation of legally independent nation-states, in contact with each other and affected by activities transcending their boundaries.

The remainder of this chapter will be concerned with the agencies and methods of international cooperation as they developed from early modern times. Consideration will be given to the diplomatic and consular services, treaties, international conferences, international administrative organization, and methods for the pacific settlement of disputes.

DIPLOMATIC AND CONSULAR SERVICES

Diplomacy has been defined as "the application of intelligence and tact to the conduct of official relations between the governments of independent states."[2] It is the science and the art of representation of states and of negotiations between them. It is a method of communication between the governments of independent states through individuals appointed for the purpose.

---

[1] See the article on "International Organization" in the *Encyclopedia of the Social Sciences,* Vol. 8, Macmillan, New York, 1932.

[2] Sir Ernest Satow, *A Guide to Diplomatic Practice,* Vol. 1, Longmans, New York, 1917, p. 1.

Diplomats are expected to "win friends and influence people" for their country and its policies. Envoys and other special representatives from one government to another were known in the ancient world. Diplomacy in its modern form began, however, with the city-states of Renaissance Italy. The diplomat was an agent and personal representative of the sovereign. The dignity and prestige of his prince was considered to be vested in him. He was entitled to be treated with due respect, and any affront or slight shown to him was received as an insult to his sovereign.

Great stress was placed upon formal honors and prestige, and there was often an unseemly scramble for precedence. The negotiations leading up to the Peace of Westphalia in 1648 were impeded for some six years because of controversies over meeting places, titles, and rank of envoys. In 1661, there was a street fight between retainers of the French and Spanish ambassadors in London over which of their coaches should be next to the royal coach in the reception of the Swedish ambassador. Another such incident took place at a court ball in London, in the winter of 1768: [3]

The Russian ambassador, Ivan Czernichew, arriving first, took his place immediately next to the Count von Seilern, ambassador of the Emperor, who was on the first of two benches arranged in the diplomatic box. The French ambassador, Comte du Chatelet-Lomon, came in late, and climbing on to the second bench, managed to sit down between his two colleagues. A lively interchange of words followed, and in the duel which arose out of the incident the Russian was wounded.

At the Congress of Vienna in 1815, and at Aix-la-Chapelle in 1818, rules of precedence were worked out in order to put an end to this type of bickering. Four grades of diplomats were recognized—ambassadors and papal legates or nuncios, envoys extraordinary and ministers plenipotentiary, ministers resident, and chargés d'affaires. The first three groups are accredited to the sovereign or chief of state; the last, to the minister of foreign affairs. Precedence within these grades is based upon length of service. Thus, the "dean" of the diplomatic corps in Washington, D.C., at any given time is the ambassador who has been at that post the longest. The present rules of diplomatic precedence are based upon the idea of the equality of states. However, they were adopted primarily for the practical purpose of finding an acceptable and automatic solution for the problem, and are of very little importance except in a ceremonial way.

Because diplomats represent the dignity of their government, and in order to expedite their work, certain privileges and immunities have been recognized for them. The official residence [4] of an ambassador or minister is inviolable. The chief of mission, his family, and servants are immune from the local juris-

---

[3] *Ibid.*, p. 19.

[4] The official residence of an ambassador is known as an "embassy"; that of a minister as a "legation."

diction. Diplomatic privileges and immunities include freedom from arrest, relief from customs duties and other taxes, and exemption for witness duty. The right of extending asylum to fugitives was formerly claimed on the basis that an embassy or legation had extraterritorial status. The recent trend has been to restrict the right of asylum on the ground that it is not permissible for a diplomat to harbor fugitives from justice. In this matter, as in other questions of diplomatic privileges and immunities, the problem is to accord sufficient freedom from local jurisdiction for the status and functions of foreign diplomatic missions, but to guard against their possible abuse or unnecessary extension.

Diplomatic representatives are appointed and sent by their governments, and they are formally received by the head of government (or foreign minister) to which they are accredited. They enter upon their work after being chosen by their own governments and accepted for the purpose by the other government concerned. An exchange of ambassadors between two countries is based upon custom and agreement, rather than upon any presumed right of legation under international law. Diplomatic representation is worked out between governments on a mutual and reciprocal basis. For example, the United States government would not send an ambassador to a foreign government which refused to return the compliment. The idea of reciprocity extends even to the rank of the officials concerned. The United States exchanges ambassadors, or exchanges ministers, with another country; it does not send an ambassador and accept a minister. The higher rank has ordinarily been reserved for the more important foreign posts, but the United States now maintains embassies in all the Latin-American republics and in some of the other smaller countries. Before an ambassador or minister is appointed, it is customary to inquire whether he is acceptable to the other government. Any indication that an individual is *persona non grata* means that he will not be appointed. Likewise, if a diplomatic official, after his appointment, becomes *persona non grata* he will be recalled or transferred immediately.

The modern means of rapid communication have had an important effect on the conduct of diplomacy. Before the days of telegraph, telephone, and radio, an ambassador in a distant country had to act on his own initiative in applying his instructions and in dealing with new situations as they arose. Today an ambassador anywhere in the world can be in almost instantaneous contact with his foreign office, and he can receive fresh instructions day by day. Not only that, but heads of governments frequently enter into direct communication with each other. For example, Prime Minister Winston Churchill and President Franklin D. Roosevelt exchanged over seventeen hundred messages and met in nine meetings, "comprising in all 120 days of close personal contact." [5] The relations between President Roosevelt and Prime Minister Churchill were unusual, of course, but in times of crisis responsible heads of state are certain

[5] Speech by Winston Churchill before House of Commons on Apr. 17, 1945.

to seek direct contact with each other. This might appear at first thought to reduce an ambassador from a position of initiative and judgment to that of a mere messenger. The diplomat himself has retained a substantial degree of importance for two reasons. For one thing, there is no substitute for the tact and skill with which instructions are interpreted to foreign governments, and the telegraph has not abolished the need for this personal touch. For another thing, the technological developments of the modern world have vastly increased the areas of human life which come within the scope of international diplomatic relations. When all is said and done, however, the centralized control of foreign policy has tended to increase. The ambassador's job is still important, but he is now a member of a team directed from the capital of his country.

The consular service is designed to expedite foreign trade and commerce, and to assist the citizens of a nation in various other ways. As Potter says, "The essential cause which has produced the modern consular system is the need for some official governmental assistance to, and supervision over, the conduct of international intercourse by the private citizens of the various nations. To this is to be added the need for protection against illegal treatment." [6] Thus, while the diplomat is concerned with the public policy of his government, the consul provides assistance to individual citizens by furnishing information on trade opportunities, keeping and certifying records, extending assistance to travelers, protecting property interests entrusted to him, and performing many other duties of a similar nature.

The consul is an official of the government which appoints him, and he receives a commission as evidence of his authority to act. While he is not accredited to a chief of state, like an ambassador, he is authorized to perform his duties in the territory of a foreign government by the issuance of a document called an "exequatur." He is a national official commissioned and authorized to act abroad for specified purposes. While diplomats are usually stationed only in foreign capitals, consular offices are to be found in all cities of commercial importance.

Consular officers are not entitled to all the privileges and immunities of diplomats, but they do receive certain rights and immunities needed for the efficient performance of their duties. These include unrestricted communication with the home government, access to fellow nationals especially when they are under arrest, maintenance of an inviolable archives, and freedom from local control in all matters pertaining to consular duties. Inviolability of premises and immunity from civil and criminal jurisdiction are not consular rights under international law but may be recognized by treaties.[7]

[6] Pitman B. Potter, *An Introduction to the Study of International Organization*, Appleton-Century-Crofts, New York, 1948, 5th ed., p. 67.

[7] For a recent case, see Lawrence Preuss, "Consular Immunities: The Kasenkina Case (U.S.–U.S.S.R.)," *American Journal of International Law*, January, 1949, pp. 36–56.

The status and functions of diplomats and consuls are defined by customary international law and by treaties.   Each nation determines the organization of its diplomatic and consular services.   Diplomats are without exception made responsible to the foreign office or its equivalent.   Consular officers are sometimes supervised by the department of commerce of their government.   Since 1924, the United States has had an integrated foreign service including both diplomatic and consular officers.[8]   Each government defines the duties of, and issues its own instructions to, its diplomatic and consular services.   The functions of the foreign service tend to be substantially similar among the various nations, and the following description will serve as an illustration of diplomatic and consular duties and activities throughout the world: [9]

The Foreign Service represents the United States abroad, interprets for its information and guidance events, situations, and opinions in the country to which the personnel is assigned, and endeavors to promote goodwill and common understanding.

The officers and employees of the Foreign Service protect the interests of the United States in accordance with treaties and international law, and advise, protect, and assist American citizens resident, traveling, or having interests abroad.   They seek to prevent or to correct practices which might discriminate against the United States or its citizens.

They negotiate treaties, conventions, and protocols regarding international intercourse, tariffs, shipping, commerce, and the preservation of the peace in conformity and in accordance with the instruction of the Secretary of State and the President.   They observe, analyze, and report on political, social, and economic conditions and trends of significance in the country in which they are assigned.   Some major subjects of these reports are legislative programs, public opinion, market conditions, trade statistics, finance, production, labor, agriculture, forestry, fishing, mining, natural resources, shipping, freights, charters, legislation, tariffs, and laws.

One of the important functions of the Foreign Service is the promotion and protection of the foreign trade of the United States.   Trade inquiries, trade disputes, and market conditions are the subject of numerous communications.   Miscellaneous inquiries on a wide variety of subjects are answered.

Other Foreign Service functions include:

    a. Issuance of passports to American citizens, registration of American citizens within the consular district of their residence abroad;

    b. Issuance of bills of health to American and foreign vessels proceeding to the ports of the United States or its possessions; submission of reports on health conditions;

    c. Issuance of visas to foreigners wishing to visit or immigrate into the United States;

    d. Dissemination of information pertaining to the United States, its policies, and its way of life;

[8] Graham H. Stuart, *American Diplomatic and Consular Service*, Appleton-Century-Crofts, New York, 1936, pp. 185–187.

[9] *The Foreign Service of the United States*, U.S. Department of State Publication 3612, Aug. 15, 1949, pp. 4–6.

e. Promotion and protection of American shipping generally and reporting on shipping conditions; entry and clearance of American ships and aircraft; relief of seamen; shipment and discharge of seamen; settlement of disputes;

f. Certification of invoices of goods shipped to the United States; investigation of and reporting on foreign market values and undervaluations of merchandise for the protection of revenues; assistance in preventing the importation of prohibited articles; administration of regulations relating to plant and animal quarantine; supervision of disinfection of merchandise intended for export to the United States;

g. Custody, administration, and settlement of estates of American citizens and seamen who have died abroad;

h. Extradition cases.

Foreign Service officers perform notarial services in accordance with United States Federal, State, and local laws, and are frequently commissioned to take testimony.

TREATIES

A treaty is a formal international agreement.[10]   If states are considered to be sovereign and legally independent, it follows that affairs of concern to two or more of them can be regulated only by mutual consent.   This consent can be based on the acceptance of customary rules and practices, or it can be given by definite acts of agreement for the settlement of specific issues or the establishment of new rules and practices.

Treaties have made an important contribution to the development of international cooperation.   Modern technology, especially in the fields of transportation and communication, has made possible a tremendous increase in the number and scope of the contacts and activities which transcend national boundaries.   A consequence has been a corresponding growth in the need for devices of agreement and cooperation.   The United States, for example, had entered into approximately three hundred treaties by 1898, but during the past fifty years it has become a party to well over twice that number.   Other countries have experienced a comparable trend.   There have also been a change and an expansion in the subjects covered by treaties.   Most treaties prior to the nineteenth century were concerned with such subjects as alliances, truces, terms of peace, and royal marriages.   The majority of modern treaties deal with social, economic, and governmental affairs, including agreements on navigation and commerce, copyright and patent law, settlement of claims, citizenship, extradition, and postal facilities.

Most early treaties were bilateral, creating obligations between two states with respect to each other.   At present, a large percentage of the treaties con-

---

10 Many other terms are used.   "Convention" has been used both for some of the great international agreements like the Hague Conventions, and also for some of secondary importance.   "Protocol" is used to describe records of discussion, articles of explanation, annexes, or even a multilateral treaty itself.   Other terms are "arrangement," "declaration," "exchange of notes," *"modus vivendi,"* "procès-verbal," *"compromis,"* "covenant," and "charter."   There is great confusion in the use of these terms.

cluded are multilateral. This tendency is to be expected with the increase in matters of common international concern. If, for example, sixty states are interested in rules of navigation on the high seas, or postal communications, or some other matter, agreement could be reached through bilateral treaties only if each state concluded fifty-nine treaties. Obviously this would be an impossibly complex procedure. A multilateral treaty with sixty signatories is the logical solution, since in this way one agreement establishes a common arrangement or standard which each accepts as an obligation with respect to all the others.

CONFERENCES

An international conference involves the consideration and discussion, with a view to agreement, of matters of common interest by the representatives of two or more states. Thus, conference in its simplest form is a technique of diplomacy, and the practice of international conferences has grown out of an extension of diplomatic negotiation. The distinguishing features of a conference are that it is arranged in advance for the consideration of designated questions and that it is attended by representatives specially appointed for the purpose. International conferences have been held on a great variety of subjects, from peace treaties to the control of opium, from the establishment of national boundaries to the prohibition of the use of white phosphorus in matches. From the Peace of Westphalia in 1648 to the third quarter of the nineteenth century, most of the international conferences [11] were concerned with the terms of peace to conclude a war. Conferences were also held to deal with important political issues of common concern. An outstanding example of this type was the concert of Europe, which attempted to maintain the European Settlement of 1815 through a series of conferences at Aix-la-Chapelle in 1818, Troppau in 1820, Laibach in 1821, and Verona in 1822.

About one hundred years ago, the use of conferences to deal with needed services and administrative questions of common international concern became increasingly frequent. Some early examples are the International Sanitary Conference at Paris in 1851, the general conference on statistics at Brussels in 1853, the Conference of Hanover to deal with navigation of the Elbe in 1861, two conferences as to marine signaling in 1864, and so on. The conference method was also used in connection with the establishment and operation of the various international administrative organizations.

Three types of international conferences may be distinguished: the *ad hoc*, the periodic, and the recurrent or continuing. The first of these is specially arranged, deals with its agenda, and at the conclusion of its meetings goes out of existence. An *ad hoc* conference is convened upon the initiative of one state (or a group of states), by addressing invitations to other states whose coopera-

[11] Or "congresses." The two terms are now used interchangeably.

tion for the purpose is sought.   The agenda is proposed by the initiating state and must have the concurrence of the other participants.   The conference usually meets on the territory of the initiating state, and it is customary to select the chief delegate of that country as presiding officer.   An illustration of the *ad hoc* conference is the Washington Conference of 1922, which was convened on the initiative of the United States.   The chief advantage of the *ad hoc* conference is that it furnishes a more expeditious method than ordinary diplomatic negotiations to deal with special issues or problems.   Its disadvantages are the special effort required to initiate the conference, the suspicion of ulterior motives often directed against the initiating state, the problem of obtaining advance agreement on the agenda, the difficulty of arranging for adequate preparatory work, and the lack of continuity.

The Hague Conferences of 1899 and 1907 and the system of inter-American conferences are examples of the periodic type.   Such conferences are designed to meet from time to time, and each arranges for the convening of its successor. Thus the special initiative of one state is not required, but there is still a lack of continuity and an inadequacy of preparatory work between the conferences.

A great improvement in the system occurred with the advent of the League of Nations, and later the United Nations.   Recurrent meetings are automatically provided for.   General international conferences are in practically continuous session.   There is no problem of inertia to be overcome; no one state has to assume the burden of the initiative; continuity is maintained; and there is a secretariat to handle the preparatory and interim work.   The various organs of the United Nations provide a method for continuing consideration and discussion, with a view to agreement, of the problems and affairs within their jurisdiction.   Also, special conferences may be called to deal with individual questions as, for example, the problem of trade and employment.

International conferences have developed from a device used on special occasions, in a quite sporadic and haphazard manner, to an institutionalized arrangement of fundamental importance in the current system of international organization.   Like the multilateral treaty, the conference technique can be used as a device of international legislation.   The states of the world, or most of them, may agree to certain rules and regulations in a general conference, and thus give their consent to designated provisions governing a matter of common concern.   In fact, it is usually by an international conference that the terms of such a treaty are agreed upon.

With all its advantages and possibilities, the device of international conferences cannot be used indiscriminately as a sort of panacea.   It is wise to adopt a somewhat critical view toward the apparent instinct to "hold a conference" at the slightest provocation.   Certain conditions must obtain if a conference is to be successful.   The question with which the conference is to deal must be fairly definite and one on which there is already a considerable area of agreement.   There must also be adequate preparation of agenda and data.   Very important, of course, are the personal qualities of the delegates.[12]

INTERNATIONAL ADMINISTRATIVE ORGANIZATIONS

One result of modern technology has been a great increase in the number, variety, and importance of activities transcending the limits of national boundaries.   These are needs and problems which cannot be met merely by international agreements and conferences, as indispensable as these devices are.   A machinery for collective action on matters of common concern is also necessary.   For this reason, administrative agencies to perform services beyond the scope of separate national action have been established.

When large numbers of people become interested in a given activity or problem, they tend to create an organization to further their joint purposes and objectives.   The area of international affairs is no exception to this rule, and many different groups have organized on a basis transcending the jurisdiction of any one nation-state.   One type is the business concern, such as Standard Oil or the Ford Motor Company, operating in more than one country.   Another type is the international humanitarian organization, of which the outstanding example is the Red Cross.   A third type is the international organization of an economic or professional interest group, such as the World Federation of Trade Unions, the International Chamber of Commerce, or the Inter-Parliamentary Union.   As Eagleton says, "There is an International Wine Office to encourage the use of wine, and an International Bureau against Alcoholism to discourage it."[13]   A recent publication[14] listed fourteen international organizations concerned with textbook revision as an aid to international understanding.   These agencies are known as "private international organizations" to indicate their nongovernmental status.   There are literally hundreds, perhaps thousands, of them in existence, ranging from large and well-known organizations of great importance to small and ephemeral groups.

The development described in the preceding paragraph was followed by the formation of "public international organizations" or, as they are sometimes called, "public international unions."   Such agencies have an official governmental status, are established by treaties, have a permanent or continuing organization, are normally open to the membership of all qualified states, and function to administer activities of interest to all the participating states.

The Universal Postal Union furnishes an instructive example of a public international organization.   A brief survey of its origin and work will give an

[12] Potter, *op. cit.*, p. 121.

[13] Clyde Eagleton, *International Government*, Ronald, New York, 1948, rev. ed., p. 159.

[14] UNESCO, *A Handbook for the Improvement of Textbooks and Teaching Materials as Aids to International Understanding*, Paris, 1949, pp. 24–32.

insight into the significance of this particular method of international cooperation. Under the original system of completely separate national postal administrations, correspondence with other parts of the world was slow, unreliable, and expensive, as the following description indicates: [15]

Not only were the rates of postage very high, but the tariffs were confused by the fact that the charges varied according to the respective route of transit. Thus, for instance, there were three different rates between Germany and Austria, five different rates between Germany and Australia, four different rates between Germany and Italy according to the particular route taken by the letter. . . . A letter from the United States to Australia would pay either five, thirty-three, forty-five, or sixty cents, or $1.02 per half ounce, according to the route by which it was sent. Mail service was by no means frequent, but the fact that a letter was prepaid for a certain route often prevented it from taking advantage of a quicker means of communication. . . . Charges in general were very high. . . . In making up a through rate, the transit charges of every country whose administration handled the letter would be included. The accounts of such mutual charges were exceedingly complicated and it took a vast amount of clerical work to keep them balanced. Further difficulty was introduced through the difference in weights and in currency, all of which had to be taken into account in computing rates. It will be apparent . . . that the service lacked the rapidity and cheapness which alone could make it a real influence in the development of world-wide business relations.

During the first half of the nineteenth century, attempts were made to improve this situation through bilateral treaties, but with little success. It became apparent that a solution could be reached only by general international action. The first postal conference was called in 1863, upon the initiative of the United States, for a discussion of the principles involved. The General Postal Union was formally established in 1875, and three years later its name was changed to the Universal Postal Union.[16] The basic purpose of this Union is to unite its members in a single postal territory for the reciprocal exchange of correspondence. Freedom of transit for the mail is guaranteed throughout the world postal territory. A uniform rate is established for foreign correspondence, and transit charges are fixed on the basis of weight and mileage. There is a Universal Postal Congress, which usually meets at five-year intervals. It reviews the basic Convention of the Union and the subsidiary agreements. Proposals involving important changes must receive a two-thirds vote, and lesser changes a simple majority. The proposed modifications are subject to ratification by the members, but in practice this has become a mere formality.

[15] Paul S. Reinsch, *Public International Unions,* World Peace Foundation, Boston, 1916, 2d ed., pp. 21–22.

[16] This was the second public international union to be established. The first was the International Telegraphic Union, formed in 1865. A few international agencies with regional or local functions were established even earlier. Apparently the first of these was the Rhine River Commission of 1804.

The Universal Postal Union maintains an international bureau, which operates under the supervision of the Swiss postal system.   It serves as an organ of liaison, information, and consultation; gives opinions on questions in dispute; acts as a clearinghouse for the settlement of postal accounts; and performs other functions of a similar nature.   In 1948, a permanent executive and liaison committee was established, composed of nineteen members elected on a geographical basis.   It meets once a year and has the functions of the maintenance of close relations with members of the Union to improve the international postal service, the study of technical questions, relations with other international organizations, and control of the activities of the international bureau.

As of September, 1948, there were eighty-eight members of the Universal Postal Union.   The members are divided into seven classes for purposes of apportioning expenses (set at an annual maximum of about $190,000 at the present time).   Each member has one vote in the Universal Postal Congress.   However, the Great Powers have special influence because of the admission of colonies to voting membership, and because in practice representation on committees is limited for the less important states.   In 1948, the Universal Postal Union became one of the specialized agencies of the United Nations.[17]

By the time of World War I, there were in existence thirty public international unions with administrative bureaus or commissions.[18]   The more important problems with which they dealt were transportation and communication facilities, disease and sanitation, economic problems, and labor legislation.   These organizations included the International Bureau of Weights and Measures, the European Danube Commission, the Wireless Telegraph Union, the International Sugar Union, the International Institute of Agriculture, the Union for the Publication of Customs Tariffs, the International Office of Public Health, the Union for the Suppression of the African Slave Trade, the International Opium Commission, the Central Bureau for the International Map of the World, and so on.   After World War I, new needs led to the creation of additional international organizations, such as the International Commission for Air Navigation, in addition to the administrative machinery of the League of Nations.

There has been great variety among the public international organizations in size and organization, but some common features are discernible.   They are established by an agreement made in an international conference, and there is nearly always provision for a periodic conference.   There is usually some kind of council or commission to act between conferences, to supervise the work carried on, and to revise the administrative regulations.   Also, there is a bureau or secretariat to perform the routine work involved in the function of the agency.   Expenses are met by contributions from the members,

[17] See p. 160.
[18] Reinsch, *op. cit.*, p. 4.

except for a few cases like the Danube Commission or the Sanitary Councils, which were self-supporting. Contributions may be allocated by dividing the members into different classes or categories, or by population, amount of commerce, length of railways, or some other factors. Inequality of voting may or may not be correlated with unequal financial contributions. The principle of unanimous consent has not been directly violated, but business has been conducted by majority vote in practice. This is accomplished by providing for consent to the basic agreements and allowing the international organization to carry out routine work and to make changes in subsidiary regulations by majority vote. A state which opposes such a change may withdraw from the organization. As a practical matter, however, the inconvenience of losing the advantages of membership is usually too strong an influence to make withdrawal a real alternative. No country can afford, for example, not to belong to the Universal Postal Union, even though it may not favor some of the regulations.

For the most part, the work of these organizations consists of research, publication, recommendation, reporting, and routine administrative tasks. Sometimes they have a limited control over individuals or over a specified activity in a given locality (the Danube Commission, for example). Basically, the control remains in the hands of the member states. The international administrative organizations are devices of cooperation, not agencies of governmental power or jurisdiction in the true sense. They offer a means of providing essential services which the member states acting separately could not provide for themselves. Their force rises from their practical indispensability. States retain power and control, but they cannot afford to do without international organization because of the compulsion of conditions and circumstances. It should be noted, also, that the international administrative organizations have furnished a valuable precedent for reconciling the legal fiction of independent sovereignty with the dynamics of modern world interdependence and with the pressing need of effective cooperative action.

PACIFIC SETTLEMENT OF DISPUTES

Contacts between nation-states and the many activities transcending national boundaries sometimes give rise to disputes and conflicts. For this reason, methods of peaceful settlement are needed if the arbitrary use of force is to be avoided. Judicial settlement in international relations is developing in a way not unlike the development of the judicial process within the state. Among primitive peoples self-help is the only form of redress for the violation of customary law. Gradually self-help gives way to arbitration, and arbitration in turn develops into the judicial process. Instead of the parties' fighting out the dispute, they began the practice of voluntarily submitting the dispute to neutral third parties. Later still the settlement of disputes was brought under the authority of the state, which assumed the prerogative of appointing the judges and of executing their judgments. With this, the settlement of the dispute became judicial proceeding in the modern sense of the term.

The handling of disputes by government agencies on the basis of law thus became a normal feature of national political organization. A development very similar to this took place with respect to the settlement of disputes between states. The process was, however, much slower and never became quite as complete. Principal reliance continued to be placed on the method of self-help. If a dispute could not be settled through diplomatic channels or by international conferences, rights could be secured only by the unilateral action of claimant states through self-help or, as it is called in international law, self-redress. This often meant a resort to some kind of coercion, ranging all the way from the threat of force, tariff discrimination, economic boycott, etc., to full-scale war. Methods of pacific settlement are intended to provide an alternative means for settling disputes. They represent a very important part of modern international organization.

Good Offices and Mediation. Though good offices and mediation are essentially negotiation, they are discussed here to illustrate the shift from self-help to arbitration and judicial settlement. After two states have gone to war or are drifting toward war, a third state may offer its good offices in bringing them together again so that their differences may be peacefully adjusted. Third states are always free to tender their good offices, and the disputant states may take no offense at the action. It involves no actual interference in the dispute, for the state tendering its good offices makes no suggestions touching the substance of the disagreement. The moment a third state comes with suggestions for conciliating the differences and bringing about a settlement of the dispute it assumes the role of a mediator.[19] Mediation is a delicate function and not lightly undertaken by governments. When mediation occurs it most generally follows upon a successful tender of good offices. States may sometimes find themselves eager to end a war in which they are engaged, but political expediency and national pride prevent them from opening direct conversations for that purpose. In such cases a tender of good offices is welcome and may be instrumental in bringing hostilities to a close. It was under such conditions that President Theodore Roosevelt was able to induce Japan and Russia to accept his good offices for bringing about a peace conference between the two countries on American soil. Roosevelt's activities during the

[19] The Hague Convention for the Pacific Settlement of International Disputes defines mediation as "reconciling the opposing claims and appeasing the feelings of resentment which may have arisen between the States at variance." The Hague Conferences sought to encourage the use of good offices and mediation by making it a friendly right of third states to offer good offices or mediation without offense to the disputant states and by regularizing the procedure.

negotiations would indicate that his services did not stop with good offices but developed into mediation.

Commissions of Inquiry. Another step forward in the use of impartial third parties in the settlement of disputes between states was made in the Hague Convention for the Pacific Settlement of International Disputes. If settlement by diplomacy fails, the parties are urged to institute an International Commission of Inquiry, with the object of facilitating "a solution of these differences by elucidating the facts by means of an impartial and conscientious investigation." It must be carefully noted that the Commission's report is limited to a statement of the facts and that the parties reserve entire freedom as to the effect to be given to the statement. Even this mild arrangement was not acceptable to most states until disagreements involving honor and vital interests had been excluded from its scope. This method of settling disputes has some notable successes to its credit, chief among which is the Dogger Bank case of 1904. In the Russo-Japanese War, a Russian squadron of warships had made a sudden attack upon an English fishing fleet, as a result of which considerable damage was done and two lives were lost. British feeling ran high, and there was considerable danger of war breaking out between the two countries. The matter was settled by the appointment of a Commission of Inquiry, three of whose members were of neutral nationality, to inquire into and report upon the facts and circumstances of the incident. As a result of the report Russia recognized its responsibility and paid the British fishermen an indemnity.

The general principle of the Commission of Inquiry was adopted and extended by Secretary of State Bryan in some thirty treaties negotiated between the United States and other countries in the years 1913 and 1914. The provisions of the Bryan treaties differ from those of the Hague Convention in several respects. The Commission is appointed in advance and is made permanent, no disagreements are excluded from its scope, and hostilities are prohibited until the Commission has made its report. The great value of the Bryan treaties lay in the fact that they provided for a "cooling-off" period in which hostilities were prohibited and for the ascertainment of facts which might become the basis of an acceptable solution.

Arbitration. The method of arbitration in the settlement of interstate disputes is almost as old as history. It had an honorable record in the history of the Greek city-states and was resorted to extensively during the Middle Ages. It is often stated that the practice lapsed throughout the early modern period and that the Jay Treaty between the United States and Great Britain in 1794 marks the beginning of the modern period of international arbitration. This is not strictly correct, for there were many cases of international arbitration throughout the seventeenth and eighteenth centuries.[20]

[20] E. O. Van Boetzelaer, *Les Arbitrages Internationaux Néerlandais de 1581 à 1794,* Drukkerij H. Buurman, Leiden, 1929.

The Hague Convention for the Pacific Settlement of International Disputes defines arbitration as "the settlement of international disputes between states by judges of their own choice, and on the basis of respect for law," with an obligation to accept the award in good faith. Arbitration, in summary, involves the settlement of interstate disputes (1) by voluntary action, (2) by judges chosen by the parties to the dispute, (3) on the basis of respect for law, and (4) with an obligation to accept the award as binding.

It is often asserted that arbitration is identical with the process of adjudication. It is pointed out that in practice the vast majority of arbitral decisions have been decided squarely on the basis of legal rules and that compromise and political expediency have seldom played a role. While this is undoubtedly true, it must nevertheless be remembered that the process of arbitration does reserve a large area for the play of equity, compromise, and expediency. The arbitrators are not always highly trained jurists; often they are diplomats and statesmen without legal training or judicial experience. Moreover, it should be remembered that the parties to the dispute agree upon, or select, those principles which shall guide the arbitral tribunal in reaching its conclusions. For these reasons arbitration may be regarded as a combination of legislative and judicial functions. While arbitration does not make changes in general international law, it often does make a change in the existing legal rights of the parties. So we may conclude that arbitration differs from judicial procedure in the strict sense of the word by (1) the selection of the arbitrators, which is made by the disputant parties themselves, for the settlement of a particular dispute, (2) the selection by the disputants of the principles upon which the tribunal shall base its award, and (3) the submission of the dispute to arbitration, which is purely voluntary.

Arbitration as a means of settling international disputes steadily gained in favor throughout the nineteenth century. One of the most notable cases of arbitration of this century was the Alabama Claims case settled in 1872. The United States charged Great Britain with not having fully lived up to its neutral duties in the Civil War. The British government had allowed confederate cruisers to be fitted out in British ports and to go out from them to prey upon American shipping, as a consequence of which the war had been prolonged and American military expenditures greatly increased. The United States government demanded an indemnity for the injuries which it had sustained. It was not until after several years of diplomatic discussion that Great Britain finally agreed by the Treaty of Washington to submit the differences between the two governments to arbitration. The court of arbitration was composed of five members; one appointed by each of the parties and one each by the King of Italy, the President of the Swiss Confederation, and the Emperor of Brazil. The tribunal awarded the American government the sum of $15,500,000 as the amount of damages due it for the injuries sustained through the failure of the British government to fulfill its neutral duties. The settlement of this serious international dispute by means of arbitration made a profound impression upon world opinion and stimulated the movement for arbitration everywhere.   ·

While resort to arbitration became more frequent as the century wore on, an attempt to institutionalize arbitration and to remove some of the defects which practice had revealed was not made until the close of the century. There were at least three serious defects in the procedure.   In the first place, recourse to arbitration was entirely a voluntary matter; there was no obligation to use this method of settlement even in cases generally regarded as most suitable for it.   In the second place, there was no permanent and readily accessible court of arbitration to which cases could be submitted.   For every case submitted arbitrators had to be chosen anew, and often the parties to the dispute found it difficult to agree upon them.   Lastly, since there was no general code of arbitral procedure for the guidance of the tribunal, the disputant states had to agree upon such a code after the dispute arose.   Negotiations to arrive at this agreement, called a *compromis,* often proved difficult and occasionally led to delay and further friction.

The First Hague Conference sought to remove these defects by setting up permanent machinery and improving the processes of arbitration.   These efforts were incorporated in an elaborate convention, called the Convention for the Pacific Settlement of International Disputes,[21] drafted and adopted at the First Hague Conference and amended at the Second.   An attempt was made to secure a provision for compulsory arbitration, if only for certain limited classes of disputes.   This effort was unsuccessful.   The best that could be obtained from the conference was the declaration of a *voeu,* a "wish," stating that the conference was unanimous "in admitting the principle of compulsory arbitration" and "in declaring that certain disputes, in particular those relating to the interpretation and application of the provisions of international agreements may be submitted to compulsory arbitration without restriction." This declaration was, of course, meaningless so far as any legal effect was concerned.   States remained free to arbitrate or not as they saw fit and as interests and expediency might dictate.[22]

The Hague Conferences also sought to set up a continuous arbitral body, but the so-called Permanent Court of Arbitration for which the Convention provides is hardly worthy of the name.   It provides for a panel of judges and a bureau, which serves as a registrar for the Court and which is housed

[21] Also commonly called the First Hague Convention.

[22] Article 38 of the Convention, which dealt with the jurisdiction of arbitration, was of the same tenor: "In questions of a legal nature, and especially in the interpretation or application of International Conventions, arbitration is recognized by the Contracting Powers as the most effective, and at the same time the most equitable, means of settling disputes which diplomacy has failed to settle.   Consequently, it would be desirable that, in disputes about the above-mentioned questions, the Contracting Powers should, if the case arose, have recourse to arbitration, in so far as circumstances permit."

at The Hague.   States which are members of the Court must keep on file with the Bureau the names of not more than four persons "of known competency in questions of international law, of the highest moral reputation, and disposed to accept the duties of arbitrators."   The same person may be selected by different powers.   The members of the Court are appointed for a term of six years, subject to renewal.   From this panel of names arbitrators must be selected whenever states care to have recourse to the Court of Arbitration for the settlement of their differences.   The number of names on the panel varies somewhat but is generally around 135.   The bureau of the Court is under the direction and control of the Permanent Administrative Council, composed of the diplomatic corps at The Hague and the Minister for Foreign Affairs, who acts as the presiding officer.

The Hague Conferences further sought to facilitate arbitration by laying down in advance, for the adoption of disputants who desired to resort to arbitration, methods of selecting the arbitrators and the rule of procedure which should govern the court.   When the parties to a dispute agree to submit it to arbitration, the question at issue, the names of the arbitrators or the method of their selection, the principles of law or equity upon which the Court is to base its judgment, and the rules to govern the procedure of the Court are all laid down in a treaty, generally called a *compromis*.   By incorporating as many of these items as possible in a general convention, ready for the use of disputants at all times, the difficulty of drawing up a *compromis* is lessened. The First Hague Convention provides a method of selecting the judges and a model code of procedure for the use of the Court.   If the disputants cannot agree on the composition of the tribunal, the Convention provides that each party shall appoint two arbitrators, of whom only one may be its own national or chosen from the persons selected by it as members of the Court.   These arbitrators together are then to choose an umpire.   Should the votes be equally divided, the choice of the umpire is entrusted to a third power, selected by agreement of the parties.   If still no agreement is reached, each party shall select a different power, and the choice of the umpire is made in concert by the powers thus selected.   If after the exhaustion of all these methods, no agreement has been reached, an umpire is chosen by lot.

It should be borne in mind that these rules of procedure thus carefully elaborated were no more than suggestions; they are in no sense binding.

This so-called Hague Permanent Court of Arbitration, which is neither a "court" nor "permanent," came into existence in 1907.   Some twenty cases were disposed of by tribunals whose membership was selected either in whole or in part from the panel of names which constitutes the Court.   At present its chief significance is as a step in the procedure for nominating judges to be elected to the International Court of Justice.[23]

The great unsolved problem of international relations is to induce states to

[23] See p. 191.

submit their disputes to arbitration or adjudication. The world is covered by a network of treaties, mostly bilateral, providing for the settlement of international disputes by arbitration, but in so far as they provide for obligatory arbitration they are almost invariably accompanied by exceptions so sweeping as to rob the commitment of all meaning. When the effort to make arbitration obligatory failed at the Hague Conference, it was hoped that practically the same end would be reached by the encouragement of the negotiation of a large number of bilateral treaties after the model of the Franco-British Treaty of 1903. Under this treaty the parties agreed to submit differences of a legal nature or involving the interpretation of treaties, provided, nevertheless, that they do not affect the vital interests, the independence, or the honor of the two contracting states and do not concern the interests of third parties.

American administrations have at various times sought to take an active part in the general movement for compulsory arbitration. The United States government negotiated and signed a number of general treaties providing for the obligatory arbitration of disputes involving legal questions, but likewise subject to the usual exception of differences involving national honor, independence, vital interests, or the interests of third states. As if this breach in the commitment to obligatory arbitration were not large enough, the Senate widened it even more. It was assumed that after the general arbitration treaty came into effect, each *compromis* or agreement for the subsequent submission of particular disputes to arbitration would be concluded by executive agreement rather than by formal treaty, for under the American Constitution a formal treaty requires the consent of the Senate for ratification, and that by a two-thirds vote. The Senate amended the arbitration treaties so as to provide that the submission of each dispute to arbitration could take place only by formal treaty. President Roosevelt objected to this and at first declined to present the amended treaties to the foreign governments for their approval, but in 1908 they were submitted and ratified. These arbitration treaties actually represent a backward step from earlier American practice, for the United States had often arbitrated differences without the conclusion of a formal treaty which had to be submitted to the Senate for prior consent. It must be remembered that it will not always be easy to get two-thirds of the Senate to favor the submission of a dispute after it arises.

The effort to relate the United States to other countries in a network of arbitration treaties more binding in their provisions was renewed by President Taft's administration. In 1911 Secretary Knox negotiated treaties with France and Great Britain respectively, in which the exceptions of national honor and vital interest were dropped and provision was made for the submission to arbitration of all "justiciable" disputes, that is, disputes involving questions of a legal nature. A joint commission was to be set up under each of these treaties for the purpose of determining in each case whether or not the particular difference was justiciable.   The Senate struck out the provision for the joint commission and inserted reservations prohibiting the submission to arbitration of a number of questions, such as the admission of aliens, debts owed by foreign states, and the Monroe Doctrine.   This mutilation of his arbitration treaties so disgusted President Taft that he withdrew them from the Senate and abandoned the whole project.

A new attack upon the problem was made by Secretary of State Kellogg. It was his idea that if the former vague exceptions of national honor, vital interests, or independence were replaced by new exceptions more precise in character, their scope would be greatly narrowed.   Secretary Kellogg therefore began the negotiation of a new series of arbitration treaties, of which the treaty of 1928 with France was the model.   While the treaty provides for the submission to arbitration of all justiciable disputes, it excepts any dispute which

(a) is within the domestic jurisdiction of either of the High Contracting Parties, (b) involves the interests of third parties, (c) depends upon or involves the maintenance of the traditional attitude of the United States concerning American questions, commonly described as the Monroe Doctrine, (d) depends upon or involves the observance of the obligations of France in accordance with the Covenant of the League of Nations.

It must be seriously doubted whether these exceptions are any narrower than the older ones they replaced, especially when we keep in mind that the parties are themselves the judge of whether a given dispute falls within these exceptions.

The high-water mark in international arbitration before World War II was reached in the Covenant of the League of Nations, which represents a collective agreement containing a broad commitment for the arbitration of disputes as an alternative to other methods.   Under Article 12 the members of the League agreed to submit either to arbitration or to inquiry by the Council any dispute arising between them likely to lead to a rupture.   Under the terms of Article 13 the members further agreed to submit to arbitration any dispute which they deemed suitable for arbitration and which could not be satisfactorily settled by diplomacy.   Furthermore, the Covenant listed certain classes of cases which are declared to be among those generally suitable for submission to arbitration.   The classes named were disputes involving the interpretation of a treaty, a question of international law, a breach of an international obligation, and the nature and extent of such breach.   After World War I there were other treaties of considerable scope providing for arbitration, among which the treaties of the Locarno Pact of 1925 were probably the most important.   A Central American Court of Arbitration after the manner of the Hague Court of Arbitration was created by agreement of the Central American states in 1923. Excluded from the jurisdiction of the tribunal were disputes involving the old vague exceptions—sovereignty, national honor, vital interests, and independence.

The defects of arbitration as a means of settling international disputes are obvious. Yet its defects are also the sources of its strength. The fact that for each particular case submitted the parties to the dispute should be free to select their own judges and include their own nationals as members of the arbitral tribunal indicated how little inclined states are to submit their disputes to the decision of impartial judges. This reluctance is further reflected in the wide reservations which are generally made in the agreements providing only for optional jurisdiction. It is not an exaggeration to say that states are willing to submit to arbitration only such unimportant disputes as the expediency and interests of the hour may dictate. It should be remembered that the decisions which proceed from arbitral tribunals are often based wholly or in part on compromise and not on strict legal rules or principles. Yet it is just these features which also constitute the merits of arbitration, for the chief problem in the maintenance of peace is that of inducing states to settle their disputes by pacific means. States can in many instances be induced to accept arbitration when they would not be willing to accept another method more nearly approaching true judicial settlement. While it is true that the most dangerous disputes, those most likely to lead to war, are seldom submitted, arbitration does nevertheless provide a method whereby a large number of irritating disputes can be removed from the field of controversy.

Judicial Settlement. This is the most highly developed form of pacific settlement. As its name implies, it involves decision by an impartial court upon the basis of law. The differences between arbitration and judicial settlement and the superiority of the latter over the former are clearly stated in Secretary Root's instructions to the American delegates to the Second Hague Conference: [24]

It has been a very general practice for arbitrators to act, not as judges deciding questions of fact and law upon the record before them under a sense of judicial responsibility, but as negotiators effecting settlements of the questions brought before them in accordance with the traditions and usages subject to all the considerations and influences which affect diplomatic agents. The two methods are radically different, proceed upon different standards of honorable obligation, and frequently lead to widely differing results. It very frequently happens that a nation which would be very willing to submit its differences to an impartial judicial determination is unwilling to subject them to this kind of diplomatic process. . . . It should be your effort to bring about in the Second Conference a development of the Hague Tribunal into a permanent tribunal composed of judges who are judicial officers and nothing else, who are paid adequate salaries, who have no other occupation, and who will de-

[24] Quoted in J. W. Garner, *Recent Developments in International Law,* Calcutta University, Calcutta, 1925, p. 667.

vote their entire time to the trial and decision of international causes by judicial methods and under a sense of judicial responsibility. These judges should be so selected from different countries that the different systems of law and procedure and the principal languages shall be fairly represented. The court shall be made of such dignity, consideration, and rank that the best and ablest jurists will accept appointment to it, and that the whole world will have absolute confidence in its judgments.

At the Second Hague Conference efforts were made to set up an International Prize Court and a Court of Arbitral Justice, but with little success in either case. Prize courts, which deal with the title to property seized on the high seas during time of war, form a part of the national governmental machinery and therefore their impartiality may be under some suspicion. There was not any great difficulty in the organization of the Court, but the convention providing for it was never ratified because there was no general international agreement with respect to prize law. The project for the Court of Arbitral Justice failed because of inability to agree on a method for the selection of judges. The small powers, led by Brazil, insisted upon the right of each state, large or small, to designate a judge. Since there were forty-one states represented at the Conference, this method would have meant a court of forty-one judges!

In connection with judicial settlement, reference should be made to the short-lived Central American Court of Justice. This Court was organized in 1907, with the active encouragement of the United States. It was opened in the following year, and in the course of its nine years of existence it adjudicated nine cases. Unfortunately the United States government, which had been instrumental in helping to create the court, also helped to destroy it. Under the terms of the Bryan-Chamorro Treaty between the United States and Nicaragua, the former was ceded not only the exclusive right to construct a canal across Nicaraguan territory, but also a naval base in the Gulf of Fonseca and two small islands in the Caribbean Sea. Costa Rica protested this treaty as violating its right to be consulted in a matter which so closely affected its interests, and it brought suit against Nicaragua before the Court. The Court sustained the claim of Costa Rica and declared the treaty void. When the United States government tacitly supported the position of Nicaragua in claiming that the Court had exceeded its competence, the other Central American states had no desire to renew the ten-year period for which the Court originally had been created.

After World War I, the Permanent Court of International Justice was established and made some very useful contributions to the judicial settlement of international disputes. The judicial organ of the United Nations is the International Court of Justice.[25]

[25] See Chap. 13.

Chapter 4

INTERNATIONAL LAW

To avoid anarchy is as essential for states as it is for individuals; hence regulation of interstate relations becomes as necessary as the regulation of the relations between man and man within states. Now it is obvious that the purpose of law has not been achieved if it prevents anarchy within the state only to create greater anarchy among states. The function of municipal and international law is the same, namely, to reduce human relations to order on principles of justice. Moreover, chaos in the international sphere will in the end cause a breakdown of many of the relations within the state. Postwar periods with their numerous political upheavals give abundant evidence of this truth.

Nature of International Law

A leading English jurist defines international law as "the body of rules and principles of action which are binding upon civilized states in their relations with one another." [1] For the purpose of completeness there should probably be added to this definition the clause, "or with the nationals of other states." Now we shall have to admit frankly that at the present moment there exists a great divergence of viewpoints with respect to the nature of international law. One school of writers maintains that international law is not law at all, but merely international morality or ethics. On the other hand, there are an increasing number of scholars who hold not only that international law is law, but that considering the facts and practices of international life the term "supranational law" should replace the term "international law," as more accurately describing its true character. [2] It is a law not merely between states but above or superior to states.

---

[1] J. L. Brierly, *The Law of Nations*, Oxford, New York, 1942, 3d ed., p. 1. Westlake, another distinguished English student of international law, simply defines international law as "the law of the society of states." *International Law*, Vol. I, Cambridge, New York, 1910, p. 1.

[2] J. P. A. Francois, *Handboek van het Volkenrecht*, Vol. I, Tjeenk Willink, Zwolle, 1931, pp. 19*ff*; J. W. Garner, "Limitations on National Sovereignty in International Relations," *American Political Science Review*, Vol. XIX, pp. 1*ff*.

The reason some people find it difficult to accept international law as law is largely that it is very different from national law in several respects. International law differs from national, or municipal, law [8] in the way it is enacted, interpreted, and enforced. Law had its origin in custom; among primitive people custom is the only source of law. A custom becomes law, generally called "customary law," when the community feels that this particular custom ought to be enforced by the application of penalties. The idea that man can consciously make law is found only in societies more or less advanced. While customary law remains an element in the law of most countries, as, for instance, the common law of the English-speaking countries, the great bulk of national law now is statute law; it has its origin in decree or legislation. International law, since it is less developed, is still largely customary law, and in so far as it has been consciously made it has come into existence by the treaty-making process and not by the decree of a sovereign or the act of a legislative body. There is neither a world sovereign nor a world legislature to enact international law.

A second important difference between national and international law is to be noted. When individuals within a state clash as to their respective rights under the law, any one of the individuals concerned may bring the case before the proper courts to have his rights defined and enforced. For centuries each state was the final arbiter of its claims under international law. If direct negotiations between two states over conflicting claims failed, the two might agree to submit the question to arbitration, but the parties to the dispute were under no obligation to do so. If negotiations between the disputant states broke down and resort was had to war, the other states in the family of nations, unless their direct interests led them to participate in the war, merely declared their "neutrality." This has all been greatly changed. By numerous bipartite treaties states have agreed to submit disputes to arbitration or judicial settlement; the members of the United Nations are under obligation to compose their differences by arbitration, judicial settlement, or conciliation. There is now an International Court of Justice, whose compulsory jurisdiction has been accepted by a large number of states.[4] States have lost a great deal of their right to be the sole and final interpreters of their rights under international law.

International law also lacks legal character, so it is frequently contended, because there is neither international executive nor police for its enforcement. It is not necessary that the agency which enforces a law should be a part of the organization or body which enacts it. England was without an effective national enforcement machinery long after the itinerant judges had firmly established a national "common law." The Catholic Church in the Middle

---

[8] The student should be careful not to confuse municipal law with city law. By "municipal law" is meant national law, as contrasted with international law.

[4] See Chap. 13.

Ages originated much law but did not itself enforce it. Even in the United States today the power which enacts law and the power which enforces it are not always organs of the same unit of government. In a few instances cases arising under Federal laws are tried in state courts, while the laws of our states are often dependent upon local courts and local administrative officials for enforcement. Thus international society still relies almost wholly upon the states themselves for the enforcement of the rules of international law.

The sanctions of international law do not differ greatly from those of national law. Municipal law must rely chiefly upon such sanctions as public opinion, habit, self-interest, and expediency, and good faith for its observance. Physical coercion is not an essential characteristic of law. John Bassett Moore points out that a large part of constitutional law is not enforced by means of specific penalties.[5] Force is at best only one means of enforcing law and its importance as a sanction is much overrated. As Laski correctly pointed out, "The will of the State obtains preeminence over the wills of the other groups exactly to the point where it is interpreted with sufficient wisdom to obtain general acceptance and no further. Should it venture into dangerous places it pays the penalty of its audacity. It finds its sovereignty by consent transformed into impotence by agreement."[6] The mere addition of penalties will not make an unpopular law enforceable. Far more important is the general recognition of law as binding and habitual obedience to it, and in this respect international law suffers little in comparison with municipal law. Though unnoticed by the public, scores of cases are daily being adjusted before national courts and in offices of foreign affairs on the basis of international law. Most treaties are faithfully executed, and it is only rarely that an arbitral decision is not carried out. The Permanent Court of International Justice under the League of Nations and its successor, the International Court of Justice, have not found their judgments flouted, even though they have had no international sheriff at their disposal. The judgments of international tribunals have almost invariably been carried out, and in many of the cases adjudicated by them national feeling ran high. Decisions of international courts are as uniformly obeyed as decisions of municipal courts. No state openly defies international law, though it may contest what the rule of law is in a particular case.

The Jay Treaty affords an interesting example of the operation of self-interest as a sanction in international law. Under this treaty the United States agreed to submit to arbitration British claims for the loss of vessels captured by French ships which had been armed in the ports of the United States. The arbitration tribunal held that the United States had failed to perform its neutral duties and awarded Great Britain $143,428. The payment of this award by the United States established the principle that a government is liable in

[5] *International Law and Some Current Illusions,* Macmillan, New York, 1924, p. 292.

[6] Harold J. Laski, *The Problem of Sovereignty,* Yale University Press, New Haven, 1917, p. 14.

damages for failure to enforce strictly its neutral duties and laid the basis for a similar claim (the Alabama Claims case) against England over half a century later. Unfortunately, statesmen and the public do not always take a long-range view of matters and hence are not sufficiently moved by the advantages of reciprocity based upon law to make this sanction as effective as it ought to be.

Some writers profess to see in war the highest and ultimate sanction of international law and even speak of intervention as the vicarious enforcement of international law. Whatever practical justification there may have been for such action under previous conditions, self-help can never be recognized as a legal sanction. It is only when used by the international community or upon its authorization that intervention or war can be regarded as possessed of legal character. We cannot speak of a sanction as having legal character in cases where the state is plaintiff, judge, and sheriff in its own cause. Self-help is essentially a mark of lawlessness. When the international community is more fully developed, self-redress will give way to collective enforcement.

RELATION OF INTERNATIONAL LAW TO NATIONAL LAW

In view of what has been said above about the nature of international law, some explanation of the relation between municipal law—probably better called national law—and international law is in order. Because international law is most generally enforced through municipal law and by national agents, the impression is conveyed that national law is superior to international law. A brief examination of the facts will show that this impression is erroneous. Some modern constitutions specifically state that international law is part of the national law. American courts and less unequivocally so the British courts have held in many decisions that international law is part of the law of the land. American courts have never deviated from the principle laid down by Chief Justice Jay in a decision in 1792 that "the United States had, by taking a place among the nations of the earth, become amenable to the law of nations" and that "it was to their interest as well as their duty to provide that those laws should be respected and obeyed." [7] In a leading English case the court held "that the law of nations, wherever any question arises, which is properly the object of its jurisdiction, is adopted in its fullest extent by the common law of England, and held to be part of the law of the land." [8]

---

[7] *Chisholm v. Georgia,* 2 Dallas 419 (1793). See also The *"Nereide,"* 9 Cranch 423 (1815), and The *"Paquete Habana,"* 175 U.S. 700 (1900). See article by Harold Sprout, "Theories as to the Applicability of International Law in the Federal Courts of the United States," *American Journal of International Law,* Vol. XVI, pp. 288ff.

[8] *Emperor of Austria v. Day and Kossuth,* 2 Giffard 628 (1861). In a more recent case, that of the West Rand Central Gold Mining Company, the court accepted this principle rather cautiously, stating that "the international law sought to be applied must, like anything else, be proved by satisfactory evidence, which must show either that the particular

A second principle observed by American and British courts is that a legislative act is assumed to be in harmony with international law unless clearly in conflict with it. In an early decision Chief Justice Marshall said, "An act of Congress ought never to be construed to violate the law of nations if any other possible construction remains."[9] Thus courts will strain a point to avoid a conflict between the two laws. Moreover, there is in all countries a large body of legislation whose direct object is the enforcement of the obligations of international law. As examples of such laws the United States statutes for the protection of diplomatic agents may be cited.

But what happens in case of a clear conflict between municipal and international law? In this event the national courts apply the statute. They cannot well do otherwise, since they are the immediate agents of their governments and receive their instructions from them. From this it must not be concluded that municipal law is superior to international law, that it can set aside a rule of international law in favor of a statute. The executive may reverse the decision of the courts, and often does. The President or the Secretry of State, either upon his own initiative or upon the demand of foreign countries invoking a rule of international law, will generally order an immediate suspension of the enforcement of the law and at once seek either the repeal of the law or the negotiation of a treaty with the state involved so as to iron out the difficulty. This was done, for example, in the case of the United States prohibition laws, which called for the arrest of rumrunners beyond the three-mile maritime belt. In this case the President, through the Secretary of the Treasury, ordered the customs officials to refrain from seizing foreign liquor smugglers beyond the three-mile limit. In the meanwhile, the State Department negotiated a series of treaties with foreign countries, under which the United States was given jurisdiction over vessels of the nations of these states beyond the three-mile limit for the purpose of enforcing its prohibition laws.

A similar conflict may arise between treaties and statutes. In a badly considered case the United States Supreme Court laid down the rule that the latest expression of the national will prevails.[10] This is the rule in nearly all countries, though there seems to be some uncertainty about the rule in Switzerland.[11] Thus Congress may nullify by unilateral action an earlier treaty as

---

proposition put forward has been recognized and acted upon by our country, or that it is of such a nature, and has been so widely and generally accepted, that it can hardly be supposed that any civilized state would repudiate it." L.R. 2 K.B. 391 (1905).

[9] The "Charming Betsy," 2 Cranch 64, 118 (1804). For an English decision of similar import see The "Annapolis," 30 L.J. P. & M. 201 (1861).

[10] Pitman Potter, "International Law and National Law in the United States," American Journal of International Law, Vol. XIX (1925), pp. 315ff.

[11] See Ruth D. Masters, International Law in National Courts: A Study of the Enforcement of International Law in German, Swiss, French and Belgian Courts, Columbia University Press, New York, 1932.

American national law, but the treaty remains binding as an international obligation. Here, too, the treaty may be saved by Executive order, as when President Wilson ordered the release of aliens drafted into the army under the provisions of the conscription act. In case there is no redress for the alien in municipal law, his government may make diplomatic presentation in his behalf. If the United States does not admit that a rule of international law has been violated or the terms of a treaty broken, the matter may be submitted to arbitration or judicial settlement. If the case is submitted to an international tribunal, the latter will apply international law, in which case international law triumphs in the end. As a matter of fact, the United States Supreme Court has several times been reversed by an international tribunal. Should the United States refuse to submit the case to arbitration or judicial settlement it would be guilty of a violation of international law or, in the case of a breach of a treaty, of failure to carry out its international obligations.

Individuals under International Law

The forerunners of Grotius recognized the individual as the subject of international law; they recognized the state as such a subject only by exception. Grotius, who is almost universally accorded the title of the father of international law, took the position that international law regulated not only the relations between one state and the subjects of another but even the relations between subjects of different states. Beginning with Hobbes, and followed by Pufendorf, the view that international law regulated only the relations between states became generally accepted. This development is very largely accounted for by the manner in which international society has developed. The growth of the doctrine of an uncontrolled absolute state sovereignty led to the exclusion of individuals and all public-law communities other than the state as subjects of international law. New juridical bodies, such as international administrative unions, the League of Nations and the United Nations, and new juridical communities, such as the mandates and trust territories, came into existence, and these became the subjects of rights and obligations under international law. The individual is again gradually emerging as a subject of international law.

The question of whether the individual is already a subject of international law has engendered much theoretical discussion, but need not detain us long. The individual is the basic unit of society and the real object of all law, and an increasing number of jurists throughout the world are taking the position that a democratic international law must place individuals in the first rank of subjects.[12] The Institute of International Law at its meeting in New York

[12] Philip C. Jessup, "The Subjects of a Modern Law of Nations," *A Modern Law of Nations*, Macmillan, New York, 1948; Nicolas S. Politis, *New Aspects of International Law*,

in 1929 adopted a Declaration of the International Rights of Man, proclaiming that it is the duty of every state to ensure each individual an equal right to life, liberty, property, freedom of religion, free choice of language, and education in this language.[13]   The opponents of this view hold that while individuals are the objects of international law, states are its sole subjects. Oppenheim gives expression to this point of view when he states that "all duties which necessarily have to be imposed upon individual human beings according to the Law of Nations are not international duties, but duties imposed by municipal law in accordance with a right granted to or a duty imposed upon the state concerned by International Law." [14]   A commission of the Economic and Social Council of the United Nations has drafted a Universal Declaration of Human Rights and is now at work on drafting an International Covenant of Human Rights.[15]

It is a well-known fact that theory generally runs ahead of practice, and for that reason it may be more profitable to survey actual international practice.   In a number of cases, such as piracy, blockade running, and the carriage of contraband, individuals have long been directly subject to the rules of international law and punishable under it.   Whereas the state enforces the rule, the authority to do so is derived not from national but from international law.   The courts of England and the United States have held that counterfeiting the money of other states is an offense against international law.[16] In addition to the rights to which the individual is subject under customary international law, the individual has also become the bearer of rights and duties under numerous treaties.   This is especially true in the case of treaties setting up international tribunals.   The extinct Central American Court of Justice had authority under certain conditions to take jurisdiction over cases of individuals against states and actually heard several such cases.   The International Prize Court, which was to have been established under the Twelfth Convention of the Second Hague Conference, was to be clothed with authority to hear cases on appeal by individuals from the national prize courts.

Carnegie Endowment, New York, 1928, pp. 18ff; Clyde Eagleton, *International Government*, Ronald, New York, 1932, pp. 177–185; J. B. Scott, "The Individual, the State, the International Community," *American Society of International Law Proceedings*, Vol. 24, 1930, pp. 15–32; and Quincy Wright, *Research in International Law since the War*, Carnegie Endowment, New York, 1930, p. 23.

[13] Sir Thomas Barclay, "New Declaration of Rights of Man," *Contemporary Review*, Vol. 140, pp. 331–336, September, 1931.

[14] L. Oppenheim, *International Law,* edited by A. McNair, Longmans, Roberts and Green, London, 1928, 4th ed., p. 21.   See also Charles Fenwick, *International Law,* Appleton-Century-Crofts, New York, 2d ed., 1924–1934, p. 85; and Amos S. Hershey, *Essentials of International Public Law and Organization,* Macmillan, New York, 1927, rev. ed., p. 157.

[15] *These Rights and Freedoms,* Department of Public Information, United Nations, 1950.

[16] *Emperor of Austria v. Day and Kossuth,* 2 Giffard 628 (1861), and *United States v. Arjona,* 120 U.S. 479 (1887).

Likewise, under the mixed arbitration tribunals set up under the Treaty of Versailles and the other peace treaties concluding World War I, individuals are given the right to present their claims without the interposition of their governments. The individual in these cases is pressing his own personal claims, not those of his government. The individual likewise has become the subject of legal obligations under a large number of treaties by which governments confer upon international bodies power to lay down regulations directly binding upon their nationals, without the specific approval of the governments in each case or the transformation of these regulations into national law. A number of commissions with such powers are found in international river law.[17] There is a growing demand that aliens by international treaty be given the privilege of suing states before an international court.

There is also the reverse side of the practice just described which needs to be presented for a balanced picture. Only states can be parties in cases before the International Court of Justice. Normally individuals can get their cases before claims commissions only if they are adopted as its own by the state. Of two equally good claims the government may accept one and reject the other for presentation before the commission, though it is not often likely to do so. Moreover, the government may sacrifice an individual's claim for political or other reasons. Since claims must be presented through a government, stateless persons, *i.e.*, persons who are citizens of no state, cannot get their claims brought before the commissions. Generally, too, the damage awarded the claimant is paid to his government and not to him directly. As a result, the individual may not always get the award after all. Thus while the individual may be a subject of international law, it should be remembered that in general he becomes the bearer of rights and duties under international law only through the intermediary of the state and in his quality as a subject of it, and that these rights will be his only so long as he remains a national of the state concerned, and only for so long as the states signatory to the treaty by which these rights and obligations are created wish to keep the treaty in force.

Sources of International Law

The sources of international law are custom, agreement, and general principles of law. In the manner of its growth, international law resembles the common law. Its chief source is custom, but not every custom in the field of international relations falls within the sphere of law. Only those practices with respect to which there has developed a general conviction that their application has become obligatory have legal character. As Article 38 of the Statute of the International Court of Justice has it, "The Court shall ap-

[17] Pitman Potter, *Introduction to the Study of International Organization,* Appleton-Century-Crofts, New York, 3d ed., 1928, pp. 176–177.

ply . . . international custom, as evidence of a general practice accepted as
law." The difficulty of determining whether a particular custom has developed into a rule of law constitutes a major problem with respect to this
source. Often this can be determined only by submission of the issue to
judicial settlement. A classic example of a court decision based upon customary international law is the case of the *Paquete Habana*, which arose in
the Spanish-American War. One of the most firmly established rules of
international law is the right of a belligerent to capture enemy vessels on the
high seas. But when an American warship brought in a couple of small fishing smacks belonging to enemy nationals the court refused to condemn them,
for the reason that "by an ancient usage among civilized nations, beginning
centuries ago and gradually ripening into a rule of international law, coast
fishing vessels, pursuing their vocation of catching and bringing in fresh fish
have been recognized as exempt, with their cargoes and crews, from capture
as prize of war." [18]

Agreement, as expressed in treaties and conventions, constitutes a second
source of international law. An analogy is sometimes drawn between the
rule of treaties in international law and that of statutes in national law, but
the analogy, while useful, is a very imperfect one, for the ordinary treaty
between two or more states cannot be regarded as an independent source of law.
Very frequently the object of a treaty is to create an obligation which does not
exist in general international law, and of course such a treaty is binding only
upon the parties to it. In other cases the object of a treaty may be to set
aside an existing rule of law. In neither of these cases can a treaty be said to
be a source of law, though binding upon the parties to it. Only a treaty setting
up an international institution or creating a new general rule governing future
conduct, ratified by a large number of states, can be regarded as a "law-making"
treaty. In a strictly technical sense even such a general treaty cannot be said
to be a "law-making" treaty unless ratified by all the states of the world, but
the ratification of such treaties in a large number of states, including all the
leading ones, has the practical effect of world legislation.

In addition to custom and agreement there is a third source of international
law, a source which has aptly been described as "original." The Statute
of the International Court of Justice refers to this source as "the general
principles of law recognized by civilized nations." Williams calls this element of international law "original law" for the reason that it has its "direct
origin in morality and the common recognition of mankind, and is the law for
the nations without the support of treaty, convention, or agreement—however
desirable for practical reasons such support may be." [19] Because so much of
international law has its source in the general principles of law or, as some

---

[18] The *"Paquete Habana,"* 175 U.S. 677 (1900).

[19] Sir John Fischer Williams, *Chapters on Current International Law and the League of Nations,* Longmans, Roberts and Green, London, 1929, p. 23.

contend, in the moral feelings of mankind, it has been exposed to the reproach of vagueness and uncertainty. The justice of this reproach cannot altogether be denied, but it should be remembered that international law is still in the early days of its development. With improvement in the process of international legislation an ever-increasing percentage of international law will become embodied in conventions, and its rules will thus take on greater precision. The common law of Anglo-Saxon countries has experienced a similar development.

Authority, while often listed as a fourth source of international law, is more generally regarded as an evidence of existing rules. Under this category come "judicial decisions and the teachings of the most highly qualified publicists of the various nations," as the Statute of the International Court of Justice phrases it. However, the Statute qualifies this source as "a subsidiary means for the determination of the rules of law." Moreover, the Statute expressly prohibits the Court from adopting the Anglo-American rule of *stare decisis,* that is, of using its decisions as binding precedents.[20] Jurists do not, of course, make law. Their writings furnish evidence of the general attitude toward rules of international law, the weight of their authority in each case being dependent upon the standing of the authors. For this reason the resolutions of the Institute of International Law have great weight as evidence of a rule of law.

Evidences of the rules of international law are also found in public documents such as the opinions of attorneys general, diplomatic correspondence, instructions for diplomatic and consular officers, the decisions of municipal courts, municipal statutes and decrees, and the records of international conferences.

The Weaknesses of International Law

Not even the most ardent internationalist will deny that international law has grave weaknesses. While these defects have, no doubt, been overemphasized by critics they are nevertheless real and cannot be ignored. Nor is it in the interest of the promotion of the rule of law in international relations to close our eyes to these defects, for the more open-eyed the world becomes to their existence, the more quickly may we expect to see them remedied.

The inadequacy of international law, and also much of its strength, flows from the fact that so large a part of its rules are derived from custom and reason. Custom develops in answer to social needs; gradually some of these customs become recognized as obligatory, as rules of law. Customary law is thus a phenomenon of living society, a product of social needs. But customary law has at least two serious defects. In the first place many of its rules lack precision and objectivity. The rules of municipal law are much more definite, for by far the larger part of these rules have their source in statutes, codes, and

---

[20] Article 59. The decision of the court has no binding force except between the parties and in respect of that particular case.

a vast body of judicial decisions. The national lawyer can go to the statute books, codes, or court reports and obtain a fairly definite answer to the question of what the rule of law is on a specific point, though of course he cannot always be sure how the courts will apply the rule in every specific case. The international lawyer lacks these definite sources. It is difficult to know when a custom has ripened into a rule of law or to obtain a common agreement as to what are general principles of law or to determine the specific rules which flow from them. While the law derived from general principles is not entirely subjective, it does leave much to be desired in the way of objectivity.

A second grave defect of customary law is the slowness with which it develops. In primitive society, where social and economic conditions change imperceptibly, this is not a serious matter, but in modern society with its vast and rapid changes customary law soon lags behind the new legal needs born of fundamental social transformations. How great this lag is, can be seen from the narrowness of the scope of international law. Some of the most vital relations between states in an interdependent world have not yet been subjected to the control of law. States are very loath to admit law into just those spheres of their activities in which dangerous conflicts arise. Armaments, tariffs, migrations, the relation of advanced to backward peoples, and the distribution of raw materials are some of the highly important subjects which have thus far escaped the regulation of international law.

The root of these defects in international law may be traced to the lack of a well-developed process of international legislation and the inability to compel states to submit disputes with each other to judicial settlement.

Treaty Making and International Legislation

We have seen that municipal law originated in custom, that customary law later became in large part judge-made law, as the judge wove the changing sentiment of the community into the law. Customary law and judge-made law change very slowly, much too slowly in a rapidly developing society. We now look to legislative bodies to make changes in the law and make new law to meet the ever-changing needs of modern society. Indeed, we have become so accustomed to look to the legislative method for the enactment of law that we forget that even today not all municipal laws are so made. Some laws reach the statute books by means of the initiative and referendum, and constitutional law, in the form of new constitutions and amendments, is generally made in a manner quite different from ordinary legislation. But none of these forms of lawmaking are found in the international community. A central international legislative body is still lacking. This is not surprising, since the international community is still primitively organized. The international community, however, is making a conscious effort to make changes in its law and to widen its scope.   The term "international legislation" has been used to describe both the process and the product of this effort.

The conscious formulation of legal rules in the international sphere originally took place by means of bipartite agreements or treaties, generally negotiated through the regular diplomatic channels.   Because the rules of the law of nations were often vague and uncertain, many inconveniences and difficulties beset the intercourse between states.   These bipartite treaties served in part to facilitate this intercourse by laying down these rules in explicit terms.   But these treaties served also to call into being a special legal relationship between the parties, whose provisions went beyond the recognized rules of international law.   By inclusion in an ever larger number of treaties between other states and by extended application, these regulations gradually become incorporated in international law.

Soon collective or multilateral treaties began to be made, increasing in number with the increasing development of international society.[21]   Multilateral treaties may be limited to the original signatory states, but treaties general in nature and legislative in character increasingly are left open for the adherence of all the states of the world.   For example, the Briand-Kellogg Pact for the renunciation of war was negotiated through the regular diplomatic channels, signed at Paris by the representatives of fifteen countries, and came into effect as soon as it was ratified by all the signatory states, but it remains open as long as may be necessary for adherence by all the other powers of the world.   Multilateral treaties are generally negotiated at conferences of representatives of the states concerned.   In the beginning these conferences were called at the initiative of one of the states, but gradually the practice of holding periodic conferences developed, since the regulations governing a subject cannot be laid down once and for all but must be periodically revised to meet changed conditions.   In some cases the state upon whose territory the conference meets is charged with the task of making the necessary preparations for the conferences; in other cases a permanent bureau is established to perform this work.   Thus have the organs of international legislation evolved over the course of the last century or more.

New international law was first made by a collective treaty at the Congress of Vienna in 1815.   This Congress laid down the ranks of diplomatic representatives, legislated against the slave traffic, and attempted to secure the free navigation of the important international rivers.   After a period of inactivity, the work of consciously developing international law was again taken in hand

[21] In terms such as "bipartite" and "multilateral," "-partite" refers to the number of parties to the treaty and "-lateral" to the nature of the obligation incurred.   Thus a bilateral treaty carries a two-sided obligation, though it may be a multipartite treaty, as for instance in the case of two or more states dealing with another state.   A treaty in which the number of signatories is more than two and the obligation runs from each to each is a multilateral treaty.

with the Congress of Paris in 1856. From this time on the movement takes on two directions, one toward the mitigation of the brutalities of war and the other toward the building of an international legal order and the creation of international organs of government. From conferences seeking to cope with the problem of mitigating the brutalities of war have emerged a series of conventions: the Declaration of Paris (1856), regulating belligerent rights of capture at sea; the Geneva Convention for the Amelioration of the Condition of the Wounded in War (1864); the Hague Conventions (1899, 1907), regulating the conduct of war and the rights and duties of belligerents and neutrals; the Declaration of London (1909), which represents an attempt to codify the laws of war at sea; and the Washington Conference resolutions (1922), seeking to regulate the use of submarines. Not all the above conventions have come into force.

Of greater significance were the advances made in the more fruitful direction of constructing an international legal order. During the past seventy-five years conferences have been held dealing with a wide variety of subjects. The Berlin Congo Conference of 1884–1885 laid down important regulations with respect to the acquisition and government of backward areas, while the two Hague Peace Conferences were successful in drawing up rules for the pacific settlement of international disputes. A series of important conferences took place from 1865 on, culminating in the formation of a number of international public unions. The first of these, the Conference on Telegraphic Correspondence which met at Paris in 1865, formed the Universal Telegraph Union, which in 1908 took the name of Telegraphic Union. Other conferences resulted in the founding of the Universal Postal Union (1874), the Union for the Protection of Industrial Property (1883), the Union for the Protection of Works of Art and Literature (1886), the Pan American Union (1890), the European Union of Railway Freight Transportation (1890), and the International Labor Organization (1919). One of the fruits of these organizatizons is the development of an international administrative law.

With the founding of the League of Nations an important advance was made in the direction of a more rapid and uniform development of international law. Though the Assembly and Council did not purport to legislate, they did have the power within a narrow sphere to pass legislative regulations, in the form of resolutions, which were binding upon the governments without their ratification. The Assembly on occasion served as a diplomatic conference for the drafting of general treaties. The chief function of the League of Nations in the work of international legislation was to direct, to stimulate, and to prepare the way for a systematic development of international law. The League instituted a number of committees of experts charged with the task of preparing treaties on special subjects. Furthermore, there were a number of technical organizations within the League, such as the Health Organization and the Communication and Transit Organization, which were continually busy with the development of international regulations within these special spheres. The work of the codification of international law was also undertaken under the auspices of the League of Nations. All these activities gave impetus, unity, and continuity to the work of international legislation. The United Nations has built upon and expanded this work.

Entitled to more than casual mention in this connection is the work of the International Labor Organization, which, though it had an organization separate from that of the League of Nations and worked independently of it, was still essentially an integral part of it. In 1946, it became a "specialized agency of the United Nations." [22] The object of the International Labor Organization is to establish an international code of labor standards and law. As a result of its work a large number of conventions and recommendations have been adopted.

The shift in treaty making from bipartite treaties negotiated through diplomatic channels to collective treaties drafted at international conferences has greatly speeded up the process of international legislation. A single multipartite treaty is the equivalent of many bipartite treaties. For example, the Briand-Kellogg Pact, to which there were sixty-two parties, would have required 1,891 bipartite treaties.

THE PROCESS OF TREATY MAKING

The first step in the process of treaty making is that of negotiation. The proposals of the various interested parties are made and discussed, views are harmonized, preliminary or tentative agreement is reached, and the treaty is drafted. Treaties may be negotiated by regular diplomatic representatives, by commissioners or delegates especially appointed for the purpose, or in special cases by a foreign minister or even a chief of state.[23] Negotiations are, of course, always conducted under the authority of the executive official responsible for the foreign relations of a state. The individual negotiators are supplied with "full powers" (or credentials) which define the scope of their instructions and authority, and which make it possible for all parties to ascertain that they are dealing with duly constituted representatives of the interested states.

The second step is signature of the treaty. This means only that the negotiators have agreed upon a draft which they undertake to refer to the consideration of the appropriate constitutional authorities of their governments. It follows that signature of a treaty does not put it into effect or give rise to a binding obligation on the states which have been parties to the negotiations. This limited significance of signing a treaty should be carefully noted because there is a rather common misconception on this point. For example, American

[22] See p. 158.
[23] For example, negotiation of the Treaty of Versailles by President Wilson and the foreign ministers of the Allied Powers.

foreign policy is sometimes criticized on the basis that a treaty has been signed before the text is publicly known. The implication of such a criticism often is that international commitments have been made by secret diplomacy. An understanding of the true significance of signing a treaty should contribute to a more accurate appraisal of the methods used in American foreign policy.

The third step in the treaty-making process is ratification, which involves acceptance of the treaty terms by the appropriate constitutional authorities of the state. Originally, the rule of ratification was designed to protect the sovereign from errors or deceit by the negotiators. Its primary importance at the present time is to provide a democratic element in foreign policy by requiring that binding international obligations cannot arise without formal concurrence of a constitutional authority representing all the people. The process for ratifying a treaty is a domestic matter, to be determined by each state for itself. In modern democracies it is quite common for treaties to be referred to the national legislative body. The United States Constitution requires that consent of two-thirds of the Senate be obtained before a treaty is ratified by the President.[24]

The fourth step is an exchange of ratifications. This gives notice of formal acceptance by the respective parties to a treaty and serves to put it into effect as between them. It is customary to take the additional fifth step of proclamation or promulgation of the treaty. This is a requirement in the United States so far as putting a treaty into effect is concerned. Treaties are a part of the supreme law of the land. Therefore, they must be formally published in order that their terms may be known.

REQUIREMENTS FOR THE LEGAL VALIDITY OF TREATIES

Which agency in the state is empowered to make treaties is a constitutional question and not a question of international law. This power is generally vested in the head of the state, subject usually to some control of the representative body.

Treaties may be written in any language. Originally, treaties were concluded in Latin; later, French was so universally used that it came to be regarded as the "official and authentic" language of diplomacy. In recent years French has lost the primacy it once enjoyed, having been compelled to share honors with English. The Covenant of the League of Nations was drawn up in French and English, and the two texts were equally authentic. The Treaty of Versailles was concluded in both French and English, but in case of doubt as to meaning the French text was decisive. There now seems to be a growing practice for states to conclude bipartite treaties in the languages of the two

[24] It should be noted that the Senate does not ratify a treaty, but merely gives its "advice and consent." After favorable Senate action, the President is free to ratify or to withhold ratification.

parties. In case both texts are regarded as equally authentic, difficulties may arise, as the two texts may not always be in perfect accord. The Charter of the United Nations was adopted in five equally authentic texts, namely, Chinese, French, Russian, English, and Spanish (Article 3).

A treaty is invalid if coercion has been used against the negotiators or against the agencies or organs of the state having to do with treaty making, but coercion applied against the state does not invalidate a treaty. Nearly all peace treaties have been signed under coercion, though, of course, the negotiators were left free to sign or not to sign. Obviously, this anomaly will continue so long as war in all its forms is not made illegal.

A new condition for the validity of treaties came into existence with the Covenant of the League of Nations. Article 18 of the Covenant prescribed that "every treaty or international engagement entered into hereafter by any Member of the League shall be forthwith registered with the Secretariat and shall as soon as possible be published by it. No such treaty or international engagement shall be binding until so registered." It was hoped that this provision would combat secret diplomacy, remove causes for distrust and conflict, promote public control, and awaken public interest. The provision on this subject in the United Nations Charter differs slightly from that in the Covenant. Instead of declaring that no treaty is binding until so registered, Article 102 of the Charter states that no party to any such treaty which has not been registered with the Secretariat "may invoke that treaty or agreement before any organ of the United Nations." The international engagements registered with the United Nations are published by it in its United Nations Treaty Series. Texts are published in the languages of negotiation, and in French and English, if either of these official United Nations languages were not used for the original texts.

REVISION AND TERMINATION OF TREATIES

Not the least important of the problems connected with international legislation is that of the revision of treaties. Burdensome and outworn treaties constitute a dangerous source of friction and may even lead to war. Some provision for their peaceful termination or revision must be provided. Even if a treaty is entirely acceptable to both parties at the time of negotiation, changed conditions may make its continuance intolerable. In the past, revision and even termination, when diplomacy failed, were obtained by going to war. If war as an instrument of national policy is to be removed from the international order, pacific means of making changes become all the more necessary. The framers of the League Covenant were not blind to this need and sought to meet it by the inclusion of the provision found in Article 19, which provides that "the Assembly may from time to time advise the reconsideration by members of the League of treaties which have become inapplicable and the consideration of international conditions whose continuance might endanger the peace of the world." This provision, one of the most important in the Covenant, remained a dead letter.

The United Nations Charter contains no specific provision with respect to the revision of treaties. It was feared that any provision of this sort, however mild, would lead to a weakening of the sanctity of treaties, as states dissatisfied with their treaty obligations would seek to invoke the aid of the United Nations to obtain release from them. The Great Powers wished to avoid including a provision in the Charter which could serve as an invitation to the former enemy states of World War II to clamor for revision of the peace treaties, as did the Central Powers between the wars. As a result of these considerations the General Assembly was not specifically authorized to recommend the revision of treaties, but it does have this power under the very broad terms of Article 14 which states it "may recommend measures for the peaceful adjustment of any situation, regardless of origin, which it deems likely to impair the general welfare or friendly relations among nations . . ." Under Chapter VI of the Charter, "The Pacific Settlement of Disputes," and Chapter VII, "Action with Respect to Threats to the Peace, Breaches of the Peace and Acts of Aggression," the Council may do the same and, in effect, go much beyond that.

Treaties may be terminated in various ways. Fulfillment of terms completes a treaty obligation. For example, a treaty for the cession of territory is "executed" or carried out when this one transaction has been completed. A treaty may expire by a time limit provided for in its text. Sometimes a treaty is made with a stipulation that it will be in effect for a certain number of years, often with some form of optional renewal for an additional period. A treaty may be replaced or superseded by a new agreement. One party to a treaty may renounce its rights; it is not to be expected, however, that a state will give up any of its rights without receiving some alternative concessions.

Another way to terminate a treaty is for one of the parties to denounce it. This is usually a controversial matter. The doctrine of *rebus sic stantibus* is sometimes invoked. This means that a treaty was concluded under a certain set of conditions, and that a material change in the relevant circumstances furnishes a legitimate reason for terminating it. However, unilateral denunciation at the option of one party is inconsistent with a stable system of dependable international agreements. Terminating a treaty without consent of the other parties is therefore considered a violation of the obligation involved. Finally, a treaty may be terminated by the extinction of one of the parties as a state.

CODIFICATION OF INTERNATIONAL LAW

The term "codification of international law" is used in several different senses. Strictly speaking, the object of codification is to make international law clearer, more precise, and more unified—to systematize an already existing body of law. "Codification" is also used to mean the work of reducing to a unified whole a body of law in which there is as yet no unity. In order to reduce many of its conflicting rules to unity it may be necessary to make changes not only of a formal but also of a material nature. When used in this sense "codification" involves not only a restatement of the law; it involves some legislation as well. Finally, the term "codification" is used to mean the creation of a uniform law by filling in gaps and correcting defects. In this sense it is used by people who desire to incorporate important reforms in the law, such as making war illegal. But this is really no longer codification; it is essentially legislation.

Several sporadic efforts to codify international law were made before the creation of the League of Nations. Aside from the field of international administrative law, where considerable progress in codification was made, the successful efforts nearly all dealt with the laws of war and neutrality. Over a dozen such conventions came out of the two Hague Conferences of 1899 and 1907. However, one of the Hague Conventions deals with the pacific settlement of international disputes. The Pan-American conferences have also been engaged in the work of furthering the codification of international law for the American continents.

During the first few years of its existence the League of Nations confined its activities in this field to promoting the codification of law in a number of special and technical subjects. Thus, the Barcelona Conference, called under its aegis, laid down the principles of international law on communication and transit. Also the League played an important part in the formation of other conventions, such as the Convention for the Simplification of Customs Formalities and the Convention on Traffic in Women and Children. In 1924 the League of Nations began actively to undertake the work of the codification of general international law. A Committee of Experts for the Progressive Codification of International Law was appointed, and the work of narrowing down the subjects considered ripe for codification was begun. Of the numerous subjects investigated three were considered to be in this category, namely, nationality, the territorial seas, and the responsibility of states. After much preparation the Council summoned the first codification conference, which met at The Hague in the early part of 1930. The conference was anything but a success, as very little agreement was reached on the statement of the law on any of the subjects before the conference. In spite of this initial failure the work is being continued.

Under the provisions of the Charter of the United Nations, "the General Assembly shall initiate studies and make recommendations for the purpose of promoting international cooperation in the political field and encouraging the progressive development of international law and its codification" (Article 13).

In pursuance of this provision the General Assembly on November 21, 1947, voted to establish an International Law Commission for the purpose of promoting the progressive development of international law and its "eventual" codification. This Commission is composed of fifteen experts on international law, representing the chief forms of civilization and the basic legal systems of the world. It has selected three topics deemed by it as ready for attempted codification, namely, the law of treaties, arbitral procedure, and the regime of the high seas.

OBSTACLES TO INTERNATIONAL LEGISLATION

While legislation is the most important problem in international relations, it is also the most difficult. States want the benefits of law but are unwilling to make the sacrifices necessary to secure these benefits. They wish to remain as free as before the act of legislation. This is an utter impossibility, of course. That kind of attitude within the state would lead to confusion worse confounded. States are still too much impressed with their surface conflict of interests and too little by their underlying common interests.

The chief obstacle to international legislation is the principle of the sovereignty of states and the concomitant rule that no state is bound by a new rule of law unless it has expressly or impliedly given assent to it. Because of this principle many writers reject the term "international legislation," for the essence of legislation is that "it binds all persons subject to the jurisdiction of the body legislating, whether they assent to it or not, whether their duly appointed representatives have assented to it or not." [25] While this is giving the term too restricted a meaning, it does nevertheless point out a great impediment in the treaty-making process. Very often the refusal of a leading or key state to ratify a treaty may cause all other states likewise to refuse ratification.

The doctrine of the equality of states likewise brings its difficulties. The smallest of states claim an equal right with large states in the formation of new law. This is, of course, an anomaly, which in time will have to disappear. While small states should be given the equal enjoyment and protection of such rights as international law may create, they cannot always expect to share equally with the great powers in the formation of that law.

What about the future development of international law? An American scholar predicts that "more and more there will be a shifting of emphasis from the rights of states to duties, from individual to collective responsibility, from national sovereignty to international control, from independence to interdependence, and ultimately the law governing the relations of states will tend to become less and less international and more and more supernational." [26]

[25] Arnold D. McNair, "International Legislation," *Iowa Law Review,* Vol. 19, 1934, p. 178.

[26] J. W. Garner, *Recent Developments in International Law,* Calcutta University, Calcutta, 1925, p. 818.

Chapter 5

THE LEAGUE OF NATIONS

No institution, and least of all a world organization, springs suddenly into existence, full-blown. The League of Nations was no exception to this rule. Violence is as old as mankind and war as old as political association, but reaction against war and plans for preventing it likewise have a long history.

EARLY PLANS

Plans for organizing peace have had their advocates over the centuries. Dante, in his *De monarchia*, which was published early in the fourteenth century, pleaded for the organization of the Christian world on an imperial basis, in the interest of unity and peace.   At about the same time, Pierre Dubois, a French lawyer, suggested a kind of permanent confederation of the various countries of Christendom as a means of maintaining peace by the application of sanctions against aggressors.   Henry IV of France in his Grand Design (1603) proposed a general council for Europe, on which each of the large states would be represented by four commissioners and the smaller ones by two. Decisions by the general council were to be binding and, if necessary, to be enforced by the collective forces of the member states.   Other noteworthy projects for organizing peace were advanced by Emeric Crucé, a Frenchman (*The New Cyneas*, 1623), William Penn (*Essay towards the Present and Future Peace of Europe*, 1694), the Abbé de Saint-Pierre (*A Project for Making Peace Perpetual in Europe*, 1714), and the German philosopher Immanuel Kant (*Essay on Eternal Peace*, 1795).

HISTORICAL PRECEDENTS

At the heart of nearly all the above plans was the international conference. This could hardly be otherwise, as consultation and conference must be at the center of all cooperation.   Moreover, there were historical precedents in abundance for associating conferences with peace, as nearly every war ended with a conference to restore peace.   From the use of conferences to restore peace to the idea of conferences to keep the peace is not a long step.   The powers which emerged victorious from the Napoleonic Wars—Austria, Prussia, Russia, and Great Britain—gave this idea formal expression in the Quadruple Alliance. The basic idea behind this alliance was that the Great Powers whose cooperation had won the victory should also ensure the peace by consulting each other in case of a threat to the peace and by common or authorized action against the disturber. France, under the clever diplomacy of Talleyrand, was admitted to this group in 1818, and the method worked quite well for a while. Four conferences were held from 1818 to 1822; revolutions in Italy and Spain, which it was feared might lead to war, were suppressed. Largely because of coolness of Britain toward the system, the practice of regular conferences was dropped, but the idea was not wholly abandoned. Known as the "concert of Europe," it continued, in the form of intermittent conferences, to regulate international affairs at critical moments, from 1822 until the outbreak of World War I.

The concert of Europe operated quite successfully in the Berlin Congress of 1878, which dealt with the situation in the Near East; the Berlin Conference of 1884–1885, which sought to regulate imperialistic competition in Central Africa; the Algeciras Conference of 1912–1913, which dealt with the dangerous situation which had developed in Morocco; and the London Conference of 1912–1913, which probably kept the Balkan War from exploding into a general conflagration. While the concert may be credited with preventing war in numerous cases, it by no means prevented all wars, and it failed to meet the crisis in 1914. The concert had many weaknesses. Peace was often preserved among the Great Powers at the expense of the smaller, weaker countries. The concert functioned only intermittently and was wholly without regular or continuous administration and conference organs, and it did nothing to cope with economic nationalism and militarism or to promote the things which made for peace.

A second strand which went into the formation of the League of Nations was the movement for limitation of armaments and the systematization of arbitration which culminated in the Hague Peace Conferences of 1899 and 1907. The development and successful functioning of a number of public international unions constituted a third element. Some of these organizations were set up to deal with an administrative problem, as in the case of the Universal Postal Union; others had considerable power to deal with local situations, such as the Rhine Commission and the European Danube Commission. Though limited in their jurisdiction, they served to suggest the possibility of international cooperation in a more integrated fashion and on a wider scale. Added to these elements and reinforcing them was the peace movement, which had many supporters in all countries. The various national associations had begun to link up in an international movement which was exerting a deep and widespread influence.

Looked at historically, the League of Nations was not a new and marvelous invention so far as its structure and methods were concerned, since ample precedents for these may be found in preceding international institutions. The League did provide for the first time a comprehensive system, with the union in one institution of a number of separate elements which had previously existed in a piecemeal fashion. The most radical departure lay in the emphasis on the principle of collective security, in contrast to the traditional nineteenth-century principle of neutrality of third states toward belligerents engaged in an international conflict.

DRAFTING OF THE COVENANT

The idea of an over-all international organization made much progress during World War I. In the midst of a sanguinary struggle men's minds naturally turned to schemes for preventing a recurrence of the tragedy. During these years, a large number of drafts of plans for the maintenance of peace were made by various individuals and peace groups. One of the most influential of these plans was that outlined by General J. C. Smuts of South Africa in an essay published on the eve of the peace conference. The movement for the creation of an international organization to prevent war and to promote peace received tremendous impetus when President Woodrow Wilson became its eloquent leader and placed behind it the backing of his government. Though it was the last of his famous Fourteen Points for the peace settlement, issued in January, 1918, it was easily the most important and most discussed item of his peace program.[1] It ran as follows: "A general association of nations must be formed under specific covenants for the purpose of affording mutual guarantees of political independence and territorial integrity to great and small states alike."

President Wilson insisted that the proposed League of Nations be created as an integral part of the general treaty of peace. He probably feared that unless this were done there might be no League of Nations, as governments might fail to ratify the constitution for the international organization if it were separated from the peace treaties. It is noteworthy that the Covenant was drafted by a relatively small number of people. The commission responsible for this task had in the beginning only ten members, two representatives from each of the five Great Powers; later, after protest from the small states, it was enlarged by nine additional members. President Wilson served as chairman of this committee.

The Covenant[2] was an unusually well drafted document. The chief explanation for this is that it was drawn up by a small group, which also happened to contain men of exceptional ability for this type of work. However, from the point of view of democratic procedure, this method has little to recommend it.

As Part I of the Treaty of Versailles, the Covenant was signed on June 28;

[1] See Appendix 3.
[2] See Appendix 4.

it likewise became Part I of the other peace treaties made in 1919–1920. After obtaining the required number of ratifications it went into effect on January 10, 1920.

Structure and Functions

The original members of the League of Nations were divided into two groups: (1) signatories of the Covenant which also ratified it, and (2) invited states, thirteen in number, which were also named in the Annex of the Covenant. Other states could be admitted to the League by a two-thirds vote of the Assembly. Any member could withdraw after two years' notice of its intention to do so, provided all its international obligations, both in general and under the Covenant, had been fulfilled at the time of withdrawal. Altogether sixty-two states were members of the League at one time or another; the largest number of members at any time was fifty-eight during 1937–1938.

The League of Nations had three main organs, the Assembly, the Council, and the Secretariat. Closely affiliated with it, in some respects a part of the League, were the Permanent Court of International Justice and the International Labor Organization. The judges of the Permanent Court were elected by the Assembly and the Council; its budget was part of the League's budget. The Court was also authorized to give advisory opinions upon "any dispute or question referred to it by the Council or by the Assembly."

The International Labor Organization was less closely tied up with the League than was the Permanent Court, but its budget was likewise a part of the League's budget. These two organs were sometimes called autonomous parts of the League of Nations. This is not altogether an accurate description of the relations between these two bodies to the League, as an institution which is dependent upon another for its budget is not wholly autonomous.

Each member could have as many as three representatives in the Assembly, but regardless of the number of representatives a state chose to send, it had only one vote. The Assembly most closely resembled a diplomatic conference; it certainly was not an international legislative body. As a general rule, substantive decisions could be made only by the unanimous agreement of the members represented at the meeting. Normally, the Assembly met annually and each Assembly chose its own president, generally from among the small states not at the time represented on the Council.

The Covenant provided that the Council was to be composed of representatives of the "Principal Allied and Associated Powers"—the United States of America, the British Empire, France, Italy, and Japan—together with four other members of the League "selected by the Assembly from time to time in its discretion." The Council could be enlarged, however, by the addition of either or both permanent and nonpermanent members. This could be done in each case by the Council with the approval of the majority of the Assembly.

As originally planned, the Great Powers were to have a very slight majority in the Council, but this they never had in fact. When the United States failed to join the League, a small state was chosen to fill the vacant seat. The ratio of Great Powers to small states in the Council membership became steadily more favorable to the latter. In the election of members to the nonpermanent seats, bloc voting developed, and since there were always smaller groups of states or isolated states which as a result had little chance of being elected, there was constant pressure for the enlargement of the Council. The number of nonpermanent members was increased from four to six in 1922, to nine in 1926, to ten in 1933, and finally to eleven in 1936. At first, there was no regulation as to the term of office of nonpermanent members, but in 1926 it was set at three years. The number of permanent members has also varied, increasing from four in 1920, to six in 1934–1935, and then declining to two at the end of 1939. The number was increased from four to five in 1926, when Germany was admitted to membership in the League and was given a permanent seat in the Council. When the Soviet Union was admitted in 1934, the number reached the peak of six, but it was to stand at this figure for only a few months. Japan's withdrawal from the League became effective in March, 1935, and the number of permanent seats was back to five. When, in October of the same year, Germany ceased to be a member of the League, the number was again reduced by one. Italy's notice of withdrawal became effective in December, 1939, the same month in which the Soviet Union was expelled from the League for its attack on Finland, and as a result only two permanent members remained, namely, France and Great Britain. The small states were now in overwhelming control of the League, but all power had departed from it.

There was no clear line of demarcation between the functions of the Assembly and the Council. The Covenant defined the powers of each in identical language; each could "deal at its meetings with any matter within the sphere of the League or affecting the peace of the world." However, the Covenant conferred on each body a number of special or exclusive functions. Among the exclusive functions of the Assembly were the admission of new members, election of the nonpermanent members of the Council, apportioning the expenses of the League among the members, and advising "the reconsideration by Members of the League of treaties which have become inapplicable and the consideration of international conditions whose continuance might endanger the peace of the world." The Council likewise had a number of exclusive functions, among which were the nomination of additional permanent members of the Council, formulating plans for the reduction of armaments, advising upon the means by which the members of the League were to preserve, as against external aggression, the territorial integrity and existing political independence of their fellow members, and supervision of the mandates system. Because of some of the special powers conferred upon it by the Covenant and because of its smaller size and its more frequent meetings, the Council did develop into something like an executive body, while the role of the Assembly was more restricted to primary action and the determination of principles.

The basic functions of the League were four in number. One of these was the formulation of plans for "the reduction of national armaments to the lowest point consistent with national safety" (Article 8). Another basic function was to "preserve as against external aggression the territorial integrity and existing political independence of all Members of the League." This was the famous Article 10 whose provisions became the predominant issue in the controversy which arose when President Wilson sought Senate approval for United States membership. Together with Article 11, laying down the principle of collective security, it constituted the core of the Covenant. The settlement of international disputes constituted the third important function (Articles 12 to 16). The fourth major function may be characterized as providing a means for peaceful change. It was incorporated in Article 19. Its provisions were weak. Under it the Assembly was authorized to "advise" the reconsideration of treaties which had become an obstacle to peaceful relations and the consideration of international conditions which were dangerous to peace. The selection of these four as the most important functions of the League is not to minimize others, such as the supervision of mandates, and the other work of the League in promoting human welfare. In the long run, these functions might have been far more important than those listed above, but unfortunately the League was not to have many decades of development. In the short run it would, and did, stand or fall with its ability to handle the four functions named.

Brief History of the League

The history of the League of Nations may be divided into three periods, as follows: 1920–1927, growth; 1927–1932, uncertainty; 1932–1939, decline and collapse.

1920–1927, *Growth.* During the first period the foundations had to be laid and the superstructure erected. Because of the failure of the United States to become a member, the League could not become what the framers of the Covenant had designed. The British, who had not been very happy about guaranteeing the territorial integrity and political independence of all members of the League, now lost all enthusiasm for it. They had hoped that the League might be the means of bringing the British and American peoples into close association and cooperation in world politics, but with the United States out of the League and the American people reverting to their former isolationist ideas, the League threatened to serve as a wedge to drive the two countries apart, and even into increasing hostility. If the British navy should be called upon to apply sanctions against an aggressor and if the United States government should assert the same neutral rights that it did before it became a belligerent in the late war, the possibility of an open clash between the two countries was not a remote one. This no sane Britisher cared to contemplate. British policy in the League of Nations, therefore, was to dilute the guarantee function.

The absence of the United States from the League also tended to drive Britain and France apart. What France desired most of all in the peace settlement was a guarantee against future attack and invasion by Germany. Clemenceau had at first demanded the detachment of the left bank of the Rhine from Germany, either by annexation to France or by the creation of a demilitarized buffer state of this area. President Wilson would not yield to this demand. As a substitute, France accepted a tripartite alliance which pledged Britain and the United States to go to the aid of France in case of attack by Germany. Great Britain and France ratified the treaty, but the United States Senate refused to give its consent to the President for ratification, and since the treaty specifically stipulated that it would be binding only if ratified by all three parties, the treaty of alliance did not become a fact. France now felt itself aggrieved. It had surrendered what it regarded as vital national interests without receiving anything in exchange. France, therefore, became very insistent that the security provisions of the Covenant be faithfully and fully enforced. Because the British would not go along with its League policy, France adopted a policy toward Germany which the British thought unreasonable and which provoked considerable British sympathy for Germany. The contrasting views of France and Britain on the League of Nations have been epitomized as follows: France regarded it as an "incomplete superstate," while Great Britain looked upon it as "a cooperative association of independent states" and "a center of influence." [3]

The absence of the United States from the new organization was also largely responsible for the failure of the plan to place all international bureaus, those already established as well as those which might be created in the future, under the direction of the League. Existing bureaus could be placed under the League only with the consent of all parties to the treaties under which they were established, but since some important countries were not members of the League, this was not possible in every case. Prewar international bureaus, like the Telegraphic Union and the Universal Postal Union, were not brought under the League. The League established a Health Organization in 1920, but the old International Office of Public Health was not abolished, because of the unwillingness of some of its members who were not members of the League to give their consent. The result was the parallel operation of two organizations with very similar functions and, in large part, with overlapping memberships.

During these early years, the League did develop a system of international administrative cooperation. Three so-called "technical organizations" were formed, namely, the Economic and Financial Organization, the Communica-

[3] Sir Alfred Zimmern, *The League of Nations and the Rule of Law, 1918–1935*, Macmillan, London, 1936, p. 339.

tions and Transit Organization, and the Health Organization. There were also created a number of permanent advisory commissions, whose functions did not differ greatly from the technical organizations. These commissions dealt with such problems as intellectual cooperation, protection of children and young people, and slavery.

During this period, the League also enjoyed a minor success in stopping a Greek invasion of Bulgaria, which occurred in the autumn of 1925. The Council, whose chairman at the moment happened to be Briand of France, acted vigorously on the basis of Article 11 and was able to restore peaceful relations between the two small states.

It was also during this period that the Locarno treaties were signed, as a result of which Germany in 1926 became a member of the League. The Locarno Pact was regarded as a long step forward in organizing the peace of Europe, and the admission of Germany to the League made the latter more of a universal organization and less of an alliance of victorious powers. However, the admission of Germany to the League, with a permanent seat on the Council, provoked a constitutional crisis, as three middle-class powers—Poland, Spain, and Brazil—likewise demanded permanent Council seats. This claim was denied them, but a significant concession was made to these states. Article 4 was amended so as to give the Assembly the power to fix by a two-thirds majority the rules dealing with the election of nonpermanent members of the Council. Under this authorization the Assembly passed a regulation whereby this body could, by a two-thirds vote, declare a member eligible for reelection. By this method these states were granted what amounted to a semipermanent seat on the Council. Upon their failure to obtain permanent seats, Brazil and Spain gave notice of their intention to withdraw from the League; however, Spain withdrew its resignation before the required two years' notice had expired. Brazil ceased to be a member in June, 1928.

1927–1932, *Uncertainty*. This period of the League's history began with a fairly hopeful movement. During 1927 and 1928, the Briand-Kellogg Pact was negotiated. It was signed August 27, 1928, by fifteen governments; it came into force on July 24, 1929. Other states were invited to adhere, and within a few years it had more adherents than the League had members. It was hoped that the Briand-Kellogg Pact, the adherents of which renounced war as an instrument of national policy, might serve as a bridge between the United States and the League. No state could go to war in violation of the Covenant without also violating the Pact, and though the latter contained no provisions for implementation, it was hoped that in case of the application of sanctions against an aggressor by the League, the United States would do nothing to hinder such action and possibly might give it some passive support. These hopes do not seem to have been wholly unfounded when it is remembered that the isolationist Senator William E. Borah, who was chairman of the important Senate Foreign Relations Committee during these years, declared that it was inconceivable that the United States would be indifferent to a violation of the Briand-Kellogg Pact.

An important factor in the troubles and uncertainties of these years was the world economic depression of 1929 and the years following. Though the World Economic Conference, convened by the League in 1927, issued what amounted to a Magna Charta for international commercial cooperation, nothing came of it in practice. With the deepening of the depression, economic nationalism became more rampant than ever. The *rapprochement* between Germany and France also came to an abrupt end in 1929, with the death of Stresemann and the election of a considerable number of National Socialists to the German parliament. In September of 1931 occurred the "incident" in Manchuria, which soon developed into a flagrant case of aggression. This clear violation of the Covenant, the Nine Power Treaty, and the Briand-Kellogg Pact was met with little coordination of action or policy between Washington and Geneva. None of the powers upon whom the enforcement of sanctions would fall were prepared to join in any form of collective action which might involve military action. On January 7, 1932, the United States government announced that it would not "recognize any situation, treaty or agreement which may be brought about by means contrary to the covenants and obligations of the Pact of Paris of August 27, 1928." In March, the Assembly adopted the Stimson nonrecognition doctrine for application by League members with respect to the Japanese violation of the Covenant. In 1932, after many years of preparation, the Disarmament Conference assembled, but by this time the world situation had so deteriorated as to doom from the start any efforts for the limitation of armaments.

1932–1939, *Decline and Collapse.* On March 27, 1933, Japan gave notice of its intention to withdraw from the League, and Germany followed by a similar action on October 24 of the same year; in conformity with the requirement of two years' notice, these two countries ceased to be members in 1935. This loss of two Great Powers was somewhat offset by the admission of the Soviet Union in September, 1934, but it had entered the League only out of fear of the rise of Hitler, who rose to power on a platform of bitter anticommunism. Encouraged by the successful defiance of the League by Japan, Germany took one step after another in setting aside provisions of the Treaty of Versailles, and in March, 1936, denounced the Treaty of Locarno. In 1935, Italy invaded Ethiopia and on May 9 of the following year declared that country annexed. League sanctions, halfheartedly applied and never extended to include military measures, failed to stop the aggression. There now began a flight from the Covenant and the League. Some members made interpretative declarations diluting their obligations under the Covenant. Others withdrew from the League altogether. Notice of withdrawal was given by Paraguay in February, 1935; by Nicaragua in June, 1935; by Guatemala in May, 1936; by Honduras in July, 1936; by El Salvador in July, 1937; by Italy in

December, 1937; by Venezuela in July, 1938; by Hungary in April, 1939; and by Spain in May, 1939.

As a result of these events there developed a movement for the reform of the League. On July 4, 1936, the Assembly of the League, in an extraordinary session, passed a resolution requesting the Council to invite governments to send in proposals to improve "the application of the principles of the Covenant," and three months later it set up a committee of inquiry to examine these proposals. The committee recommended that the Covenant should be amended so as to eliminate from it all expressions which recalled the divisions of the Great War or, in other words, to separate the Covenant from the peace treaties. There was a widespread feeling that it had been a mistake to tie the Covenant to the peace treaties and that the League was breaking down under the burden of these treaties. The committee also recommended the coordination of the various peace pacts—the Briand-Kellogg Pact and the Treaty of Rio de Janeiro of 1933—and the Covenant in order to facilitate cooperation between member and nonmember states in the maintenance of peace. There was also a strong demand for universality of membership, but this demand ran into the difficulty that anything like a general membership could be obtained only by watering down the obligations which membership would impose. However that may be, the movement for reform came to nought.

It was evident long before World War II broke out that the League would be powerless to do anything about it. Such efforts as were made to prevent the war were made outside the League. Too weak to do anything to prevent or to suppress armed hostilities, the League performed a courageous but quixotic act in expelling the Soviet Union, on December 14, 1939, for attacking Finland. After this the League became dormant. The Assembly, which had not met in several years, convened for its last session on April 8, 1946, when it took the necessary steps legally to terminate its existence and to transfer its assets to the newly created United Nations.

WHY THE LEAGUE OF NATIONS FAILED

Quite naturally, the question of why the League failed has been repeatedly raised. A multitude of answers have been given, but unfortunately there is no simple or easy answer to this query. It has been asserted frequently that the failure of the United States to join was the primary reason for the League's weakness. Few will deny that the absence of the United States was a severe blow to the League's strength and prestige, but there is no guarantee that the United States government would have continued to give the League hearty support. With the first real difficulties, the American people might easily have lapsed into isolationism again. It may be that the bitter experience of a second world war was necessary to convince them that there is no security apart from collective security. By a lukewarm or reluctant participation in the League, the United States might have been a greater detriment to the successful development of the League inside it than outside it. The League badly needed the membership of all the Great Powers, but this it would not have had even if the United States had joined. More was needed, however, than the membership of all the Great Powers. What was needed in addition was the solidarity of the Great Powers, and that was sadly lacking, especially in the 1930's. There is little to justify the belief that the mere presence of the United States at the Council table would have profoundly altered this fundamental lack of agreement.

Some critics hold that the League suffered from a grave constitutional weakness in that it permitted states to resort to war under certain conditions.[4] By permitting exceptions to the prohibition of war, the Covenant seemed to assume that war remained the normal solution of international conflicts. The rule requiring unanimity of all the members of the Council, other than parties to the dispute, in making decisions with respect to disputes has been widely criticized as unworkable. This criticism also applies, of course, to the general rule that decisions of the Assembly or of the Council required the agreement of all the members present.

From the point of view of organizing peace, the League of Nations rested upon three or four main pillars. These were the provision for the reduction of armaments (Article 8), the guarantees against aggression (Articles 10 and 16), the settlement of disputes (Articles 12 to 15 and 17), and the provision for peaceful change (Article 19). The last two dovetailed into each other somewhat, as the settlement of a dispute may involve a considerable revision of existing treaties. Because these pillars were not of equal strength, the League suffered from imbalance. The drafters of the Covenant attempted to make the guarantees against aggression very strong, while the provisions for the reduction of armaments and for peaceful change were made relatively weak. Not only was the provision for peaceful change weak, but it seems to be tacked on as an afterthought. Now it is true that order is the first condition of all civilized society and that without it justice is hardly possible, but on the other hand no amount of force can maintain a *status quo* which large numbers of peoples have come to regard as grossly unjust. Order and change must be linked together as siamese twins; the one is impossible without the other. The League Covenant probably placed too much emphasis upon order and too little upon change.

However, the failure of the League was fundamentally not due to weaknesses of constitution or structure, serious as these may have been. The basic difficulty was the absence of the will to make it work. Good machinery for

[4] Hans J. Morgenthau, *Politics among Nations*, Knopf, New York, 1948, pp. 374–375.

international cooperation can be very helpful if the will to cooperate exists, and it can make common action more effective, but without that will the best organization will be useless.

Because the League failed to provide security, which is the necessary condition for nearly everything else, the excellent work of the League and its agencies in many fields failed to receive the attention it deserved. Both the International Labor Organization and the Permanent Court of International Justice were highly successful institutions, and both survived the League in fact if not in each case in name. The League demonstrated that the difficulties of creating an international secretariat can be overcome. The Secretariat apparently was an effective and loyal body of international civil servants; at least there was very little criticism of it. The mandates system may be judged moderately successful. The League was very successful in its activities in promoting human welfare, even while it was failing dismally in its security function.

When the League of Nations is adjudged a failure, these achievements must not be forgotten.

PART II

ORIGIN, STRUCTURE, AND PROCEDURE

Chapter 6

DRAFTING THE CHARTER

Though the League of Nations had failed to provide security, the idea of an international organization to prevent war and to promote peace was not abandoned. In fact, the failure to prevent World War II strengthened rather than weakened popular demand throughout the world for an effective system of collective security. Evidence soon began to appear that at long last even the people of the United States were undergoing a change of attitude. On August 14, 1941, thus several months before the United States formally entered the war, President Roosevelt and Prime Minister Churchill met at sea and drafted the Atlantic Charter,[1] a statement of war aims somewhat like the famous Fourteen Points of President Wilson in World War I. The eighth and last point of the Charter, in speaking of a "permanent system of general security" indicated that the United States, which only a few years before had enacted neutrality legislation far more rigid than that which was on the statute books in 1914, in the vain hope of keeping out of the impending war, was now prepared to enter a system of collective security. However, one can also see in this statement the doom of the League of Nations, since it contains no reference to the League.

What were the reasons for the decision to start all over again? There was first of all the important psychological reason that it would be better to found a new organization than to try to revive one to which was attached the stigma of failure. The Covenant would in any case have to be revised; it might be less difficult to draft a new document than to modify the old. President Roosevelt probably also believed that the American people would more freely and more enthusiastically join a new world organization than they would the League, about which there had centered one of the most bitter political campaigns in American history. Moreover, the experience with the League had indicated that no security organization could be effective unless all the Great Powers were members of it. But it was highly unlikely that the Soviet Union could be induced to rejoin the League, from which it had been expelled in 1939 for attacking Finland. Thus a new security organization would have to be established if for no other reason than Soviet hostility to the League.

[1] See Appendix 6.

77

If the Atlantic Charter was the first step in the creation of the United Nations Organization, the United Nations Declaration of January 1, 1942, was the second.[2] In this important document, which was signed on New Year's Day by Roosevelt, Churchill, Litvinov, and Soong for their respective governments and by the representatives of twenty-two other states on the following day, the signatories pledged all their resources in the common struggle against their enemies until complete victory was won. They subscribed to the "program of purposes and principles" embodied in the Atlantic Charter. As other states subsequently entered the war on the side of the United Nations, they too signed the Declaration. There next followed the Moscow Declaration of October 30, 1943, signed by Molotov for the Soviet Union, Eden for Great Britain, Hull for the United States, and Foo Ping-Sheung for China.[3] From the point of view of forming a new international organization, this document was very important, since its statements on this subject were more specific than those of the Atlantic Charter, and it also definitely committed the Soviet Union to active cooperation in establishing a security organization. The four Great Power signatories declared that "they recognize the necessity of establishing at the earliest practical date a general international organization, based on the principle of the sovereign equality of all peace-loving states, and open to membership by all such states, large and small, for the maintenance of international peace and security." They agreed that they would "consult with one another and as occasion required with other Members of the United Nations with a view to joint action on behalf of the community of nations" for "the purpose of maintaining international peace and security pending the re-establishment of law and order and the inauguration of a system of general security." They also agreed to "confer and cooperate with one another and with other Members of the United Nations to bring about a practicable general agreement with respect to the regulation of armaments in the postwar period."

Shortly after the Moscow Conference, President Roosevelt, Prime Minister Churchill, and Premier Stalin met at Tehran and on December 1, 1943, issued a joint statement [4] in which they declared that the three Great Powers were determined "to work together in war and in the peace that shall follow," and that this concord would win an enduring peace. They recognized "fully the supreme responsibility resting upon us and all the United Nations to make a peace which will command the goodwill of the overwhelming mass of the peoples of the world and banish the scourge and terror of war for many generations." They further declared that they would seek "the cooperation and active participation of all nations, large and small, whose peoples in heart

---

[2] See Appendix 7.
[3] See Appendix 8.
[4] See Appendix 9.

and mind are dedicated, as are our own peoples, to the elimination of tyranny and slavery, oppression and intolerance," and that they would "welcome them, as they may choose to come, into a world family of Democratic Nations."

In these several solemn declarations all the members of the United Nations had pledged themselves to cooperate in establishing a new international organization for the maintenance of peace. The Great Powers—China, Great Britain, the Soviet Union, and the United States—had very definitely gone on record as determined to establish such an international organization. France, primarily because there was no legitimate, representative government to speak for it, was the only important country on the Allied side which was not definitely committed long before hostilities ceased. But before the conference to draft the Charter was convened, France, by becoming an adherent of the United Nations Declaration (December 26, 1944), had pledged itself in a general way to cooperate in the creation of a new security organization.

THE DUMBARTON OAKS PROPOSALS

The United Nations Conference on International Organization—the official name of the remarkable gathering of representatives of many states which gave final form to the Charter—was preceded by long and careful preparation, especially on the part of the United States government. As early as 1941, there was set up in the Department of State a group of specialists for the study of postwar problems. It was at first composed of only regular members of the Department's staff, but later a number of economists, historians, geographers, political scientists, and country and regional specialists were brought in from the outside to aid in research and the formulation of policy proposals for the peace settlement.[5] Members of Congress were frequently called in for consultation. The British government had a similar group, called the Post-Hostilities Planning Committee.

A major step in the development of the United Nations Charter was the so-called Dumbarton Oaks Conversations held at Washington from August 21 to October 7, 1944. These conversations were held in two phases. In the first phase, representatives of the United States, the United Kingdom, and the Soviet Union conferred for six weeks on the main outlines of the proposed international organization; in the second the representatives of the Soviet Union dropped out and those of China entered. The Soviet Union was then not at war with Japan, and hence felt that its neutral status as far as the war in the Pacific was concerned made it improper for its representatives to sit in a conference of this kind with China which was active only in the war in the Pacific.

[5] *Postwar Foreign Policy Preparation*, U.S. Department of State Publication 3580, General Foreign Policy Series 15, 1950.

With the American tentative proposals as a base, joint proposals were drafted. These became known as the Dumbarton Oaks Proposals.[6] In the drafting of these proposals a large number of difficult questions needed to be answered. A Department of State account of the Conversations summarizes the leading questions before the group in the early stages as follows: [7]

Should economic and social as well as security matters be included within the scope of the projected organization? Should provision be made for withdrawal from membership, for suspension of the rights of a member, and for expulsion of a member? What should be the composition of the body to give military advice to the Council? By what vote should the Council reach decisions? Should members of the Council that were parties to the dispute—including parties that were major nations with permanent membership on the Council—have the right to vote or be required to abstain from voting in decisions by the Council on the dispute? The latter was fundamental to the rights and obligations of members in the organization, to the relation of large and small nations, and to the basic principles on which the organization would function. The British came with the view that the votes of any parties to a dispute should not be taken into account. The American position, presented at this stage, was that a permanent member, like a non-permanent member, should not vote in connection with a dispute to which it was a party. The Soviet representatives held the contrary view. There was, however, no question concerning the general requirement of unanimity of the permanent members in reaching decisions on non-procedural matters of peace and security, since from the outset there was no disagreement among the three Governments on this provision.

A number of questions remained unsolved. A bomb was thrown into the Conversations when Ambassador Gromyko demanded that "the sixteen Soviet Republics" should be included among the original members of the organization. No agreement was reached on this issue, nor on that of voting in the Security Council. Nor was anything included in the Proposals on the question of colonies and of the future of the mandates system in particular. It was decided to reserve these questions for later decision.

The conversations with the Chinese representatives apparently led to no additions to or modifications of the joint proposals which had been agreed upon in the "Soviet phase." The Chinese pressed three points for adoption: [8]

1. The Charter should stipulate that, in the settlement of disputes under the United Nations, due regard should be paid to "principles of justice and international law."

2. The Assembly should promote the development and revision of the rules and principles of international law.

3. The Charter should specifically provide for the promotion of educational and other forms of cultural cooperation.

[6] Called "Dumbarton Oaks" after the name of the estate in Washington at which the meetings were held. For the text, see Appendix 10.

[7] *Postwar Foreign Policy Preparation, op. cit.*, p. 317.

[8] *Ibid.*, p. 333.

It was agreed to leave these questions open and to discuss these proposals later with the Soviet government with a view to seeking their incorporation in the charter at the coming general United Nations Conference on International Organization.

The (Dumbarton Oaks) Proposals for the Establishment of a General International Organization were published on October 9, 1944, two days after the close of the Conversations, and were sent to all the other United Nations governments for their views. In the meanwhile, the United States government was making efforts to find acceptable solutions to the more important of the unsolved questions. The Department of State worked out a formula for voting in the Security Council which was accepted by the British but rejected by the Soviet government. Agreements on the more knotty of the open questions were finally reached at a meeting of President Roosevelt, Prime Minister Churchill, and Marshal Stalin at Yalta on the Crimean Peninsula, February 4 to 11, 1945.[9]

At this conference it was decided that a United Nations conference on the proposed world organization would be convened in the United States in April, that all the United Nations and such of the Associated Nations as had declared war on the common enemy by March 1 would be invited to attend, and that the United States and British delegations to the conference would support the Soviet proposal to admit to original membership the two Soviet Socialist Republics of the Ukraine and Byelorussia. The Soviet Union now accepted the American formula for voting in the Security Council, which was that decisions on procedural matters would be made by affirmative votes of seven members but that decisions on all other matters would require the affirmative votes of seven members including the concurring votes of the permanent members, i.e., the Great Powers, except that in decisions in the pacific settlement of controversies a party to a dispute should abstain from voting.

At the Dumbarton Oaks Conversations the Chinese, Soviet, and British representatives had pressed for a discussion of proposals for a trusteeship system to replace the League of Nations mandates system, but because of a lack of agreement within the government on this matter the United States representatives were not prepared to proceed with this question. This problem had not yet been wholly solved at the time of Yalta, but sufficient progress had been made to permit the United States government to join in a preliminary agreement on territorial trusteeship. This agreement covered the following points: the Great Powers would consult each other on the question before the United Nations conference; the proposed trusteeship system would apply only to three specified categories of territories; there would be no discussion of actual territories at the conference; and the question of which territories within

[9] *A Decade of American Foreign Policy, Basic Documents, 1941–1949,* Senate Document No. 123, 81st Congress, 1st Session, pp. 27–28. For the text, see Appendix 11.

the specified categories would be placed under trusteeship would be a matter for subsequent agreements.

A final step in preparation for the United Nations Conference, at least for the American states, was the discussion of the Dumbarton Oaks Proposals at the Inter-American Conference on Problems of War and Peace held at Mexico City, February 21 to March 8, 1945. This Conference adopted a resolution which endorsed the Dumbarton Oaks Proposals as a basis for establishing international organization for promoting peace and welfare among nations, but which also expressed the desire that certain points be taken into consideration at the San Francisco Conference for incorporation in the Charter. Among these points were: [10]

the aspiration of universality as an ideal toward which the Organization should tend in the future;
the desirability of amplifying and making more specific the powers of the General Assembly in order that its action, as the fully representative organ of the international community may be rendered effective . . . ;
the desirability of extending the jurisdiction and competence of the International Tribunal or International Court of Justice;
the desirability of creating an international agency specially charged with promoting intellectual and moral cooperation among nations; and
the desirability of giving an adequate representation to Latin-America on the Security Council.

These points are of special interest and significance, as they represented the views not only of Latin-American countries but also of many other small states, and forecast the position they would take in the drafting of the Charter at the San Francisco Conference.

THE SAN FRANCISCO CONFERENCE

It had been agreed at Yalta that invitations to the Conference should be issued by the government of the United States on behalf of the governments of Great Britain, the Soviet Union, and China and of the Provisional French government. The last-named, however, would serve as a sponsor only under conditions which the United States government regarded as inconsistent with the Yalta decisions; thus the invitations to the Conference were issued in the name of the other four governments.

The United Nations Conference on International Organization convened in opening session at San Francisco on April 25, 1945, with delegations from forty-six states present. In pursuance of the Yalta Agreement, Britain and the United States sponsored the admission of the Ukraine and Byelorussia, and this proposal obtained the approval of the Conference. This was made easier

[10] *Postwar Foreign Policy Preparation, op. cit.,* pp. 405–406.

by the fact that their admission was tacitly bracketed with that of Argentina. The Latin-American delegations had no enthusiasm for admitting the first two, and the Soviet Union was opposed to the admission of the last. When Denmark was liberated, it was invited to send a delegation, which it did on June 5. The Soviet delegation demanded that an invitation be sent to the Provisional Government of Poland to send delegates, but Britain and the United States were opposed to the admission of Poland until a new representative Polish government had been formed in accordance with the agreement on this subject made at Yalta. Poland was not invited to participate in the Conference, but a place was reserved for Poland's signature of the Charter, thus making it an original member of the United Nations.

At this point it may be well to draw some comparisons between the Paris Conference which drafted the Covenant of the League of Nations and the San Francisco Conference which wrote the Charter of the United Nations. The Paris Conference met at the end of a war, while the San Francisco Conference convened at the climax of a war. President Roosevelt was convinced that it would be highly desirable to draft the Charter at a time of maximum cooperation among the United Nations. It was his idea that the Charter would extend the cooperation which had been developed in the desperate war against the Axis Powers into the peace and give it a permanent basis and organization.

President Wilson had insisted upon tying the Covenant and the peace treaties together, so that the one could not easily be taken without the other. He did this chiefly to make sure of the adoption of the Covenant, but also because he felt that serious mistakes in the peace treaties might be corrected by the League of Nations. However, between the wars many attacks were made on the League on the ground that it was the bulwark of unfair treaties. Others, less severe in their criticism, argued that the League suffered from the burden of unpopular treaties. The San Francisco Conference was not a peace conference; it had only one function, namely, to draft the Charter. In contrast with his predecessor, President Roosevelt thought it wise rigidly to separate the Charter and the new organization from the peace treaties or their enforcement. Only the future can tell which was the wiser course. After all, the international climate in which the United Nations will have to operate will be largely determined by the kind of peace treaties which are concluded among the belligerents, and the United Nations cannot but be affected by them.

The fact that the Conference was held in the United States, and on the west coast in particular, is indicative of the profound changes which had taken place in world politics in the years since 1919. It is true that because of war conditions the Conference could not have been held in Europe, or even very well in England. But the shift to San Francisco is, nevertheless, symbolic. Asia had become about as important, if not wholly as important, in world politics as Europe, and North America had become the chief center of diplomatic influence.

It is customary for the foreign minister of the host government to be chosen as the presiding officer of an international conference. This is a practice so rigidly adhered to that any departure from it is regarded as a blow to the prestige of the host country. Yet the practice was departed from at San Francisco with very little feeling. Eden for Britain and Molotov for the Soviet Union asked that the chairmanship of the public meetings be rotated among the four sponsoring governments. Eden pleaded that it was essential that the Conference make clear that the four governments were acting in unity and that this unity would continue throughout the Conference, while Molotov made co-chairmanship a matter of principle—the principle of equality. The Conference accepted the proposal for the four co-chairmen for the plenary sessions. The chief of the American delegation was made the sole chairman of the Steering Committee and the Executive Committee.

The Conference brought together a large number of very able men. Most governments sent their best. Present were Molotov of the Soviet Union; Eden, Attlee, Halifax, Cranborne, Clark Kerr, and Cadogan of England; Paul-Boncour and Basdevant of France; Spaak and Rolin of Belgium; Van Kleffens and Van Mook of the Netherlands; Koo and Soong of China; King and St. Laurent of Canada; Fraser of New Zealand; Evatt of Australia; Padilla of Mexico; Belt of Cuba; Lie of Norway; Masaryk of Czechoslovakia; Pasha Badawi of Egypt; Mudaliar of India; Romulo of the Philippines; Smuts of South Africa; and Vandenberg of the United States—to name only a few of the outstanding delegates. While there were many able men among the delegations, there was no one of the stature of Wilson or Clemenceau or Lloyd George at Paris. Neither Stalin nor Churchill was there. President Roosevelt, who had planned to attend to give the opening address, had been removed by death on the eve of the Conference. The fresh memory of his great leadership had a pervasive influence on the Conference; in the debates his name was often mentioned and his ideals were frequently pleaded. There was no one present to give the Conference great moral and dynamic leadership.

Field Marshal Jan C. Smuts, who had played a leading role in drafting the Covenant at Paris twenty-five years before, graced the Conference with his presence but his influence was not great. It is difficult to understand why this extraordinary personality played so minor a role at San Francisco. He was deeply concerned, almost obsessed, with the idea of security, and his great fear was that the Conference might prove abortive. Convinced that peace could be maintained only by the concentration of great authority in the Great Powers, he did little more than support the positions of the Big Five. His age, his illness, and his active participation in three wars probably account for this attitude. So far as the text of the Charter is concerned his chief influence was on the drafting of the preamble, which bears the impress of his idealism, but much of his felicity of expression was lost through amendments and reediting.

The Conference was divided into four commissions, and the commissions were again divided into committees, as follows:

Commission I. General Provisions
    Committee 1. Preamble, Purposes, Principles
    Commitee 2. Membership, Amendment, Secretariat
Commission II. General Assembly
    Committee 1. Structure and Procedures
    Committee 2. Political and Security Functions
    Committee 3. Economic and Security Functions
    Committee 4. Trusteeship System
Commission III. Security Council
    Committee 1. Structure and Procedures
    Committee 2. Peaceful Settlement
    Committee 3. Enforcement Arrangements
    Committee 4. Regional Arrangements
Commission IV. Judicial Organization
    Committee 1. International Court of Justice
    Committee 2. Legal Problems

The commissions served little if any purpose. The real work was done in the committees, including the Coordination Committee and the Advisory Committee of Jurists. In the closing days of the Conference these two committees had the arduous task of harmonizing the work of the "technical" committees and of ironing out defects in phraseology. The plenary sessions of the Conference and also the meetings of the commissions were open to the public, but the committee meetings were not. The United States government had prepared a slate for commission and committee chairmen, which was adopted by the Conference. Since this slate was drawn up chiefly with geographic distribution and other similar factors in mind, it was only accidentally that it produced efficient presiding officers. A few of the chairmen were excellent; some were indifferent.

Language at international conferences always constitutes a problem. It was expected that English and French would be the language of the Conference, but there was pressure for the adoption of other languages as well. Soong of China suggested that, in the interest of saving time, only English be the working language of the Conference, but his proposal received little support. In the end, English and French were made the "working" languages and English, French, Spanish, Chinese, and Russian the official languages. Speeches made in either English or French were interpreted into the other language, and speeches given in any other language were reproduced in both of the first two.   All documents were produced in each of the five official languages, which made for a tremendous amount of work.

CHIEF ISSUES

The Dumbarton Oaks Proposals had been drafted by representatives of the United States, Great Britain, and Russia, with China little more than a consultant.   Conscious of the burden which they were carrying in the war against the Axis, and convinced that the burdens of maintaining the peace would likewise fall on them, the Great Powers had reserved for themselves a special, if not a privileged, position in the Proposals which they had drafted at Dumbarton Oaks and Yalta and which became the "working paper" of the Conference.   Though France had not participated in drafting the Proposals and had refused to serve as a sponsor for the Conference, it had been given the position of a big power in the Proposals.   While the Big Five in general stood firmly together against the onslaught of the small states, there was not complete unity among them.   There was a marked solidarity between the United States and the United Kingdom; China walked a tightrope between the United States and the United Kingdom on the one hand and the Soviet Union on the other; while France exercised little force in any direction.   France had not found itself after the national disaster and was uncertain.   It was also a bit peevish, suffering from hurt pride.   The Soviet Union sometimes took positions which the Anglo-American delegations found it difficult to defend, but the Big Five succeeded in keeping a very nearly solid front.

Nor were the small states altogether homogeneous.   Some, like Canada, Brazil, the Netherlands, and Australia regarded themselves as "middle powers," entitled in some respects to a special position among the non-Great Powers. It was to fit their special position that the provision was written into the Charter that in electing the nonpermanent members of the Security Council "due regard" should be "specially paid, in the first instance to the contribution of Members of the United Nations to the maintenance of international peace and security and to the other purposes of the Organization."   A few small states voted regularly with the Big Five, either out of conviction or because they were satellite states.

In some circles in the United States there has persisted the myth of London's controlling the votes of the Dominions in international conferences. During the 1920 presidential campaign, when the League of Nations was an issue, it was frequently charged that Britain had six votes in the Assembly while the United States, if it were to join, would have only one.   This was never more than a myth, but it was one which events at the San Francisco Conference thoroughly dispelled.   The Australian, New Zealand, and Canadian delegations were among the most active in the attack on the privileged position given to the Big Five in the Proposals. Indeed, Evatt of Australia, ably supported by Fraser of New Zealand, became the leader of the small states in this struggle.

The Latin-American states occupied a peculiar position in the Conference. They are so numerous that they controlled a large bloc of votes—two-fifths of the total—and when they united on a position, as they frequently did, they could exert great influence. It is one of the anomalies of an international conference that voting power has frequently so little relation to population. The Latin-American countries have a combined population only equal to that of the United States, yet because it is divided into many states, they have twenty times the voting power of their northern neighbor.

The so-called Arab states had joined in a League not long before the Conference convened. On some questions, notably trusteeship matters, they voted regularly as a bloc.

To understand what the chief issues were, it is necessary to note briefly how the principle of great-power supremacy had been built into the structure and procedure of the Organization in the Dumbarton Oaks Proposals and the voting formula agreed upon at Yalta. The Security Council would be invested with very great power; its members would have power to take decisions binding upon all members of the United Nations. The Security Council would be composed of eleven members: the Big Five as permanent members, plus six members elected by the General Assembly for a term of two years, three retiring each year. All decisions would be made by a vote of seven, but in nonprocedural matters the seven votes would have to include the concurring votes of the permanent members, except that in the pacific settlement of disputes the parties to the dispute should abstain from voting. A permanent member could veto decisions of the Security Council to resort to enforcement measures or sanctions for breach of the peace, measures for regulating armaments, and the like. Moreover, each of the five permanent members could prevent the admission of new members and the suspension or expulsion of members and could block the appointment of a Secretary-General. Moreover, each permanent member of the Security Council would have the power to veto any amendment of the Charter.

The small states sought to whittle down the special powers which were accorded the Big Five in the Dumbarton Oaks Proposals and to improve their own relative position. Specifically, they fought for an increase of the powers of the General Assembly, where they would enjoy an overwhelming majority, for an increase in the number of nonpermanent members of the Security Council, for a decrease in the power of the Security Council, for automatic or compulsory jurisdiction for the International Court of Justice, for giving the General Assembly or the International Court power to interpret the Charter, and for an easy amending process. And, above all, they wished to make more precise and to restrict the veto power of the Big Five. It was over the voting formula in the Security Council that the most intense controversy developed.

The attack on the veto took many forms, some of them ingenious. There was an attempt made to define acts of aggression in the Charter and to make the action of the Security Council automatic in such cases. If the Council were deprived of discretionary power in a number of cases, the veto would to that extent be restricted. Another line of attack was to increase the size of the vote necessary to make all decisions, and to reduce the required number of concurring votes of permanent members from five to four or three.

It became evident during the debates on the Yalta voting formula that the sponsoring powers were not themselves wholly clear as to how far the veto extended. To obtain clarification the representatives of the small states submitted a questionnaire of twenty-three points. The statement [11] of the sponsoring states in reply was not specific on every question, but it did clarify the atmosphere on one important point. The Soviet Union, which previously had insisted that the veto also apply to the consideration of disputes by the Council, now yielded on this point and joined in a statement with the other sponsoring states that the rule of unanimity did not apply to the discussion and consideration of disputes.

Many of the delegates were unhappy about the extension of the veto to amendments. They argued that they could more easily acquiesce in some of the features they had had to accept if, in due time, these could be modified by amendments. They pleaded that they could go home and ask for ratification of a Charter with many unpopular features provided it contained a fairly liberal amending procedure. Australia was especially insistent in this matter. The Great Power answer was that unless the veto did extend to amendments the predominant position which the Charter gave them would mean nothing, for it might soon be taken away from them. The Great Powers stood adamant and there was nothing for the small states to do but to accept their stand. The provision adopted is that amendments may be added to the Charter when proposed by a two-thirds vote of the members of the General Assembly and ratified by two-thirds of the members of the United Nations, including all the permanent members of the Security Council (Article 108). The only concession made to the wishes of the small states was that a general reviewing conference may be held when desired by two-thirds of the members of the General Assembly and any seven members of the Security Council. As one of its last efforts to liberalize the amending procedure, Australia successfully proposed that the question of a review conference be placed on the agenda of the General Assembly after ten years. However, any proposal for revision must obtain a two-thirds vote of the conference and the ratification of two-thirds of the members of the United Nations, including all the permanent

[11] See Appendix 12.

members of the Security Council. Thus the predominant position of the five Great Powers is secure behind this formidable barrier against amendments or revision of the Charter without their consent.

In this contest between the Great Powers and the small states, nearly all the advantages were on the side of the former, for the reason that a United Nations organization could function effectively only with all the Great Powers as members; with one or two of the Great Powers absent it would have little, if any, value. Before this inexorable fact the small states had to bow. They were able to effect many changes, most of them improvements, in the Dumbarton Oaks Proposals, but they were unable to dislodge the Great Powers from the predominant position the latter had created for themselves in that document.

Another issue which presented considerable difficulty was that of regional arrangements. The Dumbarton Oaks Proposals not only had recognized that there should be room for them within the framework of the Charter but had provided that the "Security Council should encourage settlement of local disputes through such regional arrangements or by such regional agencies." There was the feeling in several quarters that these provisions were inadequate. The Latin-American countries and the United States wished to safeguard the traditional American policy of nonintervention from the outside in the affairs of the Western Hemisphere. Some European countries wished to make sure that treaties of mutual assistance would be legal under the Charter. Others still were concerned about creating a second line of security in case the Security Council should be unable to act because of the veto.

Article 52 gives the solution to this problem. Clause 1 of the article runs as follows:

Nothing in the present Charter precludes the existence of regional arrangements or agencies for dealing with such matters relating to the maintenance of international peace and security as are appropriate for regional action, provided that such arrangements or agencies and their activities are consistent with the Purposes and Principles of the United Nations.

This clause, together with the provision in Article 53 that where the Security Council utilizes regional arrangements or agencies for enforcement action under its authority no such action shall be taken by the regional agency (with certain exceptions) without the authorization of the Security Council, was the solution agreed upon to harmonize regionalism with universalism.

There was still another problem to which an answer had to be found. The veto in a sense creates an anomaly. According to Article 1, the first purpose of the United Nations is "to maintain international peace and security, and to that end: to take effective collective measures for the prevention and removal of threats to the peace, and for the suppression of acts of aggression or other breaches of the peace," yet the veto may prevent the Security Council from functioning. What is the effect of the veto? Does the veto free members of the duty, and even deprive them of the right, of acting against an aggressor? If it did, what a strange international security organization the United Nations would be! Article 51 gives the answer: "Nothing in the present Charter shall impair the inherent right of individual or collective self-defense if an armed attack occurs against a Member of the United Nations, until the Security Council has taken the measures necessary to maintain international peace and security."

By these provisions it was thought to harmonize the veto with collective security and regionalism with universalism.

CHARTER AND COVENANT COMPARED

The Charter is a much longer document than the Covenant and is not nearly so well drafted. The Charter is composed of 111 articles; the Covenant had only 26. The Charter is involved and repetitious; the Covenant was simple and direct. The Covenant has only a short preamble, but the Charter has, in addition to a long preamble, a chapter entitled "Purposes and Principles." The Charter has a large vestibule.

The Charter reflects far greater concern for the solution of economic and social problems, and it provides for an organ—the Economic and Social Council—whose sole function is to promote international cooperation for this purpose. The Covenant provided for no such organ.

From the point of view of general structure, the League and the United Nations were rather similar. The Council was not greatly different from the Security Council in composition, nor was the Assembly basically different from the General Assembly. Provisions in the Covenant for the Secretariat were much the same as those in the Charter. The constitution of the Mandates Commission was quite different from the complicated manner in which the Trusteeship Council is set up. The International Court of Justice is more nearly an integral part of the United Nations than was the Permanent Court of International Justice, but in structure—and in jurisdiction and procedure, as well—the new court is almost identical with the old.

While there are many similarities between the two organizations, there are also many important differences. In the League, the functions of the Council and the Assembly were not clearly differentiated; in the United Nations the functions and powers of the Security Council and the General Assembly are rather sharply divided. The maintenance of international peace and security is the primary function of the Security Council, and it has power to act and to bind all the members of the United Nations, always provided there is Great Power unanimity.

Under the League, unanimity was required (with a few exceptions) for decisions in both Council and Assembly, but only unanimity of those present. In the United Nations, the Council can make decisions by a vote of seven members, but in nonprocedural, or substantive, matters these seven votes must include the concurring votes of the five Great Powers. In the General Assembly decisions on important questions require a two-thirds vote, decisions on other matters only a simple majority. The provisions on voting in the two most important organs are thus far more liberal under the Charter than under the League. Amendments to the Covenant required the ratification of all the members of the League whose representatives composed the Council and of a majority of the members of the League whose representatives composed the Assembly. Thus, not only the permanent members of the Council, but every member had the power of vetoing amendments to the Covenant. As has already been noted, only the permanent members of the Security Council have the power to veto amendments to the Charter. With respect to voting procedure, the Charter clearly represents a considerable advance over the Covenant.

The Charter contains more comprehensive provisions with respect to dependent peoples than did the Covenant. The Charter contains a Declaration Regarding Non-Self-Governing Territories which is binding on all members of the United Nations which administer such territories. Under it they recognize an obligation to promote the social, economic, and cultural welfare of the inhabitants and to prepare them for self-government as rapidly as possible. The trusteeship system of the Charter is in many respects a continuation of the mandates system of the Covenant, but with essential differences. The territories under the trusteeship system are classified quite differently from those of the mandates system, and the Trusteeship Council has far greater power than did the Mandates Commission.

The Charter gives greater recognition to regional arrangements for the maintenance of peace and security. The Covenant (Article 21) stated, "Nothing in this Covenant shall be deemed to affect the validity of international engagements, such as treaties of arbitration or regional understandings like the Monroe Doctrine, for securing the maintenance of peace." Some of the Latin-American countries asked for clarification of this ambiguous statement but never received much enlightenment. In any case, nothing was done to implement the provision.

THE UNITED NATIONS NOT STATIC

However important the Charter may be in determining the character of the Organization, especially in its early stages, it must be remembered that the United Nations is a living institution, and no living institution can be impounded within the precise terms of a text. The determination of its members to make it work, practices which are developed in meeting new situations, interpretations of the Charter, resolutions and decisions which fill in its broad provisions—all these will have a tremendous influence in determining the future development of the United Nations. Indeed, the remarkable constitutional development the United Nations has already undergone in the few years of its existence is encouraging proof of a remarkable vitality.

Chapter 7

BASIC CHARACTERISTICS OF THE
UNITED NATIONS

The United Nations cannot be understood in its proper perspective unless its basic characteristics as an international organization are kept clearly in mind. It cannot be classified in any ready-made category, because it is not one of a large number of similar institutions or agencies. In some ways, it is unique, and therefore the possibilities of significant comparison and contrast are quite limited. In other ways, it reveals a fundamental similarity to many devices and institutions which have existed in the history of the world. We cannot assign to it a technical label, compounded from the Greek and Latin, and feel that we have it adequately placed in the labyrinth of descriptive classification. We can, however, maintain perspective and order in our study by determining the principal characteristics of the United Nations as a device of political organization.

An analysis from this point of view discloses six characteristics which can be identified as significant and basic: The United Nations is a system of international organization. Its chief purpose and function lie in the field of collective security. It developed as an extension of a wartime alliance. It gives special recognition to the principle of joint action by the Great Powers. It is primarily an association of member states. The United Nations has a legal status and international personality of its own.

A System of International Organization

Modern international organization began as a piecemeal and unsystematic affair.[1] During the nineteenth century, for example, national states were not subject to any external or superior legal control or regulation. Yet they were in contact with each other, and there were many activities which transcended national boundaries. The answer to this situation was a limited amount of voluntary cooperation. Special measures were used to meet immediate pressing needs. There were diplomats, treaties, conferences, *ad hoc* agencies, and other devices, but the agencies and methods of international

[1] See Chap. 3.

cooperation remained sporadic, mostly bilateral in form and scope, and restricted to specific needs and areas. There was no over-all system, such as now exists in connection with the United Nations.

What are the criteria by which a general system of international organization may be identified? A minimum of four tests must be applied. A system, in contrast to an unrelated and piecemeal set of devices, exists when there is a definitely constituted agency, an established continuity, generality of membership, and a broad scope of functions.

The Charter of the United Nations is a constitution for international organization. It establishes an agency with specified powers to carry out certain designated functions. This is in contrast to such methods as voluntary cooperation through bilateral diplomatic arrangements, or the convening of international conferences from time to time. A system of political organization exists when there is an interrelated pattern for the distribution of governmental functions and powers. Even when the powers delegated to a more inclusive organization are very slight, a pattern of distribution still exists. The United Nations is entrusted with certain functions, and by the Charter it is endowed with the corresponding degree of authority. This fact should not be confused with the question of the extent to which it has been able to perform its functions and to use its authority. Sometimes, for one reason or another, an organization cannot in fact use powers which have previously been granted to it. That is a matter of how it works in practice, and it will be appropriate to consider this problem later.[2] The point here is that an agency of international cooperation has been established by constitutional provision.

The matter of continuity is also important. Transitory activities and methods which come and go with great frequency do not provide the basis of stability required for a genuine system of international organization. The element of long-term duration is necessary. For example, one of the great disadvantages of the international conferences during the nineteenth century was that they adjourned *sine die* when their immediate job was done. A new conference could be convened only with great difficulty. The devices of international cooperation were temporary and discontinuous. There was usually no staff work between conferences, and there was very little carry over or accumulation of effort. The provision that meetings shall regularly take place at frequent intervals has removed great obstacles from the common discussion of matters of international concern. The United Nations includes an institutionalized system of regularly recurring conferences.

Geographic inclusiveness is a third test of a system of international organization. Universality of membership, although desirable, is not essential, provided the support and participation are sufficiently widespread to enable the agency to function on a global basis. From this point of view, the United Nations is in a stronger position than was the League of Nations. Although a number of countries have not yet become members for one reason or an-

[2] See Chaps. 14–19.

other, it does include all the Great Powers and a very large percentage of all the other countries of the world. As is well known, the United States was never a member of the League, nor did the Soviet Union join until 1934. It was anticipated, of course, that the United Nations would become a world organization in the complete sense. Therefore the Charter provided for the later admission of "peace-loving states" not numbered among the original signatories. Nine countries have been admitted under this procedure, but quite a few others remain outside. In terms of the purposes and objectives of the United Nations, this situation may be viewed as a temporary one. If the Organization is successful and if the tensions of the "cold war" are resolved, substantial universality of membership should follow as a matter of course.

The fourth criterion for a general system of international organization is that of a relatively broad scope of functions. An agency to handle one service (such as postal communications) or one technical problem (such as standard measurements) would hardly come within this definition. The scope of the United Nations, however, is as broad as the activities and possibilities of international political, economic, and social cooperation. Its purposes are to maintain international peace and security; to develop friendly relations among nations and to take appropriate measures to strengthen universal peace; and to achieve international cooperation in the social, economic, and related fields and in encouraging respect for human rights and fundamental freedoms. The only restriction on the scope of the United Nations is the provision that it shall not intervene in matters which are "essentially within the domestic jurisdiction of any state." Thus, it is potentially able to function across the whole field of modern international relations.

The United Nations, then, may be characterized as a general system of international organization because it is a definitely constituted agency, with an established continuity, generality of membership, and broad functional scope. Its six principal organs, with the subsidiary organs and affiliated specialized agencies, cover a very large proportion of contemporary international organization. The major exceptions, so far as governmental organizations are concerned, are certain regional agencies like the Pan American Union. These, however, are recognized by the Charter as being compatible with the United Nations, and in the broad sense, there is very little distinction to be made at the present time between the United Nations systems and public international organization as a whole.[3]

ORGANIZATION FOR COLLECTIVE SECURITY

"Collective security" characterizes the United Nations in terms of its chief purpose. Certainly the peoples of the world will judge it on the basis of its contribution to the prevention of war. This is consistent with the

[3] For a definition of "private international organization," see p. 31.

background of the Organization and the provisions of the Charter. The key idea in establishing the United Nations was that victory in World War II must be followed by "winning the peace." The first clause in the Preamble to the Charter speaks of the determination "to save succeeding generations from the scourge of war." The first purpose stated in Article 1 is "to maintain international peace and security." Admission to membership is open only to "peace-loving states." The General Assembly is to consider and make recommendations for the settlement of international disputes and on "the general principles of cooperation in the maintenance of international peace and security." The Security Council has the "primary responsibility for the maintenance of international peace and security." The provisions of the Charter on international economic and social cooperation are introduced with the stated purpose of creating "conditions of stability and well-being which are necessary for peaceful and friendly relations among nations."

Even a cursory reading of the Charter is sufficient to indicate that considerations of international peace and security are paramount. Disputes and situations which threaten the peace are to be handled by the General Assembly and the Security Council.[4] It is not enough, however, to deal with disputes as they arise. The conditions of lasting peace must be established in the world, if the United Nations is to succeed. In the long run, prevention is much more important than cure. For this reason, emphasis is placed upon international economic and social cooperation, upon human rights and fundamental freedoms, and upon the welfare of non-self-governing peoples. Thus, international peace and security are to be maintained by both direct and indirect methods—the former to handle emergencies and the latter to establish the basis of a lasting peace.

The United Nations represents an attempt to maintain peace through the principle of collective security. During the nineteenth century, international law and organization incorporated the principle of self-help. War was a fact outside the realm of law. When war occurred between two countries, others had a choice of joining in as belligerents or of remaining outside the conflict as impartial "neutrals." This conception of the legal status of war was abandoned by the Covenant of the League of Nations. The idea was that any nation which started a war would be opposed by the rest of the world. All third parties would come to the assistance of a victim of aggression. A potential aggressor, knowing this, would never dare launch an attack. Thus, wars would be prevented and the peace made secure. Although the League was unable to prevent World War II, the principle of concern (that an attack against one nation is an attack against all) remains valid.[5]

---

[4] See Chaps. 8 and 9.

[5] Article 11 of the Covenant provided that "any war or threat of war, whether immediately affecting any of the Members of the League or not, is hereby declared a matter of concern to the whole League, and the League shall take any action that may be deemed wise and effectual to safeguard the peace of nations."

Every organized community and every political society is based upon the principle of collective security.   An attack upon one member cannot remain a matter of indifference to the entire group.   If the rights of one are violated, an offense against the community has taken place and the agencies of the group take the appropriate action.   A murder, a burglary, an assault are not considered as affairs merely for the victim or for his family and friends.   They violate the public peace, and the entire group is affected.   This concept, as applied through the United Nations, means that joint action is to be taken by the members against any nation which commits a breach of the peace. This, if it is carried out in practice, means defeat to an aggressor and protection for the victim.   Under the United Nations system, international peace is to be maintained by a system of collective security.

EXTENSION OF A WARTIME ALLIANCE

Historically speaking, the United Nations developed from the great alliance against the Axis Powers during World War II.   The nations which united to destroy the aggressors were to cooperate in maintaining the peace after the military victory was won.   Evolution from the stage of idea and aspiration to that of institutional embodiment may be traced through a series of declarations and conferences, beginning with the Atlantic Charter and proceeding to the United Nations Declaration, the Moscow Conference, the Dumbarton Oaks Conference, the Yalta Conference, and the San Francisco Conference.[6]   Original membership was open only to states which participated in the San Francisco Conference or had previously signed the United Nations Declaration.   Enemy states and wartime neutrals were excluded from this group, and may become members only by being voted in through the usual admissions procedure.

The characteristic of the United Nations as the extension of a wartime alliance is of more than merely historical interest.   It continues to have significance in some of the situations and problems with which the United Nations must deal.   For example, the Franco government in Spain is the only remaining survivor among the collaborators with Nazi Germany and Fascist Italy.   The policy to be adopted toward Spain on this account has been the subject of one of the disagreements among members of the United Nations.   The Soviet Union has contended that the mere existence of the Franco regime is a "threat to the peace" and that therefore the Security Council should undertake to bring about its removal from power.   On the other hand, the internal governmental administration of a state is usually considered an "essentially domestic question."   The United States government took the position, in 1946, that the Franco regime was a "potential menace" to the peace but not an immediate "threat" within the meaning of the Charter.   The

[6] See Chap. 6.

majority on the Security Council were willing to go only as far as keeping Spain from membership in the United Nations and its affiliated agencies, and in recommending the withdrawal of ambassadors from Madrid. This was not sufficient to remove Franco as head of the Spanish government, and it is questionable whether the policy of suspending full diplomatic relations can be logically maintained when the policy toward other countries is on the basis that recognition does not imply approval of a government. In 1950, the General Assembly modified its position on this question.[7]

Neither Italy nor the former Axis satellites have been admitted to membership because of a difference of opinion between the Soviet Union and other members of the Security Council.[8] The Soviet Union has vetoed the applications of Ireland and Portugal on the basis of their alleged close relations and sympathies with the Axis. It has not been willing to accept Austria as a member, despite the understanding that Austria should be treated as a liberated country rather than an ex-enemy state.

The position of Switzerland is of some interest. That small European neutral has had a special relation to the development of modern international organization, and Geneva was the seat of the League of Nations. Yet Switzerland was not eligible for original membership under the policy adopted and has not applied for admission, although it has adhered to the Statute of the International Court of Justice under a special arrangement.[9]

Although the United Nations originated as the extension of a wartime alliance, it was not tied to or given responsibility for the peace treaties after World War II. The idea was that the new organization should not be shouldered with this difficult task, but should be responsible only for maintaining the peace after its basis was established. At the time the Charter was drafted, it was expected that the peace treaties would be concluded fairly soon after the end of hostilities. This has not proved to be the case. Therefore the United Nations has operated thus far in a different type of situation from the one for which it was designed. As time passes, it becomes difficult and then impossible to keep the issues of the peace settlement separate from the disputes which now threaten and disrupt international peace. Obviously, for example, the United Nations cannot ignore, or function independently of, conflicting policies in the occupation and rehabilitation of Germany.

At the present time, the efforts of the United Nations are hampered and its activities impeded by the disintegration of the partnership of nations by which it was established. Cooperation in defeating the Axis has been replaced by the "cold war," and in this fact lies the crucial problem for the eventual success or failure of the United Nations.

[7] See pp. 209–210.

[8] See pp. 141–143.

[9] For a typical Swiss view of this situation, see William E. Rappard, "The United Nations as Viewed from Geneva," *American Political Science Review,* June, 1946, pp. 545–551.

Joint Action by the Great Powers

"It was taken as axiomatic . . . that the cornerstone of world security is the unity of those nations which formed the core of the grand alliance against the Axis." [10] This axiom is reflected in the so-called principle of unanimity of the Great Powers. It is obvious that international peace and security in the modern world largely depend upon the capacity of the major powers to cooperate. Global warfare can be waged only by the leading industrial nations. Factories have become the arsenals not only of democracies, but of all fighting nations. Large-scale warfare is impossible without a huge industrial system requiring advanced scientific technology and tremendous resources of manpower and raw materials.

With the defeat of the Axis, the Great Powers among the victors had in fact almost a monopoly of the means for waging a modern global war. To reduce it to the simplest terms, as of 1945: If the United States, Great Britain, the Soviet Union, France, and China remained united and in basic agreement, how could a third world war occur? If, on the other hand, they disagreed to the point of fighting among themselves, what could the result be except a third world war? Upon this line of reasoning, the conclusion was reached that the prerequisite of a successful United Nations was unity among these five Great Powers. The Charter was drafted and the plans made in accordance with this basic assumption.

A special position was recognized for those nations which had the power to wage a modern war and which would have to accept predominant responsibility for maintaining peace. This principle was implemented by the status and functions assigned to the Security Council, which is the "enforcement arm" of the United Nations and the only constituent organ given the authority to arrive at decisions binding upon the member states.[11] It is made an agent of the entire Organization with the "primary responsibility for the maintenance of international peace and security." In the Security Council, the Great Powers are in a special category as to both membership and decision making. China, France, the Soviet Union, Great Britain, and the United States are named in the Charter as permanent members, while the other members are elected by the General Assembly for terms of two years. Decisions of the Security Council, except on matters of procedure, can be made only with the concurrence of the permanent members. In other words, the Security Council is set up in such a way that it can enforce international peace and security only to the extent that unity and agreement exist among the Great Powers. It should be noted that the permanent members cannot

---

[10] *Report to the President on the Results of the San Francisco Conference,* U.S. Department of State Publication No. 2349, Conference Series 71, June 26, 1945, p. 68.

[11] See Chap. 9.

be deprived of their special position without their own consent, since the concurrence of each is required for any amendment to the Charter.[12]

Unity of the Great Powers is necessary if the United Nations is to function successfully, but it is not sufficient to guarantee this objective. The permanent members of the Security Council cannot by themselves make affirmative decisions under the Charter. Seven votes are required, and they have only five. At least two of the nonpermanent members must agree with them if action is to be taken. Stated another way, any five of the six nonpermanent members acting as a bloc could exercise a collective veto. Actual issues, however, usually do not find states in opposition to each other on the basis of size. The basic division, thus far, has been the split within the ranks of the Great Powers, with each side attracting followers among the smaller countries.

Prior to 1945 the principle of unanimity in arriving at decisions was a basic postulate of international organization. With limited exceptions, a unanimous vote of all members was required. Even under the League of Nations, unanimity was the rule except for a few matters specifically stated in the Covenant.[13] The reason, of course, was an argument from the concept of sovereignty. If a state could be bound without its own consent, it was not considered sovereign. If it were obligated to accept the results of a majority vote contrary to its own wishes, it would be bound without its own consent. In the United Nations, all the members except the Great Powers gave up this privilege. The latter did not receive a new prerogative. They merely retained one which was normally vested in all members of previous international organizations. Relative to the others, they have a special position; but it should be recognized that decisions can be made in all organs of the United Nations by a less-than-unanimous vote. A simple or a two-thirds majority is sufficient, with the sole exception of substantive decisions of the Security Council. Here unanimity is required, not of all members as was the case for the Council of the League of Nations, but only of the permanent members. Thus, in terms of the development of modern international organization, the United Nations represents a rather sharp, but incomplete, departure from the previous rule of unanimity.

AN ASSOCIATION OF MEMBER STATES

The United Nations is primarily an association of its member states. It is a device or instrument of cooperation for the achievement of certain common ends by joint international action. It is not a superstate or a world

[12] Also, the permanent members of the Security Council are automatically entitled to representation on the Trusteeship Council.

[13] For example, in 1923, an important resolution concerning an amendment to Article 10 of the Covenant was defeated in the Assembly of the League by the sole adverse vote of Persia.

government. As a "fourth level of government" (in addition to local, state, and national) it remains in a rudimentary stage. A clear understanding of this point will enable the student to deal more constructively with the frequent questions born of frustration and impatience: Why doesn't the United Nations do thus and so? Why does it permit a few to block the majority will with impunity? The answer is, of course, that the United Nations operates by joint action based upon agreement, not by force imposed from above. Where the necessary agreement does not exist, the means for making and implementing decisions are not available.

A fundamental consideration in any system of political organization is that of the distribution of power. There are three, and only three, basic patterns, although many modifications and variations are possible. A *unitary* system places the power in a central government. Subdivisions exist, but they operate under supervision and legal control, and on the basis of authority delegated to them. A *confederation* places the power in the constituent units. Any central agencies which are established for convenience in operation obtain their authority from and remain legally subject to the component members of the confederation. Legal authority and governmental powers are decentralized, whereas under the unitary form they are centralized. The third type is the *federal* system under which power is divided by constitutional arrangement between the central government and the constituent members of the federation.

The United States is a leading example of the federal principle. The Articles of Confederation left the real powers of government with the individual states. The Constitution adopted at Philadelphia in 1787 divided these powers between the national government and the states. On the basis of the constitutional theory held in the South before the Civil War, and not entirely forgotten today, the seceding states in 1861 organized the Confederacy. Their argument was that the central government was no more than a creature of the states acting jointly, and that the attempt to make it more would enable the North unjustly to control the Union at the expense of the South.

France and Great Britain have unitary forms of government. Subdivisions exist for historic reasons and for administrative convenience, and there are issues based on localism and sectionalism, but those countries could not have a "states' rights" question in the American sense. The Soviet Union is a federation in constitutional form, but operates as a unitary system under the practice of a one-party dictatorship. Germany ran the gamut, in less than one hundred fifty years, from confederation to federal state and then to a unitary system. One of the main issues now is how much power shall be given to a central government and how much to the component states.

The United Nations would be classified as a confederation, since most of the powers of government are retained by the member states. This is obvious from the slightest knowledge of the United Nations. However, three other tests for identifying the confederal form may be mentioned. They are legislation, taxation, and enforcement directly upon individual citizens. In either a federal or a unitary system, the central government has substantial powers of legislation and taxation, and deals with individual citizens on its own account without having another level of government as a necessary intermediary. The United Nations does not have legislative authority. It does not have the power of taxation, although the members could not refuse to pay the assessments voted by the General Assembly without violating their obligations under the Charter. The United Nations does not have the authority to enforce its decisions directly upon individuals.[14] That must be done by the governments of the member states.

In addition to these general considerations, there are two principles stated in Article 2 of the Charter which are important in connection with the question of distribution of power. The "sovereign equality" of all the members is asserted, and the United Nations is prohibited from intervening in matters "which are essentially within the jurisdiction of any state." The powers of government and the status of independence from external legal control have been expressly retained by the member states. By adopting the Charter they have delegated power and accepted obligations by their explicit voluntary consent, and only to a limited degree for a specified purpose.

The term "equality" should be understood in the juridical or legal sense. No one intended to assert an obvious absurdity by any claims of equality in size, population, power, or any other material sense, just as the authors of the Declaration of Independence were aware of human differences when they wrote that "all men are created equal." Under the Charter of the United Nations, "sovereign equality" means equal legal status, equal representation, and equal voting power. Each member has one vote regardless of its size, population, wealth, influence, or any other factor. This is one of the important characteristics of a confederation or association, as contrasted with the federal type of organization. It is customary for the members of a federation to be equal in some respects. For example, in the American system of government all the states have exactly the same constitutional and legal status, and they have a guarantee of equal representation in the Senate. There is no theoretical reason that a federation could not be established with complete equality of all its members. This does not happen in practice, however, because the larger members will not agree to enter a federation on terms of complete equality of votes and influence. Thus, in the United States, the more populous states have greater representation in one House of Congress and in the electoral votes for the Presidency. It is safe to assume, therefore, that the amount of power transferred to an international organization will be comparatively slight until the principle of unequal representation is introduced in some way.

One question of interpretation of the Charter is the relation of the principle

[14] The United Nations does, of course, exercise direct supervision over its own staff.

of sovereign equality to the special position of the Great Powers. Is the latter an exception to the former? Is there an inconsistency in the Charter? It seems difficult to reconcile the concepts of "sovereign equality" and of "predominant responsibility." One should be careful not to exaggerate the discrepancy, however. All the members of the United Nations are juridical equals. They are equal in representation and voting, except that in the Security Council one permanent member can prevent the reaching of an affirmative decision but no one nonpermanent member has this power. The best interpretation seems to be that the special position of the Great Powers is an exception to the general rule of sovereign equality. Potentially, this is very important. Since the Security Council is the agent of all the members, and can make decisions binding upon them in the enforcement of international peace and security, a full utilization of all the powers granted by the Charter might destroy some of the attributes of sovereignty for all except the permanent members. For example, if a state can be obligated to use its armed forces, possibly against its own wishes, in order to help enforce a Security Council decision, what has happened to the traditional conception of sovereignty?

The reservation of "domestic jurisdiction" applies to all the organs and activities of the United Nations, with the sole exception that it cannot be used to prevent action of the Security Council in carrying out its responsibility of maintaining international peace and security. This principle of the Charter confines the scope of the United Nations to the area of the relations among the nation-states of the world. Its field is *international* cooperation. At the San Francisco Conference, the adoption of this principle in its present form was severely criticized on the ground that it would tend to weaken the new Organization unduly. However, the Great Powers insisted on it since otherwise the broad scope of the Charter might enable unwelcome interference in the domestic society and economy of the member states. Some of the smaller countries also supported the same principle because of the fear that the Security Council in the exercise of its functions might make recommendations involving essentially domestic measures and then use pressure to secure their acceptance.

In actual practice, several important problems of interpretation have arisen. In the Spanish and Czechoslovak cases, questions were raised as to whether the internal regime of a state or a change in government is essentially a matter of domestic jurisdiction. In the former case the Security Council, although it did not adopt a resolution, proceeded on the assumption that it did have the right to take action, and the General Assembly adopted a resolution containing specific recommendations. During discussion of the Czechoslovak case, the United States took the position that the matter was one of domestic jurisdiction only if there had been no interference, direct or indirect, from a foreign power. The Soviet Union, which had urged stronger action against

Franco, insisted that a change in government is exclusively within the domestic jurisdiction of a state.

The relation of governmental systems to international peace was considered in the Greek question. Also, attention has been given to this factor in voting on application for admission to the United Nations. The domestic-jurisdiction principle has been invoked in questions involving non-self-governing territories. During the Indonesian dispute, the Netherlands government claimed initially that, under international law, colonial administration is a matter of domestic concern. The Security Council did not accept this protest. The same type of problem arises under Article 73(e) of the Charter, which provides for the submission of information concerning dependent territories. The extent to which specific information can be required and reviewed has been a heated point of discussion in the General Assembly.

The application of the domestic-jurisdiction principle to questions of human rights was debated when the government of India complained to the General Assembly about the treatment of the Indian minority in the Union of South Africa. India contended that discriminatory treatment violated bilateral agreements and the United Nations Charter and that it threatened peaceful relations among nations. The Union of South Africa claimed that no international agreements were applicable and that the treatment of nationals within a country is a matter of domestic jurisdiction. This question was not explicitly decided, but the General Assembly proceeded with discussion and the adoption of a resolution which implied its authority to act. The Soviet Union has consistently held the position that any attempt to protect individual human rights by international action constitutes interference in domestic questions. That government has used its interpretation of the same principle against the proposal to establish a system of inspection in connection with the international control of atomic energy.[15]

The reservation of domestic jurisdiction is a crucial question for the future of the United Nations. Important problems and issues are no longer sharply divisible into domestic and international categories, if indeed they ever were. The great questions of our day have both aspects. Foreign and national problems are inextricably interwoven. One needs only to think of the relations between foreign aid and taxation, the "cold war" and civil liberties, export markets and full employment, and many others, to see this point. Whether the United Nations achieves a broad or a narrow scope depends largely upon the interpretation given to the domestic-jurisdiction principle, just as the scope of Federal activity in the United States depends to an important degree upon an interpretation of the balance between the implied powers delegated to the national government and the reserved powers of the states. The principle is stated in general terms, and the situation to which it applies is complex. Decisions often will depend upon viewpoints

[15] See Chap. 15.

of the Charter, so that "its interpretation will become a decisive factor in determining whether the United Nations will be an organization of large and expanding responsibilities or be kept within relatively narrow limits dictated by a strict interpretation of the provisions of the Charter." [16]

AN INTERNATIONAL PERSONALITY

We have seen that the United Nations follows the confederal form of political organization and that it is *primarily* an association of member states. It must be emphasized at once, however, that the United Nations is not a *mere* association of members. In many ways it is definitely more than that. It is a distinct entity on its own account. It may well be described as an international legal personality. It has the power to enter into treaties, and it has a headquarters, a legal status, a staff, and even a flag of its own.

An instance of the treaty-making capacity [17] is found in Article 43 of the Charter, which provides that agreements for the provision of armed forces shall be concluded between the Security Council and members of the United Nations. The capacity of an international organization to enter into commitments apart from its members is a new practice which has interesting possibilities for future development. It establishes a precedent which might be used to enlarge the scope of international action. Another type of agreement which the United Nations can make has reference to the international trusteeship system. The Charter, in this case, specifies that the terms of trusteeship arrangements must be approved by the General Assembly or the Security Council. The result is clearly to establish a relation of agreement as to the trusteeship territory between the administering authority and an organ of the United Nations. It is interesting to note also that the Charter makes it possible for international organizations to make agreements with each other. For example, under Article 63 the Economic and Social Council may enter into agreements with the specialized agencies defining the terms on which they shall be brought into relationship with the United Nations. These agreements are subject to the approval of the General Assembly.

One of the first questions in establishing the United Nations was the location of its headquarters. First it met in London, next at Hunter College in the Bronx and at other places in New York City, and then on Long Island in a reconverted gyroscope factory at Lake Success and a building at Flushing Meadows left over from the 1939 World's Fair. All these locations were temporary or interim headquarters. The selection of a permanent seat of the Organization was given careful consideration from the beginning. President

[16] Leland M. Goodrich and Edvard Hambro, *Charter of the United Nations: Commentary and Documents,* World Peace Foundation, Boston, 1949, 2d ed., p. 113.

[17] The use of the term "agreement" instead of "treaty" in the Charter has no special significance.

Roosevelt had once favored the Azores for the meeting place of the General Assembly.[18] Here the delegates would be free from undue pressure, yet air transportation would make the location easily accessible to the delegates. Another suggestion was the Black Hills of South Dakota, so that the delegates could gaze upon the dinosaurs and realize that their own job was to prevent the extinction of man. Geneva, which had been the seat of the League of Nations, did not seem a wise choice for several reasons: Switzerland was not eligible for original membership in the United Nations, public opinion might identify the new organization too closely with the League failure, and the Soviet Union was opposed to the selection of Geneva.

It was finally decided that the permanent headquarters would be established in the United States. Three different groups representing the United Nations traveled thousands of miles at an expense of over $300,000 to investigate personally a number of sites. The choice had narrowed down to Philadelphia or San Francisco, neither considered entirely satisfactory, when John D. Rockefeller, Jr., offered the United Nations a gift of a 17-acre plot of land, worth $8,500,000, along the East River in New York City. This offer was quickly accepted, and the permanent headquarters of the United Nations became a metropolitan skyscraper development. The Secretariat building, which was the first unit to be constructed, was ready for occupancy by the latter part of 1950. The specialized agencies chose to establish headquarters of their own, instead of becoming a part of United Nations headquarters.[19] The seat of the International Court of Justice is at The Hague.

Location of the headquarters of an international organization within the territory of one of its members raises some difficult problems of relationships and jurisdiction. From the international viewpoint, all the members are equally interested and have equal rights and authority. Subjection to the legal control of one national government would be unacceptable to the other members and completely inconsistent with the very idea of international organization. On the other hand, the host government has rights and duties arising from territorial jurisdiction, and it is concerned with protecting its national interests from possible harmful influences within the country but immune from legal control. Even if the status of the headquarters site itself is satisfactorily adjusted, there remain many problems of access and transit across national territory, especially as concerns the staff of the organization, fire protection, postal and other communications, taxation, administration of customs, policing of adjacent areas, and so forth.

A mutually acceptable arrangement was worked out in the form of an Agreement between the United Nations and the United States of America

[18] Sumner Welles, *Where Are We Heading?* Harper, New York, 1946, pp. 31–32. See also pp. 48–50 for Welles's opinion that the selection of New York City was a serious mistake.

[19] See Appendix 15.

regarding the Headquarters of the United Nations.   The basis for this agreement was substantially the application to this special case of the principles applying to the status of foreign embassies.   The headquarters district is under the control and authority of the United Nations, and it has power to make regulations operative there for the full execution of its functions.   The Federal, state, and local laws of the United States apply except to the extent to which they are inconsistent with regulations made by the United Nations pursuant to its authority.   The United States is not to impose any impediment to the transit to or from the headquarters district of persons attached to or doing business with the United Nations, permanent representatives are to have the same privileges and immunities as diplomatic envoys, and facilitative arrangements are agreed on for public services and protection.   Any dispute between the United Nations and the United States concerning an interpretation or application of the agreement is to be settled by arbitration.

Arrangements for the interim headquarters at Lake Success and the General Assembly sessions at Flushing Meadows follow in principle the concepts of the agreement for the permanent headquarters.   On November 8, 1949, an interesting incident occurred when the bar in the delegates' lounge at Lake Success was closed under a New York State law providing that alcoholic beverages shall not be sold on Election Day while the polls are open.   The question was raised as to why an international organization should be subject to legislation of this character.   The answer obviously is that the state law could have been made inapplicable in this case if the General Assembly had wished to pass a resolution on the grounds of necessity for the "full execution of its functions."   This was not done, but a representative of the United Nations conferred with the State Liquor Authority and the exempt status of the international bar was recognized.

The United Nations has a legal status.   Article 104 of the Charter provides that "the Organization shall enjoy in the territory of each of its Members such legal capacity as may be necessary for the exercise of its functions and the fulfillment of its purposes."   This means that the United Nations is a juridical personality with capacity to contract, to acquire and dispose of property, and to institute legal proceedings—all in its own name.   Under American law, the United Nations has in some respects the status of a corporation.   It holds title to real estate in this country, where property law is a state rather than a national affair.   In the acquisition of the headquarters site, special precautions were taken to be sure that there would be no cloud on the title or adverse claims against United Nations ownership.   The history of various parcels of land composing the site was such that this was a very complicated task indeed.   The headquarters agreement provides, in effect, that the United States has a first option in case the United Nations ever disposes of the site or any part of it.

The United Nations has a staff of its own, composed of officials and employees.   This is another indication of a distinctive organizational entity.   It involves three major questions: (1) an international civil service; (2) privileges and immunities of the staff; and (3) claims by the United Nations arising from injuries to its agents. The status and problems of an international civil service are discussed below.[20]

The question of privileges and immunities of personnel associated with the United Nations is analogous to the headquarters problem, in the sense that the status of an international organization within the territorial jurisdiction of one nation is involved. The United States does not admit that officials and employees of international organizations are entitled to diplomatic privileges and immunities under customary international law. So far as this country is concerned, such privileges and immunities must arise from treaties or from municipal legislation. In 1945, Congress passed the International Organizations Immunities Act which gives to public international organizations, recognized as such by the Secretary of State, about the same privileges and immunities as those accorded to foreign embassies and diplomatic officers. This measure is applicable to United Nations representatives and officials, but from the international viewpoint it has certain drawbacks. It is based on national comity, and not on a right under international law. The status of international organizations is compromised by certain of its provisions. For example, the Secretary of State is authorized to withhold the privileges and immunities concerned if an officer of an international organization is found unacceptable for entry into the United States.

The General Assembly approved, in February, 1946, a Convention on the Privileges and Immunities of the United Nations.[21] This Convention definitely recognizes the international status of persons associated with the United Nations in any important capacity. By the end of 1949, a total of thirty-six countries had accepted its provisions. However, the United States government has not done so. One of the stumbling blocks has been the question of United States citizens employed by the United Nations. Would not the granting of privileges and immunities to this group, including exemption from taxation [22] on their salaries, create a special class and be contrary to the idea of equal treatment of all citizens? Another problem is the interest of the United States in the activities of resident aliens within the country. From time to time, the fear is expressed in newspaper editorials and on the floor of Congress that an unsupervised entry of aliens makes an international organization an opportunity for spies.[23] Can the host government assure that its hospitality will not be abused without infringing on inter-

---

[20] See Chap. 12.

[21] For the text, see Appendix 13.

[22] See p. 189.

[23] On the other hand, in the Gubitchev case the Soviet Union accused the FBI of having access to inside information from the Secretariat.

national prerogatives, or claiming a supervisory position in relation to an organization including other national states?

No satisfactory answer to such dilemmas has been found, but the problem is an acute one. The headquarters agreement assumes the acceptance by the United States of the Convention on Privileges and Immunities. The status of the United Nations within the United States will not be definitely established until a mutually satisfactory arrangement on privileges and immunities is reached.

The assassination of Count Bernadotte in September, 1948, while he was acting as United Nations Mediator in Palestine, brought to sharp focus the question of whether the United Nations is competent to bring a claim against the responsible government for injury done to one of its agents. This question was referred to the International Court of Justice for an advisory opinion, and the Court unanimously gave an affirmative answer, saying that: [24]

In the opinion of the Court, the Organization was intended to exercise and enjoy, and is in fact exercising and enjoying, functions and rights which can only be explained on the basis of the possession of a large measure of international personality and the capacity to operate upon an international plane. It is at present the supreme type of international organization, and it could not carry out the intentions of its founders if it was devoid of international personality. It must be acknowledged that its Members, by entrusting certain functions to it, with the attendant duties and responsibilities, have clothed it with the competence required to enable those functions to be effectively discharged.

An injury to an agent is an injury to the principal. The United Nations has the competence to claim reparation, on its own account, for such an injury. In this respect it constitutes an international personality distinct from the member states which compose it.

We have seen that the United Nations has treaty-making capacity, headquarters, legal status, and a staff. It also has an official flag, a seal, and an emblem. The official emblem was designed as a circular map of the world between two olive branches. The flag consists of the emblem centered on a field of light blue. There is a flag code, stating its dimensions and proportions, and restricting its sale and use to purposes closely connected with the aims and ideals of the United Nations. It must always be treated with respect and must never be subordinated to any other flag in either size or position. Thus the symbolism of a distinctive organizational entity has begun to develop. When commercial advertising has exploited the name "United Nations," the emblem, and the flag, the Secretary-General has protested and has sought

[24] *I.C.J. Reports of Judgments, Advisory Opinions and Orders*, 1949, p. 179. See also Quincy Wright, "The Jural Personality of the United Nations," *American Journal of International Law*, July, 1949, pp. 509–516. Israel paid an indemnity of $54,628 to the United Nations in the Bernadotte case.

Federal and state legislation (unsuccessfully thus far) against such practices.

The principal organs and the specialized agencies of the United Nations have definite and important functions delegated to them. The Organization as a whole has the attributes of an international personality, as we have seen. There is also the fact that units of social organization tend to develop a life of their own. The very existence of the United Nations introduces a new factor and a new dimension into the formulation and execution of national policies. There is a strong segment of public opinion in the United States, for example, which will be critical of any policy which appears to ignore or by-pass the United Nations. The President and the State Department are under the necessity of recognizing this fact in advocating measures of foreign policy which will be supported by the American people. Although the United Nations is primarily an association of member states, it is definitely more than that. It is an international personality with real influence and as such must be taken seriously in connection with contemporary international relations and foreign policy.

Chapter 8

THE GENERAL ASSEMBLY

The General Assembly consists of all the members of the United Nations. Since this is the only one of the principal organs of which this is true, and because of some of the functions given to it, the General Assembly may be considered the central body of the United Nations. It has been called the "town meeting of the world," because it is the one place where all the members, large and small, may be heard in debate and discussion.

Each member of the General Assembly has one vote, and is entitled to a maximum of five representatives. The latter provision was the subject of considerable discussion at the San Francisco Conference. There was a desire to see that the General Assembly did not become too large for efficient operation. Also, some of the smaller countries were afraid that they would be placed at a disadvantage in relation to the larger and wealthier members. On the other hand, the broad scope of the agenda and the heavy demands of committee work indicate a need for a relatively large number of representatives. In practice, the size of delegations may be greatly increased by the appointment of alternates, advisers, and experts. The rules of procedure state that a member may have not more than five representatives and five alternates, and that the delegation may include as many advisers and experts as needed. Only the representatives and alternates, however, may sit in the General Assembly or serve as chairmen of committees.

The representatives are appointed by the respective member governments. Their qualifications are determined entirely by those governments, and in general are the same as the requirements established in each case for the foreign service. Article 8 of the Charter provides that "the United Nations shall place no restrictions on the eligibility of men and women to participate in any capacity and under conditions of equality in its principal and subsidiary organs." This, of course, merely prohibits the United Nations from discrimination on the basis of sex and does not place any restriction on the members in appointing their delegations. The representatives serve at the pleasure of their governments and may be recalled at any time. They act upon instructions and are responsible directly to their governments. In this respect the General Assembly resembles a diplomatic conference rather than a legislative body.

FUNCTIONS AND POWERS

The functions of the General Assembly are very broad in scope and of a varied nature. For convenience in discussion, they may be classified under the five headings of deliberative, supervisory, financial, elective, and constituent functions.[1]

Deliberation refers to the important provisions for discussion, study, and recommendation. The General Assembly may discuss any questions or any matters within the scope of the Charter or relating to the powers and functions of any organs of the United Nations (Article 10). It may make recommendations to the members or to the Security Council, or both, on any such questions or matters, with the sole exception that it shall not make any recommendation with regard to a dispute being handled by the Security Council unless the latter so requests. This exception is one provision of the Charter which reflects the feeling that the functions of the General Assembly and the Security Council should be more distinctly separated than was the case with the Assembly and Council of the League of Nations.

Matters for discussion by the General Assembly include the "general principles of cooperation in the maintenance of international peace and security" and principles governing the regulation of armaments. The specific reference to these matters is meant to illustrate, and not to restrict, the scope of the broad powers of discussion and recommendation conferred by the Charter. The General Assembly may call the attention of the Security Council to situations which are likely to endanger international peace and security. It has the obligation of initiating studies and making recommendations for the purposes of promoting international cooperation and assisting in the realization of human rights and fundamental freedoms. Subject to the exception of a dispute being handled by the Security Council, the General Assembly may recommend measures for the peaceful adjustment of any situation, regardless of origin, which it deems likely to impair the general welfare or friendly relations among nations.

In practice, the General Assembly has made broad use of its powers of discussion. It is a forum for the consideration of disputes or situations affecting international peace, and of matters involving the activities of the United Nations. It is only necessary to examine the agenda for one of the regular sessions of the General Assembly to confirm this. For example, the fifth session, which convened in September, 1950, first took care of the organizational details and then proceeded to a general debate, in which the heads of delegations made general policy statements. Items for discussion included, among others,

---

[1] This is the classification used by Goodrich and Hambro p. 25. This is in turn based on the description used in the report to the President by the chairman of the United States delegation to the San Francisco Conference. The terms used in this report were "to deliberate, to administer, to elect, to approve budgets and to initiate amendments."

the questions of Palestine, the former Italian colonies, Greece, China and the Far East, Korea, human rights in the Balkans, international control of atomic energy, technical assistance for underdeveloped countries, freedom of information, refugees and stateless persons, South-West Africa and other trusteeship problems, and relations with Spain.

The discussions in the General Assembly are not restricted to the debating of questions and they are not "mere talk." The term "deliberation" means discussion or consideration with a view to choice or decision, and this function of the General Assembly is in accordance with this connotation. The scope of deliberation extends beyond the actual discussion itself in two ways. First, the power of discussion implies the authorization to obtain the facts and information needed for purposes of discussion. Article 13 of the Charter requires the General Assembly to initiate studies for the purpose of promoting international cooperation in various fields. Reports and information may be requested from other organs of the United Nations and legal opinions may be sought from the International Court of Justice.

In specific disputes and questions considered by the General Assembly, there has never been any doubt of the competence to obtain relevant facts and information. The commissions appointed pursuant to resolutions in the cases of Palestine, Greece, and Korea had among their functions the making of investigations in the field and the observance of the situations on the spot. Thus, in practice, the implied power of fact finding and investigation has been broadly construed. There is no doubt that the General Assembly may authorize any study, investigation, or fact-finding procedure which is relevant to any question which it has under consideration. It is not restricted to ivory towers and cloistered walls.

Second, deliberation goes beyond "mere" discussion by arriving at recommendations. This function is specifically authorized in the Charter for the entire range of subjects which the General Assembly may discuss, with the sole exception of a dispute or situation being handled by the Security Council. The General Assembly is directed to make recommendations, as well as to initiate studies, for the promotion of international cooperation. Such recommendations have been an important factor in such questions as those of Palestine, Spain, Greece, Korea, and the Security Council voting procedure. It should be noted that "recommendations" have not been construed as referring only to formal resolutions passed by the General Assembly and addressed to other organs of the United Nations or members of the Organization. Activities undertaken under the authority of General Assembly resolutions in the cases of Palestine, Greece, and Korea included consultation, conciliation, and mediation. The commissions established in connection with these cases had among their responsibilities the function of assisting in negotiations toward an agreed settlement, both by acting as intermediaries for the parties and by making suggestions to facilitate an acceptable solution in each case.

Recommendations, of course, do not constitute legally binding decisions. They reflect the opinion and advice of the General Assembly. Their effect depends upon the force with which they commend themselves to acceptance. It is here that the separation of functions between the General Assembly and the Security Council becomes apparent. The former goes as far as it can through fact finding, discussion, persuasion, and recommendation. Enforcement action is a matter for the Security Council. This division of responsibilities is well illustrated by the Palestine case. It was generally felt that the plan of partition with economic union adopted as the recommendation of the General Assembly was *the* United Nations solution. But when this was not accepted by the parties, the Security Council did not proceed upon the basis that this plan was automatically binding and enforceable. The delegation of the United States argued that the Security Council could not take action merely to enforce a recommendation of the General Assembly against unwilling parties to the dispute, but only in the event of a finding of a threat to or breach of international peace under Article 39. This interpretation was followed, in effect, by the Security Council. The General Assembly has broad powers of study, discussion, and recommendation. It has no powers under the Charter of reaching decisions which are legally binding upon the members, or of taking enforcement action.

Although the General Assembly's powers of discussion and recommendation are very extensive, there is one important limitation. Article 2, paragraph 7, of the Charter prohibits intervention in matters which are "essentially within the domestic jurisdiction of any state." This is one of the "Purposes and Principles" of the Organization and applies to all the organs, agencies, and activities of the United Nations. Therefore, the General Assembly must observe this restriction when it undertakes to "discuss any questions or any matters within the scope of the present Charter." The growing interdependence of domestic and foreign affairs makes the interpretation of Article 2, paragraph 7, a difficult, somewhat artificial, and certainly a crucial matter.

When the question of Franco Spain was considered by the General Assembly in 1946, some delegations contended that the governmental regime of a state is "essentially a domestic matter" and therefore any attempt to deal with this case would amount to intervention contrary to Article 2(7). This argument did not convince the General Assembly, which proceeded to take action in this matter.[2]

The domestic-jurisdiction limitation has also been involved in the discussions of the treatment of non-self-governing territories. It was argued, for example, that the creation by the General Assembly of an *ad hoc* committee to examine information transmitted by members concerning the territories for which they

[2] See pp. 209–210.

are responsible was a violation of this limitation. Again, this type of opposition was unsuccessful and the General Assembly did establish such a committee.

A very interesting case involving the same question is that of the Indian minority in the Union of South Africa. In 1946, the government of India submitted a complaint regarding the treatment of this group. South Africa, supported by some other delegations, denied the right of the General Assembly to consider the case on the ground that it was a matter "essentially of domestic jurisdiction." However, the great majority supported the competence of the General Assembly, since friendly relations between two member states had been impaired. In December, 1946, a resolution was adopted stating this conclusion and affirming that the treatment of the group concerned should be in accordance with international obligations, including the provisions of the Charter. The Union of South Africa denied the General Assembly jurisdiction and did not put the resolution into effect. The next year an attempt at reaffirmation of the resolution failed of passage, and no further attempt at putting it into effect was made by the General Assembly.[3]

The United States delegation argued in this case that it would be a sign of weakness to restate a decision which had not produced the results intended. Would a firm stand against South Africa in this case have created a possible precedent for injecting the United Nations into the question of civil rights in the United States? There is an obligation under Article 1(3) of the Charter to respect the purpose of achieving international cooperation "in promoting and encouraging respect for human rights and for fundamental freedoms for all without distinction as to race, sex, language, or religion." Would it be possible for another member of the United Nations to complain that the treatment of a minority group in the United States jeopardized friendly relations among nations, and thus give the United Nations a basis for reviewing the situation?

When an internal matter becomes the subject of an international dispute, is it a question "essentially of domestic jurisdiction"? Obviously, one of the most important factors in the evolution of the United Nations will be the trend in the interpretation of this provision. If a broad and flexible construction is placed on the powers to deal with international disputes, the road is open to the establishment of a stronger international agency. A tendency to withhold from the General Assembly all matters having important domestic implications would indicate a narrow and restrictive range of international action through the United Nations.

It has been noted that, under the provisions of the Charter, recommendations of the General Assembly are not legally binding. However, there is nothing to prevent members from *agreeing in advance* to accept a particular recom-

[3] See pp. 210–211.

mendation as binding.   This occurred in connection with the question of the former Italian colonies.   The United States, Great Britain, France, and the Soviet Union were unable to agree on the disposition of these colonies when the Italian peace treaty was drafted.   They decided, however, to allow this treaty to enter into force and agreed that, if the Council of Foreign Ministers did not reach a settlement within a year, the question would be referred to the General Assembly and its recommendation accepted as binding upon the parties.

This case points to a possible method for strengthening the position and influence of the General Assembly.   It also furnishes a precedent for the exercise of a limited international legislative function.   The Charter does not confer any legislative powers.   Nevertheless, to the extent that advance agreements are made to accept as the final determination the results of a vote in the General Assembly in specific cases, an embryonic legislative function results.   If this first precedent is followed by a trend, the next step might be for the members, or some of them, to agree in advance to accept the recommendation of the General Assembly on specified types of questions.   This would be a technique analogous to the use of the "optional clause" for accepting the compulsory jurisdiction of an international court for questions capable of judicial settlement.[4]

Any proposal to give the General Assembly authority to make binding decisions must reexamine the question of voting representation.   The system of one vote for each member, large and small, is grossly unequal in terms of population.   In the General Assembly as now constituted it would be theoretically possible to get a majority (31 out of 60 votes), which would represent only 5.5 per cent of the total population of the members.[5]   A two-thirds majority could be obtained by votes representing only 11.0 per cent of the population.   On the other hand, the votes of the 21 smallest members, with 2.3 per cent of the total population, could prevent the formation of a two-thirds majority.   It seems fantastic to contemplate an arrangement under which one-eighth of the people concerned could legislate for the entire group and bind the other seven-eighths against their will, or in which 97 per cent of the people might be unable to form a two-thirds majority.

These theoretical extremes probably would not be reached in practice, but there is a real and substantial possibility that a small minority of the population would often control the decisive votes.   There is an observable tendency toward bloc voting on many issues.   This is especially important in connection with the Latin-American group.   With twenty members, they have one-third

[4] See pp. 194–195, below.   The Acheson plan, adopted in 1950, contemplates action on the basis of General Assembly recommendations in the event of an act of aggression and the failure of the Security Council to act.   See Appendix 21.

[5] These calculations are based upon the population figures given in Table 2 at the end of this chapter.

of the votes in the General Assembly but only 8.1 per cent of the population of all the members.   The American countries north of the Rio Grande have two votes, while those to the south, with a smaller total population, have twenty votes.   The Latin-American bloc, by picking up one additional vote, could exercise a veto over any General Assembly decision requiring a two-thirds majority.

Another reflection of the extreme disparity among the members is the fact that three of them (China, India, and the Soviet Union) have more than half the total population represented in the United Nations.   Representation in the General Assembly in proportion to population obviously is not the solution to the problem.   Clearly, any system of voting based solely upon population would be inacceptable to the United States and other technologically advanced countries which have to bear the financial and other burdens of carrying out United Nations decisions.   This whole question also is deeply involved in the East-West conflict.   Formulas based on a combination of population with industrial production or with educational levels have attracted some interest, but no proposal for amendment of the Charter in this respect has been made by any government.   One possibility might be to establish a double system for voting, in which a majority of all members and a majority of the population represented would be required for a decision.   Such an arrangement would make it impossible for either a group of small countries or a few large ones to bind the others without their consent, but either group would be in a position to block action.   This might lead to deadlock in the General Assembly under certain circumstances.   For example, if the Communist regime in China is admitted, that country plus the present Soviet bloc would have about 40 per cent of the vote as weighted according to population but only six out of sixty on the present basis.   India, by voting with the minority on a given issue, would create a majority of the weighted vote for a group having only seven votes out of sixty.   A comparable result could also be created by a small group of the more populous members other than India.

It might be possible to work out a compromise formula by which the larger countries would be given additional votes, but not strictly in proportion to population.   The dilemma then arises that the weighted representation would seem inadequate to the countries with the largest population, while the small countries (whose votes are needed to amend the Charter) would resist the idea of surrendering the principle of voting equality for all members.   This is a difficult and perplexing problem, but a solution is necessary if the authority of the General Assembly is to be materially strengthened.

The *supervisory* function of the General Assembly refers to its powers of control and regulation of other organs and agencies of the United Nations.   As the central body, it receives and considers reports from the other organs. While the Security Council is coordinate with the General Assembly, its annual and special reports are to include an account of measures which it has decided upon or taken to maintain international peace and security. These reports are discussed by the General Assembly, and recommendations to the Security Council or to the members may result. The annual report of the Secretary-General is important as the basis of general discussion at the opening of the regular sessions of the General Assembly.

Responsibility for the discharge of functions in the field of international economic and social cooperation is vested in the General Assembly and, under its authority, in the Economic and Social Council. Approval by the General Assembly is required for the Economic and Social Council to call international conferences, to make agreements with the specialized agencies, or to request an advisory opinion of the International Court of Justice. All the functions of the United Nations with regard to trusteeship agreements for nonstrategic areas are vested in the General Assembly, and the Trusteeship Council operates under its authority in regard to such areas. Thus, the General Assembly has definite supervisory powers over two of the other principal organs of the United Nations. It also establishes regulations for the appointment of the staff of the Secretariat, and it may make recommendations for the coordination of the various specialized agencies.

The *financial* function of the General Assembly includes its responsibility for budgetary arrangements of the United Nations and the apportionment of expenses among the members. Article 17(1) states that "the General Assembly shall consider and approve the budget of the Organization." This is an important provision because it involves the power to review the work of the other organs when their expenditure estimates are presented, and to exercise a degree of control by deciding which activities will receive financial support, and to what extent.

The General Assembly apportions the expenses of the United Nations among the members, and the resulting assessments constitute binding obligations in each case. There has been considerable debate over this apportionment. The Charter does not lay down any criteria in this connection, and the General Assembly is free to determine the criteria to be used. The basic principle has been that of ability to pay. However, there have been three major deviations from an automatic application of this concept. First, a ceiling on the maximum contribution of any one member has been recognized. In the estimates submitted by the Committee on Contributions in 1946, the United States was slated to pay almost 50 per cent of the total. It was argued by the United States delegation, however, that no one member should pay more than one-third in order that it would not have an overwhelming financial interest in the Organization. The United States finally agreed to pay 39.89 per cent temporarily. This assessment was reduced to 39.79 per cent for 1950, and to 38.92 per cent for 1951. The United States continues to support the maximum of one-third as a goal to be reached as soon as possible. For the scale of assessments recommended in 1951, see Table 1.

One of the complications in this connection arises from the location of the United Nations Headquarters in the United States. Most of the expenditures must be made in this country, but the dollar shortage in the international balance of payments creates a difficulty for many members, over and above the question of their actual financial capacity. To help alleviate this situation, some contributions have been accepted in Swiss francs and the question of extending this practice to other currencies has been investigated. This appears feasible to the extent that the United Nations spends funds in other parts of the world, as in the case of its European office and its various activities and missions elsewhere.

A second qualification on the principle of ability lies in the question of a per capita ceiling. The General Assembly has given some consideration to the argument that the per capita contribution of any member should not exceed the per capita contribution of the member bearing the highest assessment. Iceland and Sweden, for example, pay more *per capita* than does the United States. Application of a per capita limitation means, of course, that a country with a small population but a comparatively high national income would receive a reduction in its assessment. Consequently, a greater burden would fall on the poorer countries. As between two members with equal national incomes, the one with less population (and therefore more income per capita) would pay a smaller total assessment. A formula based upon national income per capita as a measure of ability to pay cannot be used at the present time without conflicting with the principle of a maximum of one-third for any one member.

A third factor which stands in the way of an automatic application of an ability-to-pay formula is the inadequacy of statistical information. Complete and comparable figures on financial capacity, national income per capita, etc., do not exist. Also the information available is subject to differing interpretations. In the actual determination of the assessments, the standard of ability to pay has been the starting point, but it has been modified by the other factors discussed above and by a process of negotiation. The present tendency is to take the figures for preceding years as a point of departure. Then the members who think their assessments are too high press for a reduction. It is for the General Assembly itself to make the final determination.

The importance of the financial and budgetary functions of the General Assembly should not be underestimated. Control of the purse strings is a potent power. This, along with the supervisory functions, provides a key position in the internal administration of the entire Organization and has a significant influence on the scope of the activities undertaken by it. Whenever the merits of an undertaking are debated, the ace of trumps is held by those with power to decide whether money shall be spent on it.

In addition to the control and apportionment of funds, the size of the United Nations budget is an important question. The General Assembly approved

TABLE 1. MEMBERS OF THE UNITED NATIONS, DATES OF ADMISSION, AND
SCALE OF ASSESSMENTS

Member	Date of ratification	Scale of assessment for 1951,[1] per cent
Original members		
Argentina	Sept. 24, 1945	1.85
Australia	Nov. 1, 1945	1.92
Belgium	Dec. 27, 1945	1.35
Bolivia	Nov. 14, 1945	0.08
Brazil	Sept. 21, 1945	1.85
Byelorussian S.S.R.	Oct. 24, 1945	0.24
Canada	Nov. 9, 1945	3.30
Chile	Oct. 11, 1945	0.41
China	Sept. 28, 1945	6.00
Colombia	Nov. 5, 1945	0.37
Costa Rica	Nov. 2, 1945	0.04
Cuba	Oct. 15, 1945	0.31
Czechoslovakia	Oct. 19, 1945	0.99
Denmark	Oct. 9, 1945	0.79
Dominican Republic	Sept. 4, 1945	0.05
Ecuador	Dec. 21, 1945	0.05
Egypt	Oct. 22, 1945	0.71
El Salvador	Sept. 26, 1945	0.05
Ethiopia	Nov. 13, 1945	0.08
France	Aug. 31, 1945	6.00
Greece	Oct. 25, 1945	0.18
Guatemala	Nov. 21, 1945	0.06
Haiti	Sept. 27, 1945	0.04
Honduras	Dec. 17, 1945	0.04
India	Oct. 30, 1945	3.41
Iran	Oct. 16, 1945	0.45
Iraq	Dec. 21, 1945	0.17
Lebanon	Oct. 15, 1945	0.06
Liberia	Nov. 2, 1945	0.04
Luxembourg	Oct. 17, 1945	0.05
Mexico	Nov. 7, 1945	0.63
Netherlands	Dec. 10, 1945	1.35
New Zealand	Sept. 19, 1945	0.50
Nicaragua	Sept. 6, 1945	0.04
Norway	Nov. 27, 1945	0.50
Panama	Nov. 13, 1945	0.05
Paraguay	Oct. 12, 1945	0.04

TABLE 1. MEMBERS OF THE UNITED NATIONS, DATES OF ADMISSION, AND
SCALE OF ASSESSMENTS (*Continued*)

Member	*Date of ratification*	Scale of assessment for 1951,[1] per cent
Original members		
Peru	Oct. 31, 1945	0.20
Philippine Republic	Oct. 11, 1945	0.29
Poland	Oct. 24, 1945	1.05
Saudi Arabia	Oct. 18, 1945	0.08
Syria	Oct. 19, 1945	0.11
Turkey	Sept. 28, 1945	0.91
Ukrainian S.S.R.	Oct. 24, 1945	0.92
Union of South Africa	Nov. 7, 1945	1.04
U.S.S.R.	Oct. 24, 1945	6.98
United Kingdom	Oct. 20, 1945	11.37
United States	Aug. 8, 1945	38.92
Uruguay	Dec. 18, 1945	0.18
Venezuela	Nov. 15, 1945	0.30
Yugoslavia	Oct. 19, 1945	0.36
Elected members		
Afghanistan	Nov. 19, 1946	0.06
Iceland	Nov. 19, 1946	0.04
Sweden	Nov. 19, 1946	1.85
Siam	Dec. 16, 1946	0.24
Pakistan	Sept. 30, 1947	0.74
Yemen	Sept. 30, 1947	0.04
Burma	Apr. 19, 1948	0.15
Israel	May 11, 1949	0.12
Indonesia	Sept. 28, 1950	

[1] From "Record of the General Assembly's Fifth Session," *United Nations Bulletin,*
Vol. X, No. 1, Jan. 1, 1951, p. 76.

budgetary appropriations of $47,798,600 for 1951.[6] On this basis, the United
States assessment would be about $18,603,215 or 12.4 cents per capita for an
entire year. The corresponding figure would be 13.6 cents for Iceland, 12.7
cents for Sweden, 11.6 cents for Canada, 10.8 cents for Great Britain, 1.7 cents

[6] *United Nations Bulletin,* Vol. X, No. 1, Jan. 1, 1951, p. 75. Since some miscellaneous
income is available, the assessments are actually a little lower than would be expected
on the basis of total expenditures of the Organization.

for the Soviet Union, and less than a penny for China.   These examples represent a wide variation, but the range in per capita national income is also very great.   The figures just quoted include only the general operating budget of the United Nations, and therefore do not account for the entire financial support being given to the activities of the Organization.   Construction of the permanent headquarters was facilitated by a $65,000,000 interest-free loan from the United States.   Each specialized agency has its own budget and scale of assessments.   With the inclusion of these amounts, the contributions of the United States reached a total of $107,268,000, or about 71 cents per capita, for the fiscal year ending June 30, 1951.

The United Nations has been completely dependent on contributions from members.   Undoubtedly its influence and activities could be strengthened if supplementary sources of income were developed.   One step in this direction is the creation of a United Nations Postal Administration under a resolution passed by the General Assembly in November, 1950.   Stamps are issued for use on official United Nations mail and for sale to philatelists, and revenues have been estimated at $300,000 for the first year of operation alone.

The budgetary function of the General Assembly also includes the responsibility of considering and approving any financial and budgetary arrangements with specialized agencies.   It also examines the administrative budgets of such agencies with a view to making recommendations to them.   It is a principle of the United Nations that the technical agencies established to meet specialized needs should be relatively autonomous, yet "brought into relation" with the Organization.   The application of this principle in budgetary terms has raised the question of the degree of control which the General Assembly may exercise over the expenditure items proposed by the specialized agencies.   During negotiations over this matter, the representatives of these agencies argued that there existed only the right to examine the budgets and to make recommendations concerning their form, but not to control their content.   The opposing view supported the principle of budgetary consolidation.

In the compromise finally reached, the specialized agencies agreed to consult concerning appropriate arrangements for the inclusion of their budgets within a general budget of the United Nations with the exact nature of such arrangements to be specified in supplementary agreements.   The pattern of these agreements varies.   Some of the specialized agencies have agreed to certain common financial practices and have submitted their budgets for discussion and recommendation, while others merely transmit copies of their reports.   However, it remains possible for the General Assembly to give publicity to the various budgetary practices and to make constructive suggestions for their improvement.

The *elective* function of the General Assembly is of two distinct types.   One has to do with the admission of new members into the United Nations.   While the Charter uses the term "admission" in this connection, it seems appropriate to think of it as an election to membership. This process is accomplished by the General Assembly upon the recommendation of the Security Council. While the Charter does not so specify, the practice has been for a prospective member to file an application addressed to the Secretary-General. It is then transmitted to the Security Council and, after its action, to the General Assembly. To the end of 1950, all applicants so recommended have been admitted, but a number of applicants have not been recommended by the Security Council. It has sometimes been argued that a *favorable* recommendation is not essential under the Charter, that the General Assembly can use its own judgment after formal consideration before the Security Council, but this point of view has not been accepted in practice.[7] It is clear that no new member can be admitted without favorable affirmative action by the General Assembly.

Another question of membership is that of the basis for losing it. A member with its contribution in arrears may lose its voting rights. A member against which preventive or enforcement action is being taken may be suspended by the General Assembly upon the recommendation of the Security Council, but the latter acting alone may restore it to the exercise of the rights and privileges of membership. A member may be expelled, by the same procedure as in the case of suspension, if it persistently violates the principles of the Charter. The right of withdrawal is not mentioned in the Charter. It does exist, however, on the basis of an agreed interpretation at the San Francisco Conference, but emphasis is placed on the "highest duty" of each member to continue its cooperation with the United Nations.

The other phase of the elective function vested in the General Assembly has to do with the choice of members for other organs. Thus the General Assembly elects the six nonpermanent members of the Security Council, all the eighteen members of the Economic and Social Council, and some of the members of the Trusteeship Council. Acting as a coordinate body with the Security Council, it participates in the election of judges to the International Court of Justice. The Secretary-General is "appointed" by the General Assembly upon the recommendation of the Security Council.

The *constituent* function of the General Assembly refers to the provision (Article 108) that amendments to the Charter are proposed, or "adopted," by that body prior to their referral to members for ratification. Also, the General Assembly participates with the Security Council in calling a general conference of members to review the Charter. If such a conference has not been held before the tenth annual session of the General Assembly (which will occur in 1955), the proposal to do so is to be placed on the agenda of that session. By the end of 1951, no amendments had been proposed and no general conference had been called.

[7] See pp. 141–143.

ORGANIZATION AND STRUCTURE

The General Assembly is required by Article 20 of the Charter to meet in regular annual sessions "and in such special sessions as occasion may require." The opening date for the annual session has been set by the General Assembly as the third Tuesday in September. Sessions are held at the headquarters of the United Nations unless the General Assembly decides otherwise. The practice of meeting occasionally elsewhere than New York City seems to be favored, although it increases the expenses of holding a session. The first part of the third session was held in Paris in the autumn of 1948, and there is considerable interest in holding a session in some other part of the world, possibly Moscow.

The General Assembly has held two special sessions (in 1947 and 1948), both on the Palestine question. Such sessions are convoked by the Secretary-General at the request of the Security Council or of a majority of the members of the United Nations.

The General Assembly elects its own President for each session. It has been the practice to choose the presiding officer from the small or middle powers, and to cover the major geographic areas of the world in succession. The Presidents for the first five regular sessions were Spaak of Belgium, Aranha of Brazil, Evatt of Australia, Romulo of the Philippines, and Entezam of Iran.

According to rules which have been adopted, no representative may address the General Assembly without having previously obtained permission of the President. This is a procedural requirement, and it does not give the President authority to use the power of recognition in order to control the viewpoints which may obtain a hearing. The President is required by the rules to call upon representatives in the order in which they signify their desire to speak. The General Assembly itself decides such questions as a time limit on speeches, closing the list of speakers, and appeals from rulings on points of order. However, the position of President of the General Assembly is an influential one. He directs the discussion and ensures observance of the rules, he may call a speaker to order if his remarks are not relevant to the subject under discussion, he makes the initial decision on a point of order, he may accord the right of reply to a member after the list of speakers is closed if this seems desirable, and of course the prestige and dignity of the position is of some consequence. His influence as a spokesman for the United Nations as a whole rivals in some ways that of the Secretary-General.

The General Assembly also elects seven Vice-Presidents for each session. If the President finds it necessary to be absent during a meeting, he appoints one of the Vice-Presidents to take his place. However, if the President becomes unable to perform his functions, a new President is to be elected for the remainder of the term.

The staff required by the General Assembly is provided and directed by the Secretary-General.   Thus, although the General Assembly has general supervision over the internal administration of the entire Organization, it does not directly supervise the staff needed for its own functions.   However, it does establish regulations for the staff of the Secretariat as a whole and it retains the supervisory and financial functions.   The General Assembly has ultimate control but not immediate responsibility in relation to the staff which it uses. It is too early to say whether this fact will have any significant influence on the trend of development in the relationships between the General Assembly and the Secretary-General, but quite possibly it will.   It is safe to assume that he who controls routine administration has the opportunity to influence the making of policy.

A very important part of the organization of the General Assembly is the committee system.   Detailed discussion and debate on a wide variety of questions would be impossible without this device.   As might be expected, therefore, most of the actual work is done by committees, of which the General Assembly has established four types.   These are the main committees, to consider substantive matters referred to them; the procedural committees, needed for the organization and conduct of business; the standing committees, with continuing functions; and the *ad hoc* committees, required from time to time for special purposes.

Six main committees are constituted at each session.   All members of the General Assembly have the right to be represented on each of them.   They consider items referred to them by the General Assembly and prepare draft recommendations and resolutions for submission to the plenary meetings. They are established on the basis of subject matter, as follows:

The First (Political and Security) Committee considers such items as admission, suspension, and expulsion of members; political and security matters within the scope of the Charter; the general principles of cooperation in the maintenance of international peace and security; the principles governing the regulation of armaments; the promotion of international cooperation in the political field; and the peaceful adjustment of situations likely to impair the general welfare and friendly relations among nations.

The Second (Economic and Financial) Committee is concerned with the economic and financial matters within the scope of the Charter, including those phases of the program of the Economic and Social Council and of the specialized agencies.   Promotion of international economic cooperation, including questions of higher standards of living, full employment, and conditions of economic progress, comes within the province of this committee.

The Third (Social, Humanitarian and Cultural) Committee considers any social, humanitarian, cultural, educational, health, and related matters within the scope of the Charter and corresponding aspects of the program of the Economic and Social Council and of the specialized agencies.   Matters of international cooperation in these fields, assistance in the realization of human rights and fundamental freedoms, and conditions of social progress are referred to it.

The Fourth (Trusteeship) Committee is concerned with the functions of the General Assembly relating to the international trusteeship system and to the Declaration Regarding Non-Self-Governing Territories.

The Fifth (Administrative and Budgetary) Committee considers matters pertaining to the budget; apportionment of expenses among the members; financial and budgetary arrangements with the specialized agencies; and staff regulations for the Secretariat.

The Sixth (Legal) Committee considers the legal and constitutional aspects of items assigned to it, matters relating to the International Court of Justice, legal questions referred by other committees, and the progressive development and eventual codification of international law.

There are two procedural committees. The General Committee consists of the President of the General Assembly, the seven Vice-Presidents, and the Chairmen of the main committees.[8] It considers the provisional agenda and applications for the inclusion of additional items. It assists the President in drawing up the agenda for each plenary meeting, in determining the priority of items, in coordinating the proceedings of all committees, and in the general conduct of his work. The Credentials Committee examines the credentials of the representatives of members, and reports on them to the General Assembly.

The standing committees have continuing functions which must be dealt with not only during the sessions of the General Assembly but also in the intervals between them. There are two committees of this type. The Advisory Committee for Administrative and Budgetary Questions consists of nine members, two of whom are financial experts. The members are selected for three-year terms on the basis of broad geographic representation, personal qualifications, and experience. This committee makes an expert examination of the budget of the United Nations, and advises the Fifth Committee. The Committee on Contributions considers the apportionment of expenses and related questions. It consists of seven members who serve for three years on a staggered basis.

The *ad hoc* committees are set up either by the plenary Assembly or by any of its Committees to handle specific problems. Thirteen such bodies, including a Permanent Headquarters Committee, Board of Auditors, Committee on Negotiations with the United States, etc., were established during the first regular session of the General Assembly. The Special Committee on Palestine, set up during the first special session, is another illustration. It is now the practice to establish an *ad hoc* (special) political committee to share the work

[8] It is customary for five of the Vice-Presidents to be chosen from representatives of the Great Powers, and for the chairmen of the main committees to come from the smaller countries.

involved in the political and security matters facing the First Committee.
The "Little Assembly," or Interim Committee of the General Assembly,
represents a special question of organization.   In September, 1947, the United
States delegation proposed that a standing committee of the whole be established to assist the General Assembly by handling preliminary and continuing
work between the regular and special sessions.   It was felt that the Assembly
could not adequately discharge its wide responsibilities during the sessions.
The Soviet Union objected to this step on the grounds that it was unauthorized
by the Charter, exceeded the power of the General Assembly to establish subsidiary organs, and represented an attempt to circumvent the Security Council
by setting up another body to handle some of the same functions.

After thorough discussion, it was decided to form such a committee on a
temporary basis.[9]   Its jurisdiction was carefully restricted to matters expressly
referred to it by the General Assembly, important disputes or situations
proposed for inclusion on the agenda of the General Assembly, and methods
of implementing the general principles of international cooperation in the
political field.   To enable the Interim Committee to discharge its functions as
an advisory body to the General Assembly, it was given the power to conduct
investigations and to advise on the matter of summoning a special session of
the Assembly.   The Interim Committee was prohibited from trespassing on
the functions of any of the other United Nations organs, and from discussing
any matter being handled by the Security Council.   Some of the matters referred to this Committee were consultation with the United Nations Temporary
Commission on Korea, the problem of voting in the Security Council, and
promotion of international cooperation in the political field.

At the end of 1950, the Interim Committee remained on a temporary basis.
The Soviet bloc has maintained its original objections and has not participated
in the work of the "Little Assembly" in any way.   The Soviet argument of
illegality under the Charter does not seem to be well taken as long as the
Committee remains in a subordinate and advisory position to the General
Assembly.   It is true, of course, that continuing deadlocks in the Security
Council tend to give a greater practical importance to the discussions and
recommendations in the General Assembly and its subsidiary organs.

In connection with questions of organization and structure, it is necessary
to make a comment on the "unofficial" aspects, such as would be represented
by the party leaders and the caucus in a legislative body.   There are no political parties in the General Assembly.   However, some tendency toward bloc
voting is discernible.   The Soviet, Arab, and Latin-American members, for
example, form distinct groups and must be reckoned with as such.   On particular issues, such as that of colonial administration, rather definite groupings
of members are apparent.   There is, too, the practice of advance consultation
which is often employed.   Information gained and attitudes expressed in this

[9] See Appendix 16.

way may influence to some degree the positions taken by members in formal debate. The contacts among delegations are a factor in the work of the General Assembly. The unofficial and informal elements of organization have evolved only to a slight extent, but the operating structure cannot be fully explained without reference to them.

PROCEDURE

The Charter provides that the General Assembly shall adopt its own rules of procedure. At the beginning of each session [10] the necessary organizational measures are taken, including the election of officers, constitution of the committees, and adoption of the agenda. General debate is opened and reports from other organs are received. Matters requiring direct action by the entire Assembly, such as the election of members to other organs, are handled in the plenary meetings held from time to time during the sessions. Other items are referred to the committees.

As a normal practice, the General Assembly does not make a final decision on any matter until it has received the report of the committee concerned. The committees perform the usual function of such devices by making a detailed study of the items referred to them, thus saving the time of the full Assembly. Since all members of the parent body are entitled to representation on each of the important committees, this division of labor is not among the members, as in a legislative body, but among different representatives of the same members. In effect, the system is one of a series of committees of the whole, which can function simultaneously because each member may have several representatives. The committees follow the European practice in having both a chairman and a *rapporteur* in each case. It is the function of the latter to report for the committee and to be its spokesman when its proposals are under consideration in a plenary meeting.

The General Assembly usually accepts the recommendations of its committees, but not always. In December, 1948, Spanish was made a third "working language" despite a committee report to the effect that it was inadvisable to impose the additional financial burden involved. In November, 1949, the plenary Assembly rejected a resolution proposed by its Trusteeship Committee which would have required members administering trust territories to submit detailed plans for leading natives to the stage of independence.

Decisions in the General Assembly are made by a two-thirds majority of those present and voting for "important" questions, and a simple majority for other matters. "Important" questions include recommendations with respect to the maintenance of international peace and security, election of members to

---

[10] A minute of silence is observed at the beginning of the first plenary meeting of each session. Despite many suggestions, it would not be possible to have a public prayer which would satisfy all beliefs.

other organs,[11] the admission of new members to the United Nations, suspension and expulsion of members, questions relating to the operation of the trusteeship system, and budgetary questions. This is a sharp departure from the former unanimity rule in international organizations.

It is notable that the basis of those *present and voting* is the least restrictive provision which is possible. When the requirement is based upon *all the members,* each absentee and each abstention amounts in effect to a negative vote. When it is based upon *all those present,* each abstention amounts to a negative vote. For example, in a body having 100 members with 10 absent and 10 present but not voting, a simple majority of all the members would mean 51 votes, as compared with 46 on the basis of those present, and 41 for those present and voting. Furthermore, in the General Assembly, any doubt as to whether a particular question requires a two-thirds majority is determined by a simple majority. Thus a bare majority of those present and voting may decide any issue except those either listed in the Charter or recognized by the majority itself to be one of the "important" questions.[12] All committees make their decisions by a simple majority vote.

A quorum in the General Assembly, under a rule effective January 1, 1950, is one-third of the members so far as the opening of a meeting is concerned, but no question can be put to a vote unless a majority of the members are present. Votes are normally taken by a show of hands or by standing, but any representative may request a roll call. When this is done, the roll is called in the English alphabetical order of the names of the members, beginning with one drawn by lot. All elections are held by secret ballot. There are no nominations except in connection with the election of judges to the International Court of Justice.

One special problem of procedure relates to the use of several official languages—English, French, Spanish, Chinese, and Russian. The first three of these are designated as "working languages." Verbatim records are drawn up and the *Journal* of the General Assembly is issued in the working languages. Summary records, and all resolutions and other important documents, are made available in all five official languages. For the speeches, a system of simultaneous translations is used. Headphones are provided and, with a switch of a dial, a representative or observer may follow the proceedings in any of the languages. The story is told of one visitor, not aware of this system, who was puzzled at the ease with which everyone else seemed to understand Chinese.

The meetings of the General Assembly and of its committees are held in public unless it decides otherwise in exceptional circumstances. Any decisions taken in closed meetings are to be promptly announced. The press, radio,

---

[11] Except for the election of judges to the International Court of Justice, which requires an absolute majority in the General Assembly.

[12] An exception to this general rule is found in Article 108 of the Charter, which provides that proposed amendments shall receive a two-thirds majority of all the members.

TABLE 2. SELECTED STATISTICS FOR MEMBERS OF THE UNITED NATIONS

Member	Area, thousands of square miles [1]	Population, thousands [2]	Birth rate [3]	Death rate [4]	Infant mortality rate [5]	Illiteracy rate [6]	Per capita income, 1949, U.S. dollars [7]
Afghanistan	251	12,000	*	*	*	*	50
Argentina	1,074	16,818	24.4	9.4	79.0	*	346
Australia	2,975	7,912	22.9	9.5	25.3	*	679
Belgium	12	8,614	17.2	12.9	57.2	5.6	582
Bolivia	413	3,990	30.7	12.7	113.1	*	55
Brazil	3,288	49,340	*	*	*	56.7	112
Burma	261	18,304	32.4	23.0	203.8	*	36
Byelorussian S.S.R.	80	5,568	*	*	*	*	(a)
Canada	3,843	13,549	26.9	9.2	42.8	3.8	870
Chile	286	5,709	33.2	18.1	169.1	28.2	188
China	3,759	463,493	*	*	*	*	27
Colombia	440	11,015	35.1	14.3	136.6	44.2	132
Costa Rica	20	838	41.0	11.8	97.4	*	125
Cuba	44	5,199	25.2	11.1	83.0	22.1	296
Czechoslovakia	49	12,463	23.3	11.5	83.2	4.1	371
Denmark	17	4,230	18.9	8.9	35.3	*	689
Dominican Republic	19	2,277	38.7	9.3	77.3	*	75
Ecuador	106	3,404	*	*	122.0	*	40
Egypt	386	20,045	43.5	21.3	152.8	85.2	100
El Salvador	13	2,150	39.5	13.2	100.4	72.8	92
Ethiopia	350	16,700	*	*	*	*	38
France	213	41,550	21.0	13.8	56.0	3.8	482
Greece	51	7,856	27.0	12.4	100.7	40.8	128

Guatemala	42	2,787	*	*	*	65.4	77
Haiti	11	3,750	*	*	*	*	40
Honduras	59	1,326	40.3	14.4	22.4	66.3	83
Iceland	40	140	27.8	8.6	130.1	*	476
India	1,197	346,000	25.5	17.2	28.8	90.9	57
Indonesia	576	72,000	28.5	20.3	*	*	25
Iran	618	18,387	*	*	*	*	85
Iraq	168	4,800	*	*	50.9	*	85
Israel	*	1,058	29.4	6.9	*	*	389
Lebanon	3	1,238	18.3	5.4	*	*	125
Liberia	43	1,648	*	*	74.9	*	38
Luxembourg	1	295	14.4	12.6	102.3	51.6	553
Mexico	760	24,448	44.6	16.8	26.8	*	121
Netherlands	16	9,956	23.7	8.1	23.8	*	502
New Zealand	103	1,881	24.9	9.1	95.1	*	856
Nicaragua	57	1,184	35.4	10.1	29.6	*	89
Norway	125	3,233	19.6	8.8	*	*	587
Pakistan	367	74,437	18.0	12.3	50.1	35.3	51
Panama	29	764	33.0	7.1	52.0	*	183
Paraguay	157	1,304	31.7	8.9	110.8	56.6	84
Peru	482	8,204	25.9	10.8	96.0	*	100
Philippines	116	19,498	32.4	16.5	139.8	23.1	44
Poland	120	24,448	24.3	13.7	*	*	300
Saudi Arabia	*	6,000	*	*	23.2	*	40
Sweden	173	6,956	17.4	10.0	*	0.1	780
Syria	72	3,135	*	*	*	*	100
Thailand	198	17,987	27.1	10.2	68.1	*	36
Turkey	296	19,623	*	*	*	79.1	125

TABLE 2. SELECTED STATISTICS FOR MEMBERS OF THE UNITED NATIONS (*Continued*)

Member	Area, thousands of square miles [1]	Population, thousands [2]	Birth rate [3]	Death rate [4]	Infant mortality rate [5]	Illiteracy rate [6]	Per capita income, 1949, U.S. dollars [7]
Ukrainian S.S.R.	223	30,960	*	*	*	*	(*a*)
Union of South Africa	472	12,112	26.7	9.1	40.1	*	264
U.S.S.R.	8,599	193,000	*	*	*	*	308
United Kingdom	94	50,363	17.0	11.7	34.1	*	773
United States	3,022	149,215	24.0	9.7	31.1	4.3	1,453
Uruguay	72	2,353	20.7	8.9	65.7	*	331
Venezuela	352	4,595	43.3	12.5	97.8	56.6	322
Yemen	75	4,500	*	*	*	*	40
Yugoslavia	99	16,040	28.3	13.6	132.3	45.2	146

* Information not given.

[1] Based upon information in the *Yearbook of the United Nations, 1947–1948*, pp. 1119, 1122. The *Statistical Yearbook* and the *Demographic Yearbook* (both published by the United Nations) give the area of each country and territory of the world in square kilometers. The figure for Indonesia has been converted from the latter source.

[2] Based upon information in the *Demographic Yearbook, 1949–1950*, pp. 71–83. Later figures, to the extent available, may be found by consulting the latest issue of the *Monthly Bulletin of Statistics*, published by the Statistical Office of the United Nations.

[3] The "crude birth rate," that is, the number of live births per 1,000 population. The information is taken from the *Demographic Yearbook, 1949–1950*, pp. 288–295. The figures are given for 1949 or the latest available year. Many of the figures are estimates, sometimes based upon incomplete information. Notes and comments in the *Yearbook* explain the significance of the data.

TABLE 2. SELECTED STATISTICS FOR MEMBERS OF THE UNITED NATIONS (*Continued*)

[4] The "crude death rate," that is, the number of deaths exclusive of stillbirths, per 1,000 population. The information is taken from the *Demographic Yearbook, 1949–1950*, pp. 380–387. The figures represent reports or estimates for 1949 or the latest available year.

[5] The number of deaths of infants under one year of age per 1,000 live births. The data exclude stillbirths. The information is taken from the *Demographic Yearbook, 1949–1950*, pp. 410–415. The figures represent reports or estimates for 1949 or the latest available year. The data used in calculating these rates are not always comparable with the data used in other columns of this table. For example, in the case of Indonesia, the *Demographic Yearbook* gives birth and death rates for the Indonesian population and infant mortality rates for Europeans only.

[6] The percentage of illiterate population at the latest census for each country. The dates range from 1928 to 1945. The United States figure is for 1930; the question on illiteracy was not asked in the 1940 census. The information is taken from *Statistical Yearbook, 1949–1950*, pp. 486–494. The percentages are given in most cases for illiterate population ten years of age or over. The lower age limit varies for a few countries. The figure 15 in this column, for example, would mean that 15 per cent of the population old enough to read and write could not do so.

[7] From *National and Per Capita Incomes of Seventy Countries in 1949 Expressed in United States Dollars*, Statistical Office of the United Nations, October, 1950. See also *United Nations Bulletin*, Dec. 15, 1950, p. 720.

(*) Included in figure for the U.S.S.R.

films, and even television are used to report its proceedings to the world.   Hundreds of visitors come to the United Nations Headquarters when important meetings are to be held.   There they can observe the sessions and see famous statesmen in the flesh.   Groups from civic organizations, and high school and college students, usually make up a large proportion of the visitors but they are by no means the only ones.   The United Nations has become quite a tourist attraction.   This, in America, is certainly a mark of success.   One has only to see the swarming lobby and the rush for tickets on a busy day to wonder what the old-school diplomats would make of it.

The General Assembly, in an attempt to improve and speed up its work, appointed early in 1949 a Committee on Methods and Procedures.   This Committee made a careful study of the factors affecting the duration of sessions and presented some recommendations.   These were considered by the Sixth (Legal) Committee and presented to the Assembly itself in November, 1949.   This study resulted in some modifications of the rules.   However, it was clear the primary factor in the length of sessions was due not to defective rules of procedure but to the number and complexity of the questions submitted and to the political problems raised by them.

Chapter 9

THE SECURITY COUNCIL

The Security Council is composed of eleven members of the United Nations. China, France, the Soviet Union, Great Britain, and the United States are named in the Charter as permanent members. Thus, the five states that were Great Powers at the close of World War II occupy a special position. These five were the leaders of the wartime alliance against the Axis nations, and they bore the brunt of the fighting and losses by which the victory was won. Also, a definite relationship between power and responsibility was sought. The members with the greatest resources of industry, technology, and manpower would necessarily take a leading part in keeping the peace of the world. It followed that they should have a leading role in making the decisions involved.

This arrangement is obviously a rigid and inflexible one, yet the list of Great Powers of the world does not remain static. Some on that list in 1945 may not belong in that classification in 2045, or 1995, or even 1965. Other countries may rise to the top in the scale of power. If this should happen, the permanent members of the Security Council would not coincide with the actual Great Powers and the argument in favor of designating permanent members would be lost. The only way to add to or substract from this category is by amendment of the Charter, and this cannot be done without the concurrence of all the permanent members. Thus, each of the five can block its removal from this group, as long as it exists as a state and remains a member of the United Nations, and no new permanent member can be added without the agreement of all five now in that category. The designation of permanent members follows the precedent of the Covenant of the League of Nations, but that arrangement was more flexible since the Council with the approval of the Assembly could create new permanent members.

The six nonpermanent members of the Security Council are elected for two-year terms by the General Assembly. These elections are staggered, so that three members complete their terms and three new ones are elected each year. The elections are held each fall during the regular annual session of the General Assembly, and the new terms begin on the following January 1. The nonpermanent members are ineligible for immediate reelection. The Charter provides two criteria for election to the Security Council. Due regard is to be paid "in the first instance to the contributions of Members of the United Nations to the maintenance of international peace and security and other purposes of the Organization." The General Assembly is the sole judge of the relevance of this qualification to the election of any particular member to a nonpermanent seat on the Security Council.

The other criterion is that of "equitable geographical distribution." Since the beginning, the actual distribution of the six elective seats has been one each for Eastern and Western Europe, two for Latin America, one for the Arab states, and one for the British Dominions.[1] Disputes concerning this matter have arisen on three occasions. In 1947, there was a heated contest between the Ukraine and India. For the former, it was argued that it had made an important contribution to winning the war, and that if it were not elected Eastern Europe would be unrepresented. Moreover, the Soviet Union was insistent that the Ukraine be elected. On behalf of India, there was the objection that the Ukraine was not an independent state and to elect it would give the Soviet Union two votes on the Security Council. Also, it was argued that India was fully qualified on the basis of ability to contribute to the purposes of the United Nations, and with Australia no longer a member of the Security Council, a geographic area with more than a half billion population would not be represented if the Ukraine were elected. After eleven ballots, India withdrew as a candidate in order to break the deadlock.

In 1949, the election of Yugoslavia (in preference to Czechoslovakia) to take the place of the Ukraine was bitterly contested by the Soviet Union. Mr. Vishinsky insisted that there was a gentlemen's agreement permitting the United Nations members in each geographic area to select the candidate for that group. This, in effect, would allow the Soviet Union to name the nonpermanent member for Eastern Europe. It was argued, on the other hand, that Yugoslavia is both a Slav and a Communist country and, as the Yugoslavs said, they had not changed their geographical position. The United States supported the Yugoslav candidacy, on the grounds that a Great Power should not be permitted to dictate the General Assembly's election of any particular country, that the geographical criterion was met, and that a Communist country independent of the Kremlin was to be preferred to one controlled from Moscow. Great Britain voted for Czechoslovakia, presumably on the grounds that it was premature to place Tito's Yugoslavia on the Security Council, and that the resulting increase in East-West tension would do more harm than good. Yugoslavia was elected by a narrow margin, but agreement on the basic issue involved was not reached.

In 1950, there was protracted balloting over the contest between Lebanon and Turkey to succeed Egypt as a member of the Security Council. On behalf of Lebanon it was argued that the seat should go to an Arab state. Those supporting Turkey contended that, under the principle of geographical representation, the Middle East and not just the Arab bloc should provide the suc-

[1] See Table 3, at the end of this chapter.

cessor to Egypt. There was also a feeling that Turkey was under special scrutiny by the Soviet Union and that, if trouble developed in that part of the world, it might be a good idea to have Turkey represented on the Security Council. A further argument against the candidacy of Lebanon was that none of the Arab countries should be selected while their differences with Israel remained unsolved. Turkey was finally elected on the fifteenth ballot.

The size of the Security Council is a problem. Because of the nature of its functions, it should be small enough to operate quickly and with a minimum of organizational complexity. On the other hand, there is considerable pressure for membership on it. A maximum of opportunity for different countries to be elected is provided by the short term of two years and by the prohibition of two successive terms for any one member. Still, six nonpermanent seats are not enough to provide continuous representation for all the major areas of the world. There is also the problem of the "middle powers." The present arrangement lumps together all countries except the Big Five. However, there is a greater disparity between Canada and Panama, for example, than between Canada and France. The League of Nations met this problem by declaring members eligible for reelection provided they obtained a two-thirds vote in the Assembly, instead of the simple majority ordinarily required. This cannot be done for the Security Council of the United Nations without an amendment of the Charter. In view of the number of small states, it is not likely that a two-thirds majority would approve such a step. And if it were done, the problem would become even more acute for all the countries not placed in the intermediate category.

Each member of the Security Council has one representative, instead of the maximum of five allowed for the General Assembly. This is another example of the emphasis on a small compact group designed to reach decisions expeditiously. The representatives to the Security Council are appointed by their respective governments and act on instructions from them.

FUNCTIONS AND POWERS

The Security Council has the "primary responsibility for the maintenance of international peace and security." In carrying out its duties under this responsibility, the Security Council acts on behalf of all the members of the United Nations. It is an agent of the entire Organization in this respect. The main functions of the Security Council may be classified under the headings of deliberation, enforcement, and election.

Deliberation includes such activities as discussion, investigation, and recommendation. The Charter contemplates a certain logical progression of steps by which international disputes would be handled, beginning with the existence of a dispute or situation "the continuance of which is likely to endanger the maintenance of international peace and security." There is, first of all, an obligation on the parties to seek a solution by peaceful means of their own choice. The Security Council may call upon the parties to settle their disputes by such means, and it is specifically authorized to "investigate any dispute, or any situation which might lead to international friction or give rise to a dispute, in order to determine whether the continuance of the dispute or situation is likely to endanger the maintenance of international peace and security." It may recommend appropriate procedures or methods of adjustment at any stage of such a dispute or situation. If the parties do not achieve a settlement by peaceful means, they are obligated to refer the matter to the Security Council.

Article 39 of the Charter provides that "the Security Council shall determine the existence of any threat to the peace, breach of the peace, or act of aggression and shall make recommendations, or decide what measures shall be taken in accordance with Articles 41 and 42, to maintain or restore international peace and security." This, in the event that pacific settlement fails, introduces a course of action which may lead to actual enforcement measures. In practice, the Security Council has been reluctant to make a formal finding of the existence of a "threat to the peace, breach of the peace, or act of aggression," and has done so only as a last resort.

The process of deliberation, both in pacific settlement and in the preliminary stages of enforcement action, is much broader than mere debate and resolution passing in the meetings at the United Nations headquarters. As in the case of the analogous function in the General Assembly, field investigations may be made. This was done, for example, in connection with the Greek, Indonesian, and Palestine disputes. Also, continuing efforts may be made under Security Council auspices to settle a dispute as between the parties. Examples of this are the establishment of the Committee of Good Offices in the Indonesian dispute, the Truce Commission and the United Nations Mediator in Palestine, and the continuing efforts of the Security Council in the Korean case.

The activities of study, discussion, and recommendation are not confined to the handling of individual disputes, but are also exercised by the Security Council in the consideration of other questions related to the maintenance of international peace and security. By Article 26 of the Charter, the Security Council is made responsible for formulating plans for the establishment of a system for the regulation of armaments. This question has been discussed, especially in the Commission for Conventional Armaments created as a subsidiary organ of the Security Council, but no basic agreement has been reached among the Great Powers. The problem of the international control of atomic energy arose after the Charter was written at San Francisco, but its relation to the major function of the Security Council is obvious. The United Nations Atomic Energy Commission was established by a resolution of the General Assembly. However, it is responsible to and operates under the supervision of the Security Council.[2]

[2] See pp. 240–244.

The *enforcement* function of the Security Council refers to the power to decide what measures shall be taken to maintain or restore international peace and security, if both peaceful settlement among the parties and recommendations of the Security Council fail in this objective. For this reason, it is often called the "enforcement arm" of the United Nations. The first step in this connection would be the application of measures not involving the use of armed force. Such measures "may include complete or partial interruption of economic relations and of rail, sea, postal, telegraphic, radio, and other means of communication, and the severance of diplomatic relations" (Article 41 of the Charter). If this is inadequate, the Security Council is authorized to take such military action as may be necessary (Article 42). Decisions made by the Security Council in the exercise of this responsibility are binding upon the members of the United Nations. This is in contrast to the League of Nations, under which it was for each member to decide for itself whether an occasion had arisen for the application of sanctions.

The armed forces and facilities necessary for the maintenance of international peace and security were to be contributed by members of the United Nations, in accordance with special agreements to be concluded with the Security Council. No agreement of this type has been reached as yet, because of the differences between the Soviet Union and the Western Powers. The size of the contribution of each permanent member has been a basic issue. The Soviet delegation has insisted on the principle of equality, as regards both strength and composition of the armed forces. The other delegations have upheld the principle of comparability, by which the contributions might differ widely as to the strength of the separate land, sea, and air components. The emphasis would be on the provision of a balanced and effective force for the Security Council, and differences in the size and composition of existing national forces would be taken into account.[3]

Obviously, if the Soviet position were accepted, each component of the United Nations armed forces would be limited initially to a strength five times the smallest contribution of that component. For example, if China were able to furnish only a nominal naval force for the Security Council, then an effective international naval force would be automatically impossible. On the other hand, if the Soviet Union should accept the principle of comparable contributions, it would be confronted with the possibility of an international armed force in which the naval and air components might be predominantly Anglo-American.

There is specific recognition, in Article 45 of the Charter, that it might become necessary for the United Nations to take urgent military action. Members are to hold national air-force contingents immediately available for

---

[3] For a summary of the opposing viewpoints concerning the armed forces to be provided, see Leland M. Goodrich and Edvard Hambro, *Charter of the United Nations: Commentary and Documents,* World Peace Foundation, Boston, 1949, 2d ed., pp. 281–286.

combined international enforcement action. However, the strength and degree of readiness of these contingents, as well as plans for their combined action, are to be determined within the limits of the special agreements mentioned above. It follows that this provision of the Charter has not been implemented as yet.

A Military Staff Committee was established "to advise and assist the Security Council on all questions relating to the Security Council's military requirements for the maintenance of international peace and security, the employment and command of forces placed at its disposal, the regulation of armaments, and possible disarmament" (Article 47 of the Charter). The Military Staff Committee consists of the Chiefs of Staff of the permanent members of the Security Council or their representatives. In addition to its duties of giving advice and assistance, it is also responsible for the strategic direction of any armed forces which may be placed at the disposal of the Security Council.

So far as the Charter of the United Nations is concerned, the problem of an international police force would be met by a system of national contingents placed under international direction for a specified purpose. This goes further than a mere combined or coordinated use of separate national forces, which was essentially the system contemplated by the Covenant of the League of Nations. However, it definitely does not represent an attempt to establish a permanent international military force.

It should be noted that the provision for national contingents to be made available to the Security Council by special agreements does not preclude the possibility of establishing an independent international armed police force, at least on a small scale. The idea of a United Nations "guard force" was suggested by the Secretary-General in 1948, and has been accepted in a modified form by the General Assembly.[4]

The Security Council's enforcement function is carefully safeguarded in the Charter. Article 51, which explicitly recognizes the inherent right of individual or collective self-defense in the event of an armed attack against a member, provides for the exercise of that right only "until the Security Council has taken the measures necessary to maintain international peace and security." Action by members under Article 51 is to be reported to the Security Council and in no way affects the authority and responsibility of the latter. Regional arrangements or agencies may be utilized for enforcement action. But no such action is to be taken by regional arrangement or agencies without the authorization of the Security Council, except for measures against the enemy states of World War II. In connection with the international trusteeship system, Article 83 of the Charter provides that "all functions of the United Nations relating to strategic areas, including the approval of the terms of the trusteeship agreements and of their alteration or amendment, shall be exercised by the Security Council."

[4] See p. 189.

The enforcement functions and powers of the Security Council are directed to its responsibility for the maintenance of international peace and security, rather than to the laying down of specific terms for the settlement of individual disputes.   If a condition of agreement and mutual confidence existed among the Great Powers, there would be a danger that they might use the Security Council in such a way as to promote their own interest in the maintenance of peace, but they are also concerned for their freedom and independence. They do not want the type of peace which results from merely forcing the weak to bow to the strong.   They want the Security Council to be capable of enforcing peace, but not capable of dictating unjust terms of settlement.   Of course, the current disagreement among the Great Powers results in a situation in which the proper function of the Security Council is likely to suffer more from deadlock than from abuse of power.   Nevertheless, from a long-term point of view, the other danger must be recognized as a possibility.

The *elective* function of the Security Council includes its responsibilities relating to the admission of new members and to the constitution of certain other organs.

As indicated above,[5] new members of the United Nations are admitted by vote of the General Assembly upon recommendation of the Security Council. As of Jan. 1, 1952, nine members had been admitted in this way.[6]   However five applicants—Albania, Bulgaria, Hungary, Rumania, and the Mongolian People's Republic—had not received the necessary seven affirmative votes to be recommended for admission.   Seven applicants—Austria, Italy, Ireland, Portugal, Finland, Transjordan, and Ceylon—failed to receive the votes of all the permanent members of the Security Council because of the opposition of the Soviet Union.[7]

Albania was not recommended for admission because of its conduct in connection with the Corfu Channel incident and the Greek case, and also because of its failure to reaffirm its pre-1939 bilateral treaties.   The Soviet government supported this application on the basis of the war record of the Albanian people.   The applications of Bulgaria, Hungary, and Rumania were not supported by most members of the Security Council because of their alleged violations of human rights contrary to treaty commitments.   Also, Bulgaria was accused of giving aid to the guerrillas in northern Greece.   The application of the Mongolian People's Republic was not approved because of doubts as to its international status.

The application of Austria was opposed by the Soviet Union on the grounds that an ex-enemy state should not be admitted until the treaty of peace with it had entered into force.   The United States took the position that commitments had been made to treat Austria as a liberated, rather than an enemy, country.

[5] P. 122.
[6] For a list of original and admitted members, see Table 1, pp. 120–121.
[7] See pp. 145–150 for a discussion of the voting procedure in the Security Council.

The British government thought that the Austrian application was premature in view of the military occupation. A resolution was proposed by Australia to recommend Austria for admission at a time and under conditions to be determined by the General Assembly. This resolution was defeated by the opposition of the Soviet Union.

The applications of Ireland, Portugal, and Transjordan were initially opposed by the Soviet Union on the basis that they did not have diplomatic relations with that government. It was also contended that Ireland was neutral, or even sympathetic with the enemy, during the war, that Portugal had special ties with Franco Spain, and that the independent status of Transjordan was questionable.

The Soviet Union supported the admission of Italy and Finland on condition that Bulgaria, Hungary, and Rumania also be admitted. That condition was not accepted by other members of the Security Council. When Ceylon applied for admission, the Soviet Union expressed doubts concerning its degree of independence and asked for a postponement of the decision. When this proposal was defeated, a favorable recommendation was prevented by an adverse Soviet vote.

These deadlocks in the Security Council led to much criticism and repeated discussions in the General Assembly. When the latter, on several occasions, passed resolutions requesting reconsideration, the members of the Security Council maintained their initial positions. Because of the widespread feeling that some members of the Security Council were not basing their votes in this matter upon the provisions of the Charter, the General Assembly also decided to request an advisory opinion from the International Court of Justice. The majority of the judges, in an opinion handed down in May, 1948,[8] reached the conclusion that a member of the United Nations "is not juridically entitled" to make its consent to admission of an applicant subject to conditions not expressly provided in Article 4, paragraph 1, of the Charter.[9]

Thus, in the opinion of the Court, there could be only five valid qualifications for membership in the United Nations. An applicant must (1) be a state; (2) be peace-loving; (3) accept the obligations of the Charter; (4) be able to carry out these obligations; and (5) be willing to do so. This would rule out the imposition of such conditions as the establishment of diplomatic relations with particular states and making the admission of one applicant depend upon the admission of another one. Six of the fifteen judges wrote dissenting opinions, in which they held that the admission of a new member was essentially a political and not merely a procedural act. The enumerated conditions are essential according to the minority view, but there is no specific

[8] See Appendix 17.

[9] "Membership in the United Nations is open to all other peace-loving states which accept the obligations contained in the present Charter and, in the judgment of the Organization, are able and willing to carry out these obligations."

statement in the Charter indicating that they are sufficient. They did not find a legal obligation upon the United Nations to admit applicant states. It is interesting to note that the decision of the Court did not divide entirely along East-West lines. Three of the minority judges, who believed that the Soviet position in this matter was legally sound, were nationals of Canada, Great Britain, and France.

After the advisory opinion of the Court, the various members of the Security Council continued to maintain their initial positions. This, of course, constitutes a refusal by the Soviet Union to accept the opinion of the majority on the Court. Even aside from this fact, it is clear that the Charter provides no automatic test of qualifications in concrete cases. Whether or not a state is "peace-loving" and "able and willing to carry out its international obligations" are matters which each member of the Security Council and of the General Assembly must determine for itself when voting upon an application.

The Security Council has an important responsibility with reference to questions of suspension and expulsion. A member of the United Nations against which preventive or enforcement action has been taken may be suspended from the exercise of the rights and privileges of membership by the General Assembly upon the recommendation of the Security Council. However, the latter may restore these rights and privileges upon its own determination. Expulsion of a member which has persistently violated the principles of the Charter is accomplished by the same procedure as in the case of suspension.

The other type of elective function possessed by the Security Council has reference to the composition of other organs. It participates in the election of judges to the International Court of Justice, and its recommendation is necessary for the appointment of a Secretary-General. Thus the responsibilities of the Security Council in this connection, while important, are not nearly so extensive as those of the General Assembly.[10]

ORGANIZATION AND PROCEDURE

The organization of the Security Council is quite simple. This might be expected from the facts that it has only eleven members and that each member has only one representative at the meetings. In a body of this size, elaborate organization is scarcely possible and obviously unnecessary.

The Charter provides that the Security Council shall be so organized as to be able to function continuously, and that each member shall be represented

[10] For the situation which arose at the expiration of the first term of the Secretary-General, when the Security Council was unable to agree on any recommendation, see p. 177. In addition to its main functions of deliberation, enforcement, and election, the Security Council also participates concurrently with the General Assembly in any proposal to call a General Conference to review the Charter, and it recommends the basis on which a state not a member of the United Nations may become a party to the Statute of the International Court of Justice.

at all times at the seat of the Organization. This is intended to give assurance that the Security Council will be able to function promptly whenever necessary to maintain peace and security. If assistance is to be given to a victim of aggression, any delay may have very serious consequences. Therefore it is intended to avoid any delays involved in convening a session of the Security Council, and in the time which it would take for the representatives to assemble. Under the rules which have been adopted, the interval between meetings shall not be longer than fourteen days.

The Charter provides that the Security Council shall decide on the method of selecting its President. A system of automatic rotation was adopted, under which the office is held by each member in turn for one calendar month according to alphabetical order in English. This method puts all the members on a basis of complete equality so far as the opportunity to preside is concerned, and it eliminates the problems and possible frictions involved in making a choice or indicating a preference. Such a system of rotation means, of course, that the Presidency of the Council cannot be an office with important functions on its own account and that there cannot be much continuity of leadership at this point. This method may also lead to a rather bizarre situation upon occasion; thus in January, 1950, when the question of China was facing the Security Council, it was the turn of the representative of China to preside. In August, 1950, it was the turn of the Soviet Union, which had been boycotting the meetings since the preceding January. The Soviet representative returned to assume the presidency of the Council and to tie it up in procedural knots for a month.

A body as small as the Security Council does not need a large number of committees. However, there have been some organizational developments of this type. The Military Staff Committee was created by provisions of the Charter as a subsidiary body of the Security Council. The United Nations Atomic Energy Commission was created by a resolution of the General Assembly, but was made responsible to the Security Council. The Commission on Conventional Armaments was established by the Security Council itself to consider the problem of the regulation of armaments other than atomic energy and weapons of mass destruction. The Committee of Experts was created at the first meeting of the Security Council in January, 1946, for the purpose of examining the Provisional Rules of Procedure and such other matters as might be entrusted to it. The Committee on the Admission of New Members has the responsibility of examining applications for membership in the United Nations. It is the usual practice for subsidiary bodies created by the Security Council for matters of general and continuing interest to be constituted as committees of the whole. In addition various *ad hoc* or special bodies have been established from time to time. Examples of these are the Committee of Good Offices on the Indonesian Question, the United Nations Commission for India and Pakistan, the United Nations Truce Commission for Palestine, and the Sub-Committee of Three to Collect Information on Candidates for Governor-ship of Trieste.

The staff for the Security Council is provided by the Secretariat. This includes clerks, translators, and other necessary personnel. The Secretary-General, or a deputy, attends the meetings.

The Charter provides that the Security Council shall determine its own rules of procedure. The first order of business is the adoption of an agenda. The rules provide that a provisional agenda shall be drawn up by the Secretary-General and approved by the President of the Security Council. In the conduct of business, the President is to call upon the representatives in the order in which they signify a desire to speak. The President decides points of order, but may be overruled by vote of the members.

There are five official languages: English, French, Spanish, Russian, and Chinese. The first two of these are working languages. A speech in one of the working languages is translated into the other. A speech in another language is translated into both working languages. Ordinarily, the Security Council uses a system of consecutive, rather than simultaneous, translation. This slows up the proceedings, and physical facilities for simultaneous translation are available. The principal reason for the slower method is probably a desire for more time to reflect upon the implications of statements made before the Council. Because of the great interest in the proceedings, both simultaneous and consecutive translations have been provided since August 1, 1950.

Verbatim records are maintained in the working languages. Resolutions, records of public meetings, and all important documents are reproduced in all five official languages. The meetings are held in public, unless it is decided otherwise for special reasons in a given case. An example of a matter dealt with in a closed meeting is the consideration of recommendations to the General Assembly for the appointment of a Secretary-General. After each private meeting, the Security Council issues a communiqué through the Secretary-General.

UNANIMITY AND THE VETO

The question of the voting procedure in the Security Council has attained such a crucial importance that it is necessary to give careful attention to this problem and its implications.

The relevant Charter provisions are found in Article 27, which provides that each member of the Security Council shall have one vote; that decisions on procedural matters shall be made by an affirmative vote of seven members; and that decisions on all other matters shall be made by seven affirmative votes, including the concurring votes of the permanent members. On matters of pacific settlement, a party to a dispute is to abstain from voting.

The requirement of concurring votes of the permanent members for decisions on important or substantive matters is based on the principle of unanimity of the Great Powers. It was a basic assumption at the San Francisco Conference that the United Nations could not succeed without agreement and unity among its leading members. In particular, it was believed that decisions to use force for the maintenance of international peace and security could not successfully be carried out against the opposition of one or more of the Great Powers. Nor could the governments of these Powers be expected to participate in an arrangement by which their armed forces could be used without their consent.

The principle that unanimity among the permanent members is a prerequisite to enforcement action finds support in practical considerations. The leading industrial nations have almost a monopoly of the means of waging a modern global war. If a reasonable degree of cooperation exists among them, it is difficult to see how a large-scale war could occur. If, however, they disagree to the point of fighting each other, the obvious result would be a third world war. Cooperation among the permanent members is essential if the Security Council is to perform its function. Since its decisions are to be taken by a procedure of voting, the outcome of the voting on a resolution indicates whether or not the necessary agreement exists. If all the members vote the same way, this shows that they agree on the measures to be taken. If some vote for and some against a proposal, this shows that they disagree and therefore are not prepared to cooperate in the suggested course of action. If four of the permanent members vote in the affirmative, and one in the negative, the proposal is thereby blocked because all of them do not concur. This is said to be a "veto." In other words, unanimity does not exist in such a case.

Some of the smaller countries at the San Francisco Conference objected to this voting procedure on the grounds that it violated the principle of "sovereign equality" of all members, and that it would weaken the Security Council by creating the likelihood that it might not be able to reach decisions necessary to the discharge of its functions. The Great Powers, however, emphasized the importance of the principle of unanimity and insisted that they were not prepared to abandon their position on this point.[11]

In the actual operation of the Security Council, the veto became almost entirely an issue between the Soviet Union and the other permanent members. By January, 1951, there had been more than forty instances in which resolutions before the Security Council had received at least seven affirmative votes but had not been carried as the result of the negative vote of one permanent member. The only veto by a member other than the Soviet Union was one by France in August, 1947, in opposing a proposal in connection with consideration of the Indonesian question. The Soviet score of vetoes includes, however, a number of negative votes on each of several issues. For example, seven

[11] See pp. 87–89.

applications for membership have been opposed by the Soviet Union, and some of these have been brought to a vote more than once.[12]

The Security Council uses two different voting procedures, depending on whether the vote is being taken on a procedural or a substantive question. However, these terms are not defined in the Charter and some difficult questions of interpretation have arisen. The governments of the permanent members made a statement on this subject at the San Francisco Conference, but this neither settles all the questions nor has any necessary binding effect on the countries which did not subscribe to it or on the Security Council itself. It is agreed that procedural matters include the internal organization and rules of the Security Council, election of its President, decisions on the time and place of meetings, adoption of the agenda, establishment of subsidiary organs, and the question of whether a particular dispute or situation is to be discussed. Decisions to take enforcement action, or to make recommendations, are clearly substantive in character.

A proposal to conduct an investigation has been considered a substantive question, on the basis that such a step may inaugurate a "chain of events" with major political consequences, in the course of which the Security Council might have to make decisions as to enforcement measures. The Soviet Union has argued that the decision to discuss a dispute or situation may start a "chain of events" leading to the necessity for substantive decisions. The Iranian dispute was the first test case of this point, and the Soviet government tacitly accepted the majority view that discussion within the Security Council, not involving an investigation, is a procedural matter.

In a doubtful case, the question of whether a proposal requires the unanimous vote of the Great Powers assumes great importance. This fact can easily be illustrated by reference to the Soviet challenge to the right of the representative of the Nationalist Government of China to continue as a member of and to preside over the Security Council. If this were considered a procedural matter involving a decision of credentials, the affirmative votes of any seven members would be controlling. If it were considered a substantive decision, any resolution would be subject to the veto of one permanent member. This would raise the further question of whether the representative of China could veto his own removal. In practice, the Security Council has made its own determination, without requesting an opinion from the International Court of Justice or any other body. Its interpretation has been guided by the principle that any doubt as to the applicable voting procedure is to be settled by a substantive vote. Thus, any question which is not clearly and admittedly procedural becomes subject to veto. The possibility of vetoing a proposal to decide a resolution by any seven affirmative votes, and then of vetoing the substance of the resolution, is sometimes called the "double veto." A precedent for mitigating the

[12] For the disputes in connection with which the veto has been used, see pp. 205–219.

effects of this procedure was established in September, 1950, when the Security Council upheld by a procedural vote a ruling of its President to the effect that the representative of China could not use the "double veto" to prevent an invitation to the Communist regime in China to participate in a discussion of the status of Formosa.

A special question relates to the effect of an abstention from voting. A party to a dispute is required to refrain from voting in connection with the process of pacific settlement. It is quite clear that this does not prevent the Security Council from reaching a valid decision without the concurring vote of a permanent member. The result of any other interpretation would be the ridiculous conclusion that the Charter requires a procedure which automatically makes the Security Council unable to fulfil one of its major functions.

But there is another aspect to the question of abstention. The Charter requires the "concurring votes of the permanent members" for a decision on a substantive matter. Suppose a permanent member is absent, or does not vote? Contrary to what one might expect from the language used, the interpretation in practice has been that an abstention from voting does not constitute a veto. Even in the most important decisions, if seven affirmative votes are cast and no permanent member casts a negative vote, the proposal is considered as adopted. This interpretation, it should be noted, makes possible some flexibility in the voting procedure, since it is possible for a permanent member to refrain from endorsing a proposal and still to allow the others to go ahead with it if they desire. In this respect, the language of the Charter has not been interpreted in as restrictive a fashion as might have been possible. This interpretation was of the greatest importance in the Korean case, since it permitted the resolutions of June 25 and June 27 to be adopted in the absence of the Soviet Union.

Dissatisfaction with the Security Council voting procedure, frequent use of the veto by the Soviet Union, and the problems of interpretation have resulted in much discussion and a number of suggestions. The General Assembly undertook the consideration of this matter as early as 1946, and this was one of the questions which the Interim Committee was instructed to place on its agenda. In April, 1949, the General Assembly passed a resolution recommending that the members of the Security Council should consider as procedural certain designated types of decisions; that the permanent members should consult among themselves whenever feasible with a view to avoiding use of the veto, and to exercise it only on questions of vital importance; and that members of the United Nations should exclude the principle of unanimity to the greatest extent feasible in agreements conferring functions upon the Security Council. On October 18, 1949, it was announced that the permanent members had agreed upon the principle and practice of consultation before important decisions are made. There was no other change in the position of these governments on the question.

The veto has become a crucial issue in the work of the United Nations, and in attitudes toward it and its prospects of success.   More than any other issue connected with the United Nations, it has acquired emotional overtones and, in the United States at least, has high headline value.   It is especially important, therefore, to consider some of the implications of this problem for the United Nations and for the practice of international cooperation in general. Since the veto is a type of negative vote, it becomes necessary to examine the question of *voting* in relation to the Security Council.

Voting is one method which is used in the process of decision making.   But there are other possible methods, of which force, diplomacy, persuasion, and informal agreement are examples.   It is often assumed that some kind of simple or qualified majority voting is the democratic way to settle all issues, but this assumption is unwarranted.   Democracy involves the protection of the minority as well as the rule of the majority.   Overwhelming majority votes do not necessarily indicate government by a democratic process, as Hitler's Germany so clearly demonstrated.   Conversely, a requirement of unanimity may exist in a democratic system.   One example of this is trial by jury, a cherished right in Anglo-Saxon jurisprudence.   It takes a unanimous vote of the jury to convict a person of a crime; not even an eleven-to-one majority can accomplish this.   Another example in the United States is the constitutional provision that no state can be deprived of equal representation in the Senate without its own consent.

There is another consideration which should not be forgotten.   Decisions can be made by voting only within the context of an agreement and a willingness to accept the results of the vote, even if it is contrary to one's interests and desires.   First principles cannot be compromised, nor can they be yielded to the expressed wishes of a majority.   Questions of honor and of vital interest cannot be settled this way.   The Civil War in the United States occurred when the opposition between the sections reached the point at which the conflicting views over states' rights and slavery were too deeply held to be settled by a process of voting.   As Lincoln said in his second inaugural, "Both parties deprecated war, but one of them would *make* war rather than let the nation survive, and the other would *accept* war rather than let it perish, and the war came."

When a powerful group refuses to subject itself to the verdict of the polls, voting ceases to be a device for arriving at decisions and for settling issues. The question, then, to be raised with respect to the Security Council is whether voting is an appropriate and useful procedure by which basic disagreements between East and West may be resolved.   Vetoes do not occur until these disagreements are brought to a vote.   To some extent, therefore, it is possible to say that the trouble with the veto is the vote.[13]

[13] For a stimulating discussion of this problem, see James B. Reston, "Votes and Vetoes," *Foreign Affairs,* October, 1946, pp. 13–22.

Decisions by voting require agreement to accept the results, even though adverse. They also require a mutually satisfactory basis of representation in the voting body. The present arrangement in the Security Council is that of one vote for each member, although there are great discrepancies among them in population, wealth, and influence. Among the permanent members, China has more than ten times the population of France. If all the members are considered, the disparity is much greater. Ecuador, for example, has a population of 3,400,000. It therefore has, in proportion to population, 136 times the voting representation of China, 57 times that of the Soviet Union, and 44 times that of the United States. Should Ecuador have equal weight with the United States, Great Britain, and the Soviet Union in arriving at decisions to take enforcement action, in view not only of the population disparity but also of the difference in the contributions which would be made in carrying out the decisions? It seems obvious that the device of voting for decision making in international organizations will be of limited usefulness until a better solution for the problem of representation is found.[14]

Another basic question in connection with the veto is that of the relation of the voting procedure in the Security Council to the whole process of cooperation through the United Nations. Defeat of a proposal in that body by one negative vote is labeled a "veto," but often other types of refusals to accept the majority opinion do not strike the public consciousness in the same fashion. For example, the Union of South Africa has refused to place the former mandate of South-West Africa under the international trusteeship despite several resolutions of the General Assembly stating that this should be done. Israel refused to accept the General Assembly recommendation that Jerusalem be internationalized. Great Britain and France served notice that they would resist any attempt to extend international supervision of colonies and that they would refuse to comply with resolutions calling for political information and plans. The United States Senate, in consenting to ratification of the Statute of the International Court of Justice, attached the reservation that virtually gives the United States government a veto over submission of cases to the Court when it is a party and alleges that the dispute is essentially a matter of domestic jurisdiction. The United States also claimed the right of veto over the status of the former Japanese mandated islands in the Pacific.

The real problem of the United Nations is the development of a sufficient degree of cooperation among its members, and especially the Great Powers. Agreement on the basis and methods for the maintenance of international peace and security is the objective. The result of a vote on a given proposal merely indicates whether or not agreement exists in that case. A veto is a reflection of disunity, rather than its cause. No solution of the problem of the veto is adequate unless it contributes to a solution of the conflict and tension among the permanent members of the Security Council.

[14] See pp. 116–117.

TABLE 3. NONPERMANENT MEMBERS OF THE SECURITY COUNCIL,
GEOGRAPHICAL DISTRIBUTION [1]

1946	1947	1948	1949	1950	1951 [2]
Australia	....	Canada	....	India	....
Brazil	....	Argentina	....	Ecuador	....
Poland	....	Ukrainian S.S.R.	....	Yugoslavia	....
Egypt	Syria	....	Egypt	....	Turkey
Mexico	Colombia	....	Cuba	....	Brazil
Netherlands	Belgium	....	Norway	....	Netherlands

[1] Leaders indicate retention of membership for the following year.

[2] In 1952 new members were Pakistan, Chile, and Greece, with Turkey, Brazil, and the Netherlands retaining their membership.

Chapter 10

THE ECONOMIC AND SOCIAL COUNCIL

It was recognized, in framing the Charter of the United Nations, that economic and social conditions have an important relation to the maintenance of international peace. Economic misery and social unrest involve frustrations and tensions which destroy order, stability, and security. Under such conditions, peace can be preserved only by the maintenance of a *status quo* backed by overwhelming force. This type of situation certainly will be a temporary and explosive one.

It was felt that the improvement of world economic and social conditions would alleviate international tensions and thus assist in the maintenance of peace and security. The United Nations, through the General Assembly and the Security Council, would deal with such disputes as might arise. But a large number of major disputes would put an intolerable strain upon these organs, and in the long run an enduring peace could be established only by preventing the rise of serious international conflicts. The Charter, in Article 55, provides that the United Nations shall assist in creating "conditions of stability and well-being which are necessary for peaceful and friendly relations among nations" by promoting:

(a) higher standards of living, full employment, and conditions of economic and social progress and development;

(b) solutions of international economic, social, health, and related problems; and international cultural and educational cooperation; and

(c) universal respect for, and observance of, human rights and fundamental freedoms for all without distinction as to race, sex, language, or religion.

Recognition of the relation of economic and social cooperation to the maintenance of international peace is very important. In the long run, the greatest opportunities of the United Nations probably lie in this field. However, it is necessary to interject a warning against a too facile acceptance of this assumption in an exaggerated form. A recent United Nations booklet, for example, opens with this sentence: "It has long been recognized that to ensure peace, it is necessary to solve the world's economic and social problems." [1]

[1] *The Economic and Social Council,* Reference Pamphlet No. 2, United Nations, 1949, p. 1.

Without detracting from the importance or relevance of this idea, one may point out that it is neither that simple nor that automatic. What is the exact relation of economic and social conditions to group conflict? The social sciences are not able, in their present stage of development, to give a definite answer. It is known, however, that there is a relationship and that the whole problem is a complex one with a number of variables.

The peoples who are economically most advanced, and who have relatively high standards of social welfare, are not always the least warlike. Napoleon's France probably had a higher "level of living" than any other country on the continent of Europe at the time. Germany in 1939 had "full employment" and was better off economically than India and many other countries. Dozens of similar examples can readily be drawn from the slightest knowledge of history. As a matter of fact, a measure of economic advancement is necessary for large-scale warfare. It is only the great industrial nations, with their huge resources and productivity, which have the capacity to fight a global war. If all the peoples of the world were poverty-stricken, small and localized wars might occur but the shadow of atomic annihilation would not hang over the entire world. Nor is the standard (or level) of living, "American" or otherwise, any guarantee of peace because of the simple psychological fact that human wants are insatiable. Sometimes those who have the most are the most dissatisfied with what they have. The extent of dissatisfaction and frustration does not bear an exact inverse correlation to the abundance of goods.

On the other hand, it is equally obvious that some tensions are associated with economic and social deprivation. The real question is the extent and incidence of the dissatisfaction with the *status quo,* and the point at which it becomes inflammable. Some insight into the nature of this complex problem will enable a more solid foundation to be laid for the important work of international economic and social cooperation. And it will forestall the frustration which would be produced in a reaction to the results of an uncritical reliance upon this type of activity as a panacea. One important consideration which presents a real opportunity at the present time is that frustration within a group seems to be at a minimum when conditions are improving and when there is a hopeful attitude concerning the attainment of significant goals by peaceful means.

Without putting all our peace-and-security eggs in the one basket of economic and social cooperation, we can recognize its special importance at the present time. Modern technology has made the nations of the world interdependent in fact. The practice of international cooperation is essential if the economic, social, and political conditions and activities are to be geared to the technological facts of life. This must be done if the evolution of modern society is to take place in an orderly fashion. The task in this connection is the fundamental one of creating the economic and social conditions of peace and security in the modern world. The foundation is not the whole house, but without it the house cannot be built.

Under the League of Nations, activities in the field of international economic and social cooperation were extensively developed.[2] The Covenant of the League provided (in Article 23) for "social and other activities," including the attempt to secure fair and humane conditions of labor; just treatment of native inhabitants of colonial territories; supervision of agreements with regard to traffic in women and children, and in opium and other dangerous drugs; supervision of trade in arms and ammunition with the countries in which the control of this traffic was necessary; maintenance of freedom of communications and transit; and steps for the prevention and control of disease. In addition to these specific provisions, both the Assembly and the Council were authorized to deal with any matter "within the sphere of action of the League or affecting the peace of the world." The work of the League of Nations in international economic and social cooperation became increasingly important and successful, but this development was overshadowed by the political crisis of the 1930's. The experience was not entirely lost, however. In addition to the concrete results obtained at the time, there was a definite influence on the recognition given to this type of international cooperation in the organization of the United Nations.

The Charter of the United Nations provides for an Economic and Social Council, which is designated as one of the six principal organs and which operates under the authority of the General Assembly. This is in contrast to the League arrangement, under which the responsibility for this type of work was vested in the political organs (Council and Assembly) and carried out by subsidiary commissions and committees. The result was to give the economic and social activities a subordinate emphasis and to allow them to be unduly influenced by political considerations.

The Economic and Social Council is composed of eighteen members of the United Nations elected by the General Assembly for terms of three years. There is a staggered arrangement, so that the terms of office of six members expire each year. There are no permanent members designated in the Charter, as in the case of the Security Council, and no criteria are specified to guide the General Assembly in electing members to the Economic and Social Council. At the San Francisco Conference, the Canadian and French delegations proposed that the countries of chief industrial importance be assured of places on the Council. The majority was opposed to making any such formal distinction, and election remains open to all members of the United Nations equally. However, since states represented on the Economic and Social Council are eligible for immediate reelection, somewhat the same result has been achieved in practice.[3] The Great Powers and the other countries of chief

[2] See p. 168.

[3] For members of the Economic and Social Council, 1946–1951, see Table 4, p. 168.

industrial importance have repeatedly been elected, and also an attempt has been made to give representation to different economic systems and a variety of interests.

FUNCTIONS AND POWERS

The functions of the Economic and Social Council lie in the areas of studies and reports, discussion and recommendations, and coordination.

Studies and reports are specifically authorized by Article 62, paragraph 1, of the Charter which states that "the Economic and Social Council may make or initiate studies and reports with respect to international economic, social, cultural, educational, health, and related matters. . . ." No one can really come to grips with the problems in these fields without the basic facts. There is a lamentable dearth of adequate statistical and other information about economic and social conditions throughout the world. There has never been an accurate census of the population in many areas, and it is difficult to make even a reasonably reliable estimate in some cases. The same difficulty applies to our knowledge of resources, productivity, and other basic factors.

Only an international agency can hope to compile factual information and to collect comparable statistics on a world-wide basis. The United Nations picked up where the League left off and has broadened its activities to a significant extent. The Economic and Social Council has made studies dealing with such subjects as the problems of refugees, the world shortage of housing, the reconstruction of devastated areas, and the economic status of women. In cooperation with the Secretariat, the Council has initiated the preparation of a statistical yearbook, a demographic yearbook, and a survey of world economic conditions. A compilation of relevant information has been a first step in the accomplishments of the Economic and Social Council and its subordinate agencies, such as the Commission on Human Rights.[4] To mention one example at this point, the Draft Declaration on the Death of Missing Persons was prepared in order to provide a common standard for declaring a missing person as legally dead. Millions had disappeared during the war. A number of practical problems hinged on the question of whether they were to be considered as dead or merely missing. In many cases, estates could not be inherited, insurance payments claimed, or other property settlements made. The remaining spouse who might wish to remarry would have a legal problem. This question involved many different countries, each with its own laws and procedures. The need for a common standard was obvious. Compilation of the relevant factual information was essential before recommendations for a common standard could be made. A by-product of this process, as happens in so many cases, is a body of information useful to scholars

[4] See pp. 131–133.

and practitioners concerned with the legal, administrative, and other phases of this particular question.

Cooperation in studying and reporting on international economic and social conditions leads in the direction of a definition of areas of agreement on important factual information and on the identification of the problems of general concern. It is an important phase of the practice of international cooperation. The difficulties are great, and the achievement is still very incomplete, for both technical and political reasons. But the reports and studies prepared under the auspices of the Economic and Social Council already are very useful in a number of ways, and much greater possibilities will be realized to the extent that secrecy of basic economic and social information ceases to become a weapon in the cold war.

Another important function of the Economic and Social Council is that of *discussion and recommendations*. The Charter authorizes the Council, in Article 62, paragraph 1, to make "recommendations with respect to any such matters to the General Assembly, to the Members of the United Nations, and to the specialized agencies concerned." This is the form taken by any decisions which the Economic and Social Council may reach. This organ of the United Nations has no authority to make decisions binding upon the members or the other organs. Its influence in this connection is measured by the extent to which its recommendations are accepted. Its method is persuasion, not force.

It is clear that the authority to make recommendations extends to international cooperation in economic, social, cultural, educational, health, and related matters. Some question has arisen concerning the competence of the Economic and Social Council in specific international disputes involving an economic or financial aspect. In 1946, the Council received proposals of the Czechoslovak and Yugoslav governments for the restoration of Danube vessels which had belonged to them, had been taken away by the German army, and were then under the control of the United States. Several delegates argued that the Council had no jurisdiction over a political dispute between interested parties, but there was general agreement that the Council had a legitimate concern with the economic situation involving the restoration of traffic on the Danube. The chairman, Mr. Sampar of Yugoslavia, stated that it was within the competence of the Council to make appropriate recommendations, since the question involved international economic issues and there was doubt as to ownership of the property. The Council finally passed a resolution recommending that a conference be held in Vienna to resolve the basic problems obstructing international traffic on the Danube.

Early in 1948, the Yugoslav government asked the Economic and Social Council to pass a resolution calling upon the United States to "cease causing damage to Yugoslavia" by further retention of gold transferred from that country and deposited with the Federal Reserve Board of New York during the war. After discussion, the Council concluded that it was not competent to deal with this question (1) because it was a particular dispute between two states, and (2) because of the juridical issues involved.

In addition to the general powers of discussion and recommendation, two specific techniques are recognized in the Charter. First, the Economic and Social Council "may prepare draft conventions for submission to the General Assembly, with respect to matters falling within its competence." The draft convention has proved to be a very useful device. Every salesman knows the value of having his papers ready, complete with dotted line, and his pen unsheathed. A draft convention furnishes the text of a proposed agreement. If a country is willing to accept the terms, all it need do is sign and ratify. The tedious work of negotiation is already done. Also, it is much easier to approach agreement on a common standard since the same draft, or model, is offered to all parties.

The other technique of discussion and recommendation stated in the Charter is found in the provision that the Economic and Social Council "may call, in accordance with the rules prescribed by the United Nations, international conferences on matters falling within its competence." The conference, as a method of international cooperation, has been discussed earlier.[5] It is an important device for discussion and recommendation. The General Assembly, at its first session, adopted this rule:

Pending the adoption, under paragraph 4 of Article 62 of the Charter, of definitive rules for the calling of international conferences, the Economic and Social Council may, after due consultation with Members of the United Nations, call international conferences in conformity with the spirit of Article 62 on any matter within the competence of the Council, including the following: international trade and employment; the equitable adjustment of prices on the international market; and health.

Later the General Assembly invited the Secretary-General to prepare, in consultation with the Council, draft rules to govern the calling of international conferences.

From the beginning the Economic and Social Council has called international conferences, some upon instructions from the General Assembly [6] and some upon its own initiative.[7] Although the criteria are not stated in the Charter and the General Assembly had not adopted definitive rules, it has been the practice that the Council may call only intergovernmental conferences and may not call them on matters "essentially within the domestic jurisdiction of any state" on account of the provisions of Article 2, paragraph 7.

The Economic and Social Council's most important function of *coordination*

---

[5] See pp. 29–31.

[6] For example, the Conference on Freedom of Information, Geneva, 1948.

[7] For example, the International Health Conference, New York, 1946; World Statistical Congress, Washington, 1947; United Nations Conference on Trade and Employment, Havana, 1947.

relates to the "specialized agencies" of the United Nations. Article 57, paragraph 1, of the Charter provides that "the various specialized agencies, established by intergovernmental agreement and having wide international responsibilities, as defined in their basic instruments, in economic, social, cultural, educational, health, and related fields, shall be brought into relationship with the United Nations. . . ." Thus, the term "specialized agencies" has a particular meaning in the United Nations system. It includes international organizations created by intergovernmental agreement and having "wide international responsibilities." The latter term, in practice, has been given both a geographic and a functional connotation. No strictly regional agencies have been included in this category. Technical or service organizations have been designated as "specialized agencies" only if they perform a function of major importance and general interest. The nature of such agencies may be indicated by a brief summary of those which have been established or initiated.[8]

The International Labor Organization (ILO) was established after World War I as an autonomous associate of the League of Nations. It seeks by international action to improve labor conditions, raise living standards, and promote economic and social stability. In December, 1946, arrangements were completed for the ILO to become a specialized agency of the United Nations. One feature of the ILO which requires special mention is its arrangement for representation of member countries. The Conference, as the highest authority of the ILO, is composed of national delegations including two government delegates and one delegate each of management and labor. Thus, one-half the representatives to the Conference are nongovernmental delegates. This is an interesting departure from the usual pattern of representation in international organizations.

The Food and Agriculture Organization of the United Nations (FAO) grew out of a conference held at Hot Springs, Virginia, in 1943. The purpose and scope of this agency is indicated by these words in the preamble to its constitution:

The Nations accepting this Constitution, being determined to promote the common welfare by furthering separate and collective action on their part for the purposes of: raising levels of nutrition and standards of living of the peoples under their respective jurisdictions, securing improvements in the efficiency of the production and distribution of all food and agricultural products, bettering the condition of rural populations, and thus contributing toward an expanding world economy. . . .

The United Nations Educational, Scientific and Cultural Organization (UNESCO) assumes that lasting peace cannot be built exclusively on political and economic arrangements, but must be founded on the intellectual

---

[8] For a description of the functions and organization of each specialized agency, see *Yearbook of the United Nations, 1948–1949*, pp. 981–1118.

and moral solidarity of mankind.   The preamble to its constitution states that "since wars begin in the minds of men, it is in the minds of men that the defences of peace must be constructed."   It is the purpose of UNESCO to collaborate in the work of advancing the mutual knowledge and understanding of peoples; to give fresh impulse to popular education and the spread of culture; and to maintain, increase, and diffuse knowledge.   These goals are sought to be realized by a wide variety of projects for international cooperation in the fields of education, science, and culture.

The International Civil Aviation Organization (ICAO) originated in a conference held in Chicago in 1944, for the purpose of laying down principles and arrangements for the development of international civil aviation in a safe and orderly manner.   The aims and objectives of ICAO, as stated in Article 44 of the Convention on International Civil Aviation, are as follows:

. . . to develop the principles and techniques of international air navigation and to foster the planning and development of international air transport so as to: (a) Insure the safe and orderly growth of international civil aviation throughout the world; (b) Encourage the arts of aircraft design and operation for peaceful purposes; (c) Encourage the development of airways, airports, and air navigation facilities for international civil aviation; (d) Meet the needs of the peoples of the world for safe, regular, efficient and economical air transport; (e) Prevent economic waste caused by unreasonable competition; (f) Insure that the rights of contracting States are fully respected and that every contracting State has a fair opportunity to operate international airlines; (g) Avoid discrimination between contracting States; (h) Promote safety of flight in international air navigation; (i) Promote generally the development of all aspects of international civil aeronautics.

The International Bank for Reconstruction and Development (called simply "the Bank") grew out of the Bretton Woods Conference of 1944 and was designed to promote the international flow of capital for productive purposes and to assist in financing the rebuilding of devastated areas and the development of resources of member nations.   The objectives were to help raise the levels of production, to assist member nations in attaining balanced economies in which exports could pay for essential imports, and thus to contribute to a healthy expansion of international trade.   In its lending operations, the Bank may make, guarantee, or participate in loans to its member countries directly, to any of their political subdivisions, or to private business enterprises in the territories of members.   First emphasis was placed on reconstruction, where there was an urgent need and also opportunity for rapid improvement in the level of productivity, but it was expected that development loans would assume a major role in the operation of the Bank.   The Bank's capital is derived from shares subscribed by member nations, in proportion to their relative economic resources.   Total subscribed capital is more than $8 billion, of which 20 per cent is paid-in capital and the remainder is in the form of a guarantee fund.

The International Monetary Fund ("the Fund") also grew out of the Bretton Woods Conference. Its purpose is to promote stability in international currency matters and to encourage the expansion of world trade. This is to be done by (1) working toward the eventual removal of restrictions on foreign exchange transactions; (2) setting up a schedule of exchange rates in terms of gold and United States dollars, so that traders who wish to buy in foreign countries can obtain the currencies they require at known and stable rates; and (3) ensuring that any major changes in foreign exchange practices will be submitted to international consultation before being put into effect. The Fund is also authorized to engage in foreign exchange and gold transactions with members, in order to provide a secondary line of monetary reserves. As the source of capital funds, a subscription quota was set for each member. This is payable partly in gold and partly in the member's own currency. These quotas vary from $500,000 for Honduras and Panama to $1,300,000,000 for the United Kingdom and $2,750,000,000 for the United States. Voting power and the amounts which may be drawn from the Fund are both related to the size of these quotas.

The Universal Postal Union (UPU) originated with the heavy increase in international mail during the nineteenth century.[9] It became a specialized agency of the United Nations on July 1, 1948. Virtually all independent nations, non-self-governing territories, and United Nations trust territories are now members of UPU, which forms a "single postal territory for the reciprocal exchange of correspondence." The basic purpose is "to secure the organization and improvement of the various international postal services, and to promote the development of international collaboration in this field." Maximum and minimum rates, weight limits, and dimensions are fixed for "ordinary mail," which is defined to include letters, postcards, commercial papers, printed matter, raised print for the blind, samples of merchandise, small packets, and phonopost articles (such as phonograph records). Supplemental agreements include provisions for other services, such as insured mail, parcel post, money orders, cash-on-delivery packages, postal checks, collection orders, and subscriptions to periodicals. Certain articles are prohibited. These include opium and other narcotics, explosive substances, immoral articles, and most live animals.

The International Telecommunication Union (ITU) is another international organization dating from the nineteenth century. Electrical telegraphy came into use in Europe about 1838, and shortly thereafter the governments concerned began to conclude agreements on standardized operation, types of conductors and apparatus, and the collection of telegraph rates. In 1865, a general treaty was signed at Paris by twenty countries, and the International Telegraph Union came into existence. Radio telegraphy was first put to use in 1899, to increase the security of maritime navigation. An International

[9] See pp. 31–33.

Radio-telegraph Union was established in 1906, since this new device could not be used effectively without international regulations. In 1932, arrangements were made to merge these two organizations into the International Telecommunication Union. The objectives of the ITU are to maintain and extend international cooperation for the improvement and rational use of telecommunication, to promote the development and most efficient operation of technical facilities, to harmonize the actions of nations in the attainment of these ends. In order to accomplish these objectives, the ITU (1) is instrumental in allocating the radio frequency spectrum and registering radio frequency assignments; (2) seeks to establish the lowest rates possible, taking into account efficient service and sound financial administration; (3) promotes measures for ensuring the safety of life through the cooperation of telecommunication service; and (4) makes studies and recommendations, and collects and publishes information for the benefit of its members. The ITU became a specialized agency of the United Nations on January 1, 1949.

The World Health Organization (WHO) is one of the new international organizations, having officially come into existence in April, 1948. This new agency was, of course, preceded by a long history of international cooperation in the field of public health. Quarantine measures have existed for centuries, and for many years international health agreements have been in force. The Health Organization of the League of Nations did much to extend this type of work. The WHO thus builds upon a long experience. Its objective is "the attainment by all peoples of the highest possible level of health," with "health" being defined as "a state of complete physical, mental and social well-being and not merely the absence of disease or infirmity." WHO is to serve as the coordinating authority on international health work, to maintain certain necessary international services, to promote and conduct research in the field of health, and to promote improved standards of teaching in the health, medical, and related professions.

The International Refugee Organization (IRO) is a nonpermanent specialized agency created to deal with the problem of refugees and displaced persons resulting from World War II. By definition, IRO is concerned with persons who were victims of Nazi, Fascist, or Falangist regimes, or were deported for forced labor, or became refugees or displaced persons for reasons of race, religion, nationality, or political opinion. It was estimated that there were about a million in these groups, in addition to the much larger number repatriated by the armies of occupation. With respect to such persons, IRO performs the functions of repatriation; identification, registration, and classification; care and assistance; legal and political protection; transport; and resettlement. Repatriation is encouraged and assisted, with due regard to the principle that no one shall be repatriated against his will. The IRO was scheduled to end operations by the end of 1951, with other organizational arrangements to be made for the refugee problem after that time.

The World Meteorological Organization (WMO) has as its objectives world-wide cooperation in the establishment of observing stations and other meteorological services; systems for the rapid exchange of weather information; standardization of meteorological observations and statistics; further application of meteorology to aviation, shipping, agriculture, and other activities; and encouragement of research and training in the field. International cooperation in meteorology was undertaken by a conference held in Brussels in 1853, primarily for the purpose of dealing with the weather and climate of the oceans, and by an organization of meteorological institutions established in 1878. The establishment of WMO converted this into an intergovernmental organization, for the purpose of strengthening the meteorological services with their respective governments and in their relations with other international organizations.

In addition to the eleven specialized agencies described above, there are two which have been initiated but not yet established: the Inter-Governmental Maritime Consultative Organization (IMCO) and the International Trade Organization (ITO).

IMCO would function in an advisory capacity to promote international cooperation in matters concerning safety at sea, shipping, removal of discriminatory action and unnecessary restrictions, and exchange of information. There are a great number of international conventions and agreements on many subjects related to shipping. There have been several international organizations dealing with some aspect of shipping. However, the need was felt for a central maritime organization to promote the objectives indicated above and to deal on behalf of shipping with agencies in such related fields as telecommunication and aviation.

ITO was planned under the auspices of the Economic and Social Council. After considerable preparatory work, a Charter was drafted at a United Nations Conference on Trade and Employment which met in Havana from November, 1947, to March, 1948. Its purposes and objectives are a balanced and expanding world economy; promotion of the economic development of underdeveloped countries, access on equal terms to needed markets and productive facilities; reduction of tariffs and other trade barriers; elimination of measures disrupting economic progress; and promotion of cooperation in fields relating to international trade.

Each of the "specialized agencies" of the United Nations has its own charter or constitution, sphere of action, structure,[10] budget, and staff, in accordance with the principle of functional organization. Although each of these agencies

---

[10] Although there are variations in details and terminology, the specialized agencies follow the same general pattern of international organization. There is an over-all conference or assembly, which meets periodically and is the highest authority of the agency; an executive board or its equivalent, which is responsible for directing the agency between meetings of its conference; and a secretariat, which performs the staff administrative functions assigned to the agency.

has a separate and distinct identity, they are not completely autonomous and unrelated to each other. They are "brought into relationship" with the United Nations, by means of agreements which are negotiated by the Economic and Social Council and approved by the General Assembly. This is necessary because of the obvious relation between their various activities and the objectives of the United Nations in the general field of international economic and social cooperation. Also, it is necessary because their various activities are not mutually exclusive but involve a considerable degree of overlapping and concern for different phases of essentially the same problems. Health, food, and refugees; aviation and meteorology; finances, currency, and international trade; labor, food, and education represent only a few of the more obvious interconnections between the work of the various specialized agencies. The principle of functional organization applied to related activities has the advantages of concentrating effort on specific areas of interest, but it does create the problem of coordination. It is a very difficult administrative task to achieve an effective working arrangement, which is neither thwarted by resistance from specialized interests nor allowed to evaporate into lip service to the general principle of coordination.

The agreements which have been concluded fall into three general patterns, with some minor variations within each group. The most detailed agreements, and the most effective from the viewpoint of coordination, are those concluded with ILO, FAO, ICAO, UNESCO, WHO, and IRO. Each of these agreements provides for reciprocal representation without vote at meetings of organs where matters of concern to the organization in question are being considered. Reciprocal proposal of agenda items is provided for. The specialized agency agrees to transmit a regular report on its activities, and provision is made for the exchange of information and documents. There are detailed provisions for cooperation in administrative matters, especially personnel, budgetary, and financial procedures. It was not possible to reach agreement on a common headquarters for the specialized agencies. The desirability of the eventual development of a unified civil service was recognized. With respect to budgetary and financial relationships, each agreement provides for consultation on appropriate arrangements for including the budget of the specialized agency within the general budget of the United Nations. Pending the conclusion of supplementary arrangements, there is consultation at the top administrative level on the preparation and transmission of the budgets and on the consideration of financial matters of common concern.

The second pattern is found in the agreements with UPU and ITU, both highly technical and long-established agencies. The provisions in these cases are more general. With respect to budgetary and financial matters, these two specialized agencies merely agree that they will transmit their annual budgets to the United Nations and that the General Assembly may make recommendations on them.   They do not promise to abide by these recommendations.

The third pattern, providing even more autonomy for the specialized agencies, is found in the agreements with the Bank and the Fund.   These two are recognized as "independent" international organizations.   The right of reciprocal representation is limited, as representatives of the United Nations are permitted to attend only meetings of the Board of Governors.   The United Nations recognizes that "it would be sound policy to refrain from making recommendations to the Bank," and there are limitations to safeguard confidential information.   The full autonomy of the Bank and the Fund in deciding the form and content of their budgets is recognized.   This position of relative autonomy and independence was justified on the basis of the special nature and responsibility of these two agencies.

It will be evident from the above discussion that the Economic and Social Council's function of coordination with respect to the specialized agencies is a very important and complex one.   Its responsibilities in this connection, together with the coordination and supervision of its own subsidiary bodies, are as broad as the wide and expanding field of intergovernmental economic and social cooperation among members of the United Nations.   Thus, the Economic and Social Council has a key role in developing the prerequisites of a stable and orderly world.   Its functions of coordination, however, are not limited to intergovernmental cooperation.   Article 71 of the Charter provides that the Council "may make suitable arrangements for consultation with non-governmental organizations which are concerned with matters within its competence."

The rapid growth of activities transcending national boundaries during the second half of the nineteenth century led to the organization of a large number of agencies concerned with a variety of interests and problems.   These were usually described as "private international organizations" to distinguish them from the public, or intergovernmental, organizations such as UPU and ITU.[11]   The term "nongovernmental organization" is more descriptive, however, and it is questionable as to whether the word "private" carries accurate connotations for such organizations as the International Federation of Agricultural Producers, the International Chamber of Commerce, or the American Federation of Labor.

Two categories of nongovernmental organizations (NGO's) have consultative status with the Economic and Social Council.   Category A includes those which have a basic interest in most of the activities of the Council and are closely linked with the economic and social life of the area which they represent.   They may submit items for inclusion on the provisional agenda of the Council.   They are permitted to present written statements limited to 2,000 words in length and, with the permission of the Council, to make ex-

[11] See p. 31.

planatory oral statements. They may also send observers to all the public meetings of the Council. Category B includes organizations which have a special competence but are concerned specifically with only a few of the fields of activity covered by the Council. They do not have the authority to submit items for the provisional agenda, but they are permitted to observe the public meetings and to present written statements limited to 500 words in length; they may also be invited to consult with committees of the Council.

By June, 1951, a total of ninety-five nongovernmental organizations had been brought into consultative arrangement with the Economic and Social Council. Nine of these [12] were in category A and the remaining eighty-six in category B.[13] The language of Article 71 of the Charter uses the term "nongovernmental organization" without the qualifying adjective "international." It was felt, however, that national organizations should normally present their views through their governments or through international organizations to which they might belong. National organizations may be included in the list after consultation with the member state concerned if they represent a field not covered by any international organization or have special experience upon which the Economic and Social Council wishes to draw. Of the ninety-five organizations with consultative status, eighty-eight are international and seven (all in category B) are national organizations.

At a meeting of the Council on February 27, 1950, unanimous approval was given to certain revisions in the procedure for consultative arrangements, on the basis of recommendations by the Council Committee on Non-Governmental Organizations (Council NGO Committee). The principal change was to emphasize the importance of consultation at the working level, in order that items coming from the NGO's would reach the Council itself only after careful preliminary consideration. It was felt that this would make possible a more effective use of the consultative arrangements and would discourage the practice of submitting items and statements for merely propagandistic purposes.

ORGANIZATION AND PROCEDURE

The Economic and Social Council has developed a rather complex organizational structure, as might be expected from its broad terms of reference and

[12] International Confederation of Trade Unions, International Chamber of Commerce, International Co-operative Alliance, International Federation of Agricultural Producers, International Federation of Christian Trade Unions, International Organization of Employers, Inter-Parliamentary Union, World Federation of Trade Unions, and World Federation of United Nations Associations.

[13] With an alphabetical range from Agudas Israel World Organization to World's Young Women's Christian Association, and with an amazing variety of interest groups. For a list, see *The Economic and Social Council, op. cit.,* pp. 97–100. The former category C was merged with category B in 1950.

the great variety of economic and social matters which come within its area of concern.   There are five types of subsidiary organs reporting to the Council: functional commissions, regional commissions, standing committees, *ad hoc* committees, and special bodies.

The functional commissions are small expert bodies designed to advise the Council on specific aspects of its work.   They vary in size from twelve to eighteen members.   States are elected as members of the commissions. They in turn nominate individuals, after consultation with the Secretary-General, in order to secure balanced representation in the various fields. These nominations must be confirmed by the Council.   Functional commissions have been set up for the following subjects: economic and employment, transport and communications, statistical, human rights, social, status of women, narcotic drugs, fiscal, and population.   In some cases, subcommissions have been established.

There are three regional commissions, one for Europe, one for Asia and the Far East, and one for Latin America.   Each consists of the members of the United Nations in its area and certain other interested states.   Each commission has the functions, for the area concerned, of facilitating concerted action for economic reconstruction and raising the level of economic activity; investigating and studying economic and technological problems and developments; and collecting, evaluating, and disseminating economic, technological, and statistical information.

The names of the standing committees are self-explanatory.   They are the Committee on Negotiations with Inter-Governmental Agencies; Committee on Arrangements for Consultation with Non-Governmental Organizations; Agenda Committee; and Interim Committee on Programme of Meetings.

Examples of *ad hoc* committees, established from time to time to deal with particular problems, are those on Genocide, Appeal for Children, and Procedure.

One of the special bodies is the Permanent Central Opium Board, composed of eight persons appointed for five years by the Economic and Social Council. Members are to be connected with and have a knowledge of the situation in drug-manufacturing and drug-consuming countries, but they are not to hold any office which puts them in a position of direct dependence upon their governments.   This Board is concerned with the general international supervision of the narcotics trade.   The supervisory body consists of four experts who make an estimate of needs for narcotic drugs for medical and scientific purposes, and publish an annual statement fixing the limits for imports and manufacture.   The United Nations International Children's Emergency Fund (UNICEF) uses contributions from governments, voluntary agencies, and individuals for the benefit of children and adolescents of countries which were the victims of aggression, for child-health purposes generally, and to safeguard the health of expectant and nursing mothers. The Administrative Committee on Co-ordination is composed of the Secretary-General of the United Nations, as chairman, and the corresponding officers of the specialized agencies. Its purpose is to implement the coordination of activities and to prevent duplication of work. The Interim Co-ordinating Committee for International Commodity Arrangements keeps informed of and facilitates consultation or action with respect to commodity problems.

In 1951, an *ad hoc* committee set up to review the organization and operation of the Council recommended that three regular sessions be held each year; that there be an annual program of work with related groups of subjects; and that items on the agenda be discussed in plenary sessions in so far as possible. Recommendations were also made for streamlining the organization of the functional commissions and subcommissions in order to reduce the organizational complexity.

Subject to the general provisions of the Charter, the Economic and Social Council determines its own rules of procedure. At least two regular sessions are held each year, one of which takes place shortly before the opening of the regular session of the General Assembly. Special sessions may be held if necessary. Each session is held at the seat of the United Nations, unless the Council decides otherwise.[14] Each year at the beginning of its first meeting the Council elects a President and two Vice-Presidents. They are eligible for reelection, but none of them may hold office after the country which he represents has ceased to be a member of the Council. The President declares the opening and closing of each meeting, directs the discussion, ensures observance of the rules of procedure, accords the right to speak, puts questions to a vote, and announces decisions.

Each member of the Economic and Social Council is permitted to have one representative at its meetings. Decisions are made by a majority of those present and voting. The meetings are held in public sessions unless the Council decides otherwise. The provisional agenda for each session is drawn up by the Secretary-General in consultation with the President of the Council. The official languages are English, French, Chinese, Russian, and Spanish. The first two of these are working languages. The system of simultaneous translation is the same as that used by the General Assembly.[15] Summary records of the public meetings of the Council, its committees and subsidiary bodies, are prepared by the Secretariat and made available to the public. The records of private meetings are made available as the Council may decide.

[14] The first regular session, early in 1946, was held in London. Beginning in 1948, one session each year has been held in Geneva.

[15] See p. 129.

TABLE 4. MEMBERSHIP IN ECONOMIC AND SOCIAL COUNCIL
1946–1951 [1]

1946	1947	1948	1949	1950	1951
Belgium			....	....	....
Canada	....			....	....
Chile	....	..../..................	....	....	....
China	....	..../..................	....	....	....
France	....	..../..................	....	....	....
Peru	....	..../..................	....	....	....
Cuba	....				
Czechoslovakia	....			....	....
India	....		....	....	....
Norway	....				
Soviet Union	............/	....	....	........../	....
United Kingdom	/	....	....	........../	....
Colombia					
Greece					
Lebanon	/..............	....			
Ukraine					
United States	/..............	....	....	/..............	....
Yugoslavia					
	Netherlands				
	Venezuela				
	Turkey				
	Byelorussia				
	New Zealand				
		Brazil			
		Poland ..../			....
		Australia			
		Denmark			
				Mexico	
				Iran	
				Pakistan	
					Philippines
					Sweden
					Uruguay

[1] The first six countries above were originally elected for three years each, the next six for two years each, and the next six for one year each. A vertical line indicates immediate reelection. Belgium resigned at the end of 1946 and was elected to a regular term beginning in 1949. Canada, Czechoslovakia and India were elected a second time after intervals of nonmembership. It is suggested that the student, on the basis of the above chart, list the expiring terms and the new members for each year to determine the extent of regional or bloc representation. Note especially how Belgium and the Netherlands have exchanged places on the Economic and Social Council and on the Security Council (see p. 151).

Chapter 11

THE TRUSTEESHIP COUNCIL

The Charter (Article 7) includes the Trusteeship Council among the six principal organs of the United Nations. It is given a position of dignity in the structure of the United Nations, but it is nevertheless a subordinate body. It functions as an auxiliary organ to the General Assembly in supervising the administration of nonstrategic trust territories, and to the Security Council in the case of strategic areas.

The Trusteeship Council is constituted quite differently from the Mandates Commission under the League of Nations. It is composed of member states, while the members of the Mandates Commission were experts appointed by the League of Nations Council and were not representatives of their governments. Undoubtedly in large measure because of this difference in character, the Trusteeship Council is a more vigorous body than was the Mandates Commission, but it is also more political. Despite the requirement of the Charter that the interests of the inhabitants of the trust territories be the first consideration in the deliberations of the Council, this is by no means always the case. It is sometimes used, as are all other bodies of the United Nations, as a forum for ideological propaganda. It may be argued that while the Charter does not set up a council of independent experts (like the Mandates Commission) it does expect the representatives of the members to be specialists on colonial problems, for Article 86, clause 2, provides that "each Member of the Trusteeship Council shall designate one specially qualified person to represent it therein." It is not clear that this was meant to be an enforceable qualification, since no one is expressly empowered to determine whether the representatives are "specially qualified." So far, no attempt has been made to disqualify a representative, and it is very doubtful whether any member would admit the authority of the Council to do so.

The Trusteeship Council is constituted in a complicated manner, because of certain basic considerations which underlie its organization. First, it was considered necessary to give automatic membership to all states administering trust territories. Secondly, it was felt that these states should be balanced by an equal number of nonadministering states. Thirdly, since all the Great Powers had a keen interest in the colonial problem and it was improbable that all of them would become administering states, provision had to be made to ensure the membership of each on the Council. This is done by giving all the permanent members of the Security Council membership in the Trusteeship Council. In summary, the Council is composed of (1) members administering trust territories; (2) such of the permanent members of the Security Council, *i.e.,* the Five Great Powers, as are not administering trust territories; and (3) as many other members elected for three-year terms by the General Assembly as may be necessary to equalize the number of members who administer and those who do not administer trust territories.

The language of Article 86 is not wholly clear as to the composition of the Trusteeship Council in case the number of members administering trust territories is less than or only equal to the number of permanent members not administering trust territories. There would then be no occasion to call on the third, or elective category, since the number of nonadministering states would equal or outnumber the administering states without the election of additional nonadministering states. Would the Council be legally constituted in this case? Presumably it would, for obviously the third category was added primarily to prevent the administering states from having a majority of votes in the Council, and secondarily to give small states representation. The drafters of this article assumed, however, that at least three of the five Great Powers would become administering states and that the above contingency was not likely to occur.

Because of the peculiar provisions governing its constitution, the Trusteeship Council could not be set up until some trust agreements had been approved and some territories thereby placed under the trusteeship system. This involved some delay, as the procedure laid down by Article 79 for approval of the agreements involved difficulties of interpretation. The procedure envisages two separate steps: (1) an agreement by "the states directly concerned," and (2) approval of the agreement by the General Assembly or the Security Council, depending upon whether the territory concerned was to be a nonstrategic or a strategic trust area. Beyond the statement that in case of territories held under mandate by a member of the United Nations the mandatory power must be a party to the agreement, the term "states directly concerned" is nowhere defined. In effect, "the states directly concerned" became the state which was in control of the territory, which in all cases but one also happened to be the mandatory power. The Soviet Union contended that all the Great Powers were included in the meaning of the disputed phrase, and that for this reason they had been made permanent members of the Trusteeship Council. However, once an agreement has been approved by the General Assembly or the Security Council, the validity of the agreement can no longer be questioned.

On December 13, 1946, the General Assembly approved agreements for eight of the former mandates, with the former mandatories named as administering states. The Trusteeship Council could now be set up. Australia, Belgium, France, New Zealand, and the United Kingdom became members of the Council as administering states, while China, the Soviet Union, and the United States became members by virtue of being permanent members of the Security Council. Since the administering states numbered five and the nonadministering members only three, two members had to be elected by the General Assembly in order to make the membership of the Trusteeship Council complete. The General Assembly elected Mexico and Iraq as members for a term of three years. The Trusteeship Council met in opening session on March 26, 1947. On the ground that it regarded the trust agreements as not in conformity with the Charter, the Soviet Union refused to participate in the elections and did not designate a representative until April 21, 1948.

As a result of the approval by the Security Council on April 2, 1947, of the strategic-area trusteeship agreement for the former Japanese mandated islands submitted by the United States, the Trusteeship Council had to be enlarged. By the change of status of the United States, the number of administering states had increased to six, while the number of nonadministering states had declined to four. Thus two additional members had to be elected to the Council. The General Assembly elected Costa Rica and the Philippines for three-year terms. When the terms of Iraq and Mexico expired in 1949, Iraq was reelected for three years and Argentina was elected to replace Mexico. To complete the unexpired term of Costa Rica, which had resigned, the General Assembly elected the Dominican Republic. The General Assembly, in 1950, reelected the Dominican Republic for a term of three years and elected Thailand to replace the Philippines.

The present (1952) members of the Trusteeship Council are as follows:

A. Administering states
   Australia
   Belgium
   France
   New Zealand
   United Kingdom
   United States of America
B. Permanent members of the Security Council not administering territories:
   China
   Soviet Union
C. Elected nonadministering states:
   Iraq (1947–1949; 1950–1952)
   Argentina (1950–1952)
   Dominican Republic (1951–1953)
   Thailand (1951–1953)

A pattern of "bloc" representation has emerged in the elections to the Trusteeship Council. Of the four elected states members, two are from

Latin America, one from the Arab League, and one from Asia. When there are so few seats to distribute, "bloc" representation becomes difficult, though the fact that several of the usual groups are assured representation as administering states or as permanent members of the Security Council simplifies the problem considerably. South Asia, the Arab countries, and Latin America are the three regions which do not have automatic representation on the Trusteeship Council; hence there is much justification for adhering to the pattern which seems to be consciously followed.

An anomalous situation arose when the 1950 General Assembly approved the trusteeship agreement for Somaliland, with Italy as the administering state. As an administering state, Italy would automatically become a member of the Trusteeship Council, if Italy were a member of the United Nations, which it is not. Its application for membership has been vetoed by the Soviet Union. To meet this difficulty, the Trusteeship Council has, in effect, accorded Italy a limited membership. It adopted twelve new rules of procedure, which gave Italy the right to participate without vote in the Council's deliberations on Somaliland and on general questions concerning the trusteeship system. Members of the Advisory Council for Somaliland, which was created by the General Assembly to assist and advise Italy in its administration of the territory, may also participate in discussions on that territory. On February 23, 1951, the Trusteeship Council passed a resolution requesting the General Assembly to include in the agenda of the sixth regular session "the question of the full participation of Italy in the work of the Trusteeship Council."

ORGANIZATION, VOTING, AND PROCEDURE

The Charter (Article 90) speaks only of a President, but the Council under its own rules has also a Vice-President. They are elected "by secret and separate ballots" at the beginning of the regular session in June from among the representatives of the members of the Council. The Council seems to have adopted the practice of alternating these positions between administering and nonadministering members; that is, when the President is a representative of a member of the first group, the Vice-President is chosen from among the representatives of the second, and vice versa. The President may appoint one of his alternates or advisers to participate in the proceedings and to vote in the Council, but in this case the President may not exercise his right to vote.

Each member of the Council has one vote. Though the permanent members of the Security Council are also permanent members of the Trusteeship Council, they do not have a veto. Decisions are made by a majority vote of the members present and voting. The Council meets in regular sessions but may be convened at any time on the request of a majority of its members.

The Trusteeship Council is authorized by the Charter to adopt its own rules of procedure.

POWERS AND ACTIVITIES

The Trusteeship Council assists the General Assembly in supervising the administration of nonstrategic trust areas and operates under its authority. It also assists the Security Council in performing "those functions of the United Nations under the trusteeship system relating to political, economic, social and educational matters in the strategic areas."

The Trusteeship Council carries out its functions chiefly in the three ways authorized by Article 87: (1) considering reports submitted by the administering authority, (2) accepting and examining petitions, and (3) sending missions to investigate conditions in the trust territories. Each administering authority must submit an annual report for each of its trust territories. In preparing this report it must follow a detailed questionnaire of nearly 250 questions prepared by the Trusteeship Council on the political, economic, social, and educational advancement of the inhabitants of the territories entrusted to its administration. Specialized agencies are invited to study these annual reports and make observations and suggestions. When the annual written report is examined by the Council, a special representative of the administering authority is given a temporary seat in order that he may give a further oral explanation and answer technical questions. Following this examination and general debate, the Council drafts a report of its own, which is incorporated in its annual report to the General Assembly, in the case of nonstrategic territories and areas, and to the Security Council in the case of strategic areas. Each report contains, in addition to a statement on conditions in the territory, the conclusions and recommendations of the Council, and also the individual views of its members.

The Trusteeship Council is also authorized by the Charter to "accept petitions and examine them in consultation with the administering authority." According to the Council's rules of procedure, petitions must, as a general rule, be presented in writing, though in certain circumstances they may be presented orally. Petitions are always presented to the administering authority for comment before the Council examines and acts on them. Petitions may be presented not only by individuals and organizations in the territories but also by others if they concern the affairs of one or more trust territories or the operation of the trusteeship system generally.

The number of petitions submitted to the Council is very large. During its first five sessions the Council considered 124 petitions and had a backlog of hundreds more. The 1949 General Assembly asked the Council to take measures to expedite their examination and disposal. Nearly a hundred petitions awaited the consideration of the eighth session (February, 1951) of the Council.   The petitions cover a wide range of subjects, such as "property claims, land titles, denial of civil and human rights, racial discrimination, poor educational services, and appeals for greater participation in local adminis-- tration.   Many of the petitioners present personal grievances.   For instance, Mr. H. O. Kallaghe, of Sumbawanga-Ulika in Tanganyika, claims the return of a dowry from his wife.   He was forced to divorce her, he says, 'without any specific reason.' " [1]

Some of the petitions, however, deal with very important problems and issues.   For example, the people of Western Samoa, through their representa- tives, petitioned for the right of self-government.   The administering author- ity, New Zealand, asked the Council to send a mission to examine the problem on the spot.   As a result, the Council sent a special mission to Western Samoa, under the chairmanship of Francis B. Sayre, the United States representative on the Council.   After spending most of July and August, 1947, in Samoa, the mission recommended some far-reaching changes in policy which were adopted by the government of New Zealand.   Other petitions have raised such questions as administrative unions of trust with nontrust territories and the unification of Ewe peoples—questions which became major issues.

The petition from the All Ewe Conference, which came before the Trustee- ship Council at its second session, raised an important but difficult problem. The Ewes are a West African tribe whose people are distributed over three territories: French Togo; Togoland, under British administration; and the Gold Coast Colony, also British.   The Ewes desire to be united under a single administration.   The consideration of this problem has taken up much time of the Trusteeship Council, and considerable time of the General As- sembly as well.   The British and French governments have set up a Con- sultative Commission elected by the Ewes and have taken other measures to satisfy the natural desire of this tribe for administrative and ultimately po- litical unification, but the Ewes do not regard them as adequate.

Lastly, the Trusteeship Council may provide for periodic visits to the trust territories, subject only to the condition that these visits must be "at times agreed upon with the administering authority."   This is a power which the Mandates Commission frequently wished it had, but which was never granted it, because of the opposition of the colonial powers in the Council of the League of Nations.   The Trusteeship Council is making regular and effective use of this means of acquiring firsthand information about the conditions and problems of the trust territories and the spirit and quality of their ad- ministration.   The first regular mission visited Tanganyika and Ruanda- Urundi in July, August, and September of 1948.   Tanganyika is a British- administered trust territory, and Ruanda-Urundi a Belgian-administered one, both in East Africa.   The second regular visiting mission went to West

[1] "Important Issues before the Eighth Session of the Trusteeship Council," *United Nations Bulletin,* Vol. X, No. 3, Feb. 1, 1951.

Africa, spending the last two months of 1949, in the four trust territories of British and French Cameroons and British and French Togoland. The third mission, in the spring of 1950, visited the trust territories in the Pacific— New Guinea, Western Samoa, Nauru, and the Trust Territory of the Pacific Islands. A fourth regular visiting mission, in 1951, visited the trust territories in East Africa. This was the second mission to Tanganyika and Ruanda-Urundi and the first to Somaliland under Italian administration. It is planned to send out one regular visiting mission each year, with the hope that each of the territories may be visited every three or four years.

Periodic visiting missions play a very significant role in the work of the Trusteeship Council in supervising the administration of the various trust territories, though apparently their organization and methods are not beyond improvement. A resolution adopted by the General Assembly in November, 1950, contains a number of suggestions for improving their organization and functional methods. The General Assembly was of the opinion that the work of the missions would be more effective if they visited fewer territories on any one trip and remained longer in each territory.

To serve as a reminder to both inhabitants and the administering authority of the special status of the territory, and as a symbol of the ideals and aspirations of the trusteeship system, the 1949 General Assembly recommended that the blue and white flag of the United Nations be flown in each trust territory, alongside the flag of the administering country.

Chapter 12

THE SECRETARIAT

The Secretariat consists of the Secretary-General and the staff of the United Nations.

It is the Secretariat, more than any other organ, which transforms the United Nations from a series of periodic meetings of Assembly and Councils into a permanent and cohesive organization. It is the main centripetal force in the international system. Without the Secretariat, the United Nations would be deprived of its center of communication and coordination, its *international* core as distinct from the national character of the delegations, which make up the Assembly and the Councils.[1]

The Secretary-General is appointed by the General Assembly upon the recommendation of the Security Council. When a candidate is being considered for recommendation, the Security Council meets in private session. The General Assembly may reject a name submitted to it. In that case, however, it cannot proceed to make its own choice but must wait until another recommendation is made. Voting on this question is by secret ballot.

The appointment of a candidate requires only a simple majority of those present and voting in the General Assembly, as contrasted with a two-thirds majority for election of states to membership on the Security Council, the Economic and Social Council, and the Trusteeship Council. The recommendation of a candidate by the Security Council, however, requires at least seven votes including the concurring votes of all the permanent members. Thus, the choice of a Secretary-General is in effect subject to the veto. This means that China, France, Great Britain, the Soviet Union, and the United States must be in agreement on a candidate if the office is to be filled. Considerable negotiation is involved, and it is to be expected that each Secretary-General will come from a small country and will not be too closely affiliated with the policies of any one of the Great Powers.

The first Secretary-General, Mr. Trygve Lie, is a Norwegian. When he was appointed on February 1, 1946, he was the unanimous choice of the Security Council and there were only three adverse votes in the General Assembly. On several occasions since then, Mr. Lie has been "in the middle" of the East-West conflict. No one could please both sides at all times, and

[1] *The United Nations Secretariat*, Carnegie Endowment, New York, 1950, pp. 8-9.

Mr. Lie has been called both a "Soviet spy" and a "running-dog of the imperialists." The present Secretary-General, fortunately, has not considered it his job to please one side or the other but has taken an international point of view and has tried to strengthen the United Nations as a true world organization.

The term of office for a Secretary-General is not specified in the Charter. A period of three years was considered at the San Francisco Conference, but this proposal was dropped when it appeared that the veto would apply to a recommendation by the Security Council. If the permanent members had to agree unanimously, a three-year term would be too short. Frequent reelection might either deprive a Secretary-General of his independence or force him to leave office as soon as he gained experience in the position. The General Assembly decided, in January, 1946, that (1) the term of appointment should be such as to enable a man of eminence and high attainment to take the position; (2) the first Secretary-General should be appointed for five years, with eligibility for reappointment; (3) the length of term might be modified later in the light of experience; and (4) it was desirable that no member should offer a retiring Secretary-General any governmental position in which the confidential information he had obtained might be a source of embarrassment to other members.

The original five-year term expired on February 1, 1951. When this question was taken up during the fall of 1950, the Security Council was unable to agree on a recommendation. The Soviet Union opposed a new term for Mr. Lie, on the grounds that he was incapable of being an objective and unbiased person. The United States indicated that it would not support any other candidate, since it would view any attempt to remove him from office as punishment for doing his duty in the Korean case. When this deadlock was not broken by a series of meetings and negotiations, the General Assembly adopted a resolution by a vote of 46 to 5, with 8 abstentions, to continue Mr. Lie in office for three more years. Only the Soviet bloc voted in the negative. The representative of China abstained from supporting Mr. Lie because he "went out of his way to circulate a memorandum which amounted to a plea" to admit the Chinese Communists to the Security Council. The Arab states abstained because they thought that Mr. Lie had not been entirely impartial in the Palestine case.

The position of Secretary-General is stronger in the United Nations than it was in the League of Nations. There are two reasons for this. One is that the Charter grants this office more important powers and functions than did the Covenant of the League. The other reason has to do with the incumbent of the office. Sir Eric Drummond, the Secretary-General of the League of Nations for the first thirteen years of its existence, did not assume responsibilities of direction and leadership. Under him, the office was a rather colorless and routine one. Mr. Lie, however, has used the powers given him in the Charter and has exercised a rather forceful leadership in behalf of the United Nations.

FUNCTIONS OF THE SECRETARY-GENERAL

Article 97 of the Charter provides that the Secretary-General shall be the "chief administrative officer" of the United Nations, and it is this title which describes his position and essential functions. The responsibilites of this office are by no means restricted to administrative duties in the routine managerial sense. It should be noted, on the other hand, that the Charter does not designate the Secretary-General as a chief executive, although he has exercised some functions which may be described as executive in type. Examples of this are his responsibilities for implementing decisions of the other organs in cooperation with the members and his capacity of spokesman for the United Nations as a whole. It would be quite misleading, however, to think of the Secretary-General's position as analogous to that of the chief executive of a national government. There are some indications of an embryonic executive authority, and as the United Nations becomes stronger, these trends may develop in a manner which it is difficult to foresee. At present, the principle of "sovereign equality" of members means that any real executive authority for the Secretary-General must exist by sufferance and be restricted to a narrow range. Conversely, all the wide variety of functions exercised by that office can be classified as "executive" in the traditional sense only in a very arbitrary way. In short, the "chief administrative officer" of the United Nations holds a unique position which can be understood to best advantage by reference to the actual duties and responsibilities involved.

The functions of the Secretary-General may be grouped under three headings—administrative and service, political, and representational.

The *administrative and service* function includes the responsibility for organizing and directing the complex and varied activities which are necessary for the operation of the Organization. The staffs of the other organs, with the exception of the International Court of Justice,[2] form a part of the Secretariat. The Secretary-General, therefore, is responsible for the performance of the essential staff work required if the General Assembly, the Security Council, the Economic and Social Council, and the Trusteeship Council are to function efficiently. The provision of space, utilities, supplies, and equipment; the recruitment of clerks, stenographers, translators, janitors, and guards; the operation of a transportation service and a cafeteria; the compilation of information and the preparation of reports; the maintenance of records and the distribution of documents—these are a sample of the elements in the complex machinery of an international secretariat.

[2] The Court has its headquarters at The Hague and has its own staff, under the direction of the Registrar.

A large number of resolutions passed by the General Assembly provide for some action on the part of the Secretary-General. This may involve, for example, communication with member governments, ascertaining the steps to be taken to give effect to the Assembly's recommendations, or the provision of information needed for consideration of a matter. He may be asked to facilitate consultation among members on a given subject, as in the case of relief plans and programs in 1947. He has been asked to prepare recommendations on the operation of a United Nations telecommunication system, the organization of a United Nations postal service, and other matters. The Secretary-General also has been given definite administrative assignments—for example, the organization of the United Nations Appeal for Children (UNAC).

The administrative and service staff work involves certain technical functions. Studies are undertaken and expert advice given to the other organs upon their request. A statistical unit has been established to examine, evaluate, and analyze statistics from governments, specialized agencies, and other sources. This unit publishes useful statistical information and coordinates the statistical activities of the specialized agencies. Some of the assignments given to the Secretariat in the field of reports and studies include analysis of information submitted on the economic, social, and educational conditions in non-self-governing territories; surveys of world economic conditions and trends; preparatory work for the International Law Commission; and preparation of suggestions concerning the form and character of reports of commissions and other subsidiary organs of the Economic and Social Council. Another technical function is the preparation of draft conventions, as in the case of the draft convention on genocide.

Important financial responsibilities also are involved in the administrative and service functions of the Secretary-General. Subject to the authority and regulations of the General Assembly, he prepares the budget of the United Nations, allocates funds, controls expenditures, collects the contributions from members, and has the custody of all funds. The Secretary-General has also been delegated the task of consulting with the specialized agencies and undertaking to develop arrangements for common fiscal controls and for common budgetary, administrative, and financial practices.[3]

A special case of an administrative responsibility imposed on the Secretary-General by terms of the Charter is found in Article 102, which provides that every treaty and international agreement entered into by any member of the United Nations must be registered with the Secretariat and published by it.

The problem of administrative coordination is a difficult one in an agency like the United Nations, with its sixty member states, six principal organs, various subsidiary organs and specialized agencies, and broad scope of functions. The centrifugal tendencies are very great, but the Organization will

---

[3] The work resulting from these responsibilities is, of course, carried out by appropriate staff assistance under the direction of the Secretary-General.

be relatively ineffective unless it can operate as an integrated system with a coherent over-all program embodying generally recognized priorities. With the natural divisions of opinion as to what should be done and how, with the inevitable vested interests in this or that activity, and with the great diversity of cultural backgrounds found among the personnel, strong leadership is needed to see that the United Nations is a real *system* and not a loose aggregation of separate blocs.

The General Assembly has certain supervisory functions, and the Economic and Social Council has coordinating responsibilities in its fields of effort.[4] It remains for the Secretary-General, however, to supply administrative coordination through staff activities and daily operations. For example, the agreements bringing the specialized agencies into relationship with the United Nations require continuous positive effort for their implementation. The Secretary-General meets with the directors of these organizations, provides personnel for liaison purposes, arranges for an exchange of documents and information, consults on the division of work, and performs other tasks in this connection.[5] Furthermore, the preparation of the various annual reports in the Secretariat offers an opportunity to describe the activities and programs in perspective and in relation to each other. This is an invaluable assistance to the General Assembly and to the Economic and Social Council in the establishment of priorities. The Secretary-General, of course, has an important task of administrative coordination in securing proper organization and teamwork of the Secretariat itself.

The Secretary-General has important functions which may be described as *political*, meaning that they require the capacity to exercise discretion and influence in the formulation of policy. The chief source of authority in this connection is found in Article 99 of the Charter, which provides that "the Secretary-General may bring to the attention of the Security Council any matter which in his opinion may threaten the maintenance of international peace and security." This goes beyond any right conferred upon the Secretary-General of the League of Nations, who could call a meeting of the Council only when asked to do so by a member.

The provisions of Article 99 make it possible for the Secretary-General to secure consideration by the Security Council of a dispute, situation, or other matter which might not be raised by a member of the Council. It also affords even greater opportunities for leadership and the exercise of influence in the United Nations. The fact that the Secretary-General may call attention to "any matter" means that he can present information or state opinions in connection with a dispute or situation already under discussion. Several

---

[4] See Chaps. 8 and 10.

[5] To formalize this arrangement, there has been created an Administrative Committee on Coordination, composed of the Secretary-General as chairman and the corresponding official of each specialized agency.

instances of this have occurred.   When the question of Iran was before the Security Council, the Secretary-General submitted a memorandum setting forth his own views on the legal aspects.   When the Greek question was being considered in 1946, he reserved the right to make his own inquiries or investigations to determine whether he should consider making any statement to the Council.   More recent examples may be found in the very active efforts of Mr. Lie to find some basis for settling the question of the representation of China in the United Nations, in his proposals for a twenty-year program of peace,[6] and in his attempts to find some basis for negotiation among the Great Powers.

Another way in which the Secretary-General exercises a political influence is through the annual report on the work of the Organization.   This is prepared each year prior to the opening of the regular session of the General Assembly, and it serves as one basis for the opening debates and statements of policy.   The report is much more than a routine summary.   It states the main issues, with the Secretary-General's own opinions and recommendations. It has a real influence and, incidentally, is an excellent source of information on the accomplishments and problems of the United Nations from year to year. In addition to presenting his annual report, the Secretary-General may propose items for the agenda of the General Assembly, the Security Council, and the Trusteeship Council.   He prepares the provisional agenda for these organs and for the Economic and Social Council, and may make written or oral statements to them.   Thus, he is in a position to exercise initiative and influence by making proposals, effecting the establishment of priorities, and advocating the viewpoints which he considers appropriate.

The *representational* function of the Secretary-General arises from the fact that he is the only person who stands for the United Nations as a whole.   All the other organs are composed of a number of members and each has a special area of responsibility.   The delegations, of course, speak only for individual countries.   There is only one Secretary-General, however, and he is concerned with the entire Organization.   The Secretary-General represents the United Nations in negotiations with other agencies and with governments, and his office is the normal channel of communication with the United Nations.   On occasion he has been empowered by the General Assembly to enter into agreements with states, as in the case of the headquarters agreement.

The Charter provision (Article 98) that the Secretary-General shall act in that capacity in all meetings of the General Assembly and the three Councils is an assurance that there will not be a tendency for each organ to develop its own little secretary-general.   In addition, the fact that the staffs serving these organs are a part of the Secretariat underscores the intention and practice of giving the Secretary-General an important central place in the work of the United Nations.

[6] See Appendix 20.

The position of the Secretary-General as chief administrative officer, with the functions indicated above, gives both an opportunity and a responsibility for leadership. The powers granted by the Charter are stated in broad terms and are not unduly restrictive on the development of this office. The force of circumstances and the personal qualities of international statesmanship combine to produce a line of development which has interesting and important potentialities. No one can say exactly what the role and status of the Secretary-General will be after a few decades, any more than the later trends in the office of President of the United States could have been predicted in 1789.

ORGANIZATION OF THE SECRETARIAT

The best method for organizing the Secretariat raised some difficult questions of public administration. One view, held by the minority, was that the staff should be organized on the basis of the bodies to be served. There would be a division of the Secretariat to serve the Security Council, one for the General Assembly, and so on. The objections to this were that it might give rise to divided loyalties, and that duplication and waste of time would be difficult to avoid. For example, the regular meetings of the General Assembly and of the Economic and Social Council are held at different times of the year. There is no reason that an economist, or any expert, might not serve one in July and the other in November. This is particularly true since many of the items on which the Economic and Social Council makes recommendations then go to the General Assembly for consideration. If different departments of the Secretariat were maintained for the two organs, separate staffs would be working on the same subject at various stages of progress. Obviously this would be very inefficient.

The majority view was that the organization should be set up on a functional basis. Each department of the Secretariat has distinctive functions but it can serve any organ as occasion requires. The Department of Economic Affairs, for example, serves primarily the Economic and Social Council, but it also is used by the General Assembly, the Trusteeship Council, and other organs as appropriate. As another example, legal experts may be needed in connection with the work of any of the organs. It is better to have one Legal Department than to have a separate legal section for the General Assembly and each of the three Councils.

Although the functional principle was adopted as the basis for organization of the Secretariat, some deviations were introduced for practical reasons. Since the Security Council has exclusive power to deal with military and enforcement measures, there are special units in the Department of Security Council Affairs to serve that organ alone. Also, there are many cases of specialization at subordinate levels; for example, one organizational unit will prepare the provisional agenda for the General Assembly and another will do the same work for the Economic and Social Council. There is no attempt to maintain absolute adherence to any one abstract principle. The conception is rather one of having the organization based on functional needs and, within this general framework, establishing a pattern which will serve the practical needs most effectively. It should also be noted that some departments of the Secretariat are more closely tied to organizational counterparts than others. For example, the Department of Economic Affairs serves primarily the Economic and Social Council, the Second (Economic and Financial) Committee of the General Assembly, and the various advisory commissions in that field; the Legal Department advises or maintains liaison with all the other organs; while the Department of Public Information serves the entire Organization and the general public.

The regional basis of staff organization remains to be mentioned. This is found in the United Nations in connection with the branch office in Geneva, the regional economic commissions, and the various visiting missions. How to secure the most efficient staffing of these groups and maintain an integrated Secretariat is a real problem of administrative management.

A brief description of each major division of the Secretariat will indicate the organizational arrangement and the principal duties of the United Nations staff:

The Department of Security Council Affairs provides such services as notification of meetings and preparation of agenda, reports, and documentation for the Security Council and for the First (Political) Committee of the General Assembly. It obtains information and prepares reports with reference to threats to peace, the pacific settlement of disputes, and the general principles of cooperation; advises the Security Council on rules of procedure; prepares studies on the political aspects of military agreements, and assists in negotiations of such agreements; makes studies on the size of armaments and traffic in arms; participates in investigations and advises on the security aspects of strategic trusteeship areas; and helps to formulate plans related to the application of enforcement measures.

The Department of Economic Affairs provides services and assistance required in connection with economic and statistical problems. It undertakes the publication of economic studies and reports; services international conferences on subjects in this field; and furnishes expert assistance, particularly for underdeveloped countries. It maintains close relations with the various specialized agencies dealing with labor, food and agriculture, trade transport and communications, banking, and finance.

The Department of Social Affairs is responsible for staffing the Third (Social, Humanitarian and Cultural) Committee of the General Assembly; the Economic and Social Council when it deals with problems of human rights, status of women, narcotic drugs, health, refugees, education, and cultural activities; and the subsidiary organs such as the Commission on Human Rights. It prepares the meetings and work programs of these bodies; carries out, according to instructions, any studies or other technical assignments in the social field; issues publications; assists in the preparation of draft conventions; and services international conferences. It keeps in touch, through documentation and reciprocal representation, with specialized agencies and other organizations concerned with labor, health, education, science and culture, and refugees.

The Department of Trusteeship and Information from Non-Self-Governing Territories carries this long and awkward title as an accurate reflection of the two different types of responsibilities for peoples who have not yet reached the stage of self-government.[7] This Department serves the Trusteeship Council, the Fourth (Trusteeship) Committee of the General Assembly, and other organs of the United Nations. It provides assistance on studies and documentation; the drafting and consideration of trusteeship agreements; formulation of questionnaires; examination of reports from the administering authorities; acceptance and examination of petitions; and periodic official visits and surveys.

The Legal Department of the Secretariat advises on legal and constitutional questions, encourages the progressive development and codification of international law, and maintains liaison with the International Court of Justice. This work involves legal assistance and opinions on interpretations of the Charter, draft treaties, resolutions, contracts, claims, and national laws of interest to the United Nations. The staff of this Department negotiates agreements such as those relating to privileges and immunities and it carries out the Secretariat's responsibility for the registration, classification, and publication of treaties.

Conference and General Services is the name of the department which makes arrangements and provides services for the meetings and conferences held under the auspices of the United Nations. It cooperates in scheduling the meetings; provides translation, interpretation, reproduction, and graphic presentation services; edits and publishes the journals and official records; provides general services such as purchasing, transportation arrangements, hotel accommodations, and buildings management; handles mail, cables, telephone, and telegraph services; and supervises the files. This, in an organization the size and complexity of the United Nations, is a tremendous managerial task. This department has about one-half the total number of employees in the Secretariat.

Administrative and Financial Services is the department which plans and executes the personnel, budgetary, and fiscal programs of the United Nations. It provides data and maintains relationships with the other organs and the specialized agencies on these questions; advises the Secretary-General on pro-

[7] See Chap. 11.

posed programs of organization prior to their adoption with respect to their personnel, budgetary, and financial implications; and it is responsible for arranging with member governments for the payment of their contributions.

The Department of Public Information advises the Secretary-General on information policy, and, working with the specialized agencies, it supervises and maintains facilities at headquarters for representatives of all information media; maintains information centers in various parts of the world; provides services for press coverage of United Nations activities and issues informative publications; organizes sales and distribution throughout the world of informative material issued by the United Nations; broadcasts accounts of United Nations activities and provides facilities for commercial and governmental broadcasting services; maintains film and photographic coverage, and encourages the production of films; provides informative material and related services to educational agencies, lecturers, and nongovernmental organizations; prepares surveys of press and radio opinion; and maintains the library and reference services of the United Nations.

Since public opinion is a crucial factor in the success of the United Nations, the information activities are of the greatest importance. A wide variety of media is used, as may be judged from the preceding paragraph. Further mention of a few selected activities is appropriate, however. A service for visitors to headquarters is maintained. They may observe any of the public meetings, subject to the availability of space. A "briefing" program explains the setup, and questions about the Organization will be answered. Experience has shown that permitting visitors to see the United Nations in action is one of the best ways to arouse interest in it. By 1950, visitors to Lake Success and Flushing Meadows were averaging over one thousand a day. When the head of the Soviet delegation, Mr. Malik, returned to assume the Presidency of the Security Council in August, 1950, as many as 23,000 visitors had to be turned away in a single day. Most of the visitors seem to take a sincere interest in the United Nations, and few are so naïve as to make the famous, and perhaps apocryphal, remark that "it's all right, but there are so many foreigners around."

One important project is known as United Nations Radio, broadcasting daily from headquarters in many different languages. When the Security Council took action in the Korean case, United Nations Radio went on the air twenty-four hours a day, seven days a week, broadcasting the news in twenty-seven different languages. In August, 1950, the Security Council became a popular television feature with a villain to hiss and a hero to cheer.

Another example of information work is the designation of various colleges and schools as volunteer educational centers. Materials are furnished and other assistance is given by the Department of Public Information in order to spread knowledge about the United Nations among teachers and through them to the general public.

Each department of the Secretariat is headed by an Assistant Secretary-General. These officials were appointed by the Secretary-General for terms of five years. At the San Francisco Conference, a proposal to have an Assistant Secretary-General of the nationality of each of the Great Powers was defeated because of the opposition of the small countries. The same result, however, has been achieved in practice. The nationalities of the department heads, as of January, 1951, were as follows: Security Council Affairs, the Soviet Union; Economic Affairs, Great Britain; Social Affairs, France; Trusteeship and Information from Non-Self-Governing Territories, China; Public Information, Chile; Legal, Czechoslovakia; Conference and General Services, India; and Administrative and Financial Services, United States.

The Assistant Secretaries-General serve almost entirely as heads of the individual departments. The development has not been in the direction of a general policy group or cabinet which would collaborate on the over-all program. There is a small Executive Office which assists the Secretary-General on those functions which he does not delegate to departments but retains as his personal responsibility. The head of this office is the Executive Assistant to the Secretary-General. If the Secretary-General is absent or unable to perform his functions, he deputizes one of the Assistant Secretaries-General to act for him.

The Staff

The staff is appointed by the Secretary-General under regulations made by the General Assembly. Members of the Secretariat are prohibited from seeking or receiving instructions from any government or from any other authority external to the United Nations. They constitute an international civil service. Upon appointment, all members of the staff must subscribe to the following oath or declaration:

I solemnly swear (undertake, affirm, promise) to exercise in all loyalty, discretion and conscience the functions entrusted to me as a member of the international civil service of the United Nations, to discharge those functions and regulate my conduct with the interests of the United Nations only in view, and not to seek or accept instructions in regard to the performance of my duties from any government or other authority external to the Organization.

A person does not lose his national citizenship by accepting employment with the Secretariat, but he serves the entire membership and his first loyalty in connection with his work belongs to the United Nations. There is, accordingly, a sharp distinction between the status of a member of the Secretariat and that of a member of a national delegation. The former performs an international function, while the latter serves the interests of his own country. Member states have an obligation not to seek influence over employees of the Secretariat. Once a staff member has been appointed, his tenure is subject solely to determination by the Secretary-General. This principle was successfully asserted in connection with Czechoslovak nationals on the staff in 1948. If delegates from Communist China are admitted as representatives of that country, the question may arise in a more complex form. It is likely that the Chinese at United Nations headquarters would be divided, at least for a time, between Nationalists functioning as international civil servants and Communists as members and employees of the delegation.

A very interesting situation arose during the Soviet absence from meetings of the Security Council between January and August, 1950. The Assistant Secretary-General for Security Council Affairs is a Russian. It became his duty to make arrangements and provide staff services for the sessions which the Soviet delegation was denouncing as "illegal." While the Soviet representatives stayed away from the meetings, the Russian Assistant Secretary-General continued to perform his duties as an international civil servant. During August two Russians sat side by side at meetings of the Security Council, Mr. Malik as President and Mr. Zinchenko as Assistant Secretary-General. On one occasion, Mr. Malik said that he had a communication to place before the Council, but since the Russian text was not available, he would ask the Assistant Secretary-General to read it. There was some grim humor in this situation: Mr. Malik's English is completely adequate, but the Soviet representative could not in any way imply that the Russian language is in a secondary position; Mr. Zinchenko is also a Russian, and it is the job of the Secretariat to see that all the required translations are available!

One of the most remarkable accomplishments of the United Nations is the success with which several thousand employees from over sixty countries [8] have been molded into an effective working staff. This is especially notable in view of the fact that the job had to be done with great speed and under very difficult world conditions. People of different languages, customs, cultural backgrounds, and administrative practices had to learn to work together effectively. Many problems remain, but the staff has functioned quite well and solid foundations have been laid for a developing international civil service.

An adequate supply of competent and efficient personnel is essential to the growth and success of the United Nations. This means more than technical expertness. An "international outlook" is indispensable. The viewpoint needed has been well described in the following words: [9]

A lack of attachment to any one country does not constitute an international outlook. A superior indifference to the emotions and prejudices of those whose world is bounded by the frontiers of a single state does not constitute an international outlook. A blurred indistinctness of attitude towards all questions, proceeding from a

[8] Nationals of nonmember states are eligible for employment.
[9] C. Wilfred Jenks, "Some Problems of an International Civil Service," *Public Administration Review,* Spring, 1943, p. 105.

freedom of prejudice born of lack of vitality, does not constitute an international outlook. The international outlook required of the international civil servant is an awareness made instinctive by habit of the needs, emotions, and prejudices of the peoples of differently-circumstanced countries, as they are felt and expressed by the peoples concerned, accompanied by a capacity for weighing these frequently imponderable elements in a judicial manner before reaching any decision to which they are relevant.

The Charter provides that the paramount consideration in the employment of staff shall be the necessity of securing the highest standards of efficiency, competence, and integrity. Some regard is to be paid to recruitment on as wide a geographical basis as possible. Yet it would be fatal to the development of a real international civil service if positions should be regarded as "spoils" allocated to the disposal of member states. The international outlook would be overshadowed, efficiency might become a secondary consideration, and the authority of the Secretary-General would be difficult to maintain. The geographic distribution of employees remains a difficult problem, especially since the trained and available personnel tends to be concentrated in a few countries. It is to be expected that the lower paid jobs must be filled for the most part by local employees. It follows that American citizens will have a very high proportion of these jobs. Of about 2,900 permanent positions at headquarters in 1950, almost 1,900 were designated as "locally recruited" and slightly more than 1,000 as "internationally recruited." [10] United States nationals held about one-third of these "international" positions. Ten members held three-fourths of them. All the Latin-American countries combined held about 8 per cent of the total, and the Soviet Union, apparently from its own desire, had only twelve positions.

Some countries whose nationals have comparatively small representation among the employees have expressed dissatisfaction with the situation. At the General Assembly session of 1947, a resolution to require allocation of positions in the same ratio as budgetary contributions was defeated by the narrowest margin. The actual distribution of jobs, however, happens to be quite close to the distribution of financial assessments. It is encouraging to note that after great efforts there has been some improvement in the geographic distribution of employees.

The salary classification plan adopted in 1946 was based on a scheme of nineteen grades with three to seven salary steps within each grade. The base salary ranged from $1,580 a year for the first step in Grade 1 to $11,000 for the position of top-ranking director.[11] The recent trend has been toward a

---

[10] The seven lowest salary grades and all linguistic positions were designated as "locally recruited." In addition to the permanent positions, there were at the time several hundred temporary positions at headquarters and about a thousand employees in other locations.

[11] The Secretary-General receives $20,000 plus a representation allowance of the same

grouping of positions in a smaller number of broad categories. A perplexing problem of equitable compensation arises from the fact that some countries exempt salaries paid to their nationals by the United Nations from income taxes, while others do not.[12] The same gross salary becomes a widely variable net salary if uniform treatment as to tax exemption does not exist. Pending the ratification by all members of the Convention on the Privileges and Immunities of the United Nations,[13] employees are in effect reimbursed for the national income taxes which they pay.

UNITED NATIONS FIELD SERVICE

In November, 1949, the General Assembly approved a proposal by the Secretary-General that a United Nations Field Service be established as a part of the staff. It is designed to provide technical and protective services for United Nations missions in the field. Guards have been regularly employed for duty at United Nations headquarters. It was felt by the advocates of the new plan that the staff service to field missions would be strengthened if the guard system were extended and the missions accompanied by aides wearing a United Nations uniform. The Field Service is not to exceed 300 persons. It is not a military force and will not carry weapons, except that side arms may be authorized on special occasions. Despite its small size and nonmilitary character, however, it is an international police force and it creates a precedent for further strengthening of the United Nations along similar lines. In addition to its protective duties, the Field Service has such tasks as handling radio communications and driving trucks.

Training of recruits includes a course in police methods, first-aid instruction, shorthand, and typewriting. Because the jeep is such an essential element in connection with field missions, the recruits are sent to a plant at Toledo, Ohio, for some concentrated instruction on how to keep a jeep in condition under all circumstances.

In addition to the Field Service itself, the General Assembly approved the establishment of a Panel of Field Observers. This consists of a list of names which can be drawn upon for observation duties in connection with truce enforcement, plebiscites, and similar matters.

---

amount, and he is provided with a furnished residence. Each Assistant Secretary-General receives $13,500 plus an allowance which has been fixed at $8,500.

[12] The United States does not exempt an American citizen employed by the United Nations from paying a Federal income tax on his salary.

[13] See Appendix 13.

Chapter 13

THE INTERNATIONAL COURT OF JUSTICE

The International Court of Justice is the principal judicial organ of the United Nations. Provision is made for the Court by Articles 92 to 96 of the Charter, and a detailed Statute to govern its functioning is made an integral part of the Charter by reference. There was some question at the San Francisco Conference as to whether the Permanent Court of International Justice, which had served as a "world court" during the period of the League of Nations,[1] should be continued or replaced by a new organization. Some delegates felt that the continuity of international judicial institutions should be preserved, that the Permanent Court of International Justice represented a great forward step and should not be scrapped, that there were references to it in a large number of treaties, and that its record was a very good one.

On the other hand, the majority thought that it was better to start with a clean slate. The former Court had lapsed so far as election of judges was concerned, and it was not feasible to reinstate the procedure. It was argued that the new Court would be intimately connected with the United Nations and should be created as a part of that system. On any other basis there would be difficulties in membership. Some countries which were not to be initial members of the United Nations had been parties to the Statute of the Permanent Court of International Justice. Conversely, some members of the United Nations (for example, the United States) had never been such parties. On the whole, it seemed better to create a new organizational entity but to preserve the continuity of concept and function. No attempt was made to revive the Permanent Court of International Justice as such, and the International Court of Justice was created as one of the six principal organs of the United Nations. However, the Statute of the present Court is specifically based upon that of the former one. The two instruments are substantially identical, with only the necessary changes in terminology. This identity is even carried to the numbering of the articles of the new Statute, to facilitate reference. For example, Article 38 of the new Statute parallels Article 38 of the earlier one. Emphasis is placed upon the fact that the principal judicial organ of the United

---

[1] See p. 90.

Nations is the successor and heir of the Permanent Court of International Justice.[2]

By provision of the Charter (Article 93), all members of the United Nations are parties to the Statute of the Court. In addition, other countries may be parties to the Statute by accepting conditions determined in each case by the General Assembly upon the recommendation of the Security Council. The conditions which have been laid down are the acceptance of the Statute and of the same obligations as United Nations members with respect to the Court, and an undertaking to contribute to the expenses an amount assessed by the General Assembly after consultation with the government concerned. By July, 1950, Switzerland and the Principality of Liechtenstein had taken advantage of this opportunity. The Court is also open to states not parties to the Statute on conditions laid down by the Security Council. The principal condition which has been established is the acceptance in advance of all the obligations of a party to the Statute for a particular dispute or a general class of disputes.

ELECTION OF JUDGES

One of the major difficulties in creating a world court has been that of a method for selecting the judges. As international organization developed, it was the practice for national governments to appoint personnel, who acted upon instructions and who represented the viewpoints and policies of their respective countries. A genuine judicial proceeding, however, requires impartial judges who do not take orders from the parties to disputes brought before the court. It was necessary, on this account, to find some acceptable method for selecting judges who could function independently of the various governments constituting a world court. But the states of the world have been reluctant to make this type of concession to the needs of international organization. The idea of sovereignty furnished theoretical grounds for insisting that "no state can be bound without its own consent." From a practical point of view, national governments have been slow to surrender the power to settle disputes into the hands of an impartial third party or agency over which they would have no control.

The method of selecting judges [3] for the International Court of Justice is based upon an ingenious and complicated compromise between the prerequisites of a world court and the demands of nationalism. First of all, it is provided that "the Court shall be composed of a body of independent judges,

[2] It is of interest to note that articles by Manley O. Hudson, published periodically in the *American Journal of International Law*, refer to both institutions as "the Court." Thus, an article in the *Journal* for January, 1950, is entitled "The Twenty-eighth Year of the World Court."

[3] The judges are known as "members" of the Court, and states are spoken of as "parties to the Statute." It is the states which are "members" of the United Nations.

elected regardless of their nationality from among persons of high moral character, who possess the qualifications required in their respective countries for appointment to the highest judicial offices, or are juriconsults of recognized competence in international law" (Article 2 of the Statute). Although the judges are to be elected "regardless of their nationality," no two of them may be nationals of the same state. Further, to assure that no one country or group will dominate the Court, it is provided that the main forms of civilization and of the principal legal systems of the world shall be represented.

In the actual procedure of selecting the judges, the first step is that of nominations by the national groups in the Permanent Court of Arbitration.[4]   No group may nominate more than four persons, not more than two of whom may be of their own nationality. (In case only one vacancy is to be filled, not more than two candidates may be nominated by each group.)   Before making these nominations, each national group is supposed to consult its highest court of justice, its legal faculties and schools of law, and its academies devoted to the study of law. When the candidates have been duly nominated, the Secretary-General of the United Nations prepares a list of the persons in alphabetical order. The General Assembly and the Security Council then proceed independently of one another to elect fifteen of these candidates to become the members of the Court. The candidates who receive an absolute majority of votes in both the General Assembly and the Security Council are considered as elected. This provision is an interesting exception to the voting procedure on all other matters. An "absolute majority" means more than 50 per cent of the total number of members, while other decisions in the General Assembly are taken by either a simple or a two-thirds majority of those present and voting. In the Security Council, an absolute majority would be six and all other decisions require at least seven affirmative votes. In electing the judges, no distinction is made between permanent and nonpermanent members, and therefore the "veto" does not apply.

The filling of vacancies and other problems of electing the judges are spelled out in the Statute in precise detail. One example may be of some interest here. Article 10, paragraph 3, of the Statute provides, "In the event of more than one national of the same state obtaining an absolute majority of the votes both of the General Assembly and of the Security Council, the eldest of these only shall be considered as elected."

The judges are elected for terms of nine years, and are eligible for reelection. The terms are staggered, so that the tenure of five judges expires every three years. Vacancies are filled in the same manner as the regular elections, and a judge elected to replace another member holds office for the remainder of his predecessor's term.

4 See p. 39. In the case of members of the United Nations not represented in the Permanent Court of Arbitration, candidates are nominated by national groups appointed for this purpose by their governments.

By the procedure outlined above, it has been possible to constitute a broadly representative world court [5] composed of a body of independent judges. Although national governments take part in the procedure of nomination and election, the judges are not appointed as representatives of their countries and do not act upon instructions. They are officials of an international judiciary, and as such enjoy diplomatic privileges and immunities.

FUNCTIONS AND POWERS

The International Court of Justice, as the principal judicial organ of the United Nations, has two types of responsibilities. It decides cases brought before it and gives advisory opinions on legal questions.

Only states may be parties in cases before the Court. Jurisdiction extends to all cases which the parties refer to it and all matters provided for in the Charter of the United Nations or in other international agreements. The Charter, however, does not provide for automatic referral of any disputes or cases to the Court.[6] Article 33, which imposes an obligation to seek pacific settlement of international disputes, refers to various methods including "judicial settlement." Under this provision, the parties might use the Court or they might resort to some other judicial procedure. Article 95, which is included in the section of the Charter dealing with the International Court of Justice, expressly provides that "nothing in the present Charter shall prevent Members of the United Nations from entrusting the solution of their differences to other tribunals by virtue of agreements already in existence or which may be concluded in the future." In this connection, it should also be noted that the Security Council in making recommendations as to methods of pacific settlement "should also take into consideration that legal disputes should as a general rule be referred by the parties to the International Court of Justice . . ." (Article 36). In short, for a case to reach the Court it must (1) involve a dispute or contending claims between states; (2) be justiciable, or subject to settlement on that basis of law; (3) be referred to the Court.

The first case brought before the International Court of Justice was the dispute between Great Britain and Albania over the mining of the Corfu Channel.[7] This referral was made by Great Britain upon the recommendation of the Security Council. The Court took jurisdiction of the case over the protest of Albania, and handed down a decision that the latter was responsible under international law for the damage and loss of human life. The amount of compensation to be paid by Albania was fixed at £843,947. Other cases sub-

[5] In 1952, the fifteen judges were nationals of Belgium, Brazil, Canada, Chile, China, Egypt, France, Mexico, Norway, Poland, El Salvador, the Soviet Union, Great Britain, the United States, and Yugoslavia.

[6] However, such an obligation might exist in a separate treaty, or because of an acceptance of the Court's compulsory jurisdiction. See pp. 194–195.

[7] See pp. 211–212.

mitted to the Court by the end of 1949 included a dispute between Great Britain and Norway over fishing rights in certain areas off the Norwegian coast, a complaint by France concerning the treatment of French nationals in Egypt, and a dispute between Colombia and Peru over the granting of asylum by the Colombian Ambassador to a Peruvian citizen.

COMPULSORY OR AUTOMATIC JURISDICTION

The question of compulsory jurisdiction has been a stumbling block in the development of international judicial institutions. One characteristic of the judicial process in every national legal system is the capacity of the courts to assert jurisdiction independently of the desires of parties to disputes. In a criminal case, the accused has no choice as to whether he will appear for trial. He is compelled to do so. In civil actions, once a court takes cognizance of a complaint the defendant must appear for the proceedings as directed. If he fails to do so, he is in contempt of court and can be summarily punished. It would be fantastic to imagine a national legal system in which the parties to a dispute could decide for themselves as to whether they would accept the jurisdiction of the courts. In international affairs, however, the situation is different. We are dealing with states, not individual citizens. We find that the idea of sovereignty and the practice of nationalism militate against an acceptance of compulsory jurisdiction in this field. Governments have been unwilling to take the step of establishing a genuine supranational legal authority.

How can the deadlock be broken between national legal independence and compulsory jurisdiction as an essential condition of international judicial settlement? A partial solution has been found in the "optional clause" device. Article 36, paragraph 2, provides:

The states parties to the present Statute may at any time declare that they recognize as compulsory *ipso facto* and without special agreement, in relation to any other state accepting the same obligation, the jurisdiction of the Court in all legal disputes concerning:
a. the interpretation of a treaty;
b. any question of international law;
c. the existence of any fact which, if established, would constitute a breach of an international obligation;
d. the nature or extent of the reparation to be made for the breach of an international obligation.

Under this provision, any state willing to do so may voluntarily accept for certain types of disputes the compulsory jurisdiction of the Court. The fiction of sovereignty is preserved by the act of state consent, and in practice the road is open for the maximum of international legal authority that national governments are willing to tolerate. Declarations under the "optional clause" may be made either conditionally or unconditionally, and may be made for a specified period of time. By July, 1949, a total of thirty-four states had signed declarations accepting compulsory jurisdiction in accordance with the "optional clause." Most of these made reciprocity a condition. That is, they would not be bound to accept the compulsory jurisdiction of the Court in connection with a given dispute unless the other party also accepted it. As to the period of time, most of the declarations were made for five or ten years, or until notice of termination.

Some states have accepted the "optional clause" with reservations. For example, members of the British Commonwealth [8] make an exception of disputes with each other, which are to be settled in such manner as the parties agree. Guatemala reserved its dispute with Great Britain concerning the territory of Belize, unless the Court would decide it *ex aequo et bono!* [9] The United States Senate, in consenting to ratification, attached a reservation making an exception of "disputes with regard to matters which are essentially within the domestic jurisdiction of the United States of America as determined by the United States of America." The first part of this clause is of no great significance because the Charter itself (in Article 7, paragraph 2) definitely excludes from the scope of the United Nations "matters which are essentially within the domestic jurisdiction of any state." The last part of the clause, however, gives the United States a sort of veto in the international judicial process, because it has a basis for nullifying the acceptance of compulsory jurisdiction for any dispute to which it may be a party. This does not necessarily lead to the conclusion that American acceptance of the Court's compulsory jurisdiction is meaningless, since an invocation of the reservation would be a very grave matter unless the dispute was clearly within the category of "domestic jurisdiction." France, Mexico, and Pakistan have made similar reservations, and the British Dominions had previously reserved matters which were in the domestic jurisdiction according to international law.

The law to be applied by the International Court of Justice includes international conventions establishing rules recognized by the contesting parties; international custom, as evidence of a general practice accepted as law; and the general principles of law recognized by civilized nations. Judicial decisions and the teachings of qualified publicists may be used as subsidiary means for the determination of rules of law. However, it is expressly provided that each decision has no binding force except between the parties and in respect of that particular case. The rule of *stare decisis,* that previous decisions constitute binding precedents for future cases involving the same issue, is not followed. The Statute of the Court in this particular case follows the practice

[8] These countries accepted the "optional clause" of the Permanent Court of International Justice. Such obligations carry over to the new Court.

[9] On considerations of right and justice, rather than solely on strict legal rules.

on the continent of Europe rather than the Anglo-American conception. Equity jurisprudence is recognized in the capacity of the Court to decide a case *ex aequo et bono* if the parties agree.

ENFORCEMENT OF DECISIONS

For the enforcement of its decisions the Court must rely upon two considerations. First is the fact that each member of the United Nations has an obligation under the Charter to comply with its decisions together with the prestige and moral weight of the Court itself. Once a case is submitted to the process of judicial settlement, the decision is likely to be accepted even by the losing party. This assumption is borne out by experience of the Permanent Court of International Justice, which handled a substantial number of cases without the development of any tendency to flout its decisions. The record here seems to be analogous to that of arbitration proceedings. The real difficulty is not with refusal to accept the results when the method is used, but with getting states to agree to use the method.

The second consideration is that if any party to a case fails to perform obligations arising from a decision of the Court, the other party may have recourse to the Security Council, which may make recommendations or decide upon measures to be taken. Presumably this authorization falls within the general framework of the enforcement powers of the Security Council and would be limited to measures necessary for the maintenance or restoration of international peace and security. It was not intended that the Security Council should act as a sort of sheriff for the Court, but that it should be able to deal with threats to the peace arising from failure to carry out a judgment of the Court.

ADVISORY OPINIONS

In addition to deciding cases referred to it, the International Court of Justice has the responsibility of giving advisory opinions on legal questions when requested by the General Assembly or the Security Council.[10] The International Court does not, of course, give advisory opinions on its own initiative. Use of the courts for legal advice to other departments of government is customary in many countries, but it is not practiced in the United States. In this country, the President relies on the Attorney-General for legal advice, and Congress on its own legal staff. Neither the executive nor the legislative branch ever requests an advisory opinion on a legal question from the Supreme Court. Conversely, the Supreme Court does not give legal advice or answer hypotheti-

---

[10] The General Assembly also may authorize other organs of the United Nations and the specialized agencies to request advisory opinions on legal questions arising within the scope of their activities.

cal questions but only entertains cases in which actual contending claims have already arisen.   The International Court of Justice, however, follows normal European practice, and it is competent to give legal advice to the other organs and agencies of the United Nations.

Although advisory opinions from the Court have great prestige and moral force, the General Assembly and the Security Council have no obligation to accept them as binding.   They represent advice, rather than decisions.   Each organ makes its own decisions on matters within its competence.   The Court is not the final authority on matters of interpretation of the Charter, in the sense that the Supreme Court exercises that function with respect to the Constitution of the United States.   The first advisory opinion,[11] on conditions of admission to membership, supported the position of the majority in the Security Council and the General Assembly, but it did not result in a change in the practice of the minority nor was it considered to have any automatic effect. The advisory opinion on reparation for injuries suffered in the service of the United Nations served to clarify and emphasize the fact that the United Nations is an international personality with legal capacity to bring claims appropriate to the discharge of its functions.[12]   Advisory opinions were also requested in connection with the dispute over the peace treaties with Bulgaria, Hungary, and Rumania, and concerning the international status of South-West Africa.[13]

It is too early to say how important advisory opinions will be in the work of the United Nations.   Definite possibilities are indicated by previous experience.   Advisory opinions definitely were useful to the League of Nations in settling international disputes.[14]   Many times disputant states consented to have the Council or Assembly ask for an advisory opinion when they were unwilling to submit a dispute to the Court for a binding judgment.   By separating the legal from the political issues and thus narrowing the controversial aspects of a dispute, advisory opinions are a great help in the work of conciliation.

ORGANIZATION AND PROCEDURE

The seat of the International Court of Justice is at The Hague.   It may, however, exercise its functions elsewhere if desirable.   The Court is required to remain permanently in session, except during judicial vacations.   The judges are entitled to periodic leave, as determined by the Court.   They are bound, unless on leave or prevented from attending by illness or other serious reason, to hold themselves permanently at the disposal of the Court.   The full Court

[11] See pp. 142–143.
[12] See p. 109.
[13] See pp. 218–219; 290–291.
[14] The Permanent Court of International Justice gave twenty-seven advisory opinions.

sits in each case, except that it may form chambers composed of three or more judges to deal with particular categories of cases; for example, labor cases or those relating to transit and communications. A quorum of nine judges is sufficient to constitute the Court.

The Court elects its own President and Vice-President for terms of three years, and they are eligible for reelection. The Registrar is appointed by the Court, which also provides for the appointment of such other officers as may be necessary. This arrangement is different from that for the other organs of the United Nations, in which cases the Secretary-General furnishes the needed staff. The official languages of the Court are French and English. Cases are initiated by a notification or application addressed to the Registrar. Provision is made for due notice to all parties concerned, representation by agents and counsel, written and oral proceedings, public hearings (unless decided otherwise), official minutes, and a judgment which states the reasons on which it is based. Within the framework of these basic requirements, the Court determines its own rules of procedure.

Decisions are made by a majority vote of the judges present. The President of the Court does not vote except in case of a tie. This is an interesting departure from the old rule of unanimity in international organization. In the first place, as we have seen, the judges do not represent the national governments, and there are only fifteen judges and not one for each party to the Statute of the Court. It is true that some concession is made to the idea of national representation by allowing each party to a dispute to have on the Court one judge of its nationality or choice (Article 31 of the Statute), but with majority rather than unanimous voting, no one party is in the position to "veto" a decision of the Court. Any judge may deliver a separate opinion if he does not agree with the majority, and rather liberal use has been made of this right of dissent during the early years of the International Court of Justice.

The expenses of the Court are borne by the parties to the Statute in a manner determined by the General Assembly. The annual expenses have been running between $600,000 and $650,000 a year. Each judge receives an annual salary, which may not be decreased during a term of office. In February, 1946, the General Assembly fixed the annual salary at 54,000 Netherlands florins, although the budget of the United Nations is voted in United States dollars. When the florin was devaluated in September, 1949, a peculiar problem was created. There was no decrease in the number of florins paid to each judge, but there was a reduction of about 30 per cent in purchasing power in terms of dollars. Many of the judges were adversely affected. For example, the American national on the Court, in so far as he returns to the United States or has expenses there, would suffer a serious disadvantage. Does this violate the stipulation against decreasing a judge's salary during his term of office?

The General Assembly was asked to direct the payment of these salaries in dollars, but no action was taken for the 1950 budget.

Something of the flavor of the Court's proceeding may be gained from the following description: [15]

Cases referred to the Court are entered on the General List, a scroll of hand-made Dutch paper, under the direction of the Registrar, Dr. Edvard Hambro. Notifications are sent at once to all concerned and to states and parties entitled to appear during the proceedings. If written statements are submitted, they are considered by the judges in private sessions. These usually are held in the Bol Room, so-called because its walls are hung with canvases by the 17th-century Dutch painter, Ferdinand Bol.

On the day announced for public hearings, the judges gather in two small council chambers decorated with portraits of Presidents and judges of previous Courts. In long black robes, with lace jabots emerging from under their stiff white collars, the members of the Court, preceded by the Registrar, file into the Great Hall of Justice, a high oak-panelled room. An usher, dressed in a black uniform, a silver chain around his shoulders, announces: "La Cour," and all present rise.

The judges proceed slowly toward a dais which occupies almost the entire length of the Great Hall. Behind it three lofty stained-glass windows show, in allegory, the development of mankind from primitive days to a time when war has been banished as an instrument of international politics.

The members of the Court take their places behind a long table, with the President in the centre, the Vice-President to his right, and the other judges seated on either side in order of seniority. The Registrar sits at a right angle to them, at one of the far ends of the table. In the first row of seats facing the Court are the agents, counsel, and advocates. Behind them is a row of seats for distinguished visitors, with the press and public occupying the remaining places on the floor and in the galleries.

After an opening address by the President, the representatives of parties concerned make their oral statements from a platform opposite the President. Official languages of the Court are English and French, although other languages may be used. In the Corfu Channel case heard in 1949, for example, Albanian and Russian were heard. Interpretation is from the floor, usually by the Court's own interpreters.

At the close of the public hearing—which may vary from the one day of the advisory opinion concerning new Members to the several weeks of the Corfu Channel dispute—the Court withdraws. Decisions are reached as soon as possible after private and secret deliberations and by majority vote of the judges present. They are announced, together with the Court's reasons, in public session, either as judgments, in cases of litigation, or as advisory opinions. The Court's judgments are final and without appeal.

[15] *United Nations Bulletin,* Vol. VIII, No. 7, Apr. 1, 1950, pp. 308–310.

PART III
WORK AND ACCOMPLISHMENTS

Chapter 14

INTERNATIONAL PEACE AND SECURITY

The most important aspect of the work of the United Nations has to do with the maintenance of international peace and security. Its chief purpose and responsibility lie in this field, and it will be judged by the degree of success achieved in this connection. Therefore it is necessary to "look at the record" of the United Nations in dealing with international disputes and to raise the question of its effectiveness.

The United Nations system for the pacific settlement of international disputes begins with the duty of members to seek a solution by peaceful means of their own choice. Article 33, paragraph 1, of the Charter provides that "the parties to any dispute, the continuance of which is likely to endanger the maintenance of international peace and security, shall, first of all, seek a solution by negotiation, enquiry, mediation, conciliation, arbitration, judicial settlement, resort to regional agencies or arrangements, or other peaceful means of their own choice." Thus, it will be seen that the United Nations Charter incorporates and builds upon the methods and procedures which had developed in an earlier stage of international organization.[1]

The obligation stated in Article 33 does not necessarily apply to all international disputes. A minor dispute unlikely to endanger peace and security might go unsettled until forgotten. The emphasis in drafting the Charter was to see that such disputes as might occur would not disrupt the peace and security of the world. The United Nations is concerned with serious disputes, and not with every little difference and disagreement which may arise in the daily conduct of international affairs. The test lies in the question of whether or not there is any real danger to peace.

In the event that the parties to a dispute do not fulfill their obligations under Article 33, provisions are made for the United Nations to assume responsibilities suited to the circumstances of the case. The Security Council, when necessary, is to call upon the parties to settle their disputes by peaceful means. The Security Council may investigate any dispute, or any situation which might lead to international friction or give rise to a dispute. In practice, this power of investigation has been broadly interpreted and has been used in such a way

---

[1] See pp. 34–43.

as to make it a very important step in the process of peaceful settlement.

Any member of the United Nations may bring any dispute or threatening situation to the attention of the Security Council or the General Assembly. The former is obligated to maintain international peace and security by measures ranging from recommendations to actual enforcement action. The General Assembly may, of course, discuss any matter within the scope of the Charter and, with one restriction, may make appropriate recommendations.[2] A state which is not a member of the United Nations may also bring to the attention of the Security Council or the General Assembly any dispute to which it is a party if it accepts in advance the Charter obligations of pacific settlement. At any stage of a dispute or threatening situation, the Security Council may recommend procedures or methods of adjustment. This would seem to exclude recommendations as to the terms, as contrasted with methods, of settlement. In practice, however, the Security Council, in view of its broad responsibilities under the Charter, has not considered its authority to be limited in this respect. If the parties to a dispute fail to settle it by pacific means, they have an obligation to refer it to the Security Council, which, in this event, may recommend appropriate terms of settlement. Also, if the parties to a dispute so request, the Security Council may make recommendations with a view to pacific settlement.

Thus, it will be seen that the Charter is based upon the idea of a series of steps in handling serious international disputes or situations which threaten to disrupt the peace. The parties have, in the first place, an obligation to use peaceful means of settlement. If this is insufficient, the Security Council or the General Assembly may undertake investigations and recommendations, either upon their own authority or upon referral by the disputants themselves or by some third party. This series of steps should not be thought of as a rigid sequence, but as a range of possibilities to be utilized as appears appropriate and feasible. The Security Council, for example, is not obligated to wait until each technique listed in Article 33 has been attempted and has failed, but may intervene whenever it seems that the parties to a dispute are not accomplishing the objective of peaceful settlement.

If a dispute is not settled by peaceful means, the Security Council is to determine "the existence of any threat to the peace, breach of the peace, or act of aggression" and shall make recommendations or decide what measures shall be taken to maintain or restore international peace and security. In the first instance, enforcement action is to be based upon measures not involving the use of armed force. These may include "complete or partial interruption of economic relations and of rail, sea, air, postal, telegraphic, radio, and other means of communication, and the severance of diplomatic relations."[3] If

---

[2] See pp. 139–140.

[3] Also, provisional measures may be applied pending a Security Council decision, in order to prevent "an aggravation of the situation."

such measures are inadequate, the Security Council "may take such action by air, sea, or land forces as may be necessary to maintain or restore international peace and security. Such action may include demonstrations, blockade, and other operations by air, sea, or land forces of Members of the United Nations." In order to implement these obligations, the Charter provides for armed forces to be made available to the Security Council and for a Military Staff Committee to be established.[4]

The Charter does not contain any detailed criteria to guide the Security Council in making its decisions, nor was any definition of "aggression" attempted. This is undoubtedly a wise approach. It would be impossible to anticipate all forms and varieties of aggression in advance, especially in view of the rapid change in the technique of warfare. A potential aggressor might twist any definition to its own purposes. Accordingly, each case must be judged on the merits. It should be noted that the Security Council itself makes decisions which are binding upon the members of the United Nations. This is in contrast with the League of Nations system, under which it was for each member to make its own decisions.[5] The binding decisions of the Security Council are limited to enforcement measures for the maintenance of international peace and security. The smaller powers at the San Francisco Conference did not want the Security Council to be given the power to decide the *terms* of settlement. They were fearful that the Great Powers would impose their will to the disadvantage of others under the guise of making a decision necessary to maintain peace. On the other hand, the smaller countries had the greatest interest in effective action by the Security Council to protect international peace and security. They wanted the Security Council to be made responsible for keeping the peace without giving it the power to make decisions which might violate considerations of justice. This was the reason for the distinction between decisions as to enforcement measures and decisions as to the terms for the settlement of disputes.

Disputes

As of September, 1951, a total of seventeen disputes or situations dangerous to peace [6] had been referred to the General Assembly, the Security Council, or both. A brief review of these cases will show how the responsibility of maintaining international peace and security has been handled.

4 See pp. 140–141 above.

5 See pp. 71–72 above.

6 The terminology "disputes or situations dangerous to peace" is used here as equivalent to the more lengthy Charter language concerning "any dispute, the continuance of which is likely to endanger the maintenance of international peace and security" and "any situation which might lead to international friction or give rise to a dispute." Fifteen of these disputes are briefly summarized in this chapter. For the cases of Korea and China, see Chap. 15.

Iran. On January 19, 1946, the government of Iran stated that interference by the Soviet Union in the internal affairs of Iran had brought about a situation which might lead to international friction, and it requested that the matter be brought before the Security Council. This request was considered, and the Security Council decided unanimously to refer the question back to the parties for further negotiation and asked that it be kept informed of the results achieved. On March 18, 1946, the government of Iran alleged that there was a dispute with the Soviet Union, the continuance of which was likely to endanger international peace and security. Specifically, the Soviet Union was charged with maintaining troops in Iranian territory contrary to treaty provisions that they would be withdrawn by March 2, 1946. The Security Council undertook a discussion of this matter, although the representative of the Soviet Union objected and refused to participate. A resolution was passed deferring action for several weeks but retaining the Iranian complaint on the agenda. After it became clear that Soviet troops had been withdrawn, further discussion was adjourned.

Greece. The Greek question was first brought before the United Nations by the Soviet Union, just two days after the Iranian complaint of January, 1946. The Security Council was requested to discuss the situation in Greece on the grounds that the presence of British troops after the termination of the war constituted interference with internal affairs and caused extraordinary tension. It appears that the complaint of the Soviet Union was really a counterpoise to the charges brought against that country by Iran. Various statements were presented, and on February 6, 1946, a resolution was passed declaring the matter closed. In August, 1946, the Ukraine brought up this matter again, declaring that a situation had arisen in the Balkans which presented a grave danger to peace. The Security Council again discussed the matter, but with no conclusive results since none of the resolutions presented received a sufficient affirmative vote to be adopted.

In December, 1946, the government of Greece requested the Security Council to give early consideration to a situation which was leading to friction between Greece and its neighbors. The Security Council discussed this matter and decided to appoint a Commission of Investigation, composed of a representative of each of the members of the Council as constituted in 1947. The Commission held a total of seventy-three meetings in the Balkans between January and April, 1947, compiled extensive evidence, and devoted sixteen meetings in Geneva to the preparation of its report. The majority of the Commission concluded that Yugoslavia and, to a lesser extent, Albania and Bulgaria had supported the guerrilla warfare in Greece, although the general condition of unrest in Greece helped to explain the situation. It was recommended that the countries concerned should attempt to reestablish normal relations and should abstain from any action likely to maintain or increase tension and unrest. Continued support to armed guerrilla bands in Greece would be considered "as a threat to the peace within the meaning of the Charter." The Soviet Union and Poland considered the evidence cited by the majority of the Commission as contradictory and inconclusive, and they challenged the reliability of witnesses who had testified on behalf of Greece. The recommendations based on the majority report were unacceptable to the Soviet Union, and the minority report was not acceptable to the other permanent members of the Security Council. Therefore, no agreement could be reached, and on September 15, 1947, a resolution was passed removing the Greek question from the agenda, so that it could be considered by the General Assembly.

The discussion in the General Assembly resulted in a resolution, adopted October 21, 1947, which "took account" of the report by the Committee of Investigation; called upon Albania, Bulgaria, and Yugoslavia to do nothing to aid the guerrillas; called upon these three countries and Greece to cooperate in settling their disputes by peaceful means; and established a Special Committee to observe and assist in implementing the recommendations. This action was strongly opposed by the Soviet bloc, which has steadfastly refused to cooperate with the United Nations Special Committee on the Balkans. The Committee has attempted to carry out its assignments by keeping the developments under observation and by preparing reports from time to time. The scope and intensity of the fighting were reduced, especially when Yugoslavia ceased its help to the guerrillas operating across the border. Conditions in Greece became somewhat more stabilized, but no real solution was reached and the situation remains a potentially explosive and dangerous one.

Indonesia. The Indonesian question was first brought before the Security Council by the Ukraine on January 21, 1946, the same day that the Soviet Union made the first complaint in the Greek case. It was alleged that the situation which had arisen in Indonesia after World War II constituted a threat to the maintenance of international peace and security. After a long discussion, proposals to establish a commission of inquiry failed of adoption.

In July, 1947, the government of Australia brought to the attention of the Security Council the hostilities in progress in Java and Sumatra between armed forces of the Netherlands and the Republic of Indonesia and urged that immediate action be taken. At the same time, the government of India called the attention of the Security Council to the situation in Indonesia. The Netherlands argued that control of colonial territory was a matter within domestic jurisdiction under international law and that therefore the United Nations had no authority to intervene. The Netherlands, however, was ready to invite a number of other governments to send representatives to report on the situation and was willing to accept a United States tender of "good offices" in the matter. On August 1, 1947, the Security Council passed a resolution calling upon the parties to cease hostilities forthwith, to settle their disputes by arbitration or other peaceful means, and to keep the Council informed of the progress of the settlement. Later the same month, the Security Council passed two additional resolutions, one requesting the members having career consuls in Batavia to instruct them to prepare a joint report on observance of the cease-fire order and the conditions in areas under military occupation. The other resolution established a Committee of Good Offices.[7]

During the latter part of 1947, the chief endeavor was to implement the cease-fire order, to arrange for the withdrawal of armed forces, and to secure the commencement of political negotiations. In January, 1948, the *Renville* settlement was signed. This agreement, concluded on board the United States auxiliary warship *Renville*, provided for a truce in military operations and acceptance of a basis of discussion for settlement of the dispute. During 1948, little significant progress was made in implementing the *Renville* agreement. There were charges and countercharges concerning an alleged economic block-ade by the Netherlands, the line of demarcation for observance of a military truce was disputed, and there was a deadlock in the negotiations for a political settlement. The Security Council and its Committee of Good Offices continued their efforts, but in December, 1948, the Netherlands government, for a sec-ond time, resorted to what it called "police action." It charged the Indonesians with violating the truce and with the instigation of sabotage and reprisals. The representative of the Republic of Indonesia denied this and accused the Nether-lands of a policy of economic and political warfare. The Security Council held several emergency meetings during Christmas week and called for a cessa-tion of hostilities and the release of certain political prisoners (including the President of the Republic of Indonesia) held by the Netherlands.

A new effort was made in January, 1949, when the Security Council con-tinued its discussions and, on the twenty-eighth of the month, adopted a resolu-tion calling for the discontinuance of military operations and guerrilla warfare, release of political prisoners, facilities for the effective functioning of the Re-publican government, cooperation in the restoration of peace and order, and resumption of negotiations. Also, the Committee of Good Offices was recon-stituted as the United Nations Commission for Indonesia and given additional functions, such as recommending the extent to which areas controlled by the Republic under the *Renville* agreement should be progressively returned to its administration, of supervising such transfers, and of recommending whether Netherlands forces should be retained temporarily in any area to assist in maintaining law and order and in observing elections.

In March, 1949, the Commission reported that the resolution of January 28 had not been followed, and that the Netherlands government proposed to convene a round-table conference at The Hague on the Indonesian question. The Security Council, on March 23, instructed the Commission to assist the parties in reaching an agreement as to implementation of the January resolu-tion and the time and conditions for holding the proposed conference. The

---

[7] Indonesia selected Australia as a member of this Committee; the Netherlands selected Belgium; and these two members selected the United States as the third member.

Indonesian question was also brought up and discussed in the General Assembly during the spring of 1949. By July, 1949, arrangements had been made for the cessation of military operations, political prisoners had been released, and Netherlands troops were evacuated from Republican territory under the observation of United Nations military observers. Dutch and Indonesian representatives met in a round-table conference at The Hague in September and October of 1949, at which an agreement was reached for an independent United States of Indonesia, associated with the Netherlands in a Union on the basis of sovereign equality. This solution was accepted by the Security Council and the General Assembly. Sovereignty was transferred to the new state on December 27, 1949, and in September of the following year, the Republic of Indonesia became the sixtieth member of the United Nations.

Syria and Lebanon. In February, 1946, the governments of Syria and Lebanon brought to the attention of the Security Council the continued presence of British and French troops in those countries, claiming that this constituted a violation of sovereignty which might give rise to serious disputes. The question was discussed and several suggestions made. The United States offered a proposal expressing confidence that the foreign troops would be withdrawn as soon as practicable. The Soviet Union proposed amendments to have the Security Council make a recommendation of immediate withdrawal. These amendments were not accepted. The United States draft resolution then received seven affirmative votes but was not adopted because of Soviet opposition. However, Great Britain and France proceeded to comply with the sentiments of the majority by withdrawing their troops from Syria and Lebanon, to the satisfaction of those countries.

Spain. The Spanish question was first discussed by the General Assembly in February, 1946, as the result of a complaint by the government of Panama. A resolution was passed recalling the decisions of the San Francisco and Potsdam Conferences that the admission of Franco Spain to the United Nations would not be supported, endorsing those decisions, and asking that members of the United Nations act in accordance with them. In April, 1946, the government of Poland brought the Spanish question before the Security Council, charging that the activities of the Franco government had caused international friction and endangered international peace and security. A subcommittee was appointed to investigate and report. The subcommittee found that, although the Franco government did not constitute a threat to the peace within the meaning of Article 39 of the Charter, it was a potential menace to international peace and security. This position was accepted by the majority, but the Soviet Union felt that definite measures should be taken to ensure the overthrow of the Franco regime, since it had been closely identified with the Axis aggressors. Most of the other members of the Security Council were unwilling to embark on such a drastic course of action.

Accordingly, no decision could be reached and the question was removed from the agenda of the Security Council on November 4, 1946, in order that the General Assembly might be free to act.

On December 12, 1946, the General Assembly passed a resolution recommending that the Franco government be debarred from membership in international agencies and conferences connected with the United Nations; that the Security Council consider the measures to be taken if a new and acceptable government were not formed in Spain within a reasonable time; and that all members of the United Nations immediately recall their ambassadors from Madrid. This recommendation was adopted despite strong opposition by some delegations. One argument was that it would constitute interference in the internal affairs of Spain contrary to Article 2, paragraph 7, of the Charter, since the internal governmental regime of a country is a matter of domestic jurisdiction. However, the majority of the General Assembly concluded that the situation in Spain was of international concern and a potential menace to peace. The other chief objection was that the recommendations calling for recall of ambassadors, and for action if a more democratic regime were not established, were matters within the province of the Security Council.

In November, 1947, the General Assembly reviewed the situation and adopted a resolution expressing its confidence that the Security Council would "exercise its responsibilities under the Charter as soon as it considers that the situation in regard to Spain so requires." Stronger proposals, including one to ask the Security Council to take enforcement measures, did not receive the necessary two-thirds vote, and the Franco regime maintained its position in Spain.

The General Assembly, in November, 1950, voted to revoke those parts of the 1946 resolution which debarred Spain from membership in the specialized agencies and which recommended that ambassadors be withdrawn from Madrid. This left each specialized agency and each member state to make its own decisions concerning Franco Spain. The arguments in favor of this action were that the specialized agencies are technical rather than political organizations, and that the maintenance of diplomatic relations does not imply approval of a regime. It was pointed out that the General Assembly condemnation of Franco remained in effect, and that the work of such agencies as the World Health Organization and the Universal Postal Union was intended to serve the peoples of the world regardless of political considerations. There was opposition from several delegations which felt that Franco Spain should not "come in by the back door." Others charged that the United States was interested in building up Spain as a strategic base against the Soviet Union. The final vote was 38 in favor of the resolution, 10 against,[8] and 12 abstentions.

Indians in South Africa. In June, 1946, the government of India requested that the General Assembly place on its agenda the question of the treatment

---

[8] All the eastern European members, and Guatemala, Mexico, Uruguay, and Israel.

of Indians in the Union of South Africa. The latter government was charged with enacting discriminatory measures, especially the Asiatic Land Tenure and Indian Representation Act of 1946 which restricted rights of Indians in regard to trade and residence. These measures, it was alleged, violated the Capetown Agreements of 1927 and 1932 between India and South Africa and were contrary to the principles of the United Nations Charter concerning human rights and freedoms. The Union of South Africa denied the General Assembly's competence to deal with the Indian complaint, on the grounds that it concerned a matter essentially within its domestic jurisdiction.

After lengthy debate, the General Assembly adopted a resolution on December 8, 1946, which stated that friendly relations between the two member states had been impaired, and that the treatment of Indians in the Union of South Africa should be in conformity with international obligations. The two governments were requested to report the measures adopted to this effect at the next session of the General Assembly. During the following year, India reported that South Africa had taken no steps to put the resolution into effect, that the situation had grown worse, and that it had been impossible to reach a common basis of discussion. South Africa still denied the General Assembly's jurisdiction and did not consider itself bound by the resolution. In particular, that government refused to accept as a basis of discussion a resolution which contained or implied a condemnation of it. Although the question was discussed at the 1947 session of the General Assembly, no new resolutions were passed. A reaffirmation of the earlier resolution was opposed by some delegations because of the feeling, expressed by the representative of the United States, that it would be a mistake and a sign of weakness to restate a decision which had not produced the expected results. The delegate of India argued, on the other hand, that failure to confirm the 1946 resolution, in face of a violation of it, meant a departure from the position taken previously and that such practices would undermine the authority of the General Assembly.

The question was again considered during the third regular session of the General Assembly. On May 14, 1949, a resolution was adopted inviting the governments of India and the Union of South Africa to enter into a discussion (with Pakistan also invited to participate) at a round-table conference, taking into consideration the purposes and principles of the Charter and the Declaration of Human Rights. The Union of South Africa, however, has maintained its original position and no generally acceptable solution has been reached.

Corfu Channel. In January, 1947, the British government brought before the Security Council a complaint against Albania, alleging that an unnotified minefield had been laid in the Corfu Channel by the Albanian government, or with its connivance, resulting in damage to two British warships with attendant loss of life. The Security Council decided to invite Albania (a nonmember of the United Nations) to participate, without vote, in the discussion, on condition that it accept for this case the obligations of membership. The Albanian government accepted this invitation. A subcommittee was appointed to examine the available evidence, and after its report the discussion was continued in the Security Council. A British draft resolution to settle the case on the basis of a finding that Albania was at fault as charged was lost by the negative vote of the Soviet Union. Thereupon, on April 3, 1947, a resolution was passed recommending that the case be referred to the International Court of Justice.[9]

Palestine. Of all the disputes referred to the United Nations, the Palestine question was one of the most complex and difficult, and it is the only situation which has resulted in the convening of a special session of the General Assembly. After World War I, Palestine had become a British mandate under the League of Nations. The question of its status after World War II was complicated by the changed position of Great Britain in world affairs, by the strategic and political importance of the Near East, and by the historic and seemingly irreconcilable rivalries between the Jews and the Arabs. In April, 1947, the British government requested that the question of Palestine be placed on the agenda of the General Assembly at its next regular session and that a special session be called to initiate a consideration of this situation. A majority of the members of the United Nations concurred in this request, and the first special session of the General Assembly opened on April 28, 1947. As a result of its deliberations a Special Committee on Palestine (UNSCOP) was set up to ascertain and record relevant facts, to examine the questions and issues involved, to conduct investigations in Palestine and elsewhere, to receive oral and written testimony, to consider the various religious interests, to prepare a report, and to submit proposals for a solution of the problem.

The work of the Special Committee resulted in two proposals. The majority recommended a plan of partition into independent Arab and Jewish states, with economic union for Palestine as a whole. The city of Jerusalem would be a separate entity, to be placed under the international trusteeship system with the United Nations designated as the administering authority. The minority proposal contemplated an independent federal state with Jerusalem as its capital. The General Assembly, after lengthy deliberations, adopted on November 29, 1947, the plan of partition with economic union, requested the Security Council to take the necessary measures to implement the plan, and established a United Nations Palestine Commission to supervise the transitional period.

The recommendation of the General Assembly was completely unacceptable to both the Jews and the Arabs. When the Palestine Commission reported to the Security Council in February, 1948, that it would be unable to maintain law and order after termination of the British mandate unless adequate mili-

[9] See pp. 193–194 below.

tary forces were made available, it became necessary for the Security Council to consider what action it should take. The situation in Palestine was critical, and Great Britain as the mandatory power was not willing to use military measures or to cooperate with the United Nations Palestine Commission in implementing the plan of partition with economic union adopted by the General Assembly. Under these circumstances, the Security Council was not in a position to use force to impose the plan, especially since some members, particularly the United States, argued that the proper function of the Council was to maintain international peace and security. rather than to enforce any specific terms of settlement. The efforts in the spring of 1948, therefore, turned in the direction, first, of bringing about a truce to prevent the spread of fighting and, second, of convening a second special session of the General Assembly to consider further the question of the future government of Palestine.

Repeated efforts to secure a truce during the spring of 1948 were unsuccessful. On May 14, 1948 (the day before the termination of the British mandate), the General Assembly decided to appoint a United Nations Mediator in Palestine to use his good offices with the local authorities, to arrange for the operation of necessary public services, to assure protection of the holy places, to promote a peaceful adjustment of the situation, and to cooperate with the Truce Commission previously established by the Security Council. By the same resolution, the United Nations Palestine Commission was relieved of further responsibilities. Count Folke Bernadotte of Sweden, Vice-President of the International Red Cross, was chosen as the United Nations Mediator.

The situation entered a new phase with the termination of the mandate, the proclamation of the state of Israel, its immediate recognition by the United States and several other countries, and the entrance of Arab armed forces into Palestine. The Security Council was finally able to arrange a temporary truce, which went into effect on June 11 for a period of four weeks. However, the Mediator was unable to secure a negotiated settlement during this time. An appeal to prolong the truce was rejected by the Arabs, and hostilities were resumed. On July 15, 1948, the Security Council passed another resolution ordering the authorities concerned to issue cease-fire orders and stating that in the event of noncompliance further action would be considered. The Mediator was instructed to bring about the demilitarization of Jerusalem and to supervise the truce, which was to last until a peaceful adjustment was reached. Many violations of the truce were reported, however, and on September 17, the United Nations Mediator was assassinated, probably by a band of Jewish terrorists. Mr. Ralph J. Bunche, of the Secretariat, was designated as Acting Mediator.

The General Assembly, at its third regular session, proceeded to a consideration of the progress report which Count Bernadotte had submitted just prior to his death. On December 11, 1948, a United Nations Conciliation

Commission for Palestine was established by the General Assembly to assist in a final settlement. During the winter and spring of 1949, the Acting Mediator was on the island of Rhodes conducting negotiations for a general armistice between Israel and the various Arab states, while the Conciliation Commission established headquarters at Lausanne to facilitate an exchange of views in relation to its general task of conciliation, the problems of territorial adjustments, the status of Jerusalem, and refugees.

Armistice agreements had been concluded for all the fighting fronts by July, 1949. The peace treaties and the definitive settlement, however, remained as unsettled issues. As of June, 1951, it had not been possible to delimit the final boundaries to the satisfaction of both Jews and Arabs, while charges and countercharges of violations of the armistice frontiers continued to be brought before the Mixed Armistice Commission and the Security Council itself. As to the status of Jerusalem, the General Assembly recommended at its fourth regular session in 1949, that the city be established as a *corpus separatum* under a special international regime administered by the United Nations. This plan could not be implemented because of its unacceptability to both parties, with the result that Israel remained in control of the new city and Jordan of the old city.

The Arab refugees presented an especially difficult problem, and one whose solution is essential to the establishment of a stable peace in Palestine. In the fall of 1950, the number of refugees was estimated at 800,000. Two-thirds of them were housed in temporary improvised quarters and the remainder in tents. This huge number is a drain on the economy of the area, and the refugees are resentful of their condition. The United Nations Relief and Works Agency for Palestine Refugees in the Near East, which was established in October, 1949, provided for rations to refugees on relief and attempted to institute a works program for employment purposes. The work projects were confined at first to the construction of roads and to forestry, since these activities involve a high percentage of hand labor. Later the scope was broadened to include archeological excavations, garment making, and handicrafts; however, the works program remained very limited in terms of the total need, because of lack of opportunities for constructive work projects, the expense in relation to the cost of direct relief, and the shortage of funds for the purpose.

Egypt. In July, 1947, the government of Egypt brought to the Security Council its dispute with Great Britain concerning the evacuation of British troops from Egypt and termination of the existing administrative regime in the Sudan. The representative of Egypt asserted that the treaty of 1936, defining relations between the two countries, had been completed under special circumstances which, with the defeat of the Axis Powers, were no longer relevant. Restrictions on Egyptian sovereignty and the stationing of British troops in that country could not be justified. The representative of Great

Britain claimed that no evidence had been offered that international peace and security were endangered by the situation and that therefore the Charter was not applicable. Moreover, negotiations for revision of the treaty in question had been conducted between the two parties and agreement had been reached on all points except that relating to the right of the Sudanese to choose their own future status. The Security Council heard these statements and discussed several draft proposals, but no resolution received a sufficient affirmative vote to be adopted and no action was taken.

India and Pakistan. The conflict between India and Pakistan was brought before the Security Council by the representative of India in January, 1948, largely on the basis that the situation in Kashmir threatened to endanger international peace and security. The Council heard the statements of the parties and, on January 17, passed a resolution calling upon them to take all measures within their power to improve the situation. The President of the Security Council conferred with representatives of the two governments in an attempt to find some common ground of agreement. The next step was the formation of a United Nations Commission for India and Pakistan, which was to investigate the situation on the spot, keep the Security Council informed, and exercise a mediatory influence. It was generally recognized that the first objective was a cessation of the fighting and that the future status of Kashmir should be determined by a fair plebiscite. The difficulty was in getting the parties concerned to agree on the terms for ending hostilities and on the basis for conducting the plebiscite.

The work of the Commission during 1948 was devoted to obtaining a cease-fire and truce agreement and to developing proposals for the organization of a plebiscite. A cease-fire order finally became effective on January 1, 1949, exactly one year after the dispute was first referred to the Security Council. Unconditional acceptance of detailed truce proposals still was not obtained, and the efforts to reconcile the opposing points of view continued. In March, 1949, Admiral Chester Nimitz was nominated as Plebiscite Administrator, but over a year later he was still waiting at United Nations Headquarters for negotiation of a truce agreement to be completed.

By a resolution adopted on March 14, 1950, the Security Council decided to appoint a United Nations Representative to replace the Commission for India and Pakistan. The chief duties of the Representative were to assist in the preparation and supervise the implementation of a plan of progressive demilitarization agreed on by the parties; to be at the disposal of the two governments for consultation and suggestions; to exercise all the powers and responsibilities formerly vested in the Commission; and to arrange at the appropriate stage of demilitarization for the Plebiscite Administrator to assume his assigned functions.

Sir Owen Dixon of Australia was appointed as United Nations representative for India and Pakistan. He spent about three months in these countries and held several conferences with their prime ministers. On September 15, 1950, he reported to the Security Council that he had been unable to achieve any agreement between India and Pakistan for implementing either demilitarization or the holding of a plebiscite. Partition of the entire disputed area might be a solution except for the Valley of Kashmir itself, which is claimed by both sides. The government of India, which had the advantage of possession, did not agree to the restrictions on her power and administration which the United Nations representative felt were essential to an independent and free expression of the will of the people concerned. A new effort was made in 1951, with the appointment of Mr. Frank P. Graham to help achieve demilitarization preparatory to a plebiscite.

Czechoslovakia. In March, 1948, the government of Chile brought to the attention of the Security Council allegations that the political independence of Czechoslovakia had been violated by interference of the Soviet Union. The question was placed on the agenda of the Security Council despite the protest of the Soviet representative, who declared that discussion of this situation would constitute gross interference in the internal affairs of Czechoslovakia and would be a violation of Article 2, paragraph 7, of the Charter. The complaints concerning Soviet interference or threats of force were categorically denied. The Security Council proceeded to discuss this matter and to hear statements from Mr. Jan Papanek, the permanent representative of Czechoslovakia to the United Nations prior to the assumption of control in that country by the Communists. The Security Council also invited the existing government of Czechoslovakia to take part in the discussion. This invitation was declined, on the grounds that the change in governmental regime was entirely a matter of domestic jurisdiction and that the complaint was a pretext for hostile maneuvering by the Western Powers. A proposal to appoint a subcommittee to investigate the situation was lost by the adverse vote of the Soviet Union,[10] and nothing further could be done by the Security Council.

Trieste. The government of Yugoslavia complained to the Security Council in July, 1948, that the United States and Great Britain, through the Allied Military Command in Trieste, were violating clauses of the peace treaty with Italy and were jeopardizing the independence of the Free Territory of Trieste. The complaint especially referred to matters of money and foreign trade, and of alleged plans to incorporate Trieste into Italy. This question was discussed by the Security Council. A proposal to condemn the measures concerned was initiated by Yugoslavia and supported by the Soviet Union and the Ukraine. However, it received only two affirmative votes, and no further action was taken by the Security Council.

Hyderabad. In August, 1948, the government of Hyderabad asked that

[10] Discussion is considered a procedural matter, but a proposal to investigate is treated as a substantive question requiring the concurrence of all the permanent members. See p. 148.

its dispute with India be brought to the attention of the Security Council. The communication charged that the Princely State had been exposed to violent intimidation, threats of invasion, frontier violations, and a crippling economic blockade.   The following month, Hyderabad reported first a threat of invasion and then an actual invasion.   The representative of India contended that Hyderabad was not competent to bring a question before the Security Council, since it was not a state and not independent.   India had been compelled to take action because of the reign of terror by private armies in Hyderabad.   All resistance to the forces of India collapsed, and while the Security Council was discussing the case, a message was received from the Nizam of Hyderabad withdrawing the complaint.   The representative of India stated that order had been restored, that the Nizam was cooperating with Indian officials, and that allegations to the contrary came from extremist agitators.   The Hyderabad delegation to the United Nations claimed that the Nizam had been coerced into cooperation with India.   The government of Pakistan, which had been invited to participate in the discussion, asked that the situation be rectified.   The discussion of this question was continued by the Security Council in the spring of 1949, but no further developments took place.

· *Berlin.*   The dispute over the Berlin blockade was placed on the provisional agenda of the Security Council on October 4, 1948, as a result of identical notifications from the governments of France, Great Britain, and the United States, calling attention to the serious situation which had arisen from the unilateral imposition by the Soviet Union of restrictions on transport and communications between the Western zones of occupation in Germany and Berlin.   The notifications stated that the Soviet action was contrary to Article 2 of the Charter and constituted a threat to peace.   Further recourse to negotiation among the parties seemed to be useless, and the Security Council was asked to consider the question at the earliest opportunity.   The Soviet Union stated that this question did not come within the competence of the Security Council, since the solution of problems relating to Germany was a matter for the governments responsible for the military occupation and since the Council of Foreign Ministers had been set up to deal with the peaceful settlement of all issues related to ex-enemy countries.   Also, the Soviet Union blamed the Western Powers, and specifically the currency reforms initiated by them, for the difficulties; the restrictions imposed by the Soviet authorities were "defensive countermeasures."   The representative of the United States asserted that the instant question did not deal with Germany as an ex-enemy country but with the threat to international peace and security growing out of the relations among the victors over Germany.

The Security Council decided to hear the question, and it was discussed at some length, although the Soviet Union refused to take part in the discussions on the basis that they were taking place illegally in violation of Article 107 of the Charter. On October 22, 1948, the six neutral members of the Security Council offered a joint draft resolution which, among other things, called upon the four governments to remove the restrictions constituting the "Berlin blockade" and to hold an immediate meeting of the four military governors to deal with the currency issue. This resolution was defeated by the adverse vote of the Soviet Union. Subsequently, a series of informal negotiations held between Mr. Jessup of the United States and Mr. Malik of the Soviet Union led to an agreement by the four governments and the lifting of the blockade in May, 1949.

Human Rights in the Balkans. In March, 1949, the governments of Australia and Bolivia raised in the General Assembly "the question of the observance in Bulgaria and Hungary of human rights and fundamental freedoms including questions of religious and civil liberties, with special reference to recent trials of church leaders." Later the question was extended to include Rumania. This item was placed on the agenda, although the Soviet Union and Poland argued that a matter of domestic jurisdiction was involved and that the application of terms and procedures of the peace treaties was not within the competence of the General Assembly. On April 30, 1949, a resolution was adopted expressing deep concern at the grave accusations made, noting with satisfaction the steps already taken by several states signatories to the peace treaties, drawing the attention of the governments concerned to their obligations, and retaining the question on the agenda.

At the fourth regular session of the General Assembly, this question was discussed again. The United States and Great Britain had attempted to follow the procedure stipulated in the peace treaties by sending notes to Bulgaria, Hungary, and Rumania accusing them of violating the clauses dealing with respect for human rights and fundamental freedoms. These governments rejected the accusations and refused to appoint their representatives on the commissions provided for in the treaties as a procedure to settle disputes arising under their terms. In these circumstances, a proposal was adopted to request an advisory opinion from the International Court of Justice on the legal issues involved. In opposition to this proposal, the Soviet Union contended that the treaty procedure was inapplicable unless the three powers (Great Britain, the United States, and the Soviet Union) jointly recognized the existence of a dispute between themselves on the one hand and the defeated countries on the other, and that this was not the case. The argument seemed to be that a dispute does not exist unless the opposing parties agree that there is a dispute. The three Balkan countries took the position, defended by the Soviet Union in the General Assembly, that the treaty procedure relating to the settlement of disputes was not applicable because they did not admit that a dispute existed.

The International Court of Justice gave as its opinion that (1) a dispute did exist within the meaning of the relevant treaty provisions; (2) Bulgaria,

Hungary, and Rumania had an obligation to carry out the measures relating to the settlement of disputes, including the appointment of representatives to the treaty commission; and (3) in the event of their failure to do so, the Secretary-General was not authorized to appoint the third member of a commission upon the request of the other party to the dispute. In practical terms, this meant that a dispute existed but the treaty procedure for handling it could not be put into effect. In November, 1950, the General Assembly adopted, by 40 votes to 3 with 12 abstentions, a resolution condemning Bulgaria, Hungary, and Rumania for willful refusal to fulfil their treaty obligations in this matter.

EFFECTIVENESS

The crucial question, of course, is whether or not the United Nations is effective in helping to maintain international peace and security. During the first five years of its existence, seventeen disputes or situations dangerous to peace were handled by the General Assembly and the Security Council. Some of them were settled, as in the cases of the withdrawal of Soviet troops from Iran and of British and French troops from Syria and Lebanon. Some of the questions, like the question of Hyderabad and the change of government in Czechoslovakia, have lapsed so far as active consideration by the United Nations is concerned. Some, like Indonesia and Palestine, have resulted in major political changes by peaceful means. Still others, notably the Korean case and the Communist Chinese intervention, have resulted in widespread hostilities. There is no doubt that the work of the United Nations has been constructive and helpful in many respects. It has provided a method and exerted an influence toward the control of international violence in the post-war world. Yet at the same time, the basic difficulties have not been solved. The divisive forces remain strong, and the "cold war" is a compelling reality. The United Nations, in this situation, is useful and helpful, but at the present time it is not a complete answer and it is certainly not a panacea.

It is apparent that a consideration of the disputes and situations referred to the General Assembly and the Security Council does not reveal the full story of the threats to international peace and security. Some questions are formulated and placed on the agenda. Others, equally important or more so, are not put forward in that way. Yet they cannot be ignored. · Such problems as the drafting of the major peace treaties, the future role of Germany, the regulation of armaments, the control of atomic energy, and the East-West conflict itself are not among the seventeen dangerous disputes and situations referred to above. Beyond the achievements of the United Nations in the settlement of this or that specific dispute, there lies the question of its effect on the general international atmosphere. Is the net result to weaken dangerous tensions and to strengthen the forces of cooperation and mutual understanding?   On the basis of a "calculated risk," does it increase the odds against a third world war in this generation?

Paradoxically, the United Nations may create disputes as well as settle them.   The town meeting of the world can be a forum for insult and vilification as well as for compromise and pacification.   Continuous conference diplomacy may lead to frustration and anger as well as to better understanding. Many of the most serious disagreements among members have occurred over questions relating to the functioning of the United Nations itself.   The problem of the veto had to do with the voting procedure in the Security Council. If there were no international organization reaching decisions by a voting process, one occasion for argument might be eliminated.   The questions of admitting new members, of electing nonpermanent members of the Security Council, and of establishing an Interim Committee of the General Assembly have involved bitter disputes from time to time.   The deadlock in the United Nations over the Chinese case, with the Soviet walkout, was based on a dispute concerning whether the Nationalist or the Communist delegation was entitled to represent China in the Security Council and other organs.

To argue, however, on the basis of the paradox stated in the preceding paragraph that the number of international disputes could be reduced by abolishing the United Nations would be like throwing out the baby to get rid of the dirty bath water.   The existence of the United Nations means that international disputes are handled at a new level and in a changed context.   The real question is that of the net effect.   On balance, does it have a helpful influence and constructive potentialities?   Its establishment grew out of the mutual interest in having an institutionalized means of settling disputes.   This signifies that international organization has developed to the stage where there is general recognition of a vital need for a system of collective security. There are disputes over the scope, interpretation, and implementation of such a system.   But when men quarrel over the methods by which disputes should be settled they are paying tribute to their tacit agreement that the methods are necessary and must be developed.   The problem of the veto and other conflicts over the functioning of the United Nations are often disheartening, but at least they show that the Organization is being taken seriously.   It is submitted that a close study of the background and work of the United Nations will lead to the conclusion that it is a big step on a long journey, as yet far from adequate but nonetheless useful, and that without giving any guarantees it does improve the chances of preventing a third world war.

The United Nations, in its work of attempting to maintain international peace and security, must rely largely on persuasion rather than force.   In connection with the disputes and situations discussed above, use has been made of the techniques of negotiation, "good offices," fact finding, conciliation, mediation, cooling-off periods, cease-fire agreements and truces, and recommendations for judicial settlement.   Only as a result of overt aggression in the

Korean case did the Security Council resort to enforcement measures. Emphasis has been on finding a solution, acceptable to the parties, which would be consistent with the maintenance of international peace and security. There are two fundamental reasons for this, in addition to the general objective of avoiding the use of armed force for the settlement of international disputes. First, only the Security Council is authorized to take enforcement measures, and it cannot decide to do so if one of the permanent members is opposed to such action. The exception in the Korean case was made possible only by the fortuitous absence of the Soviet Union over another issue. All the Great Powers plus at least two other members must agree in order to reach a decision to take action. This alone would serve to place the emphasis on attempts to work out an agreed solution. Second, the United Nations as such has no force at its disposal. The Charter provides for armed forces to be made available to the Security Council, by agreement with members of the United Nations, and for a Military Staff Committee. However, no such agreements have been concluded, and the United Nations is necessarily limited to persuasion, augmented by whatever opinion becomes mobilized behind its efforts and the pressure which member states may apply in a direction consistent with the aims of the Organization. In the Korean case the military forces were supplied by members acting under a resolution of the Security Council. This might be called an international force by designation.

Essentially, the United Nations provides an instrument of peaceful change —of real but limited usefulness under present world conditions. It attempts to rule out change by aggression, threats, and breaches of the peace, and to facilitate the use of pacific methods. In two of the questions referred to the United Nations, important changes were brought about and a major war was avoided each time. Both Israel and Indonesia became independent states and were admitted as members of the United Nations. These were certainly major accomplishments of peaceful change. But reaching an agreement, acceptable to the parties, which prevents a breach of the peace is not the whole question of peaceful change. There are also considerations of justice. The first emphasis, of course, must be placed on peace and security, since without some degree of stability and order the voice of justice has no chance to be heard. Nevertheless, a policy and a system which does not look beyond peace for its own sake will soon prove sterile. Peaceful adjustment is to be sought "in conformity with the principles of justice and international law." A dispute settled without actual fighting but, for example, by the sacrifice of the rights of small nations would not conform to the principles laid down in the Charter.

The question of treaty revision is a thorny one. Stability and order require a respect for international contractual obligations. Yet if treaty rights are as rigid as the laws of the Medes and Persians were said to be, they will eventually be neither respected nor observed. A procedure of peaceful revision is necessary. Usually, however, when the question comes up one party wants the treaty changed and the other does not, and states have been very reluctant to surrender the right to determine these matters for themselves. The Covenant of the League of Nations provided, by Article 19, that "the Assembly may from time to time advise the reconsideration by Members of the League of treaties which have become inapplicable, and the consideration of international conditions whose continuance might endanger the peace of the world." The United Nations Charter has a similar, but less definite, provision in Article 14, which authorizes the General Assembly to make recommendations for the peaceful adjustment of any situation likely to impair the general welfare or friendly relations among nations.[11]   At the second session of the General Assembly, Argentina proposed that a revision of the peace treaty with Italy be considered. However, this proposal was later withdrawn and no action was taken. Egypt, in its complaint against Great Britain in 1947, relied in part on the argument that changed circumstances had made the Anglo-Egyptian Treaty of 1936 inapplicable. Article 14 has been invoked, alone or in conjunction with the more comprehensive terms of Article 10, as a basis for consideration of the cases of Spain, South Africa, Palestine, and Korea by the General Assembly. It is not to be expected, however, that revision of treaties would be the chief emphasis during the first few years of the United Nations, when the main peace treaties after World War II cannot be written because of the "cold war." Pacific methods have been utilized by the General Assembly and the Security Council largely in an attempt to bring about a situation of international peace and security in which an orderly and just revision of obsolete treaties will be possible.

[11] One reason for not mentioning treaty revision specifically in the Charter was the fear that such a mention might be construed as an invitation to the ex-enemy states to seek a revision of the peace treaties.

Chapter 15

THE KOREAN CRISIS

The events in Korea since the surrender of Japan, and especially the invasion of the territory south of the thirty-eighth parallel by armed forces from the north, confronted the United Nations with an acute test of its ability to stop aggression and to maintain world peace. The invasion of the Republic of Korea was in a real sense aggression against the United Nations itself, for the Republic was its ward, if not its child. The military invasion constituted a bold and direct challenge to the purposes and authority of the United Nations. The League of Nations failed to meet a similar test, after which its prestige and influence waned. While the survival of the United Nations may not be at stake by what is happening in Korea, its future development will undoubtedly be greatly affected by the outcome.

Korea's geographic position in East Asia is somewhat similar to that of the Low Countries in Western Europe. It is surrounded by large countries, none of which has been willing to see it fall under the control of the others. Korea borders on China and Russia and is separated from Japan by only 120 miles of water. Assuming a world in which each state must look to its own security, Korea is of the utmost strategic importance to its three large neighbors. For centuries China regarded the peninsular kingdom, as it did nearly all neighboring states, as a vassal, but during much of this time Korea sent tribute to both Japan and China. Japan invaded Korea with large forces in the years 1592–1598, as a preliminary to the conquest of China, but the expedition failed. In 1894, the two countries went to war over the control of Korea, and in 1904, Russia and Japan clashed over the same issue. Japan succeeded in reducing Korea to a protectorate in 1905 and in 1910 formally annexed the country.

The question of the provision that should be made for Korea immediately after World War II presented the United States and its allies with no small problem. It was generally agreed that the country should have its independence, but unfortunately Koreans had had no experience with democratic political methods or modern public administration. They had had no government of their own for thirty-five years and a poor one before that. In view of all the circumstances, it seemed best to preface Korean independence with a short period of trusteeship.

223

At the conclusion of a conference at Cairo in November, 1943, President Roosevelt, Prime Minister Churchill, and Generalissimo Chiang Kai-shek issued (December 1) a joint statement outlining the war aims of their governments in the Far East. It contained the following declaration with respect to Korea: "The aforesaid three great powers, mindful of the enslavement of the people of Korea, are determined that in due course Korea shall become free and independent." At this time the Soviet Union was still neutral in the war against Japan and hence was not a signatory of this declaration, but at the Yalta Conference it agreed to enter the war in the Pacific two or three months after the conclusion of hostilities in Europe. The Soviet Union declared war on Japan on August 8, and on August 14 Japan surrendered. Rarely has a state through so little military effort acquired so much diplomatic advantage. Soviet armed forces almost immediately marched south to occupy Korean territory down to the thirty-eighth parallel, while some time later American forces established military government south of that line. The origin of this line of demarcation is shrouded in military secrecy, but presumably it was quickly decided upon by staff officers when Japan suddenly collapsed. The decision was probably made chiefly for the purpose of facilitating the disarmament and repatriation of the Japanese. But, whatever its origin and purpose, the thirty-eighth parallel became in effect the frontier between two separate and mutually hostile regimes.

MOSCOW AGREEMENT

This division of Korea into two occupational zones, governed by opposing ideologies, created all manner of difficulties. It strangled the economic life of the country and prevented any manner of political unification. An effort was made to remedy the situation at the Moscow Conference of December, 1945, at which the foreign ministers of the Soviet Union, the United Kingdom, and the United States agreed that there should be set up "a provisional Korean government," "with a view to the re-establishment of Korea as an independent state" and the "creation of conditions for developing the country on democratic principles. . . ." To assist the formation of a provisional Korean government there was to be established a Joint Commission composed of representatives of the two occupational commands. It was to consult with Korean "democratic parties and social organizations" in preparing proposals for submission to the governments of China, the Soviet Union, Great Britain, and the United States. The proposals were not, however, to envisage immediate independence but "a four-power trusteeship . . . for a period of up to five years."

The Joint Commission met in Seoul in March, 1946, but was unable to get beyond discussing the first step in the procedure. The Soviet Union demanded that all Korean groups which opposed the Moscow agreement for a trusteeship should be excluded from consultations and from the future provisional government. This would have excluded all but the Communists, as all other groups bitterly resented both the phrase "in due course" of the Cairo declaration and the five-year trusteeship directive laid down in the Moscow agreement. Indeed, the Communists were as vehement in denunciation of the trusteeship announcement as other political groups until they received the cue that they were to support it. Unable to reach an agreement on this issue of party consultation, the Joint Commission adjourned. After an appeal by Secretary Marshall to Foreign Minister Molotov, meetings were resumed in May, 1947, but all to no avail. The Soviet representatives finally proposed the creation of a "provisional assembly" of those parties which "fully support the Moscow Agreement," on the basis of equal representation of the two zones. This proposal the United States delegation rejected as inconsistent with the fact that the American zone contained approximately two-thirds of the country's twenty-nine million people. An American proposal for a four-power conference to plan a speedy implementation of the Moscow agreement, with suggestions that election be held shortly in both zones with a view to establishing zonal legislatures, representatives from which would join to compose a national provisional legislature, was accepted by China and the United Kingdom but rejected by the Soviet Union. In acknowledging this rejection the United States government expressed the view that the situation with respect to Korea could not be continued indefinitely, and that since bilateral negotiations were stalemated it would refer the problem of Korean independence to the forthcoming session of the General Assembly of the United Nations. However, at the insistence of the chief of the Soviet delegation the Joint Commission was reconvened. The Soviet Union now proposed that both governments withdraw their troops at the beginning of 1948. In the General Assembly, the Soviet delegate, Mr. Gromyko, protested that the Korean question was not within the competence of the United Nations and repeated the proposal which the Soviet representative had made to the Joint Commission, namely, that both states simultaneously withdraw their forces from Korea.

QUESTION BEFORE THE UNITED NATIONS

In the meanwhile the General Assembly had placed the Korean question on its agenda. On November 14, 1947, it adopted a modified American resolution calling for elections for a national assembly and for the establishment of a United Nations Temporary Commission on Korea, under whose "observation" the elections were to take place. The National Assembly was to form a national government, which, in consultation with the Commission, would (1) constitute its own national security forces and dissolve all other military or semimilitary formations, (2) take over the functions of government from the military commands and civilian authorities of the northern and southern zones, and (3) arrange with the occupying powers for the complete withdrawal of their armed forces as early as practicable and if possible within ninety days.

The United Nations Temporary Commission on Korea (UNTCOK) was unable to carry out its mandate for the whole of Korea because of the refusal of the Soviet commander to cooperate or even to permit it to enter North Korea. UNTCOK thereupon turned to the Interim Committee ("Little Assembly") of the General Assembly for further directives. The Interim Committee declared that in its view it was incumbent upon the Commission to implement the program outlined by the resolution of the General Assembly of November 14, 1947, in such parts of Korea as were accessible to it. The UNTCOK thereupon proceeded with plans for the elections for the National Assembly, which were held on May 30, 1948. In view of the necessarily immature character of Korean political life, the elections may be regarded as fairly successful. There was a movement, instigated from the north, to boycott the election, but this failed. About 80 per cent of the electorate registered, and of these 90 per cent voted. Because of the many parties in the field and the large number of independent candidates, the election results did not form a stable basis for government. No party won a majority of the seats; in fact, the independents constituted the largest group.

Steps to organize the new government were now taken in rapid succession. The Assembly drafted a constitution which was promulgated on July 17, 1948. Dr. Syngman Rhee was elected President by a very large majority, but his first choice for prime minister was rejected by the Assembly. On August 15, the new government took over the administration from the American occupational authorities. After receiving a report from UNTCOK on the discharge of its mandate, the General Assembly of the United Nations on December 12 declared (by a vote of 48 to 6) that the government of the Republic of Korea was "a lawful government . . . based on elections which were a valid expression of the free will of the electorate of that part of Korea . . . and that this is the only such government in Korea." A new Commission on Korea was set up to follow developments and to lend its good offices to bring about the union of south and north under one government. The United States recognized the new government on August 12. The Chinese government extended "provisional" recognition on the same day, and the Philippine government followed some days later.

The United Nations had thus helped to establish the government of the Republic of Korea, which claimed but could not exercise jurisdiction over the whole country. Almost simultaneously there was being created in the north a government which called itself the Democratic People's Republic of Korea, fashioned after the political institutions of the Soviet Union, with its capital at Pyongyang. This government, recognized by the Soviet Union and its satellites, likewise claimed jurisdiction over all Korea. Neither government was able to establish national control by peaceful means; in the end, one of them attempted to impose political unity on the country by force.

On September 18, 1948, the Soviet government notified the American government that, in response to an appeal of the Supreme National Assembly of Korea, it would withdraw its troops from North Korea before the end of the year, and it expressed the hope that the United States government would also agree to evacuate its troops from South Korea within this period. To this suggestion the United States government replied that it regarded the question of troop withdrawal as part of the larger question of Korean unity and independence. Soviet forces, with the exception of a military training mission, supposedly were withdrawn from North Korea before the end of 1948. American withdrawal took place some six months later. On June 29, 1949, the United Nations Commission for Korea (UNCOK),[1] which by a General Assembly resolution of December 12, 1948, replaced the temporary commission (UNTCOK), reported the final departure of United States occupation forces from Korea. At the request of the Korean government about five hundred officers and men remained to help train its security forces.

The United Nations Commission on Korea was no more successful than its predecessor in winning the cooperation of the northern regime in unifying the country. On February 18, 1949, it sent the Soviet Union a telegram, through the Secretary-General, requesting its good offices in establishing contact with the northern government. Some time later it sent a letter to the Premier of the Democratic People's Republic. The Commission did not receive a reply to either communication. In the meantime the northern regime was carrying on its own campaign for unification by such methods as undermining the southern government by infiltration tactics, radio appeals, manifestoes, and calls for conferences and elections looking toward political unification—under the aegis of the northern regime, of course.

Both the Republic of Korea and the Democratic People's Republic of Korea applied for membership in the United Nations. The application of the latter was not considered, while that of the former was defeated in the Security Council by a Soviet veto (April 8, 1949).

The Commission on June 29, 1949, reported that it had verified the withdrawal of United States forces from South Korea, leaving only a military advisory group of five hundred men. The Commission sent word to the Soviet Union that it was prepared to extend the same offices of observance and verification of the withdrawal of Soviet forces, but no reply was received to this offer.

That the relations between North and South Korea were getting worse and taking on a hostile character is evidenced from the resolution of the General

[1] The new Commission was composed of representatives of India (chairman), Australia, China, El Salvador, France, the Philippines, and Turkey.

Assembly of October 21, 1949, extending the life of the Commission on Korea, which was now charged with the additional function of observing and reporting developments "which might lead to or otherwise involve military conflict." This new function became the first task of the Commission. At an Independence Day celebration on March 1, 1950, President Rhee indicated that he would strive to reunite the country, by peaceful means if possible but by military measures if necessary. On the same occasion the chairman of the Commission on Korea reminded the audience that the United Nations was created to facilitate the peaceful settlement of disputes, while the United States Ambassador, John J. Muccio, warned against combating communism by other than democratic methods.

The North Korean propaganda campaign for political unification of the whole country was stepped up in June. For successive days Radio Pyongyang repeatedly broadcast an appeal for unification. In response to this appeal the Commission on Korea, on June 10, sent a representative across the thirty-eighth parallel to meet with three representatives of North Korea. They met at a point just across the parallel, but the meeting came to nought, as the northern representatives stated that they were only agents and had no authority to enter into discussion or accept documents.

INVASION OF SOUTH KOREA

The crossing of the thirty-eighth parallel by the armed forces of North Korea in the early morning of June 25, 1950, precipitated a crisis of the utmost gravity for the United Nations. In defiance of the attempt of the United Nations to unify Korea by peaceful means, the Soviet-created government now sought to achieve the same object by imposing its own regime by force. So direct a challenge to the authority and purposes of the United Nations could be ignored only at great cost to its prestige and future development. This aggression likewise confronted the United States with a most difficult decision. It was the only country which was in a position to give any real immediate aid to the South Koreans in repelling the aggression. The decision of the United States to support strong United Nations action involved tremendous military risks. Few of the American troops stationed in nearby Japan had had much combat training.

At the request of the United States the Security Council met the same day the invasion was launched. When the Council met on the afternoon of June 25, it had before it a report from UNCOK to the Secretary-General drawing attention to the "serious situation which is developing which is assuming character of full-scale war and may endanger the maintenance of international peace and security." The Council passed an amended and revised American resolution requesting the immediate cessation of hostilities and calling upon the authorities of North Korea to withdraw their armed forces to the thirty-eighth parallel. UNCOK was directed to communicate its fully considered recommendations on the situation, to observe the withdrawal of the North Korean forces to the thirty-eighth parallel, and to keep the Security Council informed on the execution of this resolution. Lastly, the resolution called upon all members of the United Nations "to render every assistance to the United Nations in the execution of this resolution and to refrain from giving assistance to the North Korean authorities." The resolution was adopted by nine votes—those of China, Cuba, Ecuador, Egypt, France, India, Norway, the United Kingdom, and the United States. The Soviet Union was absent, and Yugoslavia did not vote.

On June 26, President Truman announced that, in accordance with the resolution of the Security Council, American personnel in Korea was actively cooperating in the defense of the Republic and that steps were being taken "to expedite and augment assistance of the type being furnished under the Mutual Defense Assistance Program." On June 27, the President announced that he had ordered "United States air and sea forces to give Korean government troops cover and support." The President also stated that he had ordered a unit of the U.S. Navy to prevent any attack on Formosa and had called upon the Nationalist Chinese government to cease all air and sea operations against the mainland. "The determination of the future status of Formosa," he declared, "must await the restoration of security in the Pacific, a peace settlement with Japan, or consideration by the United Nations." The President justified these measures on the ground that the attack upon Korea had made "plain beyond all doubt that communism had passed beyond the use of subversion to conquer independent nations and will now use armed invasion and war." Communism had defied the orders of the United Nations issued to preserve peace and security. "In these circumstances the occupation of Formosa by Communist forces would be a direct threat to the security of the Pacific area and to the United States forces performing their lawful and necessary functions in that area." The measures taken by the United States with respect to China failed to receive the endorsement of many governments which supported the United Nations resolution.

The President at this time also announced that he had ordered the strengthening of American forces in the Philippines and the acceleration of military assistance to the Philippine government and similarly "to the forces of France and the Associated States in Indo-China and the despatch of a military mission to provide close working relations with those forces."

The Security Council met again on June 27. Again it had before it a resolution introduced by the United States representative. The resolution took note of the fact that its call for a cessation of hostilities had not been heeded, nor had the North Korean troops withdrawn to the thirty-eighth parallel. It also noted that the Republic of Korea had appealed to the United Nations for immediate and effective steps to secure peace and security. In view of these facts it recommended "that the Members of the United Nations furnish such assistance to the Republic of Korea as may be necessary to repel the armed attack and to restore international peace and security in the area." The resolution was adopted by a vote of seven in favor to one against. Yugoslavia cast the lone vote against it. The representatives of India and Egypt, since they had no instructions from their governments, did not participate.

The Security Council met for the third time in six days on June 30. At this meeting the representative of India reported that his government "accepted" the resolution adopted at the previous meeting, while the representative of Egypt stated that he would have abstained had he been able to participate in the voting. He explained that he would have abstained from voting for the reason, first, that the Korean conflict was but a new phase of the "deep-rooted divergencies between the Western and Eastern blocs" and secondly that the United Nations had ignored several cases of aggression in the past and could not consistently take action as it was now doing in the case of Korea. Mr. Austin, the United States representative, informed the Security Council that President Truman had that morning authorized the U.S. Air Force to conduct missions on specific military targets in North Korea wherever militarily necessary, had ordered a naval blockade of the entire Korean coast, and had authorized General MacArthur to use certain supporting ground forces.

On July 7, the Security Council met for a fourth time to consider the crisis in Korea. The Council at this meeting adopted a resolution, proposed jointly by the United Kingdom and France, recommending that all members providing military forces and other assistance, pursuant to the resolutions of June 25 and 27, make such forces and assistance available to a unified command under the United States, requesting the United States to designate the commander of such forces, authorizing the unified command at its discretion to use the United Nations flag in the course of operations against North Korean forces concurrently with the flags of the various participating nations, and requesting the United States to provide the Security Council with reports on the course of action taken under the unified command. The resolution was adopted by a vote of 7 to 0. The Soviet Union was still absent, and Egypt, India, and Yugoslavia abstained. On the next day, July 8, President Truman announced that in response to the request of the Security Council he had designated General Douglas MacArthur as the Commander of the United Nations Forces in Korea.

Nearly all the members of the United Nations responded favorably to the resolution of June 27. Secretary-General Trygve Lie was able to report on July 14 that, aside from the United States, fifty-two governments had replied favorably. All offered moral support, many material assistance, and a few military aid. Only the Chinese Nationalist government offered to make available a significant number of troops. It agreed to make available for use in Korea some 33,000 seasoned men. This embarrassing offer was turned aside by the United States government with the suggestion that, in view of the threat of invasion of Taiwan by Communist forces from the mainland, it would be desirable for the Chinese military authorities to hold discussions with representatives of General MacArthur's headquarters before any final decisions were made to reduce the defense forces on the island.

COMMUNIST VIEWS

In its report of June 26 to the Secretary-General, UNCOK stated that "all the evidence continues to point to a calculated co-ordinated attack prepared and launched with secrecy," that "South Korean forces were deployed on wholly defensive basis" and were taken "completely by surprise." The Korean Communist version as given by General Kim Usung and reported by UNCOK was that "South Korea, having rejected every Northern proposal for peaceful unification, had crowned its iniquity by launching an invasion force across the parallel, . . . thus precipitating North Korean counter attacks for which it would have to assume the consequences." This was also the view adopted by Poland, which in addition protested against "aggression of the United States on Korea, and on the territory of China, and against the announced intervention in the Philippines and in Viet Nam." The Soviet government likewise accepted the view that the events in Korea were provoked by an attack from the south, and in addition it challenged the validity of the action of the Security Council on the ground that the resolution did not have the concurring votes of all the permanent members as required by Article 27 of the Charter. The Soviet government justified its absence from the Security Council with the argument that so long as China was excluded from representation (meaning Communist China, of course) it was impossible for that body to take decisions having legal force. The United States was accused of armed intervention in Korea and of "aggression, simultaneously in a whole number of the countries of Asia."

To the Soviet allegation that the action of the Security Council with respect to Korea was illegal, the United States government replied at considerable length in a statement of June 30. It pointed out that by a long series of precedents the practice had been established whereby abstention by permanent members of the Security Council did not constitute a veto. Every member of the United Nations, including the Soviet Union, had acquiesced in this practice. It cited ten resolutions of the Council on substantive matters on which the Soviet Union had abstained but the legality of which it had never challenged. The United States statement further pointed out that the Soviet government had not questioned the legality of action taken by the Security Council in at least three instances in which it had voted with the majority but on which other permanent members of the Council had abstained. "The voluntary absence of a permanent member from the Security Council," so the United States contended, "is clearly analogous to abstention." It further drew attention to the provision of Article 28 of the Charter that the Security Council shall be so organized as to be able to function continuously and that this injunction would be defeated if the absence of a representative of a permanent member were construed to have the effect of preventing all substantive action by the Council. The United States statement also disposed of the Soviet claim about the absence of Chinese representation. The representative of the Nationalist government had been seated as the representative of China in accordance with the Rules of Procedure of the Council, and this accreditation had never been withdrawn. Therefore, the vote of the Nationalist representative on the resolutions of June 25 and 27 was the official vote of China.

A most effective refutation of the Russian arguments was made by Mr. Chauvel, the representative of France in the Security Council. He reminded the Soviet government that it always claimed to be the champion of democracy, and as such it could not consistently challenge the credentials of the Chinese representative, for that was a matter for the decision of the Council and not for any single member. With respect to the Soviet argument that the action of the Council was illegal because it had been taken without its concurring vote, Mr. Chauvel stressed the view that membership in the Council had a dual character and carried a dual responsibility. The representatives were on the one hand representatives of their governments, but on the other they were members of a body whose primary function was the maintenance of international peace and security. The latter was a collective and joint responsibility, a mandate conferred by all the members of the United Nations. This responsibility could not be shirked merely because the Council had failed to accept a member's point of view on a given matter. It was a maxim of Roman law that no one had the right to invoke his own mistakes to his own advantage. By abandoning the Council, the Soviet Union had abandoned the Charter. "When it returned to both, it would recover its right of speech, of criticism, of vote, and of veto. Until then the USSR had no moral or legal basis for contesting United Nations action."

The Soviet Union did not stop with declaring the action of the Security Council illegal. It decided to obstruct action from within by returning to the Council. Mr. Yakov A. Malik, permanent representative of the Soviet Union to the United Nations, returned to the Council on August 1 and, in accordance with established procedures, assumed its presidency for the month. He had not attended its meetings since January. Throughout the month of his chairmanship he put on a masterful exhibition of obstructionism. With the Soviet representative back in the Security Council, that body again became the international sounding board for Soviet Communist propaganda. He sought to divide the countries of the free world by driving a wedge between the United States and those countries which, though they supported the United Nations action on Korea, were not happy about American Far Eastern policy.

CHINESE COMMUNIST INTERVENTION

The first twelve weeks of military operations were very discouraging for the United Nations forces. They were pressed back behind a perimeter around Pusan, a vital seaport on the southern tip of the peninsula. They were able to hold this perimeter, however, while they were steadily building up their strength through reinforcements. In mid-September the military picture dramatically changed by the bold maneuver of General MacArthur in effecting a successful amphibious landing at Inchon near Seoul. In not many days the government of Korea was back in its capital city and the North Korean troops rapidly withdrew northward with heavy loss of men and supplies.

The northward march of the victorious armies precipitated the question of the military objectives of the United Nations forces. Were they to stop at the thirty-eighth parallel or were they to press on to the Manchurian border? It was a military question with very important political implications. India, which had recognized the Communist regime in China and had entered into diplomatic relations with it, warned that crossing the parallel might bring the Chinese Communists into the war. Moreover, India's Prime Minister was of the opinion that it would be unwise for the United Nations to attempt more than the restoration of conditions as they were before the aggression. Others were of the view that to stop at the parallel would leave everything unsettled and give the forces of aggression the opportunity to prepare for a new attack. The matter was brought before the General Assembly, which was in session. On October 7, it adopted a resolution which by implication authorized advance beyond the parallel. The General Assembly in its resolution recalled the essential objectives of its actions of 1947, 1948, and 1949 as "the establishment of a unified, independent and democratic Government of Korea," and it therefore recommended that "all appropriate steps be taken to ensure conditions of stability throughout Korea," and that "all constituent acts be taken, including the holding of elections, under the auspices of the United Nations, for the establishment of a unified, independent and democratic Government in the sovereign State of Korea." This resolution also looked toward the reconstruction of this sorely stricken land by calling upon the Economic and Social Council "to develop plans for relief and rehabilitation on the termination of hostilities" and "to expedite the study of long-term measures to promote the economic development and social progress of Korea." A United Nations Commission for the Unification and Rehabilitation of Korea (UNCURK), composed of Australia, Chile, Netherlands, Pakistan, Philippines, Thailand, and Turkey, was created to replace the United Nations Commission on Korea (UNCOK).[2]

As the United Nations forces approached the Manchurian border late in October they encountered Chinese forces, small at first but steadily increasing in number. On November 5, General MacArthur reported the fact of Chinese Communist intervention. The United Nations were now confronted with what amounted to an "entirely new war."

The United States immediately requested the Security Council to consider the new development. The Council considered a resolution sponsored by six members calling upon all "states and authorities, and in particular those responsible for the action voted above, to refrain from assisting or encouraging the North Korean authorities, to prevent their nationals or individuals or units of their armed forces from giving assistance to North Korean forces and to cause the immediate withdrawal of any such nationals, individuals, or units which may presently be in Korea." The resolution also affirmed that it was the intention of the United Nations to respect the Chinese frontier with Korea and fully to protect legitimate Chinese and Korean interests in the frontier zone. The resolution came up for a vote on November 30. It was vetoed by the Soviet Union. The United States now requested that the matter of Chinese aggression be placed upon the agenda of the General Assembly. After the failure of an attempt to bring about a cease-fire agreement, the General Assembly on February 1, 1951, by a vote of 51 to 5, adopted a resolution finding the People's Republic of China guilty of aggression in Korea and affirming that it continued to be the policy of the United Nations to bring about a cessation of hostilities in Korea and the achievement of its objectives in Korea by peaceful means.

On May 18, 1951, the General Assembly followed up this resolution with another recommending that all states apply an embargo on the shipment of arms and implements of war to Communist China and North Korea.

Efforts at Mediation

Attempts at mediation began almost immediately upon the outbreak of hostilities in Korea. Prime Minister Nehru of India on July 13, 1950, sent personal messages to Premier Stalin and Secretary Acheson proposing a solution of the Korean problem by giving Communist China a seat on the Security Council as a first step, to be followed by negotiations among the United States, the Soviet Union, and China for the permanent solution of the Korean problem. The move was rejected by the United States on the ground that yielding now to Communist demands would be tantamount to rewarding aggression.

A concession was made to Communist China when the Security Council on

[2] The resolution was passed by 47 votes in favor, with 5 opposed and 8 abstentions.

November 8 voted to invite a representative of the People's Republic of China to be present during discussion by the Council of the special report of the United Nations Command in Korea.   A little later the Political and Security Committee of the General Assembly voted to invite the Peiping government to take part in general discussions of the Korean problem, including American "aggression" in Korea.   A delegation shortly arrived from Peiping, but its only activity was bitter incrimination of American "imperialism" in the Far East.   Under the leadership of an Asia-Arab group of states, the General Assembly on December 14 passed a resolution requesting the President of the Assembly to appoint two persons to be associated with himself in constituting a team to determine the basis on which a satisfactory cease-fire could be arranged.   The President, Mr. N. Entezam of Iran, appointed Sir Benegal Rau of India and Mr. L. B. Pearson of Canada to serve with him.   The group met with no cooperation from the Chinese Communists and had to report that its efforts had ended in failure.   The Communist government in a statement to Mr. Entezam on December 22, repeated in a message of January 17 to the First Committee of the General Assembly, stated its conditions for a truce as follows: (1) the withdrawal of all foreign troops from Korea and the settlement of "Korean domestic affairs by the Koreans themselves," (2) the withdrawal of United States forces from Formosa, and (3) Chinese Communist representation in the United Nations.

The United Nations in spite of this rebuff in effect invited a continuation of efforts to reach a truce agreement.   The General Assembly resolution of February 1, which branded Red China as an aggressor, contained a request to the President of the Assembly to designate two persons who would meet with him at any suitable opportunity to use their good offices to bring about a cessation of hostilities in Korea and the achievement of United Nations objectives by peaceful means.

The United Nations forces after the intervention by the Chinese Communists were forced to withdraw from North Korea to a line south of Seoul. After a few months, however, they were again able to move forward against the enemy.   Their steady progress probably had something to do with the suggestion made by Mr. Malik, the chief Soviet delegate to the United Nations, in a radio broadcast on June 23, 1951, proposing that the time had come to settle the problem of the armed conflict in Korea and indicating that the Soviet Union would encourage discussions for a cease-fire agreement.   On June 29, General M. B. Ridgway, who some time before had succeeded General MacArthur as Chief of United Nations forces in Korea, acted on the Soviet suggestion by communicating to the Commander-in-chief of the Communist forces in Korea that he was prepared to appoint a representative if such a meeting was indeed desired.   The contact thus made resulted in the beginning of negotiations at Kaesong on July 10.   But it soon became clear that the Communists were in no hurry to reach an agreement.   Negotiations were broken off several times.   Many weary months were spent in negotiations, but no agreement had been reached in November, 1951 (time of writing).

CONCLUSIONS

The first reaction to the decision of the United Nations to resist the aggression in Korea with vigor and determination was, in general, one of hearty approval.   Some, disturbed by the steadily declining prestige of the United Nations, spoke of it as a new birth for that institution.   The more enthusiastic declared that the decision had electrified the free world, heartened the half-hearted in Europe and Asia, encouraged the fence sitters to climb down on the right side, and dispelled defeatism.   The decisive action of the United Nations in meeting aggression would in the future discourage satellites from being used by the Soviet Union and then left in the lurch.   It would unite the free world.   The lessons learned and the confidence gained from successfully repelling aggression would make it easier to meet succeeding ones.

The great gains that would come from the successful application of sanctions against an aggressor were easily discernible, and it was also easy to see what dire consequences would have come from a failure to meet the crisis squarely.   It was more difficult, however, especially in the early stages, to envisage all the problems which would have to be met and what would be the situation if the action failed or ended in a stalemate.   As the campaign to repel aggression lengthened into months and threatened to continue for years, the tensions within the free world became more and more evident.   This development was due to several factors.   A number of Asiatic countries had only just acquired their independence, and there lingered throughout Asia considerable suspicion of the large Western Powers.   The sentiment of neutralism was widely prevalent.   There was a feeling among the peoples of these new states that because of their grave internal problems and weakness they ought not to allow themselves to be drawn into either power bloc.

There was also the problem created by the fact that American policy in the Far East could not be wholly extricated from United Nations policy with respect to Korea, and later China.   American national policy in Asia by no means enjoyed universal endorsement.   India, whose moral influence in all Asia is very great, was at odds with American policy with respect to Indochina and China.   India and the United Kingdom had recognized the Communist government of China.   India disliked American support of the French in Indochina, which it regarded as intervention in support of colonialism.   It was necessary, of course, to have a unified command for the United Nations forces in Korea, and it was also clear that the commander-in-chief would have to be an American and that the only logical choice was General MacArthur.   But General MacArthur was known for his positive political views on Far Eastern policy.   All this complicated the problem and sometimes dampened enthusiasms. The Soviet Union quickly seized upon this situation and directed all of its powerful propaganda activities toward deepening this rift and sowing doubt and suspicion.

The difference became most evident in the matter of branding Communist China an aggressor and of applying some sort of sanctions against it. Many states voted for this measure with great reluctance. Some European governments feared that it might lead to a war with China, which would almost certainly draw many American divisions to Asia and away from Europe, where the real test with the Soviet Union might be precipitated just when the United States had become inextricably involved in the East. There was also a feeling that marking China an aggressor would only make a settlement more difficult without any compensating gains. To the United States it was a relatively simple moral problem. Aggression is aggression, no matter by whom it is committed. To abandon principle for expediency was only to invite disaster. Moreover, it would put the United Nations in an absurd position. If the Communist Chinese in Korea were not aggressors, then surely North Koreans, fighting in their own country, were not aggressors. If the Chinese in Korea were not aggressors, then the United Nations forces were.

One aspect of the problem is difficult to evaluate. The South Koreans had put up a heroic defense against aggression and had received much aid from the members of the United Nations; nevertheless, the war had left the Koreans impoverished and their country devastated. Even if in the end the United Nations were successful in repelling the aggression, would Korea's example inspire other small countries in a strategic position to stand firmly against aggression, or would it rather lead them to seek appeasement? The free world was not indifferent to the plight of the stricken Koreans. Measures for the relief of Korea were undertaken by the United Nations almost immediately after the invasion began, and on December 1, 1950, the General Assembly established the Korean Reconstruction Agency (UNKRA) for the relief and reconstruction of Korea. Unless outside help became available in large measure communism would still stand an excellent chance of winning all of Korea, even though it had lost on the field of battle.

The Korean experience demonstrated that the United Nations Charter had far more flexibility than even many liberal constructionists had thought possible. The absence of the Soviet Union had not blocked action by the Security Council, and when the Soviet representative returned to the Council to paralyze it, the case was shifted to the General Assembly. All in all, much was learned in every way about international cooperation in maintaining collective security. But not all the lessons were positive. Some were negative. While there were many advantages in moving the Korean issue from the Security Council to the vetoless General Assembly, it did not solve all the problems and it created some new ones. A body of sixty members is a bit unwieldy for serving as a supervisor, if not the director, of a military campaign.   It has also brought into bold relief the problem that is created by the fact that under conditions of modern, mechanized warfare only a few states can contribute any real military aid.   Not over a fourth of the members of the United Nations made any contribution to the military forces in Korea, and most of these, aside from the United States, made only token contributions. As months of hostilities followed each other the American people became restive and even resentful of the meager aid it had received, and a recrudescence of old isolationist sentiments were noticeable in American public opinion.   The large number of small states in the General Assembly who make no contribution to the United Nations cause in Korea have the controlling vote in deciding the basic policies.   This cannot be regarded as an ideal situation.   It touches the whole problem of the proper basis for representation in the United Nations organs, and especially in the General Assembly.

As the days of the United Nations police action went on interminably and the American casualty list lengthened, many Americans became frightened.   There arose the nightmare of the possibility that the Korean campaign could not be brought to a successful conclusion.   Suppose the aggressors were driven out of the country, would not a huge army have to be kept at the border indefinitely?   Strict logic would require carrying the military campaign to the Korean hinterland of Manchuria, North China, and even Siberia, but this might precipitate World War III.   General MacArthur had chafed under the directives to limit the war to Korea even though the enemy forces were supported by bases in China and were operating from this sheltered zone.   A leading candidate for the presidency of the United States was clearly appealing to a strong latent sentiment of many of his fellow countrymen by declaring the military operations in Korea "useless."

What must not be forgotten is that the situation in Korea is only a phase or a part of the whole world situation.   Can the basic issues which divide the free world from the Communist-dominated world be resolved?   If they can, the solution in Korea will be a simple matter.   As yet, however, neither force nor diplomacy has brought peace to the world.

Chapter 16

ARMAMENTS AND ATOMIC ENERGY

The regulation and control of armaments is a central problem for a system of collective security. When a nation relies on its own armed strength for protection, it has security only so long as it is stronger than any potential enemy or group of enemies. If, however, it is this strong, other nations will be too weak to protect themselves on the same basis. One Great Power, with its allies, might become so strong that no enemy dare attack it. But it is impossible for two Great Powers, or two alliances, to be that much stronger than each other. When each attempts to become stronger relative to the other, the result is an armaments race which in itself is a grave threat to international peace and security. Under the expectation of violence, each party views the other's defensive preparations as evidence of aggressive intent and speeds up the tempo of its own armament as a counterdefense. This is in turn construed as a threat, to be answered by additional measures which continue to feed the vicious spiral. One nation might possibly guarantee its security by its armed strength, but by the same token all others would be insecure and from an international viewpoint the problem would not be solved. When circumstances are such that no one nation can be overwhelmingly successful in an armaments race, all nations are insecure. Security and aggression cannot be clearly and objectively separated, with all nations strong enough to defend themselves but too weak to attack others, because the same weapons and the same bases may be used for defense or attack. The government of a Great Power does not assume that a potential enemy will never use its strength aggressively.

The Covenant of the League of Nations emphasized the idea of *reduction* of national armaments. When the attempt was made to implement this concept, it became obvious that nations would not voluntarily give up their armed forces until they had obtained security. But collective security cannot become a reality until the reliance upon competitive national armaments is ended. This is the fundamental and as yet unsolved dilemma of the armaments question. The Charter of the United Nations approaches the problem with the emphasis on regulation of armaments, with the idea that force may have to be utilized to maintain security and that minimum as well as maximum limits may have to be set. The United Nations, however, has faced the same dilemma in regulating national armaments as the League of Nations did in reducing them.

CONTROL OF ATOMIC ENERGY

A few weeks after the Charter was signed at San Francisco, an atomic bomb was dropped on Hiroshima. Consequently the United Nations began its work confronted with an overshadowing problem that had not been known to the delegates who planned the Organization. One of the first undertakings was to seek a means for dealing with this situation. The General Assembly, on January 24, 1946, unanimously adopted a resolution to establish a United Nations Atomic Energy Commission to deal with the problems raised by the discovery of atomic energy and other related matters. This Commission is composed of one representative from each of the states represented on the Security Council and also includes a representative of Canada when the latter is not a member of the Security Council. The Commission was directed to study all phases of the problem with the utmost dispatch, and to submit its reports and recommendations to the Security Council. The following terms of reference were prescribed: (1) extending between all nations the exchange of basic scientific information for peaceful ends; (2) control of atomic energy to the extent necessary to ensure its use only for peaceful purposes; (3) elimination from national armaments of atomic weapons and of all other major weapons adaptable to mass destruction; (4) effective safeguards by way of inspection and other means to protect complying states against the hazards of violations and evasions.

At the first meeting of the Commission, on June 14, 1946, the government of the United States submitted a proposed plan based upon the creation of an International Atomic Development Authority entrusted with all phases of the development and use of atomic energy.[1] The fundamental importance of immediate punishment for infringements of the rights of this Authority was stressed, and the American representative, Mr. Bernard Baruch, declared that "there must be no veto to protect those who violate their solemn agreements not to develop or use atomic energy for destructive purposes." The United States plan contained the following specific proposals:

1. The International Atomic Development Authority should conduct continuous surveys of world supplies of uranium and thorium and bring the raw materials under its control.

2. The Authority should control and operate all the primary plants producing fissionable products in dangerous quantities and all plants dealing with uranium or thorium after it had once reached the potential of dangerous use.

3. The Authority should possess the exclusive right to conduct research in

[1] This was the so-called Baruch plan. In its main outlines, it followed the recommendations of the Acheson-Lilienthal report which was published in March, 1946. The Baruch plan, however, placed more emphasis on the swift, sure, and vetoless punishment of a violator of an atomic energy agreement, and it placed less reliance on "denaturing" fissionable materials as a part of the control plan.

the field of atomic explosives, and all other atomic research should be open only to nations under license of the Authority, which would furnish them with denatured materials.

4. Dangerous activities of the Authority, and its stock piles, should be decentralized and strategically distributed.

5. Freedom for any inspection deemed necessary by the Authority should be granted by nations.

The United States proposed that, once renunciation of the bomb as a weapon had been agreed on and an adequate system of control put into effective operation with punishments set up for any violations, manufacture of atomic bombs should stop, existing bombs should be disposed of under treaty, and the Authority should be given full information as to the know-how for atomic energy production.   Subject to constitutional processes, the United States government would make available to the Authority, at successive stages, the information necessary for its effective functioning at each of these stages in its progressive assumption of control.

At the second meeting of the Commission, five days later, the Soviet Union presented its plan,[2] which was based on proposals for the conclusion of an international agreement to forbid the production and use of atomic weapons. The essentials of such an agreement would be:

1. The production and use of atomic weapons would be forbidden.

2. Within three months from the entry into force of the agreement, all stocks of atomic weapons would be destroyed.

3. Any violation of the agreement would be regarded as a serious threat against humanity.

4. Violation of the agreement would be severely punished under the domestic legislation of the contracting parties.

5. The agreement would be of indefinite duration, coming into force after approval by the Security Council and ratification by all its permanent members.

6. All states, whether members of the United Nations or not, would be obliged to fulfil all the provisions of the agreement.

The representative of the Soviet Union also proposed the creation of two committees of the whole, one to develop the exchange of scientific information and the other to prepare recommendations for outlawing and preventing the use of atomic energy for the harm of humanity.

The American and Soviet proposals of June, 1946, presented the opposing viewpoints which have persisted, with the major issues unchanged, in all the attempts to find some formula by which atomic energy might be brought under international control.   For purposes of a convenient summary, four specific points of fundamental disagreement may be recognized in the oceans of words that have poured forth on this subject.   First, there was the question of the

---

[2] This was the so-called Gromyko plan.

order in which the essential steps would be taken.   The United States insisted that the establishment of an adequate system of international control and inspection was a prerequisite to the effective prohibition of atomic weapons, and refused to share its "know-how" concerning atomic energy until there was agreement on this prior point.   The Soviet Union wanted to outlaw and destroy all atomic weapons as a first step, and then establish a system of international control.   This would, of course, put the two countries on an equality in this matter before serious negotiations on the control system were started.   The United States government did not intend to surrender the new weapon until effective safeguards were in operation and wanted to be sure that atomic disarmament would not, in effect, leave it helpless against an evader of the plan. The Soviet government, on the contrary, was unwilling to submit to a substantial degree of international control and inspection while the Americans retained a supply of atomic bombs.

The proposal that a plan of international control go into effect by successive stages was not sufficient to break this deadlock.   The problem of agreement on the first step remained.   So far as the United States was concerned, the stage of destroying its bombs and giving up its "secrets" would not be reached until an adequate system of international control and inspection had been established.   In the Soviet view, this meant that the United States would retain its advantage in the earlier stages and would be in a position to decide at what point its atomic weapons could safely be destroyed.   Therefore, the Soviet Union might consider itself as making present concessions in return for promises as to the future.   It should be noted that redemption of these promises depended in part on action by Congress, which cannot constitutionally be bound as to future action.   The American proposal on making information available to the International Atomic Development Authority contained the phrase "subject to constitutional processes."   Any agreement on atomic energy would take the form of a treaty, requiring the consent of the Senate by a two-thirds majority.   Also, the Atomic Energy Act signed by the President in August, 1946, provided that there should be no international exchange of information with respect to the use of atomic energy for industrial purposes "until Congress declares by joint resolution that effective and enforceable international safeguards against the use of atomic energy for destructive purposes have been established."

At first thought, it may seem strange that the Soviet government regarded itself as being asked to make concessions in return for insubstantial promises. After all, it was the United States which had the atomic bomb and was offering to surrender its exclusive control.   The answer lies to a considerable extent in the second point of fundamental disagreement, the question of inspection. The Baruch proposals included the stipulation that the international control authority must have unlimited rights of access for inspection purposes.   Otherwise there would be no assurance against undetected violations or evasions of an agreement on atomic weapons. The Soviet government insisted on periodic and limited inspection, feeling that greater reliance must be placed on the national governments, that continuous and unlimited rights of inspection were unnecessary and in fact would amount to supervision, and that an international agency with a majority composition of "capitalist" representatives might develop harmful policies and activities. For example, a thorough inspection would give the International Authority comprehensive information on the Soviet industrial complex and would provide data by which a potential enemy could pinpoint vital targets in the Soviet Union. This possibility was unacceptable to the Soviet government.

The third major point of disagreement involved the question of the authority to be given to an international control agency. The United States considered that complete ownership and operation of all plants producing fissionable materials was essential. The Soviet government thought in terms of an international commission which would have designated supervisory powers but which would not own and operate any plants, at least in that country. It seemed obvious that the Soviet Union would be in a minority position on the International Atomic Development Authority. The decisions would be made by a majority of "capitalist" members under the leadership of the United States. In this connection, Soviet suspicion was aroused not only by potential threats to national security, but also by fears of discrimination in the development of atomic energy for peaceful purposes. For example, a major Soviet goal is to increase industrial productivity, and its available energy per capita is quite low. Could the International Authority be expected to make decisions on the location and ownership of atomic plants in such a way as to decrease the gap in energy resources between the Soviet Union and the leading "capitalist" countries? Whatever the Soviet leaders thought at the time on this point, the maximum of international control which they would permit was far below the minimum that the American government considered essential.

In the fourth place, the question of the veto was an issue. The United States insisted that after an international agreement on atomic energy was reached the control agency must operate outside the voting procedure prescribed by Article 27 of the Charter. Suppose a plan of international control were agreed to, the United States destroyed its atomic bombs and released its information concerning atomic energy to the world, and then one of the permanent members of the Security Council violated the plan and used the veto to prevent any enforcement action to be taken against it. This was the sort of situation which the United States representative had in mind when he insisted so strongly that the veto must be eliminated for atomic matters. The Soviet Union, however, remained unwilling to sacrifice its sovereignty to this extent and stood pat on the letter of the Charter as it had so recently been written at San Francisco. The Soviet government was not going to put itself at the mercy of a voting majority of "capitalist" countries. The only concession on this point was first made in the course of General Assembly debates on disarmament during the fall of 1946, when Mr. Molotov said that the unanimity rule of the Charter had nothing to do with the day-to-day operation of the proposed international control commission. But the question still remained of whether a Great Power might violate the agreement, or be suspected of doing so, and prevent any enforcement measures against itself.

It is entirely possible that the importance of the veto question has been overemphasized in the discussions. To a large extent, it is a symbolic rather than an actual problem. If a Great Power took the drastic step of violating the international agreement, would it then acquiesce in enforcement action directed against it because of a previous commitment to be bound by a majority vote? Obviously not. It is safe to assume that attempts at enforcement would be resisted in such a case, whatever the voting procedure might be. To carry them out would mean atomic warfare, and a government which would precipitate such a situation certainly would not hesitate to break its pledge respecting a voting procedure in an international agency. Moreover, Article 51 of the Charter explicitly recognizes the inherent right in individual or collective self-defense if an armed attack occurs and the Security Council does not deal with it effectively. Therefore, a veto in the Security Council would not impede enforcement measures if the atomic violation were considered to be equivalent to an armed attack. Since a serious violation of an international agreement on atomic weapons could hardly have any other purpose than an armed attack, it is likely that measures of preventive defense could be taken by the other members of the United Nations within the framework of the Charter. Of course, there is some doubt and supposition on this point. If a violation of an atomic control plan did not constitute an "armed attack" within the meaning of Article 51, and did not result in immediate war on considerations of national security or power politics, a real difficulty in connection with the voting procedure would be involved. Since the veto question is near the crux of the whole matter symbolically, but of a much more limited importance actually, the question arises of whether it would be safe to make any concessions, in return for a satisfactory *quid pro quo* on other points, to the Soviet view that international control of atomic energy should be subordinated to the regular procedures of the Security Council.

The United Nations Atomic Energy Commission submitted its first report to the Security Council on December 31, 1946. Agreement had been reached that international control of atomic energy was technically feasible. The political basis for international control was a different matter, with all the members of the Commission, except the Soviet Union and Poland, agreeing with the substance of the Baruch proposals.

The report [3] of the Commission described the results of the work which had

[3] This report was adopted by a vote of 10 to 0 in the Commission. The Soviet Union and Poland abstained from being parties to any decision on the substance of the proposals.

been done during the year. In its general findings it stated that scientifically, technically, and practically it was feasible (1) to extend among all nations the exchange of basic scientific information on atomic energy for peaceful ends; (2) to control atomic energy to the extent necessary to ensure its use only for peaceful purposes; (3) to accomplish the elimination from national armaments of atomic weapons; and (4) to provide effective safeguards by way of inspection and other means to protect complying states against the hazards of violations and evasions. The report stated that an effective control system must be international and must be established by an enforceable multilateral treaty or convention, administered by an international agency within the United Nations. An agreement to outlaw national production, possession, or use of atomic weapons was considered essential but would not be sufficient to guarantee peaceful use or to provide effective safeguards against violations or evasions.

On the basis of these findings, the Commission recommended the creation of a strong and comprehensive system of control and inspection. An international authority possessing the power and responsibility necessary for the prompt and effective discharge of its duties would be established. The rule of unanimity of the permanent members which governed all the substantive decisions of the Security Council would have no relation to the work of this Authority. The exchange of basic scientific information should be promoted, with safeguards against dangerous uses of atomic energy itself. There would be a minimum of interference with the operations of national agencies. Representatives of the Authority would have unimpeded rights of access for the performance of their inspections. The manufacture, possession, and use of atomic weapons would be prohibited, and there would be provision for the disposal of existing stocks and for the proper use of fissionable materials. The methods for determining violations would be specified in the treaty. Enforcement measures and the punishment of violators would not be subject to veto. Finally, the treaty would provide a schedule for the completion of the transitional process leading step by step to the full and effective establishment of international control of atomic energy.

The Security Council considered the Commission's report during February and March, 1947, and adopted a resolution urging a continuation of the inquiry into all phases of the problem and the preparation of a draft convention. The Commission was also asked to submit a second report before the next regular session of the General Assembly. At a meeting on March 19, 1947, the Atomic Energy Commission instructed its committees to study particularly those questions on which agreements among its members had not been reached. A thorough consideration of the amendments and additions which the Soviet Union had proposed before the Security Council did not, however, lead the Commission to revise the findings and recommendations which it had reached in its first report.

At the Commission's meeting of June 11, 1947, the representative of the Soviet Union presented for consideration a set of "provisions on which an international agreement or convention on atomic energy control should be based." These proposals were a restatement and elaboration of the previous Soviet position, and it was decided that there was no reason to alter the program of work already laid out for the preparation of the Commission's second report [4] to the Security Council.   In the course of discussion, however, several delegations expressed a desire to have certain points clarified.   Accordingly, the representative of Great Britain addressed a letter containing eleven questions to the Soviet representative and these were answered by the latter.   In January, 1948, a detailed study of the Soviet proposals, as elaborated by this set of questions and answers, was begun.   On March 29, the British representative presented, on behalf of his own delegation and those of Canada, China, and France, a joint report analyzing these proposals.

The report stated that any effective plan for international control of atomic energy must provide against the danger of misuse of atomic materials through their diversion from legitimate uses and secret manufacture.   The Soviet proposals did not face these basic problems, as the powers and functions of the proposed international control commission were to be limited to "periodic inspection" and "special investigations," the latter to be undertaken only in case of suspicion of clandestine activities.   This would be an inadequate safeguard. Only management of the plant by an international agency would enable it to keep check on the nuclear fuels involved.   In regard to the "special investigations," the scope of inspection was to be so restricted that in practice there would be no opportunity for the international control commission to become suspicious.

Even if violations should be detected, the report continued, the international control commission would not have any powers to prevent or correct them, since it could only make recommendations to the Security Council and would not possess any independent powers of enforcing its decisions.   At best this would result in delays during which illegal activities could continue unchecked. With reference to the Soviet position that destruction of atomic weapons should take place before the conclusion of an international agreement to enforce that prohibition, the report asserted that this would give no assurance (1) that nations which were known to possess atomic weapons would in fact destroy them; (2) that nations which were not known to have atomic weapons, but which might have them, would carry out their obligations; or (3) that nations would be prevented from manufacturing atomic weapons in the future.

The joint report came to this conclusion: [5]

The Soviet Union proposals are not an acceptable basis for the international control of atomic energy.   The United Nations Atomic Energy Commission cannot

[4] Presented in September, 1947.

[5] *Yearbook of the United Nations, 1947–1948,* p. 470.

endorse any scheme which would not prevent the diversion of atomic material, which provides no effective means for the detection of clandestine activities and which has no provision for prompt and effective enforcement action. The Soviet Union Government has not only proposed a scheme that is fundamentally inadequate for the control of atomic energy, but at the same time has made the overriding stipulation that they will not agree to establish even such a feeble scheme of control until all atomic weapons have been prohibited and destroyed. It is completely unrealistic to expect any nation to renounce atomic weapons without any assurance that all nations will be prevented from producing them.

On April 5, 1948, the representative of the Soviet Union replied [6] to the arguments contained in the joint report. Concerning the question of "periodic inspection," he stated that there could not be any other kind. Any measures which had to be applied continuously in respect of productive facilities and raw materials could not be regarded as inspection but would constitute management or supervision. However, the majority proposals for management, supervision, and licensing of atomic facilities were not acceptable to the Soviet Union. There was no basis for any "special investigation" in the absence of suspicion in regard to violations. Personnel selected for this function should not be regarded as tourists who could go any place freely with or without reason. A convention prohibiting atomic weapons should be regarded as a first step in the system of establishing international control, to be followed by other important steps. International control of atomic energy as such would be useless in the absence of a convention prohibiting atomic weapons. With regard to the criticism as to the lack of enforcement powers on the part of the international control agency, it was maintained that the question of sanctions was entirely within the jurisdiction and scope of the Security Council. To place such powers elsewhere would be contrary to the letter and spirit of the Charter of the United Nations.

The Atomic Energy Commission, in May, 1948, reported that it had reached an impasse. In almost two years of work, it had succeeded in making clear the essentials of a plan for the control of atomic energy. However, the divergency of views on major principles was so great and so persistent that a draft convention on the subject could not be prepared. The Commission concluded that no useful purpose could be served by continuing its negotiations. It therefore recommended that, until such time as the General Assembly found that this situation no longer existed or the permanent members of the Atomic Energy Commission found some basis of agreement by prior consultation, negotiations in the Commission be suspended.

The Security Council discussed this report but was unable to reach any substantive decision because the same impasse prevailed there as in the Atomic Energy Commission. It did adopt a resolution, by a procedural vote, direct-

---

[6] At a meeting of the Working Committtee of the United Nations Atomic Energy Commission.

ing the Secretary-General to transmit to the General Assembly and the members of the United Nations, as a matter of general concern, the three reports of the Atomic Energy Commission and the record of the Security Council deliberations on the subject.   The suspension of work suggested by the Commission was not accepted by the Security Council.   The General Assembly considered the reports and records at its next regular meeting.   As a result, it adopted a resolution on November 4, 1948, approving the majority proposals [7] as constituting the necessary basis for establishing an effective system of international control; expressing its deep concern at the impasse in the Atomic Energy Commission; and regretting that unanimous agreement had not been reached.   It requested the six permanent members of the Commission to consult in order to determine if there existed a basis for agreement, and to report to the General Assembly.   Also, it called upon the Atomic Energy Commission to resume its sessions, to survey its program of work, and to proceed to the further study of such subjects as it considered to be practicable and useful.

As a result of this resolution, the Commission resumed its work early in 1949.   It continued its study, compilation of materials, and discussion, but the same basic impasse continued along the lines of the fundamental disagreement which had existed from the beginning.   The verification of a successful atomic explosion in the Soviet Union and the publicity about a possible "hydrogen" bomb did not alter the opposing viewpoints with respect to proposals for establishing a system of international control.   These new developments would seem to make an effective inspection all the more necessary in the opinion of the majority.   Conversely, they did nothing to alter the Soviet insistence that prohibition of atomic weapons must come first, and that the powers of an international control agency must be strictly limited.

The General Assembly, at its fourth regular session in the fall of 1949, again discussed this question and passed a resolution essentially reaffirming its former position concerning the urgent necessity of continuing the effort to reach agreement.   The President of the General Assembly, Carlos Romulo of the Philippines, addressed a special appeal to the permanent members of the Atomic Energy Commission to make every effort "to explore even the remotest possibility of an effective agreement."   He suggested that attention be directed to the possibility of (1) a short-term atomic armistice accompanied by an inspection system; (2) an interim prohibition on the use of atomic weapons, with adequate safeguards; (3) further compromises between the majority and minority plans; and (4) a new approach to the fundamental problem of control.

On December 3, Mr. Romulo said that the replies which he had received were encouraging.   Unfortunately, the consultations among the six permanent

[7] Essentially the Baruch plan, as accepted and developed by the majority on the United Nations Atomic Energy Commission.   Its main features are summarized above.

members of the Atomic Energy Commission were suspended early in 1950 as a result of the Soviet refusal to participate in any meetings with the Nationalist delegation of China, nor was any progress made after the Soviet boycott of United Nations meetings ended in August.

CONVENTIONAL ARMAMENTS

The international control of atomic energy is only a part of the question of disarmament, or regulation of armaments.   Even if atomic weapons were completely and effectively prohibited, other highly destructive means of warfare would remain available unless they, too, were eliminated or brought under effective international control.   During the second part of its first regular session, in the fall of 1946, the General Assembly considered the general principles governing the regulation and reduction of national armaments.   The discussion included a number of related topics, such as the international control of atomic energy, information on national armaments, a system of inspection, and the implementation of Article 43 of the Charter.   A resolution, representing a compromise between the various viewpoints, was adopted on December 14, 1946.   It recognized the "necessity of an early general regulation and reduction of armaments and armed forces," and recommended that the Security Council give prompt consideration to formulating practical measures; that the effective prohibition of atomic weapons be facilitated to the greatest possible extent; that an arrangement for this purpose be established within the framework of the Security Council; that the placing of armed forces at the disposal of the Security Council be accelerated; and that the armed forces of members outside their own territories be withdrawn as rapidly as possible.

This resolution was adopted while the United Nations Atomic Energy Commission was considering its first report to the Security Council, and there was an important connection between these two developments.   It was the position of the Soviet Union that the international control of atomic energy could be considered as only one aspect of the broader question of general disarmament. This position reinforced that government's contention that prohibition of atomic weapons should be the first step and also was consistent with its insistence that the whole matter be kept within the framework of the Security Council.   The United States, however, feared that the question of atomic energy, as a unique and overwhelming problem, might be submerged in the consideration of general disarmament.   It also was obvious that the veto could not be eliminated with respect to this problem except by a recognition that the usual voting procedure in the Security Council would not be applicable in enforcing an atomic-energy agreement.

The United States government at first asked that the Security Council consider the question of atomic energy before it dealt with general disarmament at all.   This proposal was not acceptable, and it was agreed that there would be simultaneous but separate discussions of atomic energy and other types of armament. A Commission for Conventional Armaments was therefore created as a subsidiary organ of the Security Council in February, 1947. This Commission proceeded to its discussions on the basis that it was to consider all armaments and armed forces except "weapons of mass destruction," which were defined to include atomic explosive weapons, radioactive-material weapons, lethal chemical and biological weapons, and any weapons developed in the future which have characteristics comparable in destructive effect to those listed. The Soviet Union continued to oppose separation of the two questions, on the basis that it was artificial and would divert the Commission from practical proposals for the general regulation and reduction of armaments.

The central issues in the deliberations of the Commission for Conventional Armaments and its Working Committee were (1) the terms of reference of the Commission in relation to atomic weapons and other weapons of mass destruction; and (2) the relationship between the general regulation of armaments and factors affecting the state of international relations. The majority on the Commission went on the assumption that a system of armament regulation and reduction could be put into effect only in an atmosphere of international confidence and security. Examples of conditions essential to such confidence were the establishment of an adequate series of agreements for forces pledged to the Security Council under Article 43 of the Charter, an adequate system for the international control of atomic energy, and the conclusion of peace settlements with Germany and Japan. The Soviet representative thought that this amounted to a refusal to implement the General Assembly's resolution of December 14, 1946, which had contained no conditions or prerequisites. Security, in the view of his government, was dependent upon the speedy formulation and implementation of practical measures for the regulation and reduction of armaments, including the prohibition of atomic weapons. The stand taken by the majority, he said, could give rise only to a new armaments race.

In September, 1948, the Soviet Union introduced in the General Assembly a draft resolution proposing that, as a first step, the permanent members of the Security Council should reduce by one-third during one year all existing land, naval, and air forces; and that atomic weapons should be prohibited as intended for purposes of aggression. This proposal was not adopted, but the General Assembly did, on November 19, 1948, pass a resolution containing (1) a recommendation that the Security Council pursue the study of the question through the Commission for Conventional Armaments in order to obtain concrete results as soon as possible; (2) a proposal that the Commission devote its first attention to obtaining and checking information from member states with regard to their armed forces and conventional armaments; and (3) an invitation to the Security Council to report to the General Assembly on the effect given to these recommendations.

The plan of work to obtain information on conventional armaments was not approved by the Security Council on account of an adverse vote by the Soviet Union. During the discussion in the fourth session of the General Assembly (fall of 1949), the representative of the Soviet Union charged that the "Anglo-American bloc had refused any reduction in armaments; was maintaining an artificial division between atomic and other weapons; and had begun an armaments race and extended their system of strategic bases and military alliances." In reply, France, Norway, Great Britain, and the United States pointed out that it was necessary to have all relevant information, and that it would be useless if not verified. No reduction of conventional armaments was conceivable unless the international control of atomic energy was achieved. This was a single question with two aspects, being handled by two separate bodies which the Security Council could coordinate. If the Western European countries were rearming with American aid, it was, they said, because they feared the intentions of the Soviet Union and not because they were opposed to disarmament.

President Truman, in his speech of October 24, 1950, before the General Assembly suggested that the work on atomic energy and conventional armaments might be more closely brought together, possibly by a new and consolidated disarmament commission. This was a change in the United States position that the two questions should be handled by separate bodies. Aggression with any weapons, and not merely the existence of the atomic bomb, had come to be the chief problem. This shift in the American approach did not imply any change in the belief that an international atomic-energy control agency must operate without the restriction of the veto. Agreement on a control plan does require unanimity; after that, the control agency would operate by majority vote. In other words, the commission which develops the agreement could follow a procedure different from that of the agency which carries out the agreement once it is made.

Although the Soviet government had insisted all along that the question of atomic energy and conventional armaments could not be separated, Mr. Vishinsky took President Truman's suggestion for a coordinated approach as a piece of "skulduggery" designed to prevent any real work on atomic control. At the time, the strategy of the Soviet government was to insist that a nation refusing to outlaw atomic bombs was automatically an aggressor.

As of this writing, no real progress has been made in resolving the substantive difficulties for international regulation of armaments, on account of the unsatisfactory relations among some of the permanent members of the Security Council. In other words, Great Powers do not agree to limit their armaments under circumstances of a "cold war."

Chapter 17

ECONOMIC AND SOCIAL COOPERATION

It is difficult to describe in a limited space the work and accomplishments of the United Nations in the field of international economic and social cooperation. There are two reasons for this difficulty. In the first place these activities cover a very broad range. Administration of postal services, lowering of trade barriers, economic reconstruction, development of rinderpest vaccine, halting of a cholera epidemic in Egypt, resettlement of refugees, facilitating international exchange of books, improvement of statistics, control of opium traffic, and steps to stabilize currency exchange rates are only a few random samples from a long and varied list of activities. Some idea of the scope and variety of this work may be gained from the fact that a catalogue of United Nations economic and social projects in 1950 listed 723 different items.[1]

The other reason for the difficulty of giving adequate treatment to this type of work in a brief space is that its results are often indirect or intangible. In some cases, the United Nations operates a definite program, and it is relatively easy to describe the specific accomplishments. One can say, for example, that during a stated period of time a given number of refugees were repatriated or resettled, and their geographic location can be indicated. Or, as another example, statistics are available as to the number of pieces of mail handled in a year through arrangements administered by the Universal Postal Union. In some cases, the work carried on under the auspices of the United Nations is one factor among many others. If one says that the International Monetary Fund approved the devaluation of the British pound from $4.03 to $2.80, the statement is true enough but what is the exact "accomplishment" of the United Nations? There is no doubt that the existence and operation of the Fund contribute to the stability of international currency exchange, but any attempt to measure the extent of this effect soon gets into a zone of uncertainty.

Much of the work of the United Nations through its various organs and specialized agencies takes the form of recommendations to states. The International Labor Organization is credited with a very definite influence in raising the standard of labor in various parts of the world. However, its work

---

[1] *Catalogue of Economic and Social Projects,* 1950 (UN Doc. E/1670).

has been persuasive, cooperative, and educational, and it is impossible to say that on a given date the ILO reduced the number of hours in a workday by so much.   Its influence is important and obvious but not subject to exact quantitative measurement.

Because of these considerations, the economic and social work of the United Nations will be indicated in this chapter by giving brief descriptions of typical work of importance in various fields.   The problems which have been attacked fall into two categories: those resulting from World War II, and those of a continuing and long-range nature.   The emphasis for the first group has been on the operation of programs to deal with immediate emergencies and needs as in the cases, among others, of UNRRA [2] and the IRO.   The first task for the long-range problems was that of preparation and organization. This preliminary stage has been largely completed, and attention has been turned to carrying out responsibilities assigned in the various economic and social fields.   This work has involved four types of activities.   First, considerable progress has been made in the collection, analysis, presentation, and dissemination of information.   Studies, reports, bulletins, yearbooks, and other publications are increasing in number and variety.   Second, conferences arranged under the auspices of agencies in the economic and social field have been a means of preparing international agreements and facilitating the cooperation of governments and experts in dealing with problems of economic development, transport, statistics, housing and town planning, cartography, child welfare, conservation of resources, and others.   Third, draft conventions have been prepared to serve as recommendations for common international standards and to remove barriers to the solution of problems of mutual concern.   This type of work has been done in such fields as human rights, genocide, freedom of information, synthetic drugs, declaration of death of missing persons, suppression of prostitution, and economic statistics.   Finally, there is the extensive field of technical assistance, in which the specialized agencies are closely associated with the work of the United Nations.

The remainder of this chapter will be devoted to the work and accomplishments of the United Nations and its specialized agencies in the fields of labor standards; transport and communications; food and agriculture; finance; economic development; health; refugees; social welfare; and education, science and culture.[3]

---

[2] The United Nations Relief and Rehabilitation Administration, an emergency agency which is no longer in existence.

[3] The specialized agencies prepare annual reports on their programs and activities.   Records and reports of the six principal organs are published.   Useful summaries may be found in the *Yearbook of the United Nations* and, upon occasion, in the *United Nations Bulletin.* The U.S. Department of State publishes a *Current Review of Economic and Social Problems in the United Nations.*   For the members of the various specialized agencies, see Table 5.

Table 5. Members of the United Nations and the Specialized Agencies
(As of August 1, 1951)

Member	UN	ILO	UPU	ITU	FAO	UNESCO	ICAO	WHO	Bank	Fund	IRO	WMO	(ITO)[1]	(IMCO)[1]
Afghanistan	x	x	x	x	x	x	x	x					x	
Albania		x	x	x				x						
Argentina	x	x	x	x	x	x	x	x				x	x	x
Australia	x	x	x	x	x	x	x	x	x	x		x	x	x
Austria		x	x	x	x	x	x	x	x	x	x		x	
Belgium	x	x	x	x	x	x	x	x	x	x	x	x	x	x
Bolivia	x	x	x	x	x	x	x	x	x	x				
Brazil	x	x	x	x	x	x	x	x	x	x		x	x	
Bulgaria		x	x	x				x						
Burma	x	x	x	x	x	x	x	x				x	x	
Byelorussian S.S.R.	x	x	x	x				x				x		
Canada	x	x	x	x	x	x	x	x	x	x	x	x	x	x
Ceylon		x	x	x	x	x	x	x	x	x			x	
Chile	x	x	x	x	x	x		x	x	x	x		x	
China	x	x	x	x	x	x	x	x	x	x		x	x	
Colombia	x	x	x	x	x	x	x	x	x	x			x	
Costa Rica	x	x	x	x	x	x		x	x	x			x	
Cuba	x	x	x	x	x	x	x	x	x	x			x	
Czechoslovakia	x	x	x	x	x	x	x	x	x	x	x	x	x	
Denmark	x	x	x	x	x	x	x	x	x	x	x		x	
Dominican Republic	x	x	x	x	x	x	x	x	x	x		x	x	
Ecuador	x	x	x	x	x	x		x	x	x			x	
Egypt	x	x	x	x	x	x	x	x	x	x		x	x	
El Salvador	x	x	x	x	x	x	x	x	x	x			x	

Ethiopia ....

Finland ....

France ....

German Federal Republic

Greece ....

Guatemala ....

Haiti ....

Honduras ....

Hungary ....

Iceland ....

India ....

Indonesia ....

Iran ....

Iraq ....

Ireland ....

Israel ....

Italy ....

Japan ....

Jordan ....

Korea ....

Lebanon ....

Liberia ....

Luxembourg ....

Mexico ....

Netherlands ....

New Zealand ....

Nicaragua ....

Norway ....

TABLE 5. MEMBERS OF THE UNITED NATIONS AND THE SPECIALIZED AGENCIES
(As of August 1, 1951) (Continued)

Member	UN	ILO	UPU	ITU	FAO	UNESCO	ICAO	WHO	Bank	Fund	IRO	WMO	(ITO)[1]	(IMCO)[1]
Pakistan	x	x	x	x	x	x	x	x	x	x		x	x	
Panama	x	x	x	x	x	x		x	x	x		x	x	
Paraguay	x		x	x	x		x	x	x	x		x		
Peru	x	x	x	x	x	x	x	x	x	x		x	x	
Philippines	x	x	x	x	x	x	x	x	x	x		x	x	
Poland	x	x	x	x	x	x	x	x	x			x	x	
Portugal	x	x	x	x	x		x	x				x		
Rumania	x		x	x				x				x		
Saudi Arabia	x		x	x	x	x		x						
Spain				x	x	x	x	x				x	x	
Sweden	x	x	x	x	x	x	x	x				x	x	x
Switzerland		x	x	x	x	x	x	x			x	x		
Syria	x	x	x	x	x	x	x	x	x	x		x	x	
Thailand	x	x	x	x	x	x	x	x	x	x		x	x	
Turkey	x	x	x	x	x	x	x	x	x	x		x	x	
Ukrainian S.S.R. .	x	x	x	x										
Union of South Africa ...	x		x	x	x	x	x	x	x	x		x	x	
U.S.S.R.	x		x	x										
United Kingdom ..	x	x	x	x	x	x	x	x	x	x	x	x	x	x
United States	x	x	x	x	x	x	x	x	x	x	x	x	x	x
Uruguay	x	x	x	x	x	x		x	x	x		x	x	
Venezuela	x	x	x	x	x	x	x	x	x	x	x	x	x	
Yemen	x	x	x											
Yugoslavia	x	x	x	x	x	x		x	x	x		x		
Total[2]	60	64	86	84	66	64	57	78	49	49	18	66	52	12

¹ Not yet formally established. The information given is for the Interim Commission of the International Trade Organization and the Preparatory Committee of the Intergovernmental Maritime Consultative Organization.

² The totals include, in addition to the members given, the following:

ILO: Viet-Nam. Japan has been admitted, but must still ratify the ILO Constitution.

UPU: Belgian Congo; French Morocco; French overseas territories; Indochina; Netherlands Antilles and Surinam; Portuguese Colonies of West Africa; Portuguese Colonies of East Africa, Asia, and Oceania; San Marino; Tunisia; United Kingdom overseas colonies, protectorates and territories under trusteeship; United States possessions; Vatican City.

ITU: Belgian Congo and territory of Ruanda Urundi; French protectorates of Morocco and Tunisia; overseas territories of the French Republic and territories administered as such; Monaco; Portuguese colonies; Southern Rhodesia; colonies, protectorates, overseas territories and territories under Mandate or Trusteeship of the United Kingdom; territories of the United States; Vatican City; Spanish zone of Morocco and the totality of Spanish possessions. Yemen has yet to accede to the ITU Convention. Korea has been approved for membership but an instrument of accession must be deposited before Korea can become a member. A few of the signatories of the ITU Convention have not yet ratified it.

FAO: Cambodia; Viet-Nam. Hungary has given notice of withdrawal, effective January 25, 1952.

UNESCO: Cambodia; Laos; Monaco; Viet-Nam.

WHO: Cambodia; Laos; Monaco; Viet-Nam. Southern Rhodesia is an associate member. Ten members have notified WHO of their withdrawal, and the World Health Assembly has resolved that their resumption of active membership would be welcomed at any time. They are: Albania, Bulgaria, Byelorussian S.S.R., China, Czechoslovakia, Hungary, Poland, Rumania, Ukrainian S.S.R., and the Soviet Union.

WMO: Belgian Congo; Bermuda; British central African territories; British east African territories; British Malayan territories; British west African territories; French Cameroons; French Equatorial Africa; French Morocco; French Oceania; French Somaliland; French Togo; French West Africa; Hong Kong; Indochina; Madagascar; New Caledonia; Portuguese East Africa; Portuguese West Africa; Tunisia. Bulgaria and Ceylon have been admitted as members, but have not yet deposited their instruments of accession to the WMO Convention.

ITO: Southern Rhodesia.

LABOR STANDARDS

Social justice to the working peoples of the world is recognized as a basic condition of a durable peace. The International Labor Organization was established in 1919 to promote the improvement of economic and social conditions among working people everywhere. Between the two world wars, the ILO completed thousands of studies, held hundreds of conferences, and sent scores of missions to give expert assistance. Some of its conventions which were adopted called for an eight-hour day and a forty-eight-hour week, holidays with pay, improved working conditions on ships, freedom of association and the right to organize, and sickness and old-age insurance. Other conventions were designed to forbid forced labor, nightwork of women, employment of women in underground mines, employment of children under fifteen years of age, and the use of white lead in paint.

At a conference in 1944, the ILO adopted the Declaration of Philadelphia which reaffirmed the principles that labor is not a commodity, that poverty anywhere constitutes a danger to prosperity everywhere, and that freedom of expression and of association are essential to sustained progress. The Declaration went on to recognize that it is a solemn obligation of the ILO to promote objectives including full employment and a living wage; extension of social security and medical care; maternity protection and child welfare; adequate food, housing, and recreation; the right to bargain collectively; equality of educational and vocational opportunity; and adequate health and safety measures.

In 1946 the ILO became a specialized agency of the United Nations. It has continued its basic program and objectives, with some change in emphasis to meet the special problems and opportunities which have existed in recent years. Manpower problems continue to have high priority in the work of the Organization. Exchanges of views and of technical experience are given by discussions in conferences and committees, the establishment of regional manpower offices to furnish technical assistance, the sending of advisory commissions upon request, and the distribution of information. The subjects of major concern in this connection include the adjustment of labor supply and demand, vocational guidance and training, and international migration. In 1949 a field office for Asia and the Far East was established, and a regional conference on technical and vocational training was held at Singapore. Later, a similar office for Latin America was opened. Advisory missions have been sent to Italy, Turkey, Egypt, and other countries in the Near East. A vitally important method for adjusting labor supply and demand is the employment service, by which workers and employers are brought into touch with each other. The ILO has encouraged the expansion of such services in various ways, and has prepared a draft convention on the subject.

The prevention of unemployment has always been one of the major objectives of the ILO. This question, which had been very prominent during the 1930's, required new attention as a substantial amount of unemployment developed in several countries in 1948 and 1949. The ILO has emphasized the importance of effective institutional arrangements for implementing full employment policy. Complete and reliable statistics also are essential for the framing and administration of full employment policies, and the ILO has attempted to obtain improvements in this connection. Comprehensive studies have been made of various technical factors relating to the maintenance of full employment. One example may be cited here: during 1949, a committee of the ILO considered the problem of instability in the construction industry and formulated several conclusions as to timing of public works and the coordination of financial resources.

Conventions adopted by the ILO in the field of social security cover employees in industry, commerce, and agriculture. They provide for compulsory insurance against sickness, old age, and death and for payment of compensation for industrial accidents and occupational diseases. New and broader social security plans have been produced by a number of governments during the past few years, and the ILO has been working toward the formulation of recommendations based on the concepts of comprehensive coverage and of social adequacy as the main criterion of benefits to be paid. A Committee of Social Security Experts met in New Zealand early in 1950 to lay the basis for this development. A questionnaire was drafted for the purpose of obtaining the views of governments on the objectives and minimum standards of social security for discussion at the thirty-fourth session of the International Labor Conference in 1951.

An example of a special problem handled with ILO assistance is the coordination of the application of national social security systems to boatmen navigating the Rhine. Since World War II, the countries bordering on the Rhine have made their social security systems more complete and more nearly equal. As the result of a conference convened by ILO in 1949, it was possible to secure uniformity of treatment for all boatmen engaged in commercial navigation on the Rhine. This is based on equality for the nationals of all participating states and the determination of social security legislation applicable to the crew of a vessel by reference to the country in which the owner of the vessel has his principal place of business. The same conference also dealt with uniform conditions of work for boatmen on the Rhine.

Freedom of association and the right to organize have always been of vital concern to the labor movement. In 1949 the ILO adopted a draft convention which would establish the right of both workers and employers to join organizations of their own choice. Ratification of this convention would place one of the fundamental rights of man in an international treaty. The most appropriate method for international examination of alleged infringements of trade-union rights has been discussed. It was decided to establish a fact-finding and conciliation commission for this purpose.

The broad field of industrial safety has been attacked from several angles throughout the history of the ILO. Conventions and recommendations have been made on such matters as inspection, prevention of industrial accidents, marking of weight on heavy vessels in sea transport, and protection of building workers. During 1949 a model code of safety regulations for underground work in coal mines was adopted, and work was begun on similar codes for civil engineering and the chemical industry. The magnitude and value of this type of work may be indicated by the fact that the revised model code of safety regulations for industrial establishments includes several thousand provisions and runs to nearly 500 pages of print. It is hoped that this model code will be especially helpful to the underdeveloped countries in building up their own codes of industrial safety regulations.

Maritime labor is another subject of special concern to the ILO. A conference held in Seattle, Washington, in 1946 resulted in the most comprehensive set of provisions governing life at sea ever drafted. Under these provisions, a seaman must have a preemployment medical examination and subsequent periodic examinations. To qualify as an able seaman, he must have three years' experience and must pass a practical test of seamanship. One convention is devoted to such matters as location of crew quarters, sleeping space, size and construction of berths, number of washrooms, lighting, ventilation, heating, the mess, and recreational facilities. Others deal with food supplies and the qualification of cooks.

The ILO constitution states as urgent requirements the provision of an adequate living wage and recognition of the principle of equal remuneration for work of equal value. In order to implement these principles, the ILO has adopted a number of conventions and recommendations and has initiated discussions and studies. These deal with such questions as the machinery for establishing minimum wages, the rate of wages adequate for a reasonable standard of living, guaranteed wages, protection against unjustified deductions, fair-wage clauses in public contracts, and equal pay for men and women. Attention is being given to questions connected with agricultural wages.

The problems of women and children have received special consideration. These include nightwork and heavy labor, minimum age limits in particular occupations, employment of women before and after childbirth, maternity benefits, provision of day nurseries, and standards for domestic work.

The ILO works by the indirect methods of discussion, fact finding, and recommendation. Therefore, its accomplishments are rather difficult to measure. It cannot reduce the hours of labor or provide an increase in wages by fiat. One cannot say that it achieved this or that tangible result on such and such a day. It is impossible, however, to make even a cursory examination of the work of the ILO without coming to the conclusion that it has had, and continues to have, an important cumulative effect upon working conditions. Its accomplishments, although incapable of precise measurement, are quite real.

One of the outstanding trends in ILO work during the past few years has been the increasing emphasis on technical assistance, which is being used to supplement the traditional methods of conference, discussion, fact finding, draft conventions, etc., in various fields of activity. Since 1948, advisory missions have made studies and recommendations on social policy and labor legislation in Turkey; facilities for vocational and technical training in ten Latin-American countries; problems of migration and land settlement in seven Latin-American countries; manpower facilities and needs in the Middle East; training within industry in eight European countries; manpower problems and vocational training in Egypt, Greece, India, and Pakistan; social security in the Philippines, Czechoslovakia, Iran, Egypt, and India; labor statistics in Venezuela; social conditions in the petroleum industry in Iran and Iraq; conditions of work on plantations in Ceylon and India; and others. Written technical advice, in contrast to visiting missions, is provided frequently on a wide variety of questions. A fellowships program has been established to encourage and provide financial assistance for study in such fields as employment organization, vocational training and guidance, social security administration, industrial relations, labor inspection, and industrial health, safety, and welfare. Also, the ILO participates in the expanded cooperative program of technical assistance set up under the auspices of the Economic and Social Council.

One effect of the technical-assistance program is to place more emphasis on agricultural questions in the underdeveloped areas, in contrast to the problems of the highly industrialized countries. The ILO has always been concerned with the welfare of agricultural labor, but work was not pursued so intensively in this field because of the urgency of industrial problems in the leading member states, the complexity of the agricultural situation, and the fact that farm workers were not as highly organized as their industrial brothers. A marked tendency to shift this emphasis has occurred as interest has grown in the idea of international cooperation for technical assistance to the underdeveloped countries.

TRANSPORT AND COMMUNICATIONS

Technological improvements in transport and communications were among the leading influences in the development of modern international organization. Of the thirteen specialized agencies in operation or being constituted, five are concerned with work in these fields.[4]

[4] Universal Postal Union, International Telecommunication Union, International Civil Aviation Organization, International Maritime Consultative Organization, and World Meteorological Organization. The first two of these are the only specialized agencies which were originally established in the nineteenth century.

The Universal Postal Union has continued its task of administering the services necessary for uniting the world in a single postal territory for the reciprocal exchange of correspondence. The importance of this work may be gauged from the fact that the number of pieces of correspondence moving internationally increased from less than 144,000,000 in 1875 to more than 3,256,000,000 in 1930. There was a sharp drop during the war, but by 1947 the figure had risen to approximately 2,000,000,000 pieces.

The twelfth Universal Postal Congress, which met in 1947, agreed on a number of revisions in its basic provisions and regulations. These included such matters as more efficient arrangements for international money order and cash-on-delivery services; and changes in the weight limits and mailing cost of printed papers and periodicals. Suggestions were made on limitations of payments to air transport companies. Minor revisions were made in the agreement concerning insured letters, parcel post, and collection of bills. The agreement on subscriptions to newspapers and periodicals remained unchanged.

The international bureau, or permanent secretariat, of UPU compiles information and issues publications of great usefulness to postal authorities. These include such reference materials as a list of air-mail services, a list of airports, maps of air-mail lines, a world map of surface communication routes, and a directory of post offices. As a means of keeping all members informed of new developments, the bureau issues a monthly journal, *L'Union Postale,* in Arabic, Chinese, English, French, Russian, and Spanish. The bureau is also a godsend to philatelists, since it receives postage stamps of all types used in the territory of each member and is required to distribute them to all other members. In 1948, for example, 2,542 different kinds of stamps were received and distributed. In addition to these and other traditional services, the bureau is developing an exchange of technical information among the various postal administrations.

The major task of the International Telecommunication Union in recent years has been concerned with the rapid developments and technical complexities of radio transmission. The Administrative Radio Conference, meeting in Atlantic City in 1947, revised the radio regulations of 1938 which had been made obsolete by scientific advances. A new world-wide frequency allocation table extending up to 10,500,000 kilocycles was set up. The recent importance of the higher frequencies is shown by the fact that in 1938 the spectrum had been charted only up to 200,000 kilocycles. Revised frequency bands were allocated, and practical machinery for putting the new allocations into effect was created. The revised regulations also cover the details of reservation of "distress frequencies" for lifesaving and rescue work; station identification signals; frequencies for air and marine navigational aids such as radar stations and for meteorological messages; and other matters relating to the efficient use of radio. The World Frequency Assignment List is a document of some 1,250 pages covering all frequencies in the radio spectrum from 15 kilocycles to 12,500 megacycles and recording the priorities of every nation for their use. This list is used in registering claims for frequencies and all negotiations between governments concerning alleged interferences are based upon the ITU records.

There is a great deal of international competition in the field of high-frequency broadcasting. The ITU is attempting to work out an equitable system for allocating space and time in each broadcasting band. The answer to this problem will not be found, however, in technical considerations alone, since strong political forces seek outlets for propaganda through international broadcasting.

The ITU also issues technical publications, including the periodical *Telecommunications Journal.*

The development of aviation has become one of the strongest influences in the field of international transport and communication. The first international commercial air service began between London and Paris a little over thirty years ago. In 1948 nearly a quarter of a million people were carried across the North Atlantic alone by air. Seventy different airlines, representing all major nations, have more than two thousand aircraft providing international service. In this situation there was obvious need to establish the International Civil Aviation Organization, in order to promote cooperation on the technical, economic, and legal aspects of international flying.

One of the most important duties of ICAO is to develop uniform standards of safety on international air routes. Traffic regulations for other types of vehicles are commonplace. Each nation has created its own rules of the road, but there are no radical differences within the confines of any one country. It is taken for granted that there must be traffic laws to prevent accidents, and that these laws must be about the same in all cities through which a motorist passes. Otherwise, travel by automobile would be impossibly dangerous. Flying is more swift and complex, and an airplane may cross several countries within a very short time. Lack of uniformity in flight rules and regulations would result in confusion and a large number of accidents.

ICAO attempts to achieve technical uniformity at a high level of quality. For example, an airplane must be structurally sound, and must carry enough fuel; the crew must have certain experience, knowledge, and skill; they must be physically fit; and adequate weather reports must be available for the planned route. The standards which have already gone into effect include those on personnel licensing; aeronautical maps and charts; rules of the air; meteorological codes; dimensional practices, to be used in air-ground communications; operation of aircraft on international scheduled services; aircraft nationality and registration marks; airworthiness; and facilitation of international air transport.

Another accomplishment of ICAO is the creation of a network of ocean weather stations in the North Atlantic, which has the greatest volume of transoceanic traffic and some of the most unpredictable weather in the world. The vessels operating this network cruise at designated locations. They send helium-filled balloons to a height of 60,000 feet, with mechanisms attached to give readings of the humidity, temperature, and pressure of the air. The upper-air observations are made every six hours, and surface weather conditions are recorded every three hours. These ships provide the current weather data which air transport requires, they are communications relay points for aircraft, and they serve as rescue posts for planes in distress. As a result of this service, a dramatic rescue took place in October, 1947, when sixty-nine passengers were saved from the *Bermuda Sky Queen*. About a year later, four crew members were saved from a sinking U.S. Air Force plane. In addition, passengers of sinking ships have been rescued and at least one ship saved from the ice.

Another ICAO project is the Icelandic joint-support agreement. Iceland is the logical location for weather observations, radio aids, and an area traffic center. These services are very costly, however, and residents of Iceland would not derive much direct benefit from them. Should each Icelander be expected to pay $4 a year to maintain them for airlines of other countries? The result is that ten nations share in the cost of providing area traffic control, meteorological stations, and communications services in Iceland.

The development of aviation has brought many legal problems. A typical task undertaken by ICAO is the conclusion of a convention on the international recognition of rights in aircraft. The chief importance of this convention lies in the fact that the very mobility of the airplane makes for difficulty in taking out mortgages. If a person loans money and takes a mortgage on aircraft, the property might be seized in another country for debt, and the investor would lose his money. The new convention makes it possible for mortgages and other property rights contracted in one country to be generally recognized. It will be much easier, therefore, for operators to borrow money for the purchase of new equipment.

The ICAO issues a periodic bulletin and other publications.

The Inter-Governmental Maritime Consultative Organization (IMCO) will parallel ICAO in the field of ocean shipping. The need for one central organization to perform administrative services under the numerous maritime conventions has been evident for a long time. The immediate impetus for the new organization, however, came from Allied experience during and after World War II in a series of intergovernmental shipping organizations.

The World Meteorological Organization was established to take over the work of an older nongovernmental organization in this field.[5] Millions of dollars depend upon taking advantage of favorable weather and upon adequate warning of bad weather. Such industries as aviation, shipping and trucking, agriculture, outdoor movies, resorts, sports, and building trades require ac-

[5] See p. 33.

curate information daily. Ships and planes need detailed information on weather conditions over wide areas. The international exchange of weather information is essential to permit accurate forecasting within national borders and to facilitate international travel. Under the procedures used by the WMO, meteorological information is made available from all parts of the world to experts who make the forecasts. As a result of this work, the vocabulary of meteorology has become an international language. In conjunction with the International Telecommunication Union, special frequencies have been set aside for transmitting weather information and warnings by radio. International standards for flight weather reporting have been worked out with the International Civil Aviation Organization.

The Transport and Communications Commission of the Economic and Social Council has considered and made recommendations on such international problems as inland transport; movement of persons and goods; transport statistics; standardized highway marking systems; and the coordination of activities in the fields of aviation, shipping, and telecommunications with respect to safety of life at sea and in the air. Passports and frontier formalities have been considered by experts on the subject, and the Economic and Social Council has expressed the view that it is desirable for these formalities to be reduced and simplified to the extent consistent with national security.

FOOD AND AGRICULTURE

The production and distribution of food is one of the most important problems of international cooperation in the economic and social field. A large proportion, probably two-thirds, of the world's population is perpetually undernourished, and millions of people are constantly subject to the threat of famine. The Food and Agriculture Organization of the United Nations was created in the recognition that hunger is a breeding ground for social unrest and conflict, and in the belief that ways could be found to develop and maintain an adequate food supply. The FAO encourages the use of modern tools and methods to increase crop yields. It promotes conservation of existing food supplies and searches for new sources. It studies problems of maldistribution and provides a forum for review of national policies. This agency does not operate a huge program of its own, but cooperates with governmental and other agencies in studies, reports, technical assistance, demonstration projects, conferences, and similar methods. A wide variety of projects has been undertaken. It is possible here only to indicate the nature of this work by brief descriptions of some of these activities.

The first thing done after the organization had been established was to make a survey of the world's food supplies in relation to needs. The World Food Survey, made by a group of experts and published in 1946, covered seventy countries and about 90 per cent of the world's population. This constituted a fundamental document on food supplies and estimates of the needs. This revealed that food supplies would have to be increased by more than 100 per cent in twenty-five years to bring the diets of the ill-fed up to a reasonably good level and to allow for population growth. Therefore, the world food problem is one of expansion and distribution, not one of overproduction and surpluses.

The FAO was established to deal with work of a long-term nature. However, it soon appeared that more immediate functions would have to be assumed because of the critical postwar food shortage. Starving people were not interested in long-term programs. The FAO assumed some of the agricultural rehabilitation work begun by the United Nations Relief and Rehabilitation Administration, a temporary agency. Another emergency job was the initiation of the International Emergency Food Council to recommend the allocation of scarce foodstuffs and some other products among importing countries. If this had not been done, the food situation in many countries would have been even worse. This work was later absorbed by the FAO. Although the allocated authority consisted only in the power to make recommendations, the extent to which the latter were carried out showed that international cooperation was a real factor in this important matter.

Rice is a staple food for half the world's population. In 1949, the FAO organized an International Rice Commission, which is the first international body to be concerned expressly with problems of the production and use of one food. Its projects include the scientific cataloguing of rice varieties and the launching of work on rice breeding.

Rinderpest is a deadly virus disease of bovine animals that is especially widespread in the Far East, Asia, and Africa. It kills close to a million cattle a year in China alone. FAO veterinarians, with the cooperation of the Chinese Ministry of Agriculture, developed an improved vaccine and assisted in working out an annual program of vaccination for fifteen million animals. With use of the vaccine developed in China, similar programs have been set up in a number of other countries in Africa and Asia. Considerable work also has been done on other animal diseases, such as hog cholera, erysipelas, foot-and-mouth disease, tuberculosis of cattle, and poultry diseases.

One very interesting project has to do with rotenone, the insecticide which places the gardener on somewhat equal terms with the insects. In China before World War II, modern insecticides were used by only a few of the richest farmers. However, native plants had been used for centuries to kill insects. One plant, derris, was known as "fish poison." It had been discovered long ago that if the roots of the derris vine were thrown into a pond, the fish would be killed and rise to the top. The fish killed in this manner could be eaten without ill effects to human beings. Derris root, in short, has the characteristic of being poisonous to cold-blooded animals and harmless to warm-blooded ones. The insecticide manufactured from it is called "rotenone."

Derris grows in China in both a wild and a cultivated state, but methods of applying it were limited and provincial. Some farmers, for example, make their own insecticides by grinding derris root and mixing it with clay. An FAO team in China found a boarded-up war plant in Shanghai and undertook the manufacture of rotenone. They made an extractor from kerosene drums, pipe, and junk, and took other technical short cuts. Simple sprayers and dusters were also made. As a result, rice production increased by four or five bushels per acre.

Other FAO projects include, among others, a fight on predatory locusts; hybrid-maize breeding; soil-fertility practices; improvement of forestry programs and fisheries resources; and control of infestation of food in storage by rats, molds, and fungi. A catalogue of genetic stocks has been undertaken. This will include data on all varieties of food plants wherever they may be found. A plant breeder, needing some particular quality for a strain which he hopes to produce, will have the world's total varieties of that plant under his survey through the FAO catalogue. Another service which has been started is a seed stock of outstanding varieties of cereals, grasses, legumes, oil seeds, and vegetables. This stock is maintained at Rome, Italy, and samples are distributed for experimental purposes to plant breeders around the world. Some excellent studies and statistical reports have been made. These range from the surveys of world food and agriculture to such specialized subjects as salted cod.

FINANCE

The flow of investment capital and the stability of exchange rates are of great importance for the promotion of international trade, and therefore for international cooperation in the economic field. Countries with surplus funds need foreign investment outlets, and other countries need to borrow capital to develop their economies. The International Bank for Reconstruction and Development is the first international organization for long-term foreign lending. Creditor as well as debtor countries are represented on its board; thus it affords the unique opportunity for both lenders and borrowers to participate in drafting its policies.

Immediately after World War II the attention of the Bank was directed to Europe, where the need was urgent and the best opportunity existed to raise levels of productivity quickly. Loans for reconstruction purposes included $250 million to France, $195 million to the Netherlands, $40 million to Denmark, and $12 million to Luxembourg. The agreements provided for the purchase of specific commodities which the borrowing countries needed to step up production and to contribute to the reconstruction of Europe. The funds were used mainly for industrial and agricultural machinery, transportation equipment, and basic raw materials. Other loans made by the Bank to the European area included $12 million to four Dutch shipping companies for the purchase of six merchant vessels, and $16 million to Belgium for reequipment of its steel and power industries.

As time went on the major attention of the Bank was shifted in two ways. When the Marshall Plan went into operation, reconstruction loans for Western Europe were available through the Economic Cooperation Administration. The Bank, accordingly, used its funds to serve other parts of the world. The other change was a shift in emphasis from reconstruction to development. The more recent loans have been made for developing productive facilities and resources rather than for repairing wartime damage.

Loans of a development type include $16 million to instrumentalities of the Chilean government for the development of hydroelectric power and water resources, and the importation of modern agricultural machinery; $34.1 million to agencies of the Mexican government for electric-power development; and $75 million [6] to a Brazilian corporation for the expansion of hydroelectric-power facilities and telephone installations. India was the first country in Asia to receive a loan from the Bank. Transportation is a critical problem there, and $34 million was made available for the reconstruction and development of state-owned railways. Proceeds will be used to finance part of the purchase price of locomotives, boilers, and spare parts.

An interesting project in India arose from the fact that much good agricultural land had gone out of cultivation because of the inroads of a weed known as "kans grass." This is a stubborn plant with deep roots. The Indian government had made experiments to eradicate it by deep ploughing, using tractors left by the U.S. Army. The experiments were successful, and the government proposed to tackle the job in many parts of central India over a total area as large as the state of Connecticut. Since this plan offered a cheap means for a very urgent increase in food production, a loan of $10 million was made for the importation of tractors and other equipment to clear the land.

Loans have been made for the development of timber resources in Finland and Yugoslavia, and for the construction of a hydroelectric plant in El Salvador. In July, 1950, two loans were made to Turkey, where inadequate harbor facilities had resulted in overcrowding and excessive port charges, thereby limiting both foreign trade and essential coastwise traffic. A loan of $12.5 million was made for the development of Turkey's major ports over a period of twenty-five years. In addition, a loan of $3.9 million was made to finance the construction of grain-storage facilities. These should play an important role in agricultural development. Grain is Turkey's largest crop, but present storage facilities are inadequate and poorly equipped. In 1950, loans for development projects were also made to Australia, Colombia, Ethiopia, Thailand, and Uruguay. By 1951, the total amount of loans had passed the billion-dollar mark.

[6] Later increased to $90 million.

Before a loan is made, the Bank satisfies itself that the borrower would be unable to obtain the loan in the private-capital market under reasonable conditions, that the project is soundly conceived, and that the borrower will be able to repay. The process of assuring itself that these conditions have been met has led the Bank into providing a useful service of surveys and advice to governments. Some twenty countries have been visited, advice and assistance have been made available, and loan negotiations are in progress.

The accomplishments of the International Monetary Fund are difficult to state, because of the highly technical and confidential nature of its work and because so many different factors enter into the international financial situation. The Fund was designed to provide machinery for consultation on international monetary problems, and to facilitate the expansion and balanced growth of international trade; to promote stability of currency exchange, and to avoid competitive depreciation; to eliminate foreign-exchange restrictions on current transactions; and to make available short-term financial assistance, so that temporary maladjustments in the balance of payments could be corrected without resort to restrictive measures.

The Fund has provided the machinery of consultation, and it has worked toward the other objectives. By 1950, par values of more than forty national currencies had been established by international agreement. During its first two years of operation, the Fund extended credits to seventeen of its members in a total amount of $725,500,000. Although this type of activity was intended to eliminate short-term maladjustments, a substantial portion of the credits went to countries in which far-reaching economic adjustments would be necessary to establish a genuine equilibrium in the balance of payments. The major underlying problem is that of a dollar shortage. The countries which need goods from the United States have been unable to earn the dollars to pay for them. Greatly increased production in those countries and a basic realignment of export-import transactions are necessary to change this situation. In the meantime, the Fund has made a significant contribution, but its assistance represents only a small percentage of the total dollar aid which has been made available through the Economic Recovery Administration (Marshall Plan) and in other ways. The Fund is in a position to correct temporary balance-of-payment maladjustments in a genuine multilateral trading system, but it cannot cure the world's deep-seated economic ills.

The most dramatic test of the Fund came with the devaluation of the British pound and a number of other currencies in 1949. The measures were taken in cooperation and consultation with the Fund, which played a useful role in securing a proper range of currency relationships. These devaluations were not followed by a cycle of competitive depreciations, such as occurred in the 1930's, but how much of this was due to the International Monetary Fund and how much to basic economic factors is a moot point.

The financial work of the United Nations is not limited to that of the Bank and the Fund. The Economic and Social Council is interested in financial questions and has established a fiscal commission as a subsidiary organ. In 1947 the Council requested the Secretary-General to build up a fiscal information service. Information has been compiled and various studies made in this field. Publications have been issued on such subjects as public debt and international tax agreements.

Economic Development

The specialized agencies of the United Nations deal with the major phases of international economic and social cooperation. There is, however, a need for coordination, and there are certain over-all problems of economic development which cannot be handled adequately on the basis of separate functional agencies. The Economic and Social Council is responsible for the general coordination of programs in this field, and it has undertaken to promote world economic development by the establishment of regional economic commissions, the promotion of international trade, conferences on certain basic problems of general interest, and a program of technical assistance.

The Economic Commission for Europe, created by a resolution of the Economic and Social Council in March, 1947, was the first regional agency of the United Nations. Later, two other regional economic commissions were established, one for Latin America and one for Asia and the Far East. Their functions are to initiate and participate in measures for concerted action; to make or sponsor studies of economic and technological problems and developments; and to undertake or sponsor the collection, evaluation, and dissemination of economic, technological, and statistical information. These regional economic commissions operate on very small budgets, and they can take no action without agreement of the countries concerned. They provide a forum for discussion and a clearinghouse for information. Arrangements are made for representatives of various countries to meet and to talk over the common problems of the area. The result is collective, rather than individual, examination of economic questions of mutual interest.

The type of work done by the regional economic commissions can best be explained by a few illustrations. One of the greatest recovery needs in postwar Europe was an increase in coal production. The United States seemed the most likely source for machinery to modernize the mines, but through a list and detailed description of mining machinery needs it was found that a large proportion of the items could be supplied by manufacturing resources in Europe. Another difficult problem was the shortage of wood to reinforce the coal pits. The deficit in 1948 amounted to twenty-five million pit props. The Coal Committee of ECE provided a forum through which the various countries could see how much pitwood was available and decide how it should be shared. The allocations arrived at in this way were only recommendations, not binding decisions, but nonetheless a helpful service was provided. Another example was the shortage of refractories to reline steel furnaces needed for economic recovery in Italy. Silica bricks could be made in the British and American zones of occupied Germany if the necessary quartzite could be obtained from the French zone. Labor was not available at the quartzite mines, and the Italians offered to send the manpower and accept the material produced in payment. The Americans helped by supplying information on methods of mining quartzite in Alaska, thus making it possible for work to proceed during the winter months. Action followed, the French government gave priority to the job, including extra cigarettes to the miners, and the silica brick crisis was met. The regional economic commissions cannot finance or operate huge projects, but they can be very helpful in ironing out difficulties and providing a cooperative method for eliminating bottlenecks which could not be removed by individual countries acting separately.

The expansion of international trade is essential to the development of a sound world economic order. Three major conferences to negotiate on tariff reductions have been held since 1946: one in Geneva; one at Annecy, France; and one at Torquay, England. A fifty-six-nation conference on trade and employment met in Havana during the winter of 1947–1948. A charter was drafted, by which the countries ratifying it would agree to negotiate for the reduction of tariffs, to observe certain detailed rules for the reduction or elimination of other trade barriers, to refrain from the use of quotas except under carefully defined circumstances, to refrain from certain restrictive business practices, and to comply with equitable principles in concluding commodity agreements. When this charter is accepted by enough governments, the International Trade Organization (ITO) will come into existence as a specialized agency of the United Nations. Its function will be to provide a forum for discussion and a mechanism for settling disputes in this field. In the meantime, an Interim Commission is doing preparatory work. The United States, which took a leading part in initiating the proposed ITO, has not ratified the agreement. Until this is done, there seems to be very little hope for its establishment or effectiveness.

There have been important developments with respect to commodity problems. In August, 1949, the International Wheat Agreement entered into force between four exporting and thirty-two importing countries. By June, 1950, sales totaling 14,551,000 metric tons of wheat annually had been guaranteed under the terms of this agreement. Other commodities which have been under study and discussion include tin, cotton, and sugar.

As an example of a conference on an important subject of general concern, the United Nations Conference on the Conservation and Utilization of Resources may be mentioned. This Conference was held at Lake Success in 1949, and was the first occasion on which scientists and other experts from all over the world met at the invitation of the United Nations to exchange information and discuss common problems. A total of 706 experts from more than fifty countries attended. In addition, 22 nongovernmental organizations and 152 learned scientific societies sent representatives. The topics of chief concern were minerals, forests, fuels and energy, water, land, and fish and wildlife. It was decided to publish the full records and documentation of the Conference. There was general agreement that many of the ideas and suggestions should be followed up in connection with various programs with which the United Nations is concerned.

The program of technical assistance to underdeveloped areas [7] has become one of greatest importance in the field of international cooperation. The rate of technological progress in different geographic areas has been very unequal, and many parts of the world do not share in the advantages of modern techniques. It was estimated that in 1949 more than half the world's population received annual incomes averaging less than $100 per capita, as compared with better than $1,400 for the United States. The economy of the underdeveloped areas is typically agrarian, but the average output per person in agriculture is less than one-tenth that in the more advanced countries. Average life expectancy is low, illiteracy is widespread, communicable diseases are prevalent, malnutrition is the rule, and starvation often occurs.

The gap between the most and the least highly developed countries has been increasing, in spite of the growing interdependence of the modern world. Higher levels of output and better economic organization make it easier to produce capital for further development. Technological progress has a cumulative effect, so that the less developed countries fall farther behind, relatively speaking. The people in these areas, however, are becoming more aware of and dissatisfied with their situation, and they are anxious to increase productivity and raise their living standards. It is also obvious that the wide gap between great wealth and grinding poverty constitutes a source of unrest and instability. Added to these considerations is the recognition that prosperity is indivisible or, to put it another way, that prosperous customers are good for business. Here, then, is a program which appeals to internationalist idealism by proposing to help the world's underprivileged peoples, and which offers the hard-boiled realist bigger and better markets. It also seems to provide an opportunity to allay some of the unrest and dissatisfaction which tend to erupt in open violence and which are a continual menace to international peace.

The United Nations had been providing technical assistance for economic development in various ways. In December, 1948, the General Assembly passed a resolution calling for an expansion of this program. The next month President Truman, in his inaugural address, proposed "a bold new program for making the benefits of our scientific advances and industrial progress

[7] The term "underdeveloped" is now used instead of the more patronizing and resented word "backward."

available for the improvement and growth of under-developed areas." He said, in part, that [8]

Our aim should be to help the free peoples of the world, through their own efforts to produce more food, more clothing, more materials for housing, and more mechanical power to lighten their burdens.

We invite other countries to pool their technological resources in this undertaking. Their contributions will be warmly welcomed. This should be a cooperative enterprise in which all nations work together through the United Nations and its specialized agencies wherever practicable. It must be a world-wide effort for the achievement of peace, plenty, and freedom.

Early in 1949 the Economic and Social Council passed a resolution requesting the Secretary-General, in consultation with the interested specialized agencies, to prepare a plan for an expanded cooperative plan of technical assistance for economic development. At its session in the fall of 1949, the General Assembly unanimously endorsed this program. In extending technical assistance, the participating organizations are instructed to observe certain general principles, including the following: (1) assistance shall be given only on request in agreement with the government concerned; (2) the assistance furnished shall not be a means of foreign economic and political interference; (3) distinctions arising from the political structure of the country requiring assistance, or from the race or religion of its population, shall be avoided; and (4) in establishing priorities, due regard shall be paid to the urgency of needs and the geographical distribution of applicants.

The amount of $288,000 for technical assistance had been included in the United Nations budget for 1949. This was increased to $508,420 for 1950, and the same amount for 1951. Under the regular 1950 program, sixteen countries requested expert advice, and approximately fifty experts of some twenty different nationalities were made available. The forms of the proposed assistance are technical advisory services, training, demonstration projects, pilot plants, and dissemination of technical information. At a conference in June, 1950, representatives of fifty governments pledged contributions of about $20 million, over and above the regular United Nations budget. Under the expanded program, 265 requests were received from fifty-five governments by the end of 1950.

One of the advantages of this program is that it can achieve substantial results with a very small expenditure of funds. The export of know-how does not need to be a costly operation. Slight technical improvements, which may be quickly suggested by an expert, can make a real difference in food production per acre, for example. All this is valuable and useful work, and should not be underestimated. The problem of economic development on a large scale, however, raises the question of capital investments in many times

[8] This was the famous "Point Four" proposal.

the amounts yet made available.   Private investors are not likely to be interested unless the loans are made in areas with stable social and political conditions, or unless they receive government guarantees against loss.   The only alternative, so far as private investment is concerned, is the type of speculative capital which asks for enormous profits as compensations for unusual risks. This is obviously an undesirable method in the circumstances.   Direct government financing raises the specter of economic imperialism, unless a genuine internationalized system of capital investment can be worked out through the United Nations.   In the meantime, the program of technical assistance for economic development goes ahead in a modest way.   This is potentially one of the most significant trends in the field of international economic and social cooperation.[9]

HEALTH

It has been recognized for a long time that the protection of health requires international cooperation.   Germs do not respect international boundaries, and they enter a country without the sanction of passport or visa.   At the San Francisco Conference in 1945, health was considered a field of United Nations concern.   One of the first acts of the Economic and Social Council was the creation of a technical preparatory committee to prepare for an international health conference.   This conference, which was held in June, 1946, drafted the constitution of the World Health Organization (WHO).   The interim preparatory commission for WHO was granted unusual operating powers in view of the acute postwar health problems.   Thus activities could be undertaken before the formal establishment of WHO itself.

One of the first projects was a malaria-control program in Greece, where this disease attacked one to three million persons annually and resulted in thousands of deaths.   A nationwide campaign was started by the Greek government in 1946 with the assistance first of UNRRA and later of a WHO mission.   Some 96,000 acres of malarious swamps were sprayed from airplanes with DDT, and several hundred thousand houses were sprayed by hand. After two years the death rate had dropped sharply, and in some regions the incidence had fallen from 85 to 5 per cent.   The control of malarial mosquitoes and the Dacas fly also made possible a substantial increase in rice and olive production.   In 1949, antimalarial operations were carried on in twenty different countries.

For the first time in history, tuberculosis is being fought on an international scale by the coordinated efforts of medical and health personnel, with laboratory and other technical facilities.   This program calls for tuberculin testing of 50,000,000 children in Europe alone.   Tuberculosis centers were established

[9] For a description of this program, see *United Nations Work and Programs for Technical Assistance*, UN Department of Public Information, April, 1951.

and studies begun in countries of Asia, Africa, and Latin America. In India, WHO installed the first BCG (vaccine) laboratory in that country. By December, 1949, tests for tuberculosis had been given to 18,000,000 children and young adults, and 8,400,000 had been immunized against infection.

A dramatic success for international cooperation in the field of health was scored in connection with the outbreak of a serious cholera epidemic in Egypt in the autumn of 1947. Cholera has always been a dread disease, and strict quarantines have been enforced against its spread. Modern transportation, however, creates new problems. The incubation period for cholera is about five days. Formerly a traveler who contracted the disease would fall sick before his ship could reach a distant point, and quarantine regulations could be enforced. With air travel, an American tourist might pick up the germ in Cairo, for example, spend a day or two in Paris and London, and be back in New York or Washington before he showed any symptoms. Under these conditions a serious cholera epidemic could spread far and rapidly.

In the Egyptian epidemic, 20,877 cases with a mortality rate of almost 50 per cent were reported within eight weeks. The interim commission of WHO was consulted by cable and immediately went into action. Thirty-six countries connected with Egypt by land, sea, or air routes, as well as the WHO epidemiological station at Singapore and the Pan American Sanitary Bureau at Washington, were kept informed on the situation, thus enabling them to take the necessary quarantine measures. WHO collected information on the potential production of cholera vaccine; supplied the vaccine promptly at greatly reduced cost; served as a procurement agency and sent large quantities of essential drugs and medical supplies to Egypt by chartered plane; and provided the Egyptian government with information on current methods of cholera control. That government, with WHO advice and assistance, undertook to inoculate every person in Egypt. As a result of these measures, an all-time world's record for halting a major epidemic was established.

The WHO has provided the assistance of experts and demonstration teams to help member countries to organize or expand programs in the six priority fields of malaria, tuberculosis, venereal diseases, nutrition, maternal and child health, and environmental sanitation. The international disease-reporting services have been expanded, so that quarantine officers may receive faster and more complete information. Assistance is given to governments for the organization of public health services, and about two hundred fellowships a year are awarded for the training of public health personnel. The technical services of WHO include the fields of biological standardization, international pharmacopoeia, health statistics, and revision of international sanitary conventions.

The WHO has a strong interest in the program of technical assistance for economic development, on the thesis that the world cannot rise to economic health on the backs of unhealthy people. Throughout the underdeveloped areas of the world, there is much suffering and countless human lives are wasted on account of diseases which could be prevented by relatively simple procedures. Other diseases in the same areas could be controlled only by techniques requiring much greater professional training and an organized large-scale effort. In any case, economic development cannot progress very far without adequate measures for the protection of public health.

REFUGEES

At the end of World War II there were about eight million refugees and displaced persons in Central Europe. About seven million were repatriated by the allied armies and by UNRRA, but most of the remaining million would not voluntarily return to their countries of origin. The great majority of these were from areas to which the Soviet system had been extended, and they either were opposed to communism or feared punishment. Many, however, did not want to return to communities where memories of Nazi persecution would haunt them, and there were some who could not return immediately to distant homes because of practical difficulties. In addition to these one million persons, there were smaller groups stranded in Asia and Africa.

In 1947 the International Refugee Organization inherited the task of protecting and resettling the refugees and displaced persons. The IRO is an outstanding example of international administration. It has been an operating agency, rather than a forum for study and discussion. The magnitude of the task carried out by IRO is indicated by a few statistics. It assumed initially the responsibility for complete maintenance of about 720,000 persons in the displaced-persons camps of central Europe. (The remainder of the million had some assets of their own, or were able to work in the local economies or for the occupation forces.) This meant the provision of food, shelter, and medical care for a group of people as large as the population of Cincinnati or Buffalo. In this connection, for example, IRO had one of the largest housing programs ever operated by a single authority.

By May 31, 1951, about a million refugees and displaced persons had been reestablished. About 930,000 chose to settle in new homes, and the remainder were assisted in returning to their countries of origin. Repatriation has been the primary objective, but IRO has followed the principle that no individual should be repatriated against his will. The Soviet Union was strongly opposed to this position, insisting that the decision in each case should be made by the government of the person's nationality or place of origin, and none of the Soviet countries assisted in this work.

At the peak of its operations, IRO was one of the largest mass transportation agencies in the world. During the summer of 1949 it had a fleet of thirty to thirty-five chartered ships and was using an average of twenty-seven trains a month for movements within Europe. The cost of maintenance and transportation largely explains the fact that IRO has spent more money than all the rest of the United Nations and the specialized agencies combined. Its largest annual budget was $155 million, but the simple arithmetical process of dividing this figure by the number of refugees will show that no great extravagance was lavished upon them. It may be taken as an axiom of government that the assumption of major operating responsibility involves the expenditure of money in large amounts.

The IRO operated an International Tracing Service for three years, seeking to establish the fate of persons who disappeared during the war. In 1948, for example, 48,121 requests about missing persons were received. It was possible to give some information in response to 18,113 of these inquiries, and in 16,367 cases either the missing person was found or proof of death established. One of the most tragic situations was that about 19,000 unsolved inquiries about missing children were still on file at the end of 1949.

The IRO is a temporary agency. It was originally scheduled to terminate at the end of June, 1950, but this term was extended to the end of 1951. The General Assembly has made provision for a High Commissioner's Office for Refugees, to exercise continuing responsibility for the protection of refugees and stateless persons. One of the big remaining problems is that of the so-called "hard core." This includes persons who are chronically ill, the aged, and others debarred by the various national immigration laws. Some, who would be eligible themselves, have relatives with severe handicaps and are not willing to break up their families. A special problem is that of the "forgotten elite"—professional persons such as doctors, artists, and teachers whom no country seems to want as immigrants. Every effort, however, is being made to resettle this group before the termination of IRO. It is slow work, but some countries like Norway, Israel, and France have undertaken to help with the "hard core" in one way or another.

A new problem arose in 1948, as a result of the hostilities in Palestine, with about 750,000 Arabs becoming refugees. The General Assembly created an emergency relief program and appealed for voluntary contributions. The Palestine Conciliation Commission established an economic survey mission to study the situation and make recommendations. The report, submitted in November, 1949, proposed a combined relief and works program under which direct relief would be gradually replaced by useful projects furnishing employment to the refugees. The mission determined that useful work could be found in view of the opportunities to improve and reclaim land, increase the supply of water, extend road systems, and improve sanitation and shelter. On the basis of this report, the General Assembly established a new agency, the United Nations Relief and Works Agency for Palestine Refugees in the Near East, to carry out a relief and works program over an eighteen-month period. The estimated cost of $54,900,000 was to be financed by voluntary governmental contributions. The question of Palestine refugees is of the greatest importance, not only from the social and humanitarian point of view but also because it is a major problem in arriving at a definitive settlement between the Jews and the Arabs.

SOCIAL WELFARE

Various activities in the field of social welfare have been undertaken by the United Nations. The international control of narcotic drugs began before World War I on the initiative of the United States, which was concerned with the problem of drug addiction in the Philippines. Later the League of Nations did much useful work in this field. In 1946 the United Nations assumed the responsibility for international cooperation to prevent or restrict the abuse of narcotics. A Commission on Narcotic Drugs was established as a direct successor to the League's Advisory Committee on this subject. The first task of the Commission was to deal with problems of organization and to reestablish the controls which had lapsed during the war. Attention was then directed to limits on the production of raw materials and to those narcotics now covered by existing international agreements. The discovery of new synthetic drugs has created an urgent situation. Amidone, for example, has the same effects as morphine, is possibly more dangerous, and can be easily produced. A protocol approved by the General Assembly in 1948 places new drugs under international control and provides that the World Health Organization shall decide whether a particular drug is habit-forming. The decision of WHO is automatically binding.

One problem to which the Commission has devoted considerable attention is the coca leaf, from which cocaine is made. This leaf is chewed in many parts of South America. In 1949, a commission of inquiry was sent at the request of the governments of Bolivia and Peru to study the effects of coca chewing in the Andes, and to investigate the possibilities of limiting the production and distribution of coca leaves.

Another welfare activity of the greatest importance has been the work of the United Nations International Children's Emergency Fund (UNICEF). Millions of children in Europe and Asia were in a desperate plight as a result of the war. By 1950, assistance had been given through UNICEF in providing a daily supplementary meal for over five million children and nursing or pregnant mothers in thirteen different countries. UNICEF contributed to the meal, which was ordinarily a school lunch, the protective foods such as milk, meat, fish, fats, and fish-liver oil. The government of the assisted country provided bread or cereals, potatoes, sugar, or whatever other foods were available locally. The supplementary meal amounted to 400 to 600 calories daily, a small but important part of a child's nutritional needs. UNICEF has also attacked the problem of building up the local production of milk. Its activities are not restricted to food supply, however, and it has helped to supply clothing and to cooperate with other organizations in the protection of child health.   In 1950 the emphasis shifted from emergency relief to long-term projects for child welfare throughout the world.   Funds for UNICEF were raised through voluntary contributions from governmental and private sources. By January, 1951, a total of $152 million had been received for this program. About half this amount came from the United States.

Other social-welfare activities of concern to the United Nations include supervision of the various international conventions for the suppression of traffic in women and children and of obscene publications, and discussion, studies, and dissemination of information in such fields as crime prevention, family life, and administration of social-welfare services.   A test of whether relief could be made available in a particular emergency came with the earthquake in Ecuador on August 5, 1949.   A special representative of the Secretary-General and experts from the specialized agencies were sent to the scene to help in any way possible.   More concretely, $340,000 was made available from UNICEF funds.   At the peak, this provided food, blankets, and soap for over 53,000 children.

EDUCATION, SCIENCE, AND CULTURE

One of the best known of the specialized agencies is the United Nations Educational, Scientific and Cultural Organization (UNESCO).   In its constitution occurs the oft-quoted statement, "since wars begin in the minds of men, it is in the minds of men that the defences of peace must be constructed." As its name implies, UNESCO is concerned with a broad range of programs and activities in the fields of education, science, and culture.   The task of UNESCO was conceived as collaboration to advance mutual knowledge and understanding of peoples through all means of mass communications; to give fresh impulse to popular education and to the spread of culture; and to maintain, increase, and diffuse knowledge.   This, on a budget averaging between $8 million and $9 million a year, is a large order, and one of the perplexing problems has been the definition of concrete objectives within such a broad field.

The situation arising from wartime destruction of thousands of schools, museums, and libraries gave UNESCO one of its first tasks.   A balance sheet of needs and resources was established, direct assistance was given where the need was greatest, and a world-wide campaign to obtain voluntary contributions was organized.   A Temporary International Council for Educational Reconstruction was set up to plan relief campaigns and to coordinate the work of the separate national voluntary agencies.[10]   National bodies, especially in the United States, contributed many million dollars' worth of aid in the form of educational materials, books, fellowships and study grants, and technical advisory commissions for war-devastated countries.   Direct UNESCO grants were made, on a much smaller scale, for books and periodicals, sound projectors

[10] In UNESCO circles, this was known as Operation TICER.

and radios for schools, microfilm equipment, and museum and laboratory supplies. Token grants have been made for various types of emergency aid to war-devastated areas and for such cooperative activities as voluntary international work camps. These token grants represent a small drop in a large bucket, so far as the total need is concerned, but their main purpose is to stimulate voluntary contributions and action on a much larger scale.

One of the major concerns of UNESCO has been the problem of fundamental education, especially in relation to the adjustment of peoples at various stages of development to modern industrial civilization. A quarterly journal and an annotated monthly bibliography of relevant literature in fundamental education are published as a technical information service. Conferences and educational missions have been organized on such subjects as illiteracy and adult education. Basic studies designed to assist in improving the quality of textbooks and teaching materials have been undertaken. Teaching about the United Nations and the specialized agencies has been encouraged by such methods as international essay and poster competition, and the issuance of pamphlets with suggestions and bibliography.

Another type of attack on the problem of fundamental education was the initiation of a pilot project in the Marbial Valley in Haiti, to show how to attack poverty, disease, and ignorance in an underdeveloped area with 97 per cent illiteracy. A sociological survey was completed and steps were taken to standardize Creole spelling and grammar, preliminary to the preparation of schoolbooks in the local language. A small clinic and a school were opened, and plans for agricultural development were made. The success of the project was limited, however, in the sense that accomplishments represented a very small beginning on a very big job. For example, the patients at the clinic responded to the treatment for yaws, but the problem of malnutrition remained. The scope of the project may be indicated by the fact that in 1949 the government of Haiti and UNESCO each contributed $13,500. In 1950, the UNESCO contribution was increased to $20,000.

In the area of the natural sciences, one of the principal projects has been the establishment of field science cooperation offices in Asia, the Middle East, and Latin America to act as liaison agents between the more scientifically advanced countries and the less highly developed areas. UNESCO has cooperated with international scientific organizations by means of grants-in-aid and conferences on abstracting of scientific literature and other problems. As a project in the popularization of science, discussions were initiated in 1949 on the theme "Food and People." Excellent background material was prepared in collaboration with FAO, WHO, and the United Nations Secretariat. The subject of "Energy in the Service of Man" was decided on as the topic for 1950.

One of the important projects in the social sciences is a study of international prejudices and tensions and possible techniques of correction. This includes a comprehensive analysis of forces that influence understanding among peoples and shape their social attitudes. The principal forces being considered are nationalism, technology, population trends, cultural heritages, and ideological conflicts. A scientific study of international organization has been initiated, a limited documentation service is provided, and a quarterly journal (*International Bulletin of the Social Sciences*) is being published.

UNESCO has an extensive cultural program in the arts, literature, and philosophy. It helped to establish the International Theatre Institute. A long-range project has been launched to promote the translation of the most important works of literature of every country. A system of book coupons has been developed to enable soft-currency countries to purchase books in hard-currency countries. In effect, UNESCO acts as a banker, exchanging the currency of one country for that of another and thus eliminating, within the limits of available funds, the foreign-exchange problem in the purchase of books. In the field of philosophy, UNESCO has laid special emphasis on the philosophic bases of human rights.

In connection with the international exchange of persons, UNESCO has given priority to the collection and publication of information about the availability and conditions of fellowships and scholarships; the analysis of obstacles to the free movement of persons between countries, with recommendations for their elimination; and the administration of a limited number of fellowships, and the stimulation of others from both governmental and private funds.

Another important part of UNESCO's program is concerned with mass communication. Surveys of the technical facilities of press, radio, and films in forty-five countries have been completed and published. An international agreement to facilitate the circulation of visual and auditory materials has been opened to signature. A study is being made of the current variations in the Braille system throughout the world, with a view to reaching agreement on principles of uniformity and rationalization. UNESCO has been active in disseminating the Universal Declaration of Human Rights and in the preparation of exhibits and other materials on this subject.

A unique clause in UNESCO's constitution provides for an element of direct participation by the peoples of the member states. National cooperating bodies exist in some thirty countries. The United States National Commission for UNESCO comprises 100 persons, of whom not more than 60 may be representatives of national voluntary organizations interested in educational, scientific, and cultural matters. Not more than 10 may be officials of the Federal government, and not more than 15 of state and local governments. The remaining 15 are chosen at large. This organizational feature, as well as the objectives and program, emphasizes the fact that the main purpose of UNESCO is to aid in creating a climate of intellectual cooperation among the peoples of the world.

Chapter 18

NON-SELF-GOVERNING
TERRITORIES AND TRUSTEESHIP

As a result of the imperialist movement in the centuries following the period of exploration, a large part of the non-European world was brought under the control of Western European states. These territories were called "colonies," though strictly speaking only territories settled by peoples of the so-called mother country are colonies. Noncontinguous territories inhabited by a relatively dense indigenous population are more properly called "dependent territories" or "dependencies."

Thus the British territories in North America, Australia, and New Zealand were properly called colonies. In these colonies, institutions of self-government were established almost immediately upon the arrival of the colonists and the demand for independence developed rapidly. The thirteen British colonies in North America, which subsequently became the United States of America, took up arms and won their independence before the end of the eighteenth century.

The territories, dependent on the other hand, were nearly all found in the Tropical Zone and had climates which did not attract Europeans as permanent settlers. During the first centuries of the imperialist movement, the native peoples of these conquered territories received harsh treatment and frequently were ruthlessly exploited. Gradually other ideas began to penetrate the thinking of the West and in course of time the administration of the colonies became more enlightened. A number of factors contributed to this development. Though belatedly, an increasing number of people began to demand the application of Christian principles to all phases of social life. The slogan of the French Revolution, "Liberty, Equality, and Fraternity," had its influence, as also the humanitarian movement of the nineteenth century. The rapid advance of democracy and democratic ideas not only helped to improve colonial administration, it undermined the whole institution of colonialism and brought it into ill repute. An ever-growing number of people found it difficult to harmonize imperialism with democratic principles. So long as people in the colonies remained passive, the issue did not become acute, but with the development of nationalism in these territories the democratic peoples of the West found themselves in a position which steadily became more distasteful and costly to them. There also developed among peoples of states which had no colonies a feeling that the power over dependencies was used to favor commercially the nationals of the metropolitan country.[1] There developed a widespread conviction that imperialism was an important cause of war.

Imperialism was a lively issue in the early decades of this century. An American scholar characterized imperialism as "the most impressive achievement and the most momentous world problem of our age."[2] On the eve of World War I nearly a third of the world's population lived in non-self-governing territories. In the fifth of his Fourteen Points, President Wilson in January, 1918, gave expression to the feeling which at the time generally prevailed with respect to the colonial issue and the peace settlement. He declared:

A free, open-minded, and absolutely impartial adjustment of all colonial claims, based upon a strict observance of the principle that in determining all such questions of sovereignty the interests of the population concerned must have equal weight with the equitable claims of the government whose title is to be determined.

It is interesting to note that President Wilson placed the interests of the indigenous population only on a level with the "equitable claims" of the states seeking authority to govern them. He did not propose that the Peace Conference make arrangement for colonies in general. No colonial power would have accepted that. However, a mild provision applicable to all non-self-governing territories of states members of the League of Nations was inserted in the Covenant. Under Article 23(b), the members of the League "undertake to secure just treatment of the native inhabitants of territories under their control."

The Peace Conference could deal in an effective manner only with the colonies of the former enemy countries. It was generally agreed on the one hand that the former German colonies and Turkish territories should not be restored to their former rulers and on the other that they were not ready for independence. President Wilson was unalterably opposed to annexation, and in this position he was backed by a strong world opinion. There remained, thus, only two solutions: (1) direct administration by the proposed new international organization, and (2) administration by a designated country subject to supervision of the League of Nations. The first was not feasible be-

---

[1] The term "metropolitan country" instead of "mother country" is now generally used to designate the dominant state. The latter expression is clearly inappropriate when the people in the dependency are of a different race from the inhabitants of the controlling state. Since "metropolis" means "mother city," it is really no more appropriate than "mother country" for these dependencies. Sometimes, following the French, the term "metropole" is used.

[2] Parker Thomas Moon, *Imperialism and World Politics,* Macmillan, New York, 1926, p. 1.

cause it was unacceptable to the chief Allied Powers which had conquered these territories. Furthermore, it was thought to be unwise to burden the League of Nations with an experiment in the international administration of colonies. National administration subject to international supervision remained as the only feasible solution. The mandates system, as the arrangement was called, can therefore be regarded as a compromise between the views of those who were hostile to territorial annexation and colonialism on the one hand, and the desires of the chief Allied Powers which had conquered these territories and wanted to annex them, on the other. Secondly, it was an attempt to solve the problem of securing administration in the interests of the native population and of the world rather than in the interests of the administering country in such territories as, in the euphemistic language of Article 22 of the Covenant, "are inhabited by peoples not yet able to stand by themselves under the strenuous conditions of the modern world."

THE LEAGUE MANDATE SYSTEM

The outlines of the mandates system were laid down in Article 22 of the Covenant. It stated as the basic principle to be applied to the mandated territories that "the well-being and development of such peoples form a sacred trust of civilization" and that "the best method of giving practical effect to this principle is that the tutelage of such peoples should be entrusted to advanced nations who by reason of their resources, their experience or their geographical position can best undertake this responsibility, and who are willing to accept it, and that this tutelage should be exercised by them as Mandatories on behalf of the League."

It provided for three types of mandates, which later were designated as A, B, and C. The former Turkish territories were regarded as having "reached a stage of development where their existence as independent nations can be provisionally recognized subject to the rendering of administrative advice and assistance by a Mandatory until such time as they are able to stand alone." These mandates, classed as A mandates, were intended to be of relatively short duration, but only one of these territories, Iraq, had acquired its independence before World War II. It became independent in 1932, and at the same time it became a member of the League of Nations. Only Great Britain and France held A mandates. The former was the mandatory for Iraq and Palestine (including Transjordan), and the latter for Syria and Lebanon.

The former German territories in Africa were described as being "at such a stage that the Mandatory must be responsible for the administration of the territory" under conditions which would guarantee freedom of conscience and religion, and prohibition of certain abuses such as slave trade and arms and liquor traffic, and would secure "equal opportunities of trade and commerce of other Members of the League." These territories were designated as B mandates. The mandatory power for Tanganyika, West Togo, and the western Cameroons was Great Britain; for East Togo and the eastern Cameroons, France; and for Ruanda-Urundi, Belgium.

The remaining former German territories were classified as C mandates. The Covenant stated that these, "owing to the sparseness of their population, or their small size, or their remoteness from the centers of civilization, or their geographical contiguity to the territory of the Mandatory, and other circumstances," could be best administered under the laws of the Mandatory "as integral portions of its territory." The large but sparsely settled South-West Africa was assigned to the Union of South Africa as a mandatory; the former German islands in the Central Pacific, north of the equator, became the mandated territory of Japan; Western Samoa was placed under the administration of New Zealand; and North-East New Guinea was entrusted to Australia as mandatory. The small island of Nauru was placed under the joint administration of Great Britain, Australia, and New Zealand.

It will be noted that the chief difference between the three types of mandates consisted in the amount of administrative authority conferred upon the mandatory. The authority of the mandatory power was restricted to rendering "administrative advice and assistance" in case of the A mandates, while in the case of B mandates the administering state had complete governmental power, subject to a few express restrictions. The C mandated territories could be administered "under the laws of the Mandatory as integral portions of its territory."

The degree of authority, control, or administration to be exercised by the mandatory was determined in each case by an agreement between the Council of the League of Nations and the mandatory, but in every case the mandatory was under the obligation of rendering an annual report of its administration to the Council. The Covenant further provided for the institution of a permanent commission "to receive and examine" the annual reports and "to advise the Council on all matters relating to the observance of the mandates."

Such in brief outline was the mandates system. The system was not without weaknesses and inconsistencies, but in general it may be said to have been successful. It made for high standards of administration in the interests of the native population and it also served to stimulate the administrations of other dependencies to achieve higher levels of native welfare.

THE CHARTER AND NON-SELF-GOVERNING TERRITORIES

The Dumbarton Oaks Proposals did not contain a single reference to colonial questions. At the time of the Dumbarton Oaks Conversations, the participating governments were not yet prepared to discuss this subject. The United States government, which was expected to take the lead in this matter, found itself in a peculiar position. Americans, largely because of their historical background, have always been strongly anticolonial, and now that many colonial territories in the Pacific were being freed of the enemy by American armed forces, many argued that the American government had a special responsibility to ensure their freedom. However, events in the war had also aroused other sentiments, especially in the armed forces. Japan had fortified the islands in the Pacific over which it exercised a mandate under the League of Nations. This was done in violation of the Covenant and of the terms of the mandate. These islands, athwart the sea lanes from Hawaii to the Philippines, were conquered by American armed forces at great cost. Regarding these islands primarily from the point of view of American defense, the Army and Navy quite naturally desired their annexation in outright sovereignty.

Had the United States government yielded to this demand of the defense departments, its moral influence in the movement for some sort of international regulation of the colonial problem would have been destroyed. The Department of State, therefore, adamantly resisted the demands for outright annexation. It was not until this internal conflict had been solved that the American government could exercise any vital leadership in this matter. The difficulty was solved by a compromise. It was agreed that the United States government would press for a special kind of trusteeship for the former Japanese mandated islands which would give it the right to fortify them and to close all or parts of them for reasons of security.

At Yalta, President Roosevelt, Prime Minister Churchill, and Marshal Stalin reached agreement on the basic principles of an international trusteeship system which would apply to (1) existing mandates of the League of Nations, (2) territories detached from the enemy as a result of the present war, and (3) any other territory which might voluntarily be placed under trusteeship. It was to apply to no other territories. It was further agreed that the five powers which were to have permanent seats on the Security Council would consult each other on this question before the San Francisco Conference. These consultations did not take place before the Conference, but were held while the trusteeship provisions of the Charter were being drafted.

The articles finally hammered out at the Conference are grouped in three chapters and deal with two types of dependencies. Chapter XI deals with all non-self-governing territories except those which are under trusteeship, whereas Chapters XII and XIII outline the position of territories which have been placed under the international trusteeship system. Most of the dependent territories in the world fall under the first group. It was not to be expected that states would accept much United Nations interference in the administration of territories over which they had acquired jurisdiction decades ago. What they accepted in Chapter XI was a general declaration of principles governing the administration of their non-self-governing territories. Thus the United States as a member of the United Nations has agreed to be guided by these principles in governing Alaska, the Hawaiian Islands, Puerto Rico, and its other dependencies. The second group of dependencies falling within the scope of the Charter provisions are the territories placed under the international trusteeship system. It may be argued that Chapter XI applies to all dependencies, trust territories as well as others, for it lays down the goals of administration of "territories whose peoples have not yet attained a full measure of self-government." However that may be, it is a matter of little significance, since the basic objectives of the trusteeship system are stated at length in Article 76, and these objectives include practically all, if not actually all, of those listed in Article 73 for the administration of non-self-governing territories.

Dependencies Not under Trusteeship

As has already been indicated, Chapter XI constitutes a general declaration of principles governing the administration of territories "whose peoples have not yet attained a full measure of self-government." Under Article 73 all members of the United Nations "which have or assume responsibilities" for the administration of non-self-governing territories accept a number of far-reaching obligations. They "recognize the principle that the interests of the inhabitants of these territories are paramount, and accept as a sacred trust the obligation to promote to the utmost . . . the well-being of the inhabitants of this territory." To this end administering states are to ensure their political, economic, social, and educational advancement, to develop self-government, "to assist them in the progressive development of their free political institutions," "to further international peace and security," and "to promote constructive measures of development." They also agree to "transmit regularly to the Secretary-General for information purposes, subject to such limitation as security and constitutional considerations may require, statistical and other information of a technical nature relating to economic, social, and educational conditions in the territories for which they are respectively responsible. . . ."

Article 74 stipulates that the policy of the members of the United Nations in administering non-self-governing territories "must be based on the general principle of good-neighborliness." This provision seems quite superfluous, since the obligation to pursue a policy of "good-neighborliness" is assumed throughout the Charter and is explicitly stated in many articles.

Chapter XI of the Charter is an extension and an elaboration of Article 23(e) of the Covenant of the League. It starts from the basic principle that all questions of colonial policy and administration are international in character and therefore subject to a measure of world accountability. Unfortunately, its provisions are frequently vague and repetitious and occasionally inconsistent. The language of Chapter XI gives no answer to the question of what constitutes a non-self-governing territory or who is to determine what territories fall within the scope of the Declaration. The District of Columbia is not self-governing, yet it is quite clearly not the intention of the Charter to include such territories within the scope of Article XI. Since the General Assembly may "discuss any questions or any matters within the scope" of the Charter and make recommendations to the members "on any such questions or matters" (Article 10), it may presumably also specify in recommendatory form the territories which fall within the scope of the Declaration. In practice it is left to the members to determine which of their territories are non-self-governing. Very much the same is true of other vague clauses of the chapter. It is the administering government which in first instance decides what these clauses mean, subject always to such pressure as the General Assembly can exert through discussion and recommendation.

Administering states are "to promote to the utmost . . . the well-being of the inhabitants of these territories," but "within the system of international peace and security established by the present Charter." It does not seem possible that a policy of promoting the well-being of dependent peoples could endanger international peace and security, except in a negative way. Moreover, the last clause is an unfortunate qualification of the sound general principle stated in the first. In a seriously disturbed world this qualification may easily be used to annul the general principle. The question may also be raised as to whether it is wise or fair to require of peoples which are regarded as not yet ready to govern themselves that they make positive contributions to international peace and security.

The heart of the Declaration is found in Article 73(e), which requires the administering states to transmit information regularly to the Secretary-General on conditions in their non-self-governing territories. However, this obligation is qualified by a number of restrictions. Only information of a technical nature need be transmitted, the term "political" having been purposely omitted from the clause; the obligation to transmit information is "subject to such limitation as security and constitutional considerations may require"; and the transmission of the reports to the Secretary-General is "for information purposes." It must not be forgotten, however, that this information can be used by the General Assembly as the basis for discussion and recommendation, and this is being done increasingly.

The great majority of the members of the United Nations are states which have no colonies, and many of them have memories of a former colonial status. It is natural that these countries should press for the largest measure of international accountability possible under the terms of Chapter XI. Some sought to require administering states to submit political information. This movement was bitterly opposed by the states with colonial responsibilities and was defeated. A resolution of the General Assembly (November 3, 1947) states that the voluntary transmission of information on the development of self-governing institutions in non-self-governing territories and its summarizing by the Secretary-General "are entirely in conformity with the spirit of Article 73 of the Charter, and should be . . . encouraged." Some governments supply political information; others refuse to do so.

Somewhat similar differences arose over the use to be made of the information transmitted to the Secretary-General. By a resolution of December 14, 1946, the General Assembly recommended that the information transmitted in the course of 1947 should be "summarized, analyzed and classified by the Secretary-General and included in his report to the second session of the General Assembly," and that the Secretary-General communicate to the specialized agencies the information transmitted, with a view to making all relevant data available to their expert and deliberative bodies. The resolution provided further that the Secretary-General convene an *ad hoc* committee composed in equal numbers of representatives of members transmitting information and of representatives elected by the General Assembly, and that the *ad hoc* committee examine the Secretary-General's summary and analysis of the information transmitted "with a view to making recommendations to the General Assembly regarding the procedures to be followed in the future. . . ." The basic procedures of the above resolution were extended indefinitely by a series of resolutions adopted by the General Assembly on November 3, 1947.

A third controversy arose over the question of whether the Secretary-General may receive or collect information from sources other than the governments of the administering states. The colonial powers insist that only information furnished by their governments be considered.

There is a strong inclination on the part of the noncolonial states to minimize the differences in status under the Charter of non-self-governing and trust territories and to assimilate the former to the latter. There was, for example, the drive to make of the *ad hoc* examining committee a duplicate of the Trusteeship Council. The representative of China actually proposed to confer upon the Trusteeship Council this examining function. The colonial powers resent the sharp criticisms of their administration frequently made by the representatives of countries whose standards of social welfare are not above those of the dependencies concerned and whose progressive development in democratic government leaves much to be desired. They frequently remind the General Assembly of the differences between Chapter XI on the one hand and Chapters XII and XIII on the other, and point out that the competence of the United Nations under the first is much less than under the other two.

In conclusion it should be noted that the problem of dependent territories has greatly diminished, at least quantitatively, since World War II. Lebanon, Syria, Palestine, and Transjordan, the former A mandates in the Near East, became full-fledged members of the family of nations. The 450 million people on the subcontinent of India have acquired national independence, as have also the Philippines with 19 million population; Indonesia, with 80 million people; and Burma with a population of 17 million. Ceylon with over 7 million people, attained dominion status in the Commonwealth of Nations. The peoples of Indochina have been granted self-government within the French Union. Korea is no longer a Japanese dependency, although it is not yet a happy land. The combined population of non-self-governing territories is now reduced to something like 150 million.

The original list of territories (1946) under Chapter XI contained seventy-four dependencies, but this number has been considerably reduced. Because of protests of the Republic of Panama, the United States no longer reports on the Panama Canal Zone. The United Kingdom has ceased to report on Malta, and France has ceased sending in reports on a number of territories, presumably because of change in their constitutional status.

The Trusteeship System

The basic objectives of the trusteeship system are laid down in Article 76. They are practically the same as those outlined in Article 73 for the administration of non-self-governing territories. Superficially there seems to be at least one important difference. In the case of non-self-governing territories the administering states are under obligation "to develop self-government," whereas in the case of trust territories the basic political objective is declared to be the progressive development of the inhabitants "towards self-government or independence as may be appropriate to the particular circumstances of each territory and its peoples and the freely expressed wishes of the peoples concerned, and as may be provided by the terms of each trusteeship agreement." The representatives of some of the noncolonial countries at the San Francisco Conference wished to have independence stated as the goal for the administration of both kinds of territories, but this proposal was bitterly opposed by the delegates of the colonial powers. As a compromise it was included for the one and not the other. It was argued that self-government included the possibility of independence but that it was unwise to emphasize the latter as a goal, since independence might not be feasible for all territories, as for example small or isolated territories. Moreover, when a people attains a certain level of social and economic development it cannot be denied its independence if it really desires it. The emphasis should therefore be placed upon social and economic development. If that is done the political development will largely take care of itself.

The trusteeship system applies to three types of territories, namely, former League of Nations mandates, territories detached from the enemy as a result of World War II, and territories voluntarily placed under the system.[3] Because the Union of South Africa has refused to place South-West Africa under the system, the question of whether members of the United Nations are under

---

[3] For the territories under the trusteeship system, see Table 6.

legal obligation to place former mandated territories under the trusteeship system has been much discussed.   Article 77 states that "the trusteeship system shall apply to such territories in the following categories as may be placed thereunder by means of trusteeship agreements."   It is obvious that a state cannot be compelled to enter into an agreement against its wishes, but it has been argued that the word "may" must be interpreted to mean that the administering state has the choice of either placing the territory under trusteeship or of giving it independence.   The administering state need not propose an agreement, but in that case it loses the right to govern the territory.   The General Assembly in 1946, 1947, and 1948 urged the Union to propose a trusteeship agreement, and finally, in 1949, it asked the International Court of Justice for an advisory opinion on the question of the Union's international obligations with respect to the territory.

The International Court of Justice gave its advisory opinion July 11, 1950. The Court declared as its opinion that South-West Africa is a territory under international mandate assumed by the Union of South Africa on December 17, 1920, that the General Assembly is legally qualified to exercise the supervisory functions previously exercised by the League of Nations with regard to the administration of the territory, and that the Union of South Africa is under an obligation to submit to supervision and control of the General Assembly and to render annual reports to it.   The Court was further of the opinion that the competence to determine and modify the international status of the territory did not rest with the Union acting alone, but with the Union acting with the consent of the United Nations.   However, the Court was further of the opinion that the provisions of the Charter do not impose on the Union of South Africa a legal obligation to place the territory under the trusteeship system. While the advisory opinion of the International Court of Justice offers no support for United Nations action to compel South Africa to place the territory under trusteeship, it would seem to block rather effectively any plans of the Union to incorporate the territory within its own domain.

Of the second category of territories named in Article 77, Italian Somaliland was placed under the trusteeship system in 1950.   Unable to reach an agreement among themselves on the disposition of the former Italian colonies, the United States, Great Britain, France, and the Soviet Union finally placed the matter before the General Assembly for decision.   In accordance with resolutions of this body, Libya obtained its independence on December 24, 1951; Somaliland was placed under Italian administration within the United Nations trusteeship system for ten years, after which it is to be independent; and Eritrea was federated with Ethiopia as an autonomous unit under the Ethiopian Crown.

Under the terms of the Treaty of Peace with Japan signed at San Francisco on September 8, 1951, Japan must concur in any proposal of the United States to the United Nations to place under the trusteeship system, with the United

States as the sole administering authority, the Ryukyu, Bonin, Rosario, Volcano, Parece Vela, and Marcus Islands.

Not many people believe that any dependencies will voluntarily be placed under the trusteeship system. Certainly there has been no rush by colonial powers to place their dependencies under the system. Yet the possibility of this happening should not be wholly discounted. The pressure of world public opinion, especially as it expresses itself through the United Nations, for extensive educational facilities and social services makes colonial administration very expensive and bars any significant economic advantage to the administering country. Under these conditions states may not always wish to retain the expensive luxury of administering colonies, though national pride makes them reluctant to withdraw. But in this case the state would wish to free itself completely from the responsibility of administering the dependency, and would therefore be inclined to grant it independence.

The system set up by the Charter is very much like the mandates system of the League of Nations, with some important differences. As in the case of mandates, a territory comes under the system only by an agreement, called the "trusteeship agreement," which states "the terms under which the trust territory will be administered," and designates "the authority which will exercise the administration of the trust territory." The administering authority may be one or more states or the Organization itself. Only in the case of one trust territory does the administering authority consist of more than one state. Australia, New Zealand, and the United Kingdom are named as the joint administrators of Nauru, but in fact the island is administered by Australia alone. Condominiums have not been very successful, as witness the Anglo-Egyptian Sudan and the New Hebrides, and it is not likely that this form will be used. Administration by the Organization itself is somewhat of an anomaly in a trusteeship system, since the function of the United Nations in this case would not be supervisory but administrative. To date no territory has been placed under the administration of the Organization. The General Assembly by a resolution of November 29, 1947, recommended that "the city of Jerusalem shall be established as a *corpus separatum* under a special international regime and shall be administered by the United Nations." This resolution, reinforced by another one of December 9, 1949, which would have placed Jerusalem under the administration of the Trusteeship Council, could not be implemented because of the opposition of Israel and Jordan.

STRATEGIC AREAS

As has already been indicated, the United States insisted upon a special kind of trusteeship to meet what is regarded as its military requirements in the former Japanese mandated islands in the Pacific. This was provided for in Article 82 of the Charter which stipulates "that there may be designated, in any trusteeship agreement, a strategic area or areas which include part or all of the trust territory to which the agreement applies, without prejudice to any special agreement or agreements under Article 43." Whereas the functions of the United Nations with regard to trusteeship agreements for nonstrategic territories "including the approval of the terms of the agreements, and of their alteration or amendment" are exercised by the General Assembly, assisted by the Trusteeship Council, in the case of strategic areas, these same functions are exercised by the Security Council, where each of the permanent members— the five Great Powers—has the power of veto. The basic objectives of the system are equally applicable to the people of all trust territories. Moreover, the Security Council must, "subject to the provisions of the trusteeship agreements and without prejudice to security considerations," make use of the assistance of the Trusteeship Council in performing the functions of the United Nations under the trusteeship system relating to political, economic, social, and educational matters in strategic areas.

There is only one trust territory of the strategic type, and that is the Trust Territory of the Pacific Islands, which are the former Japanese mandated islands, and which before World War I had been colonies of Germany. The agreement,[4] approved by the Security Council on April 2, 1947, designates the United States of America as the administering authority. The right of the administering state to close any areas of the territory is recognized in Article 13 of the agreement.

This trust territory was first administered by the United States Department of the Navy, but in 1951 it was placed under civilian rule, and the Security Council has turned over to the Trusteeship Council its functions regarding political, economic, social, and educational matters. Since security matters remain under the jurisdiction of the Security Council, the United States can prohibit inspection of its military bases on the islands by representatives of any of the United Nations organs.

The United States demanded the inclusion in the agreement of the provision that "the administering authority may determine the extent of their applicability to any areas which may from time to time be specified by it as closed for security reasons" (Article 13). There was objection to this as establishing a dangerous principle, but it was nevertheless accepted. In spite of objections, the United States practically acquired the right to administer the islands as a part of the United States (Article 3). The draft which the United States submitted did not contain a provision for independence as a goal of the administration. To meet Soviet objections, a compromise on this issue was reached. Independence was accepted as an aim, but subject to the qualifying clause, "as may be appropriate to the particular circumstances of the trust territory and its peoples and the freely expressed wishes of the peoples concerned" (Article 6).

[4] See Appendix 14 for text of the agreement.

The trusteeship system, in contrast with the mandates system, not only expects the trust territories to contribute to the maintenance of peace but emphasizes their obligation to do so. The Covenant (Article 22, clause 5) stipulated that in the B mandates the administering states were to prohibit traffic in arms and to prevent "the establishment of fortifications or military and naval bases and of military training of the natives for other than police purposes and the defence of territory." The first basic objective of the trusteeship system, according to Article 76 of the Charter, is "to further international peace and security," and Article 84 specifically lays upon the administering authority the duty to ensure that the trust territory play its part in the maintenance of international peace and security, and to this end it may "make use of volunteer forces, facilities, and assistance from the trust territory in carrying out the obligations toward the Security Council undertaken in this regard by the administering authority. . . ." This provision applies to both strategic and nonstrategic areas.

REGIONAL COMMISSIONS

An effect of colonial expansion and rivalry has sometimes been the fragmentation into a number of small, unnatural administrative units of regions which could be governed much more effectively as one. The Caribbean is such a region. During the early days of World War II, the islands of the Caribbean became isolated, as a result of the German submarine campaign, and economic and social conditions, which already were bad, became worse. To meet the emergency the British and American governments created the Anglo-American Caribbean Commission. The Commission proved so successful that it was put on a permanent basis by an agreement of 1946, with the governments of France and the Netherlands also as members, and renamed the Caribbean Commission. The object of the Commission is to encourage and strengthen cooperation among the members and their territories "with a view toward improving the economic and social well-being of the peoples of those territories." This is to be done by "promoting scientific, technological, and economic development in the Caribbean area and facilitating the use of resources and concerted treatment of mutual problems, avoiding duplication in the work of existing research agencies, surveying needs, ascertaining what research has been done, facilitating research on cooperative basis, and recommending further research."

A similar commission was set up for the islands of the South Pacific by an agreement of 1947, with the governments of Australia, France, New Zealand, Great Britain, and the United States as signatories. The South Pacific Commission, like the Caribbean Commission, is a consultative and advisory body to the participating governments "in matters affecting the economic and social development of the non-self-governing territories within the scope of the Commission and the welfare and advancement of their peoples."

This kind of cooperation is in pursuance of the pledge made by members of the United Nations in Article 73 of the Charter, "to cooperate with one another and, when and where appropriate, with specialized international bodies with a view to the practical achievement of the social, economic, and scientific purposes set forth in this Article."

CONCLUSIONS

It is fortunate that the colonial problem as such has greatly declined in magnitude in recent years, for the United Nations has not demonstrated its suitability for dealing with it.   The Big Four struggled over the disposition of the former Italian colonies for several years, took one position and then another on what should be done with them, and finally left it to the General Assembly to decide.   In the meanwhile there was uncertainty and stagnation in the territories.   Moreover, no one who knows anything about conditions in the former Italian colonies believes that they are ready for independence.   A Big Four commission which visited the territories for the purpose of making an investigation of this problem in 1948 declared that an overwhelming majority of Libyans are illiterate and the degree of political understanding is low.   Libya has nevertheless been made a sovereign state and is now on its own.   It is inconceivable that Somaliland can be prepared for independence in ten years.   The interests of the inhabitants had very little to do with the decisions for the disposition of these territories.   Confusion, dictatorship, or domination from the outside may well be the lot of these two territories unless some special regime is set up under the United Nations to prevent their collapse.

In the modern world, good government and self-government are closely related.   Self-government is never secure where there is bad government, and in any case it is not of very great value there.   On the other hand, colonial powers have been prone to set the standards unnecessarily high and to use them as an excuse for delaying the grant of independence.

There was much criticism of the demand of the United States for a "strategic" type of trusteeship in the Charter and for its "take it or leave it" attitude with respect to the trust agreement it submitted to the Security Council for the former Japanese mandated islands.   It looked like a thinly veiled scheme of annexation.   By placing the territory under civilian administration and by requesting the shift of the nonmilitary supervisory functions to the Trusteeship Council, the United States government has done much to allay criticism. In viewing the American position certain factors should be kept in mind, such as the special geographic position of these islands, their strategic importance for the defense of the United States, and their minor economic value and small population. There is no danger that the inhabitants are going to be exploited; it is more likely that they will be pampered. The American costs of administration (exclusive of military expenditures) run to several million dollars a year for the 60,000 inhabitants. It is not probable that the islands will ever be wholly self-supporting. Nevertheless, by demanding a highly special regime for the territory, which already had an international status, the United States did lose considerable moral authority in the matter of dependent areas.

The colonial question has entered a strange stage. The overwhelming majority of the members of the United Nations are underdeveloped countries, many of them with memories of former colonial status. Their representatives in the General Assembly and in the Trusteeship Council reflect a strong feeling against colonialism. The Soviet Union and its satellites are opposed on principle to all dependencies—that is, non-Communist ones—hence no administration of non-self-governing territories has ever a good feature in their eyes. Administering states are thus held up to standards of civil and political rights and social welfare which few of the critics have attained at home. In effect, the international community will no longer tolerate the political domination of one people by another unless the latter are wholly unprepared for independence, the standards of administration are high, and the interests of the inhabitants are made paramount. It is not surprising that the administering states have regarded some of the demands and criticisms as irresponsible and have reacted sharply. The atmosphere has become so embittered that fruitful cooperation is difficult.

The inhabitants of most non-self-governing territories, and especially of trust territories, are more fortunate than the citizens of many independent underdeveloped countries. They have moral claims upon technologically advanced metropolitan countries for help in raising their standards of living. Puerto Rico is making perceptible progress by means of generous help from the United States. Her less fortunate neighbors may have to wait for aid. The Philippine Republic still benefits from its former position as a dependency of the United States. In addition to huge sums of money poured, directly and indirectly, into the country (nearly $2 billion between 1945 and 1949) the American government has agreed to aid its former dependency to the extent of $50 million annually for five years (1950–1955). The hard-pressed British already before the war had their colonial development and welfare fund.

The colonial problem has moved into a new phase. The many countries with their large populations which won their independence in recent years are faced with grave economic problems. Political independence did not solve any of the basic social and economic problems of these underdeveloped countries; it merely shifted the responsibility for solving them to the inhabitants of these territories, but unfortunately most of these peoples are without adequate financial resources, technology, or administrative experience. President Truman's fourth point of his inaugural address (1949)— his bold new program for extending technological assistance to underdeveloped countries—as well as the United Nations program of technical assistance are aimed at filling this void. So long as these countries remain economically weak they will remain politically and militarily weak and an easy prey to communism. This is an urgent problem of vast magnitude, and one beset by very great difficulties.

TABLE 6. TERRITORIES UNDER THE TRUSTEESHIP SYSTEM

Trust territory	Administering authority	Population	Area, square miles
New Guinea	Australia	1,006,200	93,000
Ruanda-Urundi	Belgium	3,718,646	20,916
Cameroons	France	2,702,500	166,797
Togoland	France	944,446	21,236
Western Samoa	New Zealand	72,936	1,133
Tanganyika	United Kingdom	7,079,557	392,688
Cameroons	United Kingdom	991,000	34,081
Togoland	United Kingdom	382,200	13,040
Nauru	Australia	3,162	82
Trust Territory of Pacific Islands	United States of America	60,000	687
Somaliland	Italy	1,300,000	194,000
Total		18,260,647	937,660

Chapter 19

HUMAN RIGHTS AND FUNDAMENTAL FREEDOMS

One of the principal functions of the United Nations is to promote universal respect for and observance of human rights. This is considered one of the most important aspects of the fundamental task of establishing the conditions of a lasting peace. Handling dangerous international disputes and preventing a resort to aggression do not by any means constitute the full responsibility of the United Nations. It is important to do these things when and if necessary, but in the long run the major objective is the attainment of an international order in which disputes will always be settled by pacific means.

The Charter of the United Nations makes seven definite references to the matter of human rights. The drafters of the Charter did not merely pay it lip service, but made it a really important foundation stone. The preamble refers to the determination "to reaffirm faith in fundamental human rights, in the dignity and worth of the human person, in the equal rights of men and women and of nations large and small. . . ." Article 1 of the Charter mentions, as one of the purposes of the United Nations, "to achieve international co-operation in . . . promoting and encouraging respect for human rights and for fundamental freedoms for all without distinction as to race, sex, language, or religion." Article 13 makes it the responsibility of the General Assembly to initiate studies and make recommendations for the purpose, among others, of assisting in the realization of human rights and fundamental freedoms. The provisions of the Charter dealing with international economic and social cooperation, as necessary for peaceful and friendly relations among nations, include an obligation to promote "universal respect for, and observance of, human rights and fundamental freedoms for all without distinction as to race, sex, language, or religion" (Article 55). The Economic and Social Council is authorized to make recommendations for this purpose (Article 62) and is instructed to set up commissions in economic and social fields and for the promotion of human rights (Article 68). Finally, one of the basic objectives of the trusteeship system, as stated in Article 76 of the Charter, is "to encourage respect for human rights and for fundamental freedoms for all without distinction as to race, sex, language, or religion, and to encourage recognition of the interdependence of the peoples of the world."

It is of the greatest importance that the Charter of the United Nations, as the constitution of modern international organization, incorporates a democratic ideology. The repeated emphasis on "human rights and fundamental freedoms" puts organized international cooperation in the attainment of world peace and security on a basis springing from a cultural and political heritage friendly to the ideals of American democracy. Moreover, it is quite clear that peace is not conceived as the mere absence of war and aggression, but as an affirmative condition with the positive qualities of welfare for the human race. As the world became more interdependent and life more complicated, the problem of human rights became universal and more directly related to the conditions for maintaining international peace and security. Violations of elementary human rights had been a major contributing cause of World War II, and it became apparent after the publication of the Dumbarton Oaks proposals that the peoples of the world were determined to create strong international machinery to prevent a recurrence of that experience. Inspiration for this movement was also derived from the "four freedoms" as stated by President Roosevelt,[1] the Atlantic Charter of August, 1941, and the Declaration by the United Nations of January 1, 1942.

The Charter of the United Nations does not contain a bill of rights. The content and scope of "human rights and fundamental freedoms" were left for later elaboration. Americans are accustomed to thinking of a bill of rights as an essential part of a constitution, in order to protect the individual against excessive or arbitrary governmental power. The original draft of the Federal constitution, however, did not contain a bill of rights, but this portion of the Constitution came into existence as a series of ten amendments ratified in 1791. Very limited powers were granted to the United Nations, so that a bill of rights was not needed in order to prevent it from abusing its authority. The problem is not to protect individuals against the United Nations as American citizens are protected against arbitrary action by governmental agencies and officials. The problem is to achieve a greater degree of international cooperation in promoting human rights among and within the member states. In the United States, certain restrictions on the states are found in the Federal constitution and its amendments. In the United Nations system the only restrictions on the members are those found in the general obligations of the Charter itself and in the subsidiary commitments which may be accepted. As yet, the United Nations acts through its members and has no direct way of assuring rights and freedoms to individual citizens.

---

[1] In his state of the Union message of January, 1941. The "four freedoms" are freedom of religion and of speech, and freedom from fear and from want. See Appendix 5.

THE COMMISSION ON HUMAN RIGHTS

The Economic and Social Council in February, 1946, established a preliminary Commission on Human Rights and on June 21, 1946, adopted the terms of reference of the permanent Commission and determined its membership. This Commission consists of representatives of eighteen members of the United Nations. Thus, it was decided that the Commission on Human Rights would consist of representatives of governments, rather than of experts serving in their individual capacities. The Economic and Social Council selects the eighteen members of the United Nations to be represented. Each member then selects its representative for the Commission. With a view to securing balanced representation in various fields, however, the Economic and Social Council directed the Secretary-General to "consult with the governments of the members so selected before the representatives are finally nominated by these governments and confirmed by the Council." The term of office is three years, on a staggered basis, and members are eligible for reelection.

The Commission on Human Rights was directed to submit proposals, recommendations, and reports concerning an international bill of human rights; international declarations or conventions on civil liberties, the status of women, freedom of information and similar matters; the protection of minorities; the prevention of discrimination on grounds of race, sex, language, or religion; and any other matter concerning human rights. It does not have the authority to take action in individual cases involving human rights. For basic documentation, the Secretary-General was requested to make arrangements for the compilation of a yearbook on human rights; collection and publication of information on the activities relating to human rights of all organs of the United Nations; collection and publication of information concerning human rights arising from trials of war criminals, quislings, and traitors; preparation of a survey of the development of human rights; and the collection of plans and declarations on human rights by specialized agencies and nongovernmental organizations.

When the Commission met, it soon became apparent that the drafting of an international bill of human rights would have to be done in several stages. The first task was to elaborate a Declaration defining the fundamental human rights and freedoms. This was conceived "as a common standard of achievement for all peoples." It would be a statement of principles, rather than a binding and enforceable legal obligation, and its influence would be moral and educational. The next step was to be an international convention or treaty, setting forth in precise terms the provisions which governments are willing to accept as legally binding. Finally, it was obvious that there would be a need for machinery to ensure the observance of human rights and to deal with violations. This required the development of "measures of implementation."

In accordance with this conception of its threefold task, the Commission first undertook the writing of a Declaration on Human Rights. This work was done in a very careful and meticulous way. Using documentation furnished by the Secretariat, a drafting committee prepared a first draft. In the light of comments from member governments, the Commission as a whole revised it. Then the revised draft was circulated, the drafting committee met again, and the Commission prepared its final proposal. This went to the Economic and Social Council, and then to the General Assembly which referred the proposal to its Third Committee. This Committee made a very detailed examination, going over the draft almost word by word. The resulting document went to the General Assembly, which adopted the Universal Declaration of Human Rights [2] on December 10, 1948, by a vote of 48 to 0, with 8 abstentions and 2 members absent.

All this careful, detailed work was necessary because of the great differences in cultural, philosophic, and legal views. If the Declaration were to command respect and allegiance, and if it were to be more than a string of maxims, it was essential to reach the fullest possible understanding about every word and clause. In the drafting of the Declaration, three basic issues could be discerned. The first had to do with the relation between the individual and the state. Most of the members believed that the fundamental individual freedoms should be expressed, and that human and not state rights should be emphasized. The representatives of the Soviet members, however, stressed the duty of man to the state and the community, and urged the inclusion of more explicit safeguards of the sovereign rights of the "democratic state." The discussion of the meaning, and ambiguity, of this phrase was one of the most important debates in the Commission. Traditional bills of rights in the Western world, notably those of France and the United States, have been concerned with protections of the individual against arbitrary governmental action. The bill of rights in the Soviet constitution is written in terms of guarantees to the individual by the state. In the former, individual rights are to be preserved by directing governments not to take forbidden action. In the latter, the concern is with governmental responsibility for taking affirmative action.

The second basic issue related to the emphasis to be given the traditional individual-personal rights, as compared with the so-called economic-social rights. All members wanted to see both types of rights confirmed, and the Universal Declaration as adopted actually does this. The Soviet representatives interpreted the problem as being essentially one of the duty of the state to guarantee economic and social rights to "the broad masses of the people." They considered the traditional rights formal and empty without the guarantee of the new economic, social, and educational rights. A declaration of rights, without provisions for their guarantee by the state and society, reminded the

[2] For text, see Appendix 19.

Soviet representative of a saying from the Russian fairy tales, "Only the toes are left, the body is gone." The British and American representatives laid greater stress on the personal, civil, and political liberties, and held the view that governments are in a position only to promote, not guarantee, economic, social, and educational rights. The representative of France took an intermediate position. He did not want to overlook the traditional values, but to him "social security" belonged to the essence of human rights, and he thought that it required special emphasis because it was not well established.

The third issue was the underlying one of the nature and origin of human rights. On what basis does man possess them? If they are "natural" rights, every person possesses them because he is a human being; they are "inalienable." The state does not have, and cannot have, any legal right or authority to abrogate them, but is obligated to recognize and respect them. If, on the other hand, human rights are conferred by society or the state, they may also be withdrawn by the authority which grants them. The Universal Declaration accepts the natural-rights philosophy. The first clause in the preamble is: "Whereas recognition of the inherent dignity and of the equal and inalienable rights of all members of the human family is the foundation of freedom, justice and peace in the world." Article 1 of the Declaration reads: "All human beings are born free and equal in dignity and rights. They are endowed with reason and conscience and should act towards one another in a spirit of brotherhood."

In addition to these basic issues, there was some disagreement as to the kind of document the Declaration should be. All the members agreed that it should be short and concise, so as to be readily understandable. However, the approach of the United States, Great Britain, and China was to emphasize the positive side of rights and freedoms, and whenever possible to leave the restrictions to the Covenant to be drafted later. The representative of France wanted the Declaration to be more explicit, and thought it should go further than any previous declarations of human rights. The Soviet states thought that, in addition to an enumeration of rights and freedoms, there should be provisions indicating the action to be taken to realize them. They also wanted certain limitations stated: for example, freedom of speech, etc., should be denied to Nazis, Fascists, and others who work against democratic interests. Furthermore, they wanted it made clear that the realization of rights and freedoms is subject to the laws of the countries concerned.

The work of the Commission was further complicated by the existence of five official languages and by different connotations of key terms. Great care had to be taken to see that the same meaning was understood by all the representatives. The value of the Declaration would be considerably lessened if there were too many ambiguities and uncertainties as to the precise scope of the various provisions. A few examples will illustrate the type of questions which came up in the discussions.

To an American, the statement "All men are created equal" may seem perfectly obvious in meaning. But there were two objections to it. First, in some countries, where the emancipation of women is recent or still in progress, the term "men" might not be understood in the generic sense. It had to be made clear that women were included too. The other objection came from those who did not wish to endorse the idea of a divine creator. Therefore, the statement became, "All human beings are born free and equal in dignity and rights." This also, it will be noted, gives some content or explanation to the term "equal."

Article 2 states that everyone is entitled to rights and freedoms "without distinction of any kind, such as race, colour, sex, language, religion, political or other opinion, national or social origin, property, birth or other status." The word "birth" was added to an earlier draft after a long discussion as to whether "class" or some other word would better convey the idea sought for.

A proposal was made for inclusion of the statement, "Everyone is entitled to a good social and international order." The Soviet representative, Professor Pavlov, argued that an order which permitted private ownership of the means of production, and the resulting exploitation of one group by another, could not possibly be "good." The statement was revised and finally became, "Everyone is entitled to a social and international order in which the rights and freedoms set forth in this Declaration can be fully realized" (Article 28).

The Universal Declaration of Human Rights, as adopted, contains a preamble and thirty articles. The first two articles constitute an affirmation of human rights and freedoms, and they are meant to apply to everyone, everywhere. Articles 3 through 15 state the traditional rights as they have been known in the Western world. These include the right to life, liberty, and security,[3] to recognition as a person before the law, and to a fair trial. Slavery, torture, cruel and inhuman punishment, arbitrary arrest, and arbitrary interference with home, family, or correspondence are prohibited. All persons are entitled to equal protection of the laws. Ex post facto laws are forbidden. There is recognition of the right to a nationality, to freedom of movement, and to seek asylum from persecution in another state. Article 16 states the equal right of men and women to marry and to found a family. Article 17 deals with the right to own property. The next two articles affirm the basic freedoms of thought, conscience, religion, opinion, and expression. Articles 20 and 21 state the rights of peaceful assembly and association, and to a share in the government of one's country.

The next six articles proclaim the economic, social, and educational rights. Article 22 is of special interest as a concise statement of the philosophy underlying this conception of human rights. It states that "everyone, as a member of society, has the right to social security, and is entitled to realization, through

---

[3] Is it a commentary on the modern world that "security" replaces "pursuit of happiness" in the classic American trinity of human rights?

national effort and international cooperation and in accordance with the organization and resources of each State, of the economic, social and cultural rights indispensable for his dignity and the free development of his personality." Specific rights in this area include work, protection against unemployment, just remuneration, trade unions, rest and leisure, periodic holidays with pay, an adequate standard of living, education, and participation in the cultural life of the community. The branding of children as "illegitimate" is prohibited by the statement that "all children, whether born in or out of wedlock, shall enjoy the same social protection." To counteract such activities as the Nazi youth movement, it was provided that "parents have a prior right to choose the kind of education that shall be given to their children."

Article 28 refers to the social and international order. Article 29 is a statement of duties, rather than rights. It says that everyone has duties to the community "in which alone the free and full development of his personality is possible." Exercise of rights and freedoms is subject only to limitations determined by law for the purpose of securing recognition of the rights of others and meeting the "just requirements of morality, public order and the general welfare in a democratic society." The rights and freedoms may in no case be exercised contrary to the purposes and principles of the United Nations. The final article reflects a precaution against the technique of using freedoms to destroy a democratic order by providing that nothing in the Declaration shall be interpreted to give any state, group, or individual a basis for destroying any of the rights and freedoms which it defines.

The Universal Declaration of Human Rights was adopted by the General Assembly without a dissenting vote. Two countries, El Salvador and Yemen, were absent when the vote was taken. There were eight abstentions. Saudi Arabia refused to approve the Declaration on account of Article 18 which recognizes the right to change one's religion. The delegate from Saudi Arabia thought this was contrary to the Koran, but other Mohammedan countries did not follow this interpretation. The Union of South Africa abstained because of the opinion that the Declaration "went too far" in being progressive. The remaining six abstentions were accounted for by the Soviet Union and the other Communist countries. They considered it as an unprogressive eighteenth-century document, with no guarantees that the stated rights would be achieved. They also objected to the idea of inalienable rights of the individual, on the grounds that the concept of an isolated individual is contrary to social reality.

After the adoption of the Universal Declaration of Human Rights by the General Assembly, the Commission on Human Rights undertook the next stage of its work. The principal task in this connection is to prepare a draft covenant, which will be an international convention or treaty legally binding upon all the states which ratify it. The signatory states will be responsible for seeing to it that their internal regimes conform to the obligations of the

Covenant, and thus the agreements reached in the area of human rights will pass from the realm of principle to that of enforceable law.   Measures of implementation have also been considered in connection with this state of the Commission's work, since it is necessary to lay down some basis for enforcement machinery in the proposed Covenant on Human Rights.

A draft was prepared in 1949 and circulated to member governments for their comments.   The Commission on Human Rights revised this document at its meeting during March, April, and May, 1950, and referred it to the Economic and Social Council.   It then went to the General Assembly, which adopted a series of resolutions [4] concerning it after extensive debate in the Third (Social, Humanitarian and Cultural) Committee.   Several features in the Covenant as drafted were declared unacceptable, and it was decided that the Commission on Human Rights should rewrite the draft and submit it to the next regular session of the General Assembly.

The first question which arose in connection with the draft covenant was that of its scope in relation to the Universal Declaration of Human Rights. The definition of precise legal obligations which governments are willing to accept at the present time is quite a different matter from statements of principles or of aspirations.   For example, what is the legal counterpart of the principle that everyone has a right to "life, liberty and security"?   The right to live is of course the most important of all.   Without it, all the others are entirely meaningless.   This right was asserted in the Declaration.   For the Covenant, however, a number of possible exceptions or limitations were put forward, most of them by the United States.   These included circumstances in which it would be considered lawful to deprive a person of life, such as suppression of rebellion or riot, self-defense, accident, killing for violation of honor, to prevent an escape, by the military in time of war, medical operation in the absence of gross negligence or malpractice, through a voluntary medical experiment, or by officers of the law to prevent a crime.   The British approach was to emphasize that no one should be deprived of his life "intentionally," and to list the limitations.

In the traditional bills of rights in the Western world, the "right to life" has really consisted of constitutional and legal protection against illegal deprivation of life by the state.   It is manifestly absurd to think of a governmental guarantee against death.   The right to life may be inalienable, but it is not absolute.   The most that can be done by a positive approach is to combine the traditional protections with the responsibility of the state to maintain adequate conditions of human living.   The latter might include jobs, social security, healthful environment, and so forth.   In 1950 the Commission on Human Rights decided to take the position that the right to life must be protected by law, and drafted the statement that "to take life shall be a crime, save in the execution of a sentence of a court, or in self-defense, or in the case

[4] On Dec. 4, 1950.

of enforcement measures authorized by the Charter." Limits were also placed on capital punishment.

The problem of freedom of the press offers another example. To Americans, this "right" usually means absence of censorship, that Congress and the state legislatures may pass no laws "abridging the freedom of the press." To the Soviets, it means access to supplies such as ink and newsprint. To them, unless the state assures this access to supplies by "democratic" interests and denies the privilege to Fascists, the "freedom of the press" is only a camouflage by which the exploiters of the people maintain their monopolistic position. The provision of the draft covenant on this point is based on the idea that states shall not interfere illegally or arbitrarily with the right recognized in Article 19 of the Universal Declaration that "everyone has the right to freedom of opinion and expression; this right includes freedom to hold opinions without interference and to seek, receive and impart information and ideas through any media and regardless of frontiers."

As one more example of the problem of specific legal definition of a human right, Article 5 of the Declaration says that "no one shall be subjected to torture or to cruel, inhuman or degrading treatment or punishment." In this connection, some of the inhuman Nazi medical experiments come to mind. But how can such things be categorically outlawed without at the same time prohibiting, for example, compulsory sterilization of mental incompetents as practiced in some countries? After thorough consideration, and consultation with the World Health Organization, the Commission arrived at this statement: "In particular, no one shall be subjected against his will to medical or scientific experimentation involving risk, where such is not required by his state of physical or mental health."

The nature of the permissible limitations on human rights posed an important issue. To what extent, and by what justification, may states place restrictions upon the rights and freedoms of individuals within their jurisdiction? It is established constitutional doctrine in the United States, for example, that the guarantees of the Federal bill of rights are subject to limitations of public policy and the rights of other individuals. Freedom of religion does not include the right to practice polygamy or human sacrifice, or to handle poisonous snakes in public. The freedoms of speech and of the press do not extend to libel, obscenity, incitement to riot, or yelling "fire" in a crowded theater. Maintenance of a balance between individual rights, social obligation, and the public welfare is a matter of interpretation and practice. The problem is that the specific recognition of limitations may give governments a pretext for nullifying the individual rights. If restrictions can be justified where the public welfare requires, how can governments be prevented from abusing the scope of this limitation? If individual rights can be restricted when this is necessary and reasonable in the public interest, what then is the meaning of "necessary and reasonable"? If only arbitrary

nitations are allowed, who decides what is "arbitrary"? The difficulty
compounded by the suspicion that the countries in which individual rights
e most in need of protection would be the first to whittle down the rights
/ broad interpretations of the allowable limitations.

The issue of limitations also raised the question of whether they should be
ated in one all-embracing article, as the United States suggested, or whether
e precise limitations should be stated in each article, as Great Britain wished.
he draft covenant as it came from the Commission on Human Rights was
compromise between the American and British views. It attempts to state
e limitations as concisely and definitely as possible, and to restrict them to
justifiable range. The basic freedoms, for example, are subject only to
ch limitations as are pursuant to law and are necessary for the protection of
ublic safety (and national security), public order, health or morals, or the
ghts and freedoms of others. It will readily be seen that a great deal will
ill depend upon interpretation and practice.

The question of derogation is a special aspect of the problem of limitations.
his referred to the modification or withdrawal of rights and freedoms be-
use of war or other national emergency. The governmental right of deroga-
on is recognized in the countries with the most advanced conception of civil
berties, but in such countries it is also limited to the strict necessities of the
ccasion. During war, censorship is established to the extent necessary to
rotect national security, and martial law may be invoked when, for example,
n invasion makes it impossible for the civil courts to function. Other exam-
les of derogation will occur to the reader. However, if the draft covenant
iould state that individual rights and freedoms may be annulled in case of
ublic emergency, an avenue of arbitrary and unreasonable restriction would
e left open. This problem is handled by strictly limiting the right of deroga-
on to an emergency or disaster, and by providing that in any case there may
e no derogation from certain rights such as those against torture and unlawful
eprivation of life.

Another important problem of transforming a declaration of principles into
gally binding obligations lay in the question of provisions on applicability to
deral states and non-self-governing territories. The federal question is espe-
ially important for the United States, in which much of the legal authority
oncerning human rights lies in the states, while the national government has
e responsibility for enforcing treaty obligations. It can be foreseen that
treaty increasing the power of the national government at the expense of
states' rights" would meet great difficulties in the Senate. The United States
rged a text which would recognize its constitutional division of powers, while
any other delegations protested that the result would be an unfair disparity
f obligations as between federal and unitary states.

The majority in the Third Committee were in favor of a stipulation that the
ovenant would apply automatically to all the non-self-governing territories

administered by a signatory country. The British and several other deleg
tions argued that this would deprive the non-self-governing peoples of the rig
to decide for themselves.

Another question of the scope of the covenant was how many of the righ
and freedoms it should codify. One viewpoint was that it should compri
the basic individual, civil, and political rights, while some delegations want
to extend it to include the economic and social rights as well. It becar
obvious that the complexity and controversial nature of the latter area wou
make it impossible to draft a covenant expeditiously if an attempt should
made to put into legal form all the rights mentioned in the Universal Declar
tion. The Commission on Human Rights decided, therefore, that the trac
tional field would be covered as an initial step and that the resulting draft wou
be a *first* covenant of human rights. Work could then proceed on the drafti
of a *second* covenant embodying the economic and social rights. Howeve
this decision was rejected by the General Assembly, which affirmed that bo
categories should be included in the draft covenant.

The problem of implementation was another fundamental issue which ha
to be considered in connection with the draft covenant. There were tw
different conceptions of this problem. The Soviet Union conceived impl
mentation as the realization by each state in its own way of the rights ar
freedoms concerned. Under this view, there would be no international m
chinery to supervise or assure the observance of the declaration and the cov
nant. Human rights and freedoms, according to the Soviet Union, invol
the relation between the individual and the state. This is held to be a matt
of domestic jurisdiction, and international machinery would be a violation
Article 2, paragraph 2, of the Charter.

Others had a conception of implementation which would allow for son
supervision or review of the condition of human rights within the states ratif
ing the covenant. They did not consider that human rights were the e
clusive domestic concern of each state and, even if they were, the situatic
would be changed by the ratification of the proposed international covenar
The non-Soviet delegates wished to devise some measures by which the Unite
Nations could do something about human rights when and if they were vi
lated. There was a variety of opinions on what these measures should b
Some thought of the Commission on Human Rights as the proper agency f
this task. Others would set up separate organs, perhaps a special commissic
or even an international court of human rights. The representative of Chir
stressed the importance of a more positive view. He would emphasize th
realization of human rights by education and cooperation, rather than th
punishment of delinquencies in this field.

Still another issue related to the question of petitions. There was agre
ment that signatory states should have the right of initiating complain
concerning violations of the covenant. When it came to the question

ether individuals, groups and organizations could submit petitions, there
s sharp difference of opinion.   The Soviet Union was opposed to such a right
principle, arguing that it would introduce a disruptive element into the
itural relationship" between the state and its citizens.   Later, this position
s modified to admit the possibility that organizations of a "wide demo-
tic basis" might submit petitions.   The second attitude was held by the
ited States, Great Britain, and China.   They were not opposed in principle
t wanted to exercise caution, lest false hopes might be aroused as to the
ual force of international guarantees in the near future.   The third school
thought, led by Australia and India, wanted an immediate recognition of the
ht of petition for individuals and groups.   Among other arguments, they
;ed that granting the right need involve no commitment as to how the peti-
ns would be handled, and that it would be a mockery to tell people they had
tain rights and then refuse to listen to complaints that these rights had
n violated.

The machinery for implementation, as recommended in the first draft cove-
it, would consist of a Human Rights Committee, composed of seven mem-
s elected by the parties to the covenant for five-year terms on a staggered
sis.   Any party to the covenant could complain to another party alleged
be violating any of its provisions.   If satisfaction were not obtained, a
nplaint could then be made to the Committee, whose function would be to
estigate the facts, offer its "good offices," and make a report on the situation.
us, it will be seen that the cautious approach was adopted for purpose of
draft covenant.   Only signatory states would be represented on the Hu-
n Rights Committee.   A country unwilling to ratify and place its own
iation under scrutiny would not have an opportunity to file complaints con-
ning other countries.   Individuals and groups would not as yet be given
right of petition.   No international court of human rights was to be estab-
ied, and the international machinery to be instituted was to have no co-
ive or enforcement powers.

These draft provisions were severely criticized during the debate in the
neral Assembly's Third Committee during November, 1950.   On the one
id, the representative of the Soviet Union stated that all articles dealing
h measures of implementation were unacceptable as infringing on the
nestic jurisdiction of signatory states.   On the other hand, the majority
the Committee felt that there should be provisions for consideration of
itions from individuals and organizations on alleged violations of human
hts.   These provisions might be inserted in the covenant itself or in sepa-
e protocols.   There was also a widespread feeling that the economic, so-
l, and cultural rights should be included in the first draft covenant.   As a
ult of this dissatisfaction, the Commission on Human Rights was requested
submit a revised draft.

Anyone who wishes to study the ideological struggle of the modern world

would do well to make a careful examination of the proceedings of the Co
mission on Human Rights. The place of the individual in the social ord
the authority of government, all the fundamental issues of rights and freedo
have been exhaustively stated and reviewed there by representatives of
the major cultures, philosophies, and legal systems. It has furnished a for
without parallel in history for the most searching comparative analysis
ideas and views on the crucial problems of liberty and authority.

It must be recognized that the question of human rights and freedoms
far-reaching implications. Their effective international guarantees wo
mean a fundamental change in the relation between the individual and
state. As was indicated above,[5] the object is not to limit the power of
United Nations but to protect individual rights and freedoms against ab
by their respective governments. It is well to remember that, under
Constitution of the United States, there was for many years very little ba
for Federal protection of the rights of citizens against their respective st
governments. The first ten amendments, or Bill of Rights, consisted of
strictions on the Federal government. The only *Federal* restrictions on
freedom of a state to treat its own citizens as it pleased were those enumera
in Article 1, Section 10, of the Constitution. Of these, the only ones wh
dealt directly with human rights were the prohibitions against bills of
tainder and ex post facto laws. The adoption of the Fourteenth Amendm
after the Civil War first opened up a wide area for Federal action to sec
individual rights against the state governments. This power was used i
limited way for many years, and Federal action still does not occupy this wh
field of governmental authority.

Even though the draft covenant has not been submitted for ratificati
some jurisprudence is beginning to develop on the subject of human rig
There is, first of all, a possibility that the Universal Declaration may of its
have some significance for the development of international law. It is p
sible to argue that the Declaration constitutes an authoritative definition a
interpretation of the provisions of the Charter on this subject, and that i
a contribution to "the general principles of law recognized by civilized
tions." In a Canadian case (*In re Drummond Wren*), the Supreme Co
of Ontario ruled restrictive covenants illegal as in conflict with the Uni
Nations Charter. Mr. Justice Black, of the United States Supreme Co
asked in a concurring opinion (*In re Oyama v. Calif.*), "How can this
tion be faithful to this international pledge if state laws which bar land ov
ership and occupancy by aliens on account of race are permitted?" In Ap
1950, the California appellate court ruled that a state law restricting la
ownership by aliens was invalid as in conflict with the Charter of the Uni
Nations. There has been considerable criticism of this decision on the grou
that the provisions of the Charter on human rights are not self-executing, t

[5] See p. 299.

they have no specific content and legal force in this country until Congress
islates on the subject.[6] The point remains open to question for the present,
ce the case has not been reviewed by the United States Supreme Court.
It is easy to see, however, that ratification of the proposed covenant by the
ited States might have some interesting and important constitutional and
al consequences, even though an international court in this field is not
templated at this time. The Federal government doubtless would gain
thority in the field of civil rights, and the scope of "states' rights" would be
respondingly narrowed. It is possible that governmental power would be
reased in another way if the Federal government were considered inter-
tionally responsible for violations of human rights by individuals or groups
thin its territory.

Obviously, the question of an international covenant on human rights is a
ry real and practical one. It is a mistake to think of this matter as some ab-
act proposition with no relevance to actual conditions. In this connection,
is of interest to take note of some of the criticism of the proposed Covenant.
e American Bar Association has been especially prominent in this con-
ction and seems to have four major reasons for its position. One of its
ticisms, that the source of human rights is placed in legislative fiat, does not
m to be supported by the language of the Declaration and draft Covenant
elf. Second, the Association objects to the so-called economic, social, and
ucational rights on the ground that they embody a collectivist philosophy.
the third place, some of the passages are considered vague and ambiguous.
nally, the American Bar Association points to alleged implications as to
anges in the American form of government, especially if jurisdiction is given
an international court, and considers that ratification of the draft covenant
the United States would constitute an improper use of the treaty power.[7]

The suggestion has been made that the present work of the Commission on
uman Rights might be based on the rights and freedoms essential to the
nctioning of the United Nations itself.[8] These might include, for exam-
e, freedom to travel to the headquarters of the Organization, the right to be
formed about meetings and decisions of the United Nations, the right to
press an opinion on the policy of one's government in the United Nations,
d other rights applicable in this connection. The Commission, however,
ntinues to work on the basis of securing a maximum area of agreement among
vernments on international cooperation in the protection of human rights
d fundamental freedoms for everyone, everywhere.

6 Manley O. Hudson, "Charter Provisions on Human Rights in American Law," Ameri-
n Journal of International Law, July, 1950, pp. 543–548. Another viewpoint is ex-
essed by Quincy Wright in "National Courts and Human Rights—The Fujii Case,"
merican Journal of International Law, January, 1951, pp. 62–82.
7 "International Human Rights," Law and Contemporary Problems, 1949, pp. 451–478.
8 Ibid., pp. 428–429.

OTHER WORK ON HUMAN RIGHTS

Activities of the United Nations in the field of human rights and fun mental freedoms have not been confined to the work of the Commission Human Rights. Selected problems have been handled as separate items un the auspices of the Economic and Social Council and the General Assemb Among the most important of these have been freedom of information and the press, genocide, and the status of women.

Freedom of Information and the Press. It has been recognized from beginning that freedom of information is closely linked with the maintenar of international peace and security. The General Assembly pointed out in resolution of February 13, 1946, that "the United Nations cannot achieve purposes for which it has been created unless the peoples of the world fully informed of its aims and activities." The General Assembly furth stated in a resolution of December 14, 1946, that "freedom of information a fundamental human right and is the touchstone of all the freedoms to wh the United Nations is consecrated," and that "understanding and cooperati among nations are impossible without an alert and sound world opinion whi in turn, is wholly dependent upon freedom of information."

To help define this concept and to determine the attendant responsibiliti a United Nations Conference on Freedom of Information was convened Geneva during the spring of 1948. All members of the United Nations a several nonmember states were invited to participate in this Conference, a the specialized agencies and a number of nongovernmental organizations we invited to attend. Delegates representing fifty-four governments were pr ent, and three others sent observers. The concept and problems of freedo of information were thoroughly discussed and debated for about four wee! The results of the conference took the form of a series of resolutions a three draft conventions—on the gathering and international transmission news, on the institution of an international right of correction,[9] and on fre dom of information.

A Sub-Commission on Freedom of Information and of the Press was esta lished as a subsidiary organ of the Commission on Human Rights.[10] Th Sub-Commission consists of twelve experts who serve in their personal capac ties, not as official representatives. They are elected by the Commission

[9] By this right a state which feels that news reports, which are likely to injure its inte national relations and which have been disseminated abroad, are false or distorted m submit its version of the facts to the state in whose territory the reports were publishe The latter then has the obligation to make the statement of "correction" available to ne enterprises.

[10] The Commission also had a Sub-Commission on Prevention of Discrimination a Protection of Minorities.

uman Rights for three-year terms subject to the consent of their governments.   The Sub-Commission has undertaken studies and made recommenda-
ons in connection with the provisions on freedom of information and of the
ress in the Universal Declaration of Human Rights and in the draft cove-
ant.   It has also held several conferences for the purpose of discussion and
riving at recommendations.   Throughout these sessions, the fundamental
fference between the Western and Soviet concepts of a "free press" has been
aintained rather than resolved.   The Soviet representatives have repeatedly
ade the argument that information should be used in the interests of the
eople and not of big capitalist newspaper monopolies.   They have em-
hasized that an international convention on the subject should be an instru-
ent in the struggle for peace and against war propaganda.   Censorship in
e Soviet Union is allegedly directed not against freedom of information, but
gainst the spreading of false and distorted information.   They contend that
e whole field of mass information in the United States and Great Britain is
ontrolled by "big business."   The Polish representative said on one occasion
at the assertion that all in the United States are equally free to influence
ublic opinion is just as true as the assertion that the Waldorf-Astoria is open
millionaires and beggars.

Members from the Western countries, on the other hand, continue to stress
e concept of a free press, which is familiar in the American tradition.   They
adily admit that distorted or malicious information may be disseminated,
ut they feel that the best corrective is in the competition of ideas and the
ealthy lash of public criticism.   Repressive government censorship would
eate more evils than it could possibly eliminate.   They believe that peo-
le should be allowed access to news from all sources and to all kinds of differ-
t opinions.   According to this conception, the effort to control ideas and
formation by an authoritarian regime is the most dangerous of all govern-
ental controls and the very negation of a free press.

It can be readily understood how difficult it is to reconcile such divergent
oints of view as those held by the Communist countries on the one hand and
e Western European and English-speaking countries on the other.   The
oviet bloc received considerable support from Latin-American and Middle
astern countries.   A proposed Mexican amendment, for example, would
ave authorized censorship on the basis of "national dignity," "national
restige" and "national security"!   Such "permissible restrictions" would
stify practically any curb on the transmission of news, and the convention
which such provisions were incorporated would afford not protection but
gal justification for suppressing freedom of information.

Genocide.   "Genocide" is a new name for an old crime.   It means the de-
ruction of groups of human beings.   The destruction may take the form of
assacres, executions, or deprival of food and housing.   The birth rate may
e restricted by the forced segregation of the sexes, or the special character-

istics of the group may be destroyed by such means as the forced transfer ·
its children to other groups. Massacres, pogroms, and mass killings were a
old story in human history long before Cato's slogan *Carthago delenda es*
and this sorry record by no means stopped with the sacking of Carthage. I
Nazi Germany, genocide was practiced on a large scale as a deliberate polic
of state carried out with scientific ingenuity. The punishment of these crime
became one of the war aims of the Allied nations. The Nuremberg tria
included, as one part of the indictment, crimes against humanity, namely mu
der, extermination, enslavement, deportation, and other inhuman acts com
mitted against any civilian population before or during the war, or persec
tions on political, racial, or religious grounds committed in connection wit
the war. The trial and conviction of the Nazi leaders by the Internation
Military Tribunal were endorsed by a resolution of the General Assembl
However, there was a feeling that penal repression of this kind should not I
limited to acts connected with war, but should be of universal application.

The convention on genocide seeks to make this offense an internation
crime. There is some precedent for this in the treatment of piracy, traff
in women and children, and the slave trade, which are now recognized a
offenses against humanity and the law of nations. The purpose is to secu
general agreement to placing genocide in the same category as an internation
crime. The convention was drafted by an *ad hoc* committee established t
the Economic and Social Council, and was approved by the General A
sembly on December 9, 1948, after consideration by the Sixth (Legal) Con
mittee. Genocide is defined in the draft convention as any of the followin
acts committed with intent to destroy, in whole or in part, a national, ethni
racial, or religious group as such: (1) killing members of the group; (2
causing serious bodily or mental harm to members of the group; (3) d
liberately inflicting on the group conditions of life calculated to bring abo
its physical destruction in whole or in part; (4) imposing measures intende
to prevent births within the group; and (5) forcibly transferring the childre
of the group to another group.

The Soviet representative wanted to extend the definition to include "cu
tural genocide," meaning any deliberate act committed with the intention
destroying any language, religion, or culture or any national, racial, or re
ligious beliefs. The majority agreed that crimes like the destruction c
churches, schools, and libraries, or other measures of cultural exterminatio
were barbarous, but that this question belonged to the field of human right
To extend the genocide convention to cover this field would make it too broa
and general, even vague, and would weaken the purpose of preventing an
punishing the physical destruction of entire human groups.

The United States representative wished to include "political" group
among those to be protected against genocide, but the majority decided again
this. Some held that such groups are not sufficiently defined to be include

ıd some thought that to include them might lead to interference in the in-
ırnal affairs of countries.

Violations are to be tried by "a competent tribunal of the State in the ter-
tory of which the act was committed." An international jurisdiction is not
tablished by the convention, although the way is left open for its possible
ıture development by providing the alternative of "such an international
ınal tribunal as may have jurisdiction with respect to those Contracting
arties which shall have accepted its jurisdiction."

The question naturally arises of the value of the genocide convention. In
ıe discussions in the Sixth Committee of the General Assembly the greatest
essimism was expressed by the British delegate. He argued that individual
ınocide is already punishable by the laws of all countries, whereas genocide
ımmitted by states is punishable only by war. A regime committing such
crime would not hold back on account of a convention or surrender itself for
ial by an international tribunal. No steps should be taken, he thought, to
ad people to believe that some great forward step had been taken when noth-
ıg had really been changed. The representative of Czechoslovakia said that
lthough the existence of a convention on genocide might not have deterred
litler, it would have at least precluded a spirit of toleration toward him and
ould have made it difficult to conclude agreements such as the one at Munich.

The feeling prevailed that it was important to give a precise definition of
enocide and to make a solemn international affirmation of its outlawry.
'here would then be a legal basis for collective international safeguards. De-
ıite the fact that some representatives retained a degree of skepticism and
ıat many were not fully satisfied by all the provisions, the convention on
ınocide was adopted by a unanimous vote of the General Assembly. It went
ıto effect in January, 1951, three months after it had been ratified by twenty
ountries.[11]

Status of Women. The status of women has been recognized by the
Inited Nations as a special problem. One of the prohibited discriminations
ı the field of human rights and fundamental freedoms is that on account of
ıx, and Article 8 of the Charter provides that "the United Nations shall place
ıo restrictions on the eligibility of men and women to participate in any ca-
acity and under conditions of equality in its principal and subsidiary organs."

In June, 1946, the Economic and Social Council established a Commission
ın the Status of Women, to serve as an expert body on matters pertaining to
ıis question. Its functions are to prepare recommendations and reports
ın the promotion of women's rights in political, economic, social, and educa-

---

[11] Not including the United States. For an elucidation of the arguments pro and
ın, see *Hearings before a Subcommittee of the Committee on Foreign Relations on Execu-*
ve O, The International Convention on the Prevention and Punishment of the Crime of
enocide, United States Senate, 81st Congress, 2d Session (Government Printing Office,
)50).

tional affairs. It was also instructed to watch for, study, and make recor
mendations on urgent matters requiring immediate attention. The Commi
sion is composed of fifteen members. The representatives are nominated l
the governments of the elected countries after consultation with the Secretar;
General. The nominations then go to the Economic and Social Council f«
confirmation. By this procedure it is possible to get members with expe
knowledge on all aspects of women's status. It has been the practice for a
fifteen representatives to be women.

The Commission has advocated political rights for women, to include un
versal adult suffrage; equal rights to vote, to be elected, and to hold offict
and equal participation in government. In civil matters, the aim is fu
equality. With respect to marriage, the Commission seeks freedom «
choice, dignity of the wife, monogamy, equal rights to dissolution of ma
riage, equal rights to guardianship of children, and the right of a marrie
woman to retain her own nationality if she wishes. As to legal capacity, tl
Commission declared that women, single or married, should have equal righ
to enter into contracts, and to acquire and dispose of inherited property. I
order to prevent economic and social discrimination against women, equ;
rights with men are sought in regard to such matters as labor, wages, and hol
days.

The Commission has taken the position that women are entitled to speci;
protection in certain circumstances, such as before and after childbirth. Als«
an effective system of health and social insurance legislation is advocate«
Some of the subjects which have been emphasized in the studies, conference
and recommendations of the Commission are political rights, especially th
suffrage and office holding; nationality of married women; property rights «
married women; application of penal law to women; and educational of
portunities for women.

PART IV

FUTURE

Chapter 20

STRENGTHENING THE UNITED NATIONS

The United Nations is a going concern. Its record of activities and accomplishments during its first six years is an impressive one, considering the difficulties which have existed. Yet a secure world peace has not been established, and even the optimist will agree that the road ahead is long, difficult, and dangerous. It is in relation to these facts that the necessity and possibilities of strengthening the United Nations must be judged.

Making Effective Decisions

It is essential to the success of the United Nations that it be capable of making effective decisions. If a stalemate develops between opposing groups, the Organization will be unable to accomplish its purposes and it will lose the support and respect of governments and peoples. If agreement is limited to formal resolutions which pay tribute to the principles of the United Nations but do not affect the actual course of events, the label of hypocrisy will be added to that of impotence. The basic question is, "What steps can be taken so that the organs of the United Nations can reach decisions more expeditiously and implement them more effectively?"

At the San Francisco Conference, the Charter was drafted on the basis that decisions could be made in the General Assembly by a simple or two-thirds majority, and in the Security Council by seven votes out of eleven with the concurrence of all the permanent members. Agreement and joint action by the Great Powers were considered indispensable to the maintenance of international peace and security. Decisions would be reached if the Big Five and a sufficient number of other members were in agreement. The decisions would be practically effective if the same countries supported them and put them into operation. Of course, no one expected that the Great Powers would see eye to eye on every question; rather, the hope was that there would be a sufficient degree of cooperation to permit a mutually acceptable solution for disputes and situations dangerous to peace and security.

The development of the "cold war" placed emphasis on security *against* an opposing bloc rather than on security *with* other members of a general

world organization. East-West antagonism presents a cleavage too w
to be bridged by mutual confidence and agreed cooperation. This unf
tunate fact alters the situation in which the United Nations functions, a
it radically changes the problem of reaching effective decisions. Under t
"rule of unanimity" the Great Powers must be in agreement; in a time
"cold war" they are in fundamental disagreement. It is difficult for th
to cooperate in the achievement of collective security when they are thi
ing in terms of security from each other. This means that there is const
danger of a stalemate on questions of critical importance. Consequently
need is felt for some alternative means of arriving at significant decisions.

The small countries at the San Francisco Conference had opposed the Gr
Power veto, but the Big Five, and especially the United States and the Sov
Union, had insisted on it. After the frightful possibilities of atomic bon
became apparent, there was considerable discussion in many countries abc
the establishment of some form of world government in place of the Unit
Nations. The idea of "eliminating the veto" became a slogan and rallyi
point for many who were convinced of an urgent necessity for a much stron
world organization than the United Nations as it existed. The veto questi
also became a symbol of high emotional value to the American public as t
Soviet Union played its role of a minority of one among the permanent me
bers of the Security Council.

The campaign to "eliminate the veto," however, tended to confuse cav
with effect. One negative vote, blocking unanimity of agreement, was mer
a reflection of the power and inclination of the Soviet Union to pursue polic
not acceptable to the other Great Powers. It does no good to reach decisic
by a majority vote if the minority has the power to prevent the decisions fr
being carried out. In such cases, the majority can prevail only by induci
the minority to cooperate or by finding some means to make its oppositi
ineffective. Reaffirmation by balloting that the majority is the majori
certainly does not reach the heart of this problem.

A more practical and promising approach was to seek a basis for eliminati
the so-called "abuse of the veto." This would recognize the propriety of refu
ing to be bound by majority voting in matters considered vital to national sec
ity or involving actual enforcement measures. On the other hand, frivolous a
obstructive use of the unanimity rule would be precluded. There is a wi
latitude for interpretation and negotiation on this point, since the Charter
far from definitive on the question of vetoable items. Some, like the ado
tion of the agenda and the election of a presiding officer, are clearly procedur
Others, like the use of enforcement measures, are obviously substantive a
therefore subjective to the rule of unanimity. But there is much doubtf
ground between these clear-cut extremes. Does the proposal to discuss
matter involve a substantive decision? How about a proposal to establish
commission of inquiry? These are only two of the many questions whi

uld be raised concerning the elusive and controversial distinction between
procedural" and "substantive" matters.

In 1948 the General Assembly, upon the proposal of the United States,
ve an extensive consideration to this subject. A list of various types of
questions which appeared appropriate for decision by a procedural vote was
scussed. As a result, recommendations were made to the Security Council
at the permanent members agree not to exercise the privilege of the veto
questions of pacific settlement, the admission of new members, and other
atters not involving decisions on enforcement measures. These recom-
endations have not been accepted by the Soviet Union, which has continued
exercise its prerogatives of a negative vote on much the same basis as be-
re. However, the permanent members of the Security Council did announce
eir acceptance of the General Assembly's recommendation that they resort
consultation in order to hold the number of vetoes to a minimum. This
chnique has some promise. Informal discussion may provide an opportunity
r exploring areas of agreement and thus promote a "meeting of the minds."
lso, it may help to ease the situation in the respect that there are no vetoes
hen questions are not brought to a formal vote. Forcing a vote on a proposi-
on known to be unacceptable to the minority invites a veto and may increase
ther than alleviate tension, especially in terms of public opinion.

One result of stalemate in the Security Council has been an increased em-
hasis on the General Assembly. In the latter organ, "important" decisions
ay be made by a two-thirds majority of the members present and voting.
here is no veto. Although the decisions of the General Assembly are recom-
endations rather than binding obligations, there are ways of making its
fluence felt in dispute concerning which the permanent members of the Se-
urity Council are not able to agree. The Greek case, for example, was re-
oved from the agenda of the Security Council, and the General Assembly
roceeded to consider the matter and to appoint the United Nations Special
ommittee on the Balkans. The situation in Korea was not referred to the
ecurity Council prior to June, 1950. The General Assembly had undertaken
find a solution and, among other things, had appointed the United Nations
ommission which was in Korea when the war broke out. The prompt report
f an impartial international body was an important factor in making pos-
ble the swift and decisive action of the Security Council.

One obvious way to strengthen the General Assembly is to enable it to
nction continuously. The Charter provides for regular annual sessions and
r special sessions which may be called upon the request of the Security
ouncil or a majority of the members of the United Nations. Most of the
gular sessions have lasted about three months or a little less, although the
hird Assembly reconvened in the spring of 1949, because its business was not
ompleted the preceding December. Two special sessions have been held,
oth to deal with the situation in Palestine. The Interim Committee of the

General Assembly (or "Little Assembly") was established in 1947 as a com
mittee of the whole to function between sessions.   This provided a means fe
continuous study and discussion of matters related to the work of the Gener
Assembly, and for the preparation of recommendations to the parent bod
It could also exercise a limited amount of delegated authority, as when
authorized the United Nations Temporary Commission on Korea to procee
with the supervision of elections in the southern part of the country in 194
The Soviet Union objected to the creation of the Interim Committee and ha
never participated in its work, on the grounds than an illegal attempt was b
ing made to undermine the Security Council and transfer its functions to
subsidiary organ of the General Assembly.

At the fifth Assembly in 1950, the United States delegation presented for
recommendations "designed to increase the effectiveness of United Natio
action against aggression." [1]   After some modification, these proposals we
introduced as a joint resolution by Canada, France, the Philippines, Turke
Great Britain, the United States, and Uruguay.   The purpose was to strength
the General Assembly in the event of the Security Council's inability to de
with an act of aggression because of the veto.   The proposals were (1)
provision for calling the General Assembly into emergency session upon twenty
four hours' notice; (2) the establishment of a "peace patrol" to observe situa
tions dangerous to world peace and report upon them; (3) a plan for th
designation of units within national armed forces to be ready for prompt ser
ice on behalf of the United Nations; and (4) the establishment of a com
mittee to study and report on means which might be used to carry out the pu
poses and principles of the Charter.

The "Uniting for Peace" resolution [2] was adopted by the General Assembl
on November 2, 1950, by a vote of 52 to 5, with 2 abstentions.   This make
possible prompt consideration by the General Assembly if the Security Counc
is prevented from acting in case of an act of aggression.   An emergency ses
sion could be convened within twenty-four hours, instead of two weeks a
required under the previous rules.   The General Assembly may discuss th
situation and adopt a recommendation by a two-thirds majority.   This woul
not constitute action nor would it represent a binding obligation under th
Charter.   Nevertheless, as Mr. John Foster Dulles said in his speech of Octo
ber 9, recommendations can be equally effective if made to a responsive mem
bership. [3]

[1] See address of Secretary of State Acheson before the General Assembly, Sept. 2
1950; speech by John Foster Dulles before the Political and Security Committee on Oct. 9
speech by Andrei Vishinsky before the same Committee the next day; and subsequer
debates.

[2] This resolution incorporated the four points of the joint resolution and also the mai
principles of a Chilean draft resolution on the strengthening of democratic principles as
means of contributing to the maintenance of peace.   For the text, see Appendix 21.

[3] It may be noted in this connection that the Security Council resolutions of June 25 an
27, 1950, on the Korea case took the form of "requests," not directives.

The adoption of these proposals provides a method for making decisions without the requirement of unanimity among the permanent members of the Security Council. The effectiveness of any such decisions will depend entirely upon the extent to which they were accepted and carried out by member states. The Soviet Union objected to the proposals on the basis that they were intended to destroy the basic principle of joint responsibility of the Great Powers and that they violated the Charter by attempting to deprive the Security Council of its legitimate powers. This was not an unnatural opposition, since the practical effect of the plan is to enlarge the area of decisions which can be taken without the consent of the Soviet Union.

In gauging the probable effectiveness of the proposals in question, it must be kept in mind that, under the Charter, the General Assembly cannot take over the functions and prerogatives of the Security Council, and that neither Soviet power nor Soviet intransigence can merely be voted out of existence. But it may be possible to create a situation in which the majority take action sanctioned by the United Nations without the prerequisite of an affirmative vote of all the permanent members of the Security Council. There may be occasions when the Soviet Union, for example, will oppose and vote against a resolution but not interfere with measures taken by others to carry it out. The Korean case, in fact, already furnishes an example of this. The Soviet Union certainly opposed United Nations armed assistance to the Republic of Korea, and a veto of the Security Council resolutions was not interposed only because of a boycott of the meetings over another issue. Nevertheless, at this writing the Soviet Union has not taken up arms in support of the North Korea regime which it sponsored. The very existence of a capacity to make effective decisions without unanimity among the Great Powers will tend toward acceptance of such decisions and will reduce the significance of the veto. This fact will have profound consequences for the future development of the United Nations. The advance knowledge that one member can block the wishes of the majority puts a premium on obstruction by a determined minority. When this obstacle is removed, the minority is more likely to seek maximum concessions to its point of view through negotiations.

Article 51 of the Charter refers to the inherent right of individual and collective self-defense in the event of an armed attack and the failure of the Security Council to maintain international peace and security. No machinery was established, however, for reaching decisions to invoke the right of collective self-defense under Article 51. One interesting suggestion [4] is that members be invited to conclude a multilateral treaty agreeing that they would accept a two-thirds vote of the General Assembly, including at least three of the Great Powers. A formal treaty to this effect is not necessarily involved in the proposals under discussion, but it is anticipated that in an emergency the

[4] Advocated, for example, by the American Association for the United Nations. This is the idea of the Thomas-Douglas resolution (Senate Concurrent Resolution No. 52, 81st Congress, 2d Session).

members would vote responsibly in the General Assembly and be responsive to a resolution adopted by a two-thirds majority.

A second point in the proposals was the establishment of a "peace observation commission," or "peace patrol," preferably not to include any of the Great Powers. Such a commission could go or send observers to areas of friction, with the consent of the countries whose territories would be visited. It might draw upon the panel of field observers already established by the General Assembly. The very presence of a United Nations Commission should operate to discourage aggression, and in the event it did occur, the Security Council and the General Assembly would have prompt and reliable information. When fighting breaks out between countries, each side takes great pains to prove that the other was the aggressor. The position of a United Nations commission is likely, therefore, to have considerable practical value, especially in determining the position of peoples with no direct interest in the particular controversy itself. This conclusion does not depend upon speculation, however, since commissions created by the General Assembly have already proved their value in Greece and Korea.

A consideration of the distinction between effective decisions and "mere resolutions" cannot overlook the question of an international police force. Article 43 of the Charter provides for armed forces to be made available by agreement between the members and the Security Council. This provision has not been implemented because of the basic disagreements among the Great Powers. The United Nations Guard has been established in the Secretariat under the authorization of the General Assembly. This, of course, is a very small nonmilitary armed force by designation. The members were requested to furnish the necessary assistance to protect the Republic of Korea from aggression and to restore peace. The United States carried a large share of the burden, but it should be noted that within three months after the initial attack sixteen different countries had committed military forces for use under the United Nations flag.[5]

The resolution adopted by the fifth Assembly included a plan by which each member would designate within its national armed forces one or more United Nations units. They would be specially trained and equipped and continuously maintained in readiness for prompt service on behalf of the United Nations. This does not involve a specific earmarking of forces, or the establishment of an international army as such. It merely means that the members should be ready to use armed force on behalf of the United Nations if the necessity should arise and if the appropriate decisions are made. Technical advice on organization, training, and equipment of such units might be made available by means of attaching to the Secretariat a panel of military experts. This proposal contemplates the same type of international armed force as does

[5] *United Nations Bulletin*, Vol. IX, No. 7, Oct. 1, 1950, pp. 305–307. Many more offered economic assistance, medical supplies, etc.

Article 43 of the Charter, namely, a system of national contingents to be placed under international command for specified purposes. Since, however, the necessary agreements with the Security Council have not been concluded, the members would establish the national contingents upon the recommendation of the General Assembly.

How Strengthen the United Nations?

The necessity and desire to strengthen the United Nations raise the question of method. Three main approaches may be identified. They are (1) amendment of the Charter; (2) interpretation of the Charter and of the powers of the United Nations; and (3) actual use of the Organization.

About six weeks after the Charter was signed at San Francisco, an atomic bomb was dropped on Hiroshima. Many who knew what a future atomic war might mean began to ask whether a Charter written in the preatomic age were not obsolete before it was ratified. Some of the nuclear physicists and various other people talked about a world government strong enough to administer world law and to ensure world peace. Books like *An Anatomy of Peace* by Emery Reves, *Modern Man Is Obsolete* by Norman Cousins, and *Peace or Anarchy* by Cord Meyer, Jr., commanded a wide attention. New interest was aroused by the idea, advocated by Clarence Streit since 1938, of a federal union of democracies to strengthen the forces of freedom and to serve as a nucleus for an eventual world government. Ely Culbertson, the bridge expert, publicized a pet plan of his own. A group of scholars centered at the University of Chicago drafted a constitution to show what a federal republic of the world "might look like." For a while there was an epidemic of plans and movements, practically all of them on the theme that the United Nations would be too weak and must be replaced (or greatly altered) by some kind of stronger world government.

When questions were raised as to how this would be brought about, the tendency was to insist that it could be done because it must be done. Unspeakable catastrophe was the only alternative, and time was short. In fact, however, none of these plans had an answer for the basic dilemma of world government—that of effectiveness and acceptability. Obviously a plan is useless unless it would be effective in practice. No plan has a chance to be tried out in practice unless it is widely acceptable, especially to those who control the governments of the leading nations. Any proposal which had a chance of being widely accepted, in fact as well as in theory, was likely not to be sufficiently effective to control the policies of governments.

The procedure for amending the Charter (Article 108) requires the concurrence of all the permanent members of the Security Council. Thus, amendatory proposals are themselves subject to the veto. It does not seem logical to suppose that a Great Power ready to veto resolutions offered within the scope of the Charter would be willing to accept amendments giving greater powers to an international organization and taking away the right of veto. The real problem has not been one of constitution making. There was nothing in the Charter which prohibited or restricted the maximum amount of international cooperation which was obtainable in practice. On the contrary, there were scope and authorization under it for vastly more cooperation than was being attained. The world-government advocates were well-intentioned, but their efforts were misdirected because of a misapprehension as to the nature of the problem at issue. The function of a constitutional document is to record a consensus which has been reached. It can even influence the extent to which a consensus is achieved, and it can be an important element in the maintenance of a subsequent unity. All this can be illustrated from the development and history of the United States Constitution. One thing a constitutional document cannot do, however, is to create a consensus and a unity in the absence of the essential social, economic, political, and psychological factors.

Another method for strengthening the United Nations is by interpretation of the Charter. There are enough general terms, and ambiguous provisions, to offer many opportunities for a broad construction of the functions and powers of the United Nations. This field would expand tremendously if the Great Powers had more confidence in each other, but already important precedents have been established. The Security Council intervened in the Indonesian case despite the contention of the Netherlands government that the dispute was between a state and one of its colonies and therefore a matter within domestic jurisdiction. In several instances, the Security Council has handled a dispute without making a formal finding under Article 39. It has not shown a tendency to evade its responsibilities by hiding behind legal technicalities or a narrow literalism. The General Assembly has been inclined to give a broad interpretation to its mandate to discuss, and make recommendations on any matters within the scope of the Charter.

Even in connection with the veto there are some liberalizing precedents. The most notable of these is concerned with the significance of an abstention from voting. The Charter, Article 27, refers to the "concurring votes" of the permanent members of the Security Council. If one of the Big Five abstains from voting, does it show its concurrence? Or is an affirmative vote necessary? The interpretation in practice has been that a resolution is adopted when there are at least seven affirmative votes and when no permanent member casts a negative vote. In other words, the veto has been modified by interpretation even at the expense of straining the language of the Charter. This has had the most important consequences. The Security Council could pass the resolution on Korea in June, 1950, in the absence of the Soviet Union because of the ruling that nonvoting is not a veto. If the precedents had been that "concurrence" requires a definite affirmative vote, the resolutions could have been vetoed by the absence of the Soviet Union. If it is true that the Korean case represents the real turning point in the United Nations, the interpretation that an abstention is not a veto will rank in historic significance with the case of *Marbury v. Madison* in the constitutional development of the United States.

At the San Francisco Conference it was assumed that the United Nations could not use force to maintain peace without the unanimity of the Great Powers. In the Korean case it did use force without the concurrence of all the Great Powers. The significance of this fact is the destruction of the veto to the extent that the overwhelming majority show a united determination in a crisis. It has been established that no one member, no matter how powerful, can block action by the United Nations. This has been done by interpretation and practical action, not by amendment of the Charter.

Basically, the way to strengthen the United Nations is to use it. All methods and actions which are appropriate to the purpose and not prohibited by the Charter may be utilized. Accomplishments [6] have a cumulative effect upon subsequent developments, since success feeds on success and failure leads to failure. The United Nations, in six years of operation, has become a reality which cannot be ignored. The member states, however, remain the depositories of power. The United Nations, although an international personality and an influential institution in its own right, is still primarily an association of members. The confederation has become stronger, but it has not been transposed into a federation.

Under these circumstances, a prime requisite is genuine and constant support in terms of national policies. This does not imply an admonition to altruism on the part of the nations. There is room for enlightened selfishness in two respects. First, most governments, and certainly their peoples, have a vested interest in peace and security. The statesman and the citizen can be interested in the success of the United Nations on the same basis as that on which they want their community to have adequate police and fire departments. Second, the United Nations presents an opportunity for the mobilization of support for national policies. For example, let us assume that it is in the strategic interest of the United States to resist a conquest of South Korea by a Communist regime. How, except for the United Nations, could the backing of fifty-two other countries be obtained for international action against the aggressor? Conversely, the Soviet Union has opportunity to benefit from the fact that many important countries (India is an outstanding example) have not written a blank check in favor of the United States, but show themselves capable of picking and choosing among various aspects of American policy.

The concept of regionalism offers one approach to the coordination of national policies with general collective action. Articles 52 and 53 of the

[6] For a descripiton of accomplishments, see Chaps. 14–19.

Charter specifically recognize the validity of regional arrangements within the over-all pattern of the Organization. The elements of geography, historic tradition, and immediacy of interest unite to give force to this concept. It is impossible to escape the conclusion, however, that regionalism offers a technique of limited value rather than a solution to the problem. There are many reasons for this. Regions are not mutually exclusive. Boundaries cannot be drawn to eliminate overlapping security zones. Germany, Iran, Korea, and many other places are of interest to both East and West. Often there is a gradation of interests as between close neighbors and more distant areas, but a remote geographic area may be considered of vital importance, as for example in the case of American policy toward Korea. Even if regional boundaries could be objectively determined, there would remain the question of outposts and advance bases needed to defend one's region against attack. These outposts and bases would be in someone else's region. With the interdependence of the modern world, and in view of the far-flung security zones of the Great Powers, the problem of world peace must be solved on a global scale if it is to be solved at all.

The breakdown of the principle of unanimity changed the significance of regionalism within the United Nations. The compelling problem shifted from subsidiary arrangements within a general system to methods for security against another member of that system. The more notable organizational results are found in the Soviet bloc, on the one hand, and the North Atlantic Pact, on the other. The latter was devised as a means for collective self-defense under Article 51 of the Charter, rather than as a regional arrangement under Article 52. The situation which produced it was not contemplated at the time of the San Francisco Conference, and it seems fair to conclude that the North Atlantic Pact is neither expressly sanctioned nor prohibited by the Charter. If it helps to stabilize the world political situation by forestalling a potential armed attack on Western Europe, it will eventually contribute to the strengthening of the United Nations. If, as the Soviets claim, it is designed as a basis for aggression, or even if it contributes unnecessarily to international tension, it is of course inconsistent with the principles and purposes of the United Nations. At present, any judgment on that question has to do with the integrity and wisdom of national policies.

The question of what the peoples of the world can do to strengthen the United Nations involves the problem of public opinion. It is easy to speak glibly of "world public opinion," but upon analysis this term may represent little more than a figure of speech or a sentimental abstraction. It is true, however, that the United Nations has begun to capture popular imagination in the United States and many other countries. Foreign offices feel impelled to defend their policies in terms of United Nations principles and decisions. Support of the United Nations is avowedly a cornerstone of American foreign policy, and any Secretary of State who proposed to go in the contrary direction would have a lot of explaining to do.   It may be premature to talk about world public opinion, but certainly there is a parallel development in many countries.   Out of this there begin to emerge a common international institution and symbolism.

CONCLUSION

Strengthening the United Nations is a process involved in the development of international society.   One of the most notable facts about the United Nations is that it has been strengthened during the past six years.   In terms of an effective organization for the maintenance of international peace and security, however, it is an infant requiring a long period of growth to reach maturity.

The United Nations has placed foreign affairs and international relations in a new context.   Decisions of national policy must now be made from a different perspective.   The United Nations has demonstrated that it can prevent or stop small wars.   It cannot, of course, prevent a Great Power from making war if it is determined to do so.   It has created a situation, however, in which even the Great Powers are impelled to justify their policies, in terms of the principles of the United Nations.   More than that, it provides a broader range of methods for preventing a resort to hostilities.   When there seems no other way out of an impasse, it may possibly reach some solution or adjustment through the United Nations.   The possibilities of the United Nations are along lines which were stated as follows in connection with the Berlin blockade: [7]

So long as the Great Powers are deadlocked, the Security Council cannot coerce one or the other into a settlement; when the possibility of agreement exists, the United Nations machinery can focus the attention of the world and provide the way to work out the settlement; above all, the constant application of the principles of conciliation embodied in the Charter can operate to prevent the irreparable and disastrous rupture of negotiations.

The very existence of the United Nations presents increased opportunities for peaceful settlement and encourages the use of pacific methods.

One of the most significant developments in the United Nations is the emergence of what might be called a "third force."   There are great dangers in a bipolar world, with all countries lined up on opposing sides in the East-West conflict.   Such a situation involves two gigantic blocs, mutually hostile to each other and with little room for the operation of conciliating influences. If, however, there are members of the United Nations which will throw their weight against any aggressor, a better balance will be achieved.   The role

[7] A. H. Feller, *Annual Review of United Nations Affairs, 1949,* edited by Clyde Eagleton, New York University Press, New York, 1950, p. 8.

of India in relation to the Korean conflict is a leading example in point.   The government of India endorsed the use of force to stop the attack from North Korea, but did not approve all proposals made by the United States.   The need for support from other countries tends to modify policies of both the United States and the Soviet Union.   Moreover, the United Nations provides a forum in which small countries collectively can exert a real influence.

From the viewpoint of practical international politics, a "third force" is taking shape within the general organization rather than on a regional or geographic basis.   This fact points to the basic fallacy in all proposals to attempt a reorganization of the United Nations so as to exclude the Soviet Union. Certainly many important nations would resent and resist an ultimatum to line up on one side.   Such a step would increase the tension between East and West, at precisely the place where an alleviation of tension is most needed. Moreover, the emerging "third force" would be destroyed and one of the most hopeful trends in the present situation would be brought to an abrupt end.

The United Nations presents a method, an institution, and an opportunity. Its influence and prestige have increased as it has dealt with succeeding crises in the postwar world.   The problem of strengthening the United Nations in the future is essentially one of contributing to the achievement and maintenance of international peace and security.   This is no simple and easy task, nor is it one which can be done in sheltered isolation from the social, economic, and political problems of the modern world.   The challenge is as broad, and as important, as the building of a stable and peaceful world order.   The success of the United Nations is linked with the future of modern civilization.

BIBLIOGRAPHIC NOTE

The purpose of this bibliographic note is to provide an introductory guide to the literature concerning the United Nations. In a volume of this scope, a definitive bibliography on the United Nations and related topics is not feasible because a mere listing of items would require a considerable monograph verging on the encyclopedic. For example, a catalogue of the titles of the publications issued by the United Nations itself during 1949 alone constituted a booklet of forty-eight printed pages. More important, however, is the fact that an inclusive bibliography is not necessary for an introduction to the United Nations. Accordingly, this bibliographic note is designed to provide a reference to the publications of greatest value to the student and interested citizen, and to mark a point of departure for further study.

The United Nations publishes the official records of the various organs. These are, of course, a basic source for reference work. The *Yearbook of the United Nations* gives a detailed account of the structure and activities of the Organization. This publication contains a wealth of information and includes such items as the texts of the more important resolutions, verbatim rules of procedure of the various organs, membership of all the organizational units and delegations, and a summary record of activities with citations to the basic documents. *Everyman's United Nations* (3d ed., 1952) is published as a ready reference guide to the organization, functions, activities, and accomplishments of the United Nations.

The *Annual Report of the Secretary-General* provides a very useful summary and interpretation of the work of the Organization each year. The specialized agencies also publish reports concerning their activities. The *United Nations Bulletin* is an official periodical prepared by the Department of Public Information. It is issued on a semimonthly basis and is indispensable for following the current proceedings.

Many reports, bulletins, and pamphlets on a variety of topics are published by the United Nations. A list of *Current United Nations Publications* is issued from time to time by the Sales and Circulation Section of the Department of Public Information. The *United Nations Study Kit* contains a selection of pamphlets and booklets of general interest; it is especially useful for discussion groups and for persons who wish a brief over-all introduction to the United Nations and its activities. The sales agent in the United States for all United Nations publications is the International Documents Service, Columbia University Press.

The United States government publishes annually a report of the President to Congress on *United States Participation in the United Nations*. The material in these reports is based on drafts made by officers of the Department of State who have taken part in the work described. The result is a useful summary of the work of the United Nations from the American viewpoint. The Department of State

Bulletin and *Documents and State Papers* contain many articles on topics related to the United Nations, and the Department issues various pamphlets on individual questions.

Most recent books on world affairs and international relations devote attention to the United Nations. Some of the more useful books with that Organization as their major focus of attention are:

Eugene P. Chase, *The United Nations in Action*, McGraw-Hill, New York, 1950. A textbook giving a nontechnical but fairly comprehensive explanation of the origin, development, and work of the United Nations.

Vera Micheles Dean, *The Four Cornerstones of Peace*, McGraw-Hill, New York, 1946. A "primer" of four international conferences leading to the establishment of the United Nations. There is also a chapter entitled "The American Voter and International Organization."

Clyde Eagleton (ed.), *Annual Review of United Nations Affairs*, New York University Press, New York, 1950, 1951. The proceedings of the first and second New York University Institutes for Annual Review of the United Nations.

Herbert Vere Evatt, *The United Nations*, Harvard University Press, Cambridge, Mass., 1948. A small book based on lectures at Harvard University; reflects the "small power" viewpoint of which Mr. Evatt has been a leading spokesman.

Herbert Vere Evatt, *The Task of Nations*, Duell, Sloan & Pearce, New York, 1949. A discussion and interpretation of the third General Assembly.

Leland M. Goodrich and Edvard Hambro, *Charter of the United Nations: Commentary and Documents*, World Peace Foundation, Boston, 1949. A systematic account of the constitutional development of the United Nations. Contains a useful bibliography.

L. Larry Leonard, *International Organization*, McGraw-Hill, New York, 1951.

Trygve Lie and others, *Peace on Earth*, Hermitage House, New York, 1949. A discussion by various United Nations officials.

Useful books for further exploration of the development and significance of international organization are:

Clyde Eagleton, *International Government*, Ronald, New York, 1948.

Pitman B. Potter, *An Introduction to the Study of International Organization*, Appleton-Century-Crofts, New York, 1948. Contains a valuable bibliography of the standard works on international organization, politics, and law; diplomacy and treaties; the conference system; international administration, methods of peaceful settlement; and the League of Nations.

Harold M. Vinacke, *International Organization*, Appleton-Century-Crofts, New York, 1934.

There is a considerable body of periodical literature on the United Nations and related subjects. The *Bulletin* has been mentioned above. The *United Nations World* is a monthly publication of general interest. It contains interpretative articles and special features.

International Organization, a quarterly publication of the World Peace Foundation, is concerned largely with information and articles on the work of the United Nations and the specialized agencies. It is supplemented by the quarterly *Documents of International Organizations*.

Other periodicals which devote a substantial amount of space to the United Nations include *International Conciliation, Foreign Policy Reports, The American Journal of International Law, The American Political Science Review,* and *Foreign Affairs.* This is by no means an exhaustive list. Consultation of an index to periodical literature, or even a cursory examination of the periodical collection of any library, will show that all publications concerned with contemporary affairs necessarily devote some attention to the United Nations.

The United Nations does not function in a vacuum. The student of international organization will do well, therefore, to consult some books on general world politics for background. Among the many good books in this field the following will be found useful:

Hans Morgenthau, *Politics among Nations,* Knopf, New York, 1948. An analysis of international politics within reasonable compass, with a power-politics point of view.

Walter R. Sharp and Grayson Kirk, *Contemporary International Politics,* Rinehart, New York, 1940. An excellent, comprehensive survey as of the eve of World War II.

Robert Strausz-Hupé and Stefan T. Possony, *International Relations: In the Age of the Conflict between Democracy and Dictatorship,* McGraw-Hill, New York, 1950. A comprehensive survey and keen analysis of current forces in world politics. Useful and significant documents are dispersed throughout the text. The authors adhere rather strongly to the power-politics school.

APPENDIXES

Appendix 1

CHARTER OF THE UNITED NATIONS

WE THE PEOPLES OF THE UNITED NATIONS
DETERMINED

to save succeeding generations from the scourge of war, which twice in our lifetime has brought untold sorrow to mankind, and to reaffirm faith in fundamental human rights, in the dignity and worth of the human person, in the equal rights of men and women and of nations large and small, and
to establish conditions under which justice and respect for the obligations arising from treaties and other sources of international law can be maintained, and
to promote social progress and better standards of life in larger freedom,

AND FOR THESE ENDS

to practice tolerance and live together in peace with one another as good neighbors, and
to unite our strength to maintain international peace and security, and
to ensure, by the acceptance of principles and the institution of methods, that armed force shall not be used, save in the common interest, and
to employ international machinery for the promotion of the economic and social advancement of all peoples,

HAVE RESOLVED TO COMBINE OUR EFFORTS
TO ACCOMPLISH THESE AIMS.

Accordingly, our respective Governments, through representatives assembled in the city of San Francisco, who have exhibited their full powers found to be in good and due form, have agreed to the present Charter of the United Nations and do hereby establish an international organization to be known as the United Nations.

CHAPTER I

PURPOSES AND PRINCIPLES

Article 1

The Purposes of the United Nations are:'
1. To maintain international peace and security, and to that end: to take effective collective measures for the prevention and removal of threats to the peace, and for the suppression of acts of aggression or other breaches of the peace, and to bring about by peaceful means, and in conformity with the principles of justice and inter-

national law, adjustment or settlement of international disputes or situations which might lead to a breach of the peace;

2. To develop friendly relations among nations based on respect for the principle of equal rights and self-determination of peoples, and to take other appropriate measures to strengthen universal peace;

3. To achieve international cooperation in solving international problems of an economic, social, cultural, or humanitarian character, and in promoting and encouraging respect for human rights and for fundamental freedoms for all without distinction as to race, sex, language, or religion; and

To be a center for harmonizing the actions of nations in the attainment of these common ends.

Article 2

The Organization and its Members, in pursuit of the Purposes stated in Article 1, shall act in accordance with the following Principles.

1. The Organization is based on the principle of the sovereign equality of all its Members.

2. All Members, in order to ensure to all of them the rights and benefits resulting from membership, shall fulfill in good faith the obligations assumed by them in accordance with the present Charter.

3. All Members shall settle their international disputes by peaceful means in such a manner that international peace and security, and justice, are not endangered.

4. All Members shall refrain in their international relations from the threat or use of force against the territorial integrity or political independence of any state, or in any other manner inconsistent with the Purposes of the United Nations.

5. All Members shall give the United Nations every assistance in any action it takes in accordance with the present Charter, and shall refrain from giving assistance to any state against which the United Nations is taking preventive or enforcement action.

6. The Organization shall ensure that states which are not Members of the United Nations act in accordance with these Principles so far as may be necessary for the maintenance of international peace and security.

7. Nothing contained in the present Charter shall authorize the United Nations to intervene in matters which are essentially within the domestic jurisdiction of any state or shall require the Members to submit such matters to settlement under the present Charter; but this principle shall not prejudice the application of enforcement measures under Chapter VII.

CHAPTER II

MEMBERSHIP

Article 3

The original Members of the United Nations shall be the states which, having participated in the United Nations Conference on International Organization at San Francisco, or having previously signed the Declaration by United Nations of January 1, 1942, sign the present Charter and ratify it in accordance with Article 110.

Article 4

1. Membership in the United Nations is open to all other peace-loving states which accept the obligations contained in the present Charter and, in the judgment of the Organization, are able and willing to carry out these obligations.

2. The admission of any such state to membership in the United Nations will be effected by a decision of the General Assembly upon the recommendation of the Security Council.

Article 5

A member of the United Nations against which preventive or enforcement action has been taken by the Security Council may be suspended from the exercise of the rights and privileges of membership by the General Assembly upon the recommendation of the Security Council. The exercise of these rights and privileges may be restored by the Security Council.

Article 6

A Member of the United Nations which has persistently violated the Principles contained in the present Charter may be expelled from the Organization by the General Assembly upon the recommendation of the Security Council.

CHAPTER III

ORGANS

Article 7

1. There are established as the principal organs of the United Nations: A General Assembly, a Security Council, an Economic and Social Council, a Trusteeship Council, an International Court of Justice, and a Secretariat.
2. Such subsidiary organs as may be found necessary may be established in accordance with the present Charter.

Article 8

The United Nations shall place no restrictions on the eligibility of men and women to participate in any capacity and under conditions of equality in its principal and subsidiary organs.

CHAPTER IV

THE GENERAL ASSEMBLY

Composition

Article 9

1. The General Assembly shall consist of all the Members of the United Nations.
2. Each Member shall have not more than five representatives in the General Assembly.

Functions and Powers

Article 10

The General Assembly may discuss any questions or matters within the scope of the present Charter or relating to the powers and functions of any organs provided for in the present Charter, and except as provided in Article 12, may make recommendations to the Members of the United Nations or to the Security Council or to both on any such questions or matters.

Article 11

1. The General Assembly may consider the general principles of cooperation in the maintenance of international peace and security, including the principles govern-

ing disarmament and the regulation of armaments, and may make recommendations with regard to such principles to the Members or to the Security Council or to both.

2. The General Assembly may discuss any questions relating to the maintenance of international peace and security brought before it by any Member of the United Nations, or by the Security Council, or by a state which is not a Member of the United Nations in accordance with Article 35, paragraph 2, and, except as provided in Article 12, may make recommendations with regard to any such questions to the state or states concerned or to the Security Council or to both. Any such question on which action is necessary shall be referred to the Security Council by the General Assembly either before or after discussion.

3. The General Assembly may call the attention of the Security Council to situations which are likely to endanger international peace and security.

4. The powers of the General Assembly set forth in this Article shall not limit the general scope of Article 10.

Article 12

1. While the Security Council is exercising in respect of any dispute or situation the functions assigned to it in the present Charter, the General Assembly shall not make any recommendation with regard to that dispute or situation unless the Security Council so requests.

2. The Secretary-General, with the consent of the Security Council, shall notify the General Assembly at each session of any matters relative to the maintenance of international peace and security which are being dealt with by the Security Council and shall similarly notify the General Assembly, or the Members of the United Nations if the General Assembly is not in session, immediately the Security Council ceases to deal with such matters.

Article 13

1. The General Assembly shall initiate studies and make recommendations for the purpose of:

   a. promoting international cooperation in the political field and encouraging the progressive development of international law and its codification;
   b. promoting international cooperation in the economic, social, cultural, educational, and health fields, and assisting in the realization of human rights and fundamental freedoms for all without distinction as to race, sex, language, or religion.

2. The further responsibilities, functions, and powers of the General Assembly with respect to matters mentioned in paragraph 1(b) above are set forth in Chapters IX and X.

Article 14

Subject to the provisions of Article 12, the General Assembly may recommend measures for the peaceful adjustment of any situation, regardless of origin, which it deems likely to impair the general welfare or friendly relations among nations, including situations resulting from a violation of the provisions of the present Charter setting forth the Purposes and Principles of the United Nations.

Article 15

1. The General Assembly shall receive and consider annual and special reports from the Security Council; these reports shall include an account of the measures

that the Security Council has decided upon or taken to maintain international peace and security.

2. The General Assembly shall receive and consider reports from the other organs of the United Nations.

Article 16

The General Assembly shall perform such functions with respect to the international trusteeship system as are assigned to it under Chapters XII and XIII, including the approval of the trusteeship agreements for areas not designated as strategic.

Article 17

1. The General Assembly shall consider and approve the budget of the Organization.

2. The expenses of the Organization shall be borne by the Members as apportioned by the General Assembly.

3. The General Assembly shall consider and approve any financial and budgetary arrangements with specialized agencies referred to in Article 57 and shall examine the administrative budgets of such specialized agencies with a view to making recommendations to the agencies concerned.

Voting

Article 18

1. Each member of the General Assembly shall have one vote.

2. Decisions of the General Assembly on important questions shall be made by a two-thirds majority of the members present and voting. These questions shall include: recommendations with respect to the maintenance of international peace and security, the election of the non-permanent members of the Security Council, the election of the members of the Economic and Social Council, the election of members of the Trusteeship Council in accordance with paragraph 1(c) of Article 86, the admission of new Members to the United Nations, the suspension of the rights and privileges of membership, the expulsion of Members, questions relating to the operation of the trusteeship system, and budgetary questions.

3. Decisions on other questions, including the determination of additional categories of questions to be decided by a two-thirds majority, shall be made by a majority of the members present and voting.

Article 19

A Member of the United Nations which is in arrears in the payment of its financial contributions to the Organization shall have no vote in the General Assembly if the amount of its arrears equals or exceeds the amount of the contributions due from it for the preceding two full years. The General Assembly may, nevertheless, permit such a Member to vote if it is satisfied that the failure to pay is due to conditions beyond the control of the Member.

Procedure

Article 20

The General Assembly shall meet in regular annual sessions and in such special sessions as occasion may require. Special sessions shall be convoked by the Secretary-

General at the request of the Security Council or of a majority of the Members of the United Nations.

Article 21

The General Assembly shall adopt its own rules of procedure. It shall elect its President for each session.

Article 22

The General Assembly may establish such subsidiary organs as it deems necessary for the performance of its functions.

CHAPTER V

THE SECURITY COUNCIL

Composition

Article 23

1. The Security Council shall consist of eleven Members of the United Nations. The Republic of China, France, the Union of Soviet Socialist Republics, the United Kingdom of Great Britain and Northern Ireland, and the United States of America shall be permanent members of the Security Council. The General Assembly shall elect six other Members of the United Nations to be non-permanent members of the Security Council, due regard being specially paid, in the first instance to the contribution of Members of the United Nations to the maintenance of international peace and security and to the other purposes of the Organization, and also to equitable geographical distribution.

2. The non-permanent members of the Security Council shall be elected for a term of two years. In the first election of the non-permanent members, however, three shall be chosen for a term of one year. A retiring member shall not be eligible for immediate re-election.

3. Each member of the Security Council shall have one representative.

Functions and Powers

Article 24

1. In order to ensure prompt and effective action by the United Nations, its Members confer on the Security Council primary responsibility for the maintenance of international peace and security, and agree that in carrying out its duties under this responsibility the Security Council acts on their behalf.

2. In discharging these duties the Security Council shall act in accordance with the Purposes and Principles of the United Nations. The specific powers granted to the Security Council for the discharge of these duties are laid down in Chapters VI, VII, VIII, and XII.

3. The Security Council shall submit annual and, when necessary, special reports to the General Assembly for its consideration.

Article 25

The Members of the United Nations agree to accept and carry out the decisions of the Security Council in accordance with the present Charter.

Article 26

In order to promote the establishment and maintenance of international peace and security with the least diversion for armaments of the world's human and economic resources, the Security Council shall be responsible for formulating, with the assistance of the Military Staff Committee referred to in Article 47, plans to be submitted to the Members of the United Nations for the establishment of a system for the regulation of armaments.

Voting

Article 27

1. Each member of the Security Council shall have one vote.
2. Decisions of the Security Council on procedural matters shall be made by an affirmative vote of seven members.
3. Decisions of the Security Council on all other matters shall be made by an affirmative vote of seven members including the concurring votes of the permanent members; provided that, in decisions under Chapter VI, and under paragraph 3 of Article 52, a party to a dispute shall abstain from voting.

Procedure

Article 28

1. The Security Council shall be so organized as to be able to function continuously. Each member of the Security Council shall for this purpose be represented at all times at the seat of the Organization.
2. The Security Council shall hold periodic meetings at which each of its members may, if it so desires, be represented by a member of the government or by some other specially designated representative.
3. The Security Council may hold meetings at such places other than the seat of the Organization as in its judgment will best facilitate its work.

Article 29

The Security Council may establish such subsidiary organs as it deems necessary for the performance of its functions.

Article 30

The Security Council shall adopt its own rules of procedure, including the method of selecting its President.

Article 31

Any Member of the United Nations which is not a member of the Security Council may participate, without vote, in the discussion of any question brought before the Security Council whenever the latter considers that the interests of that Member are specially affected.

Article 32

Any Member of the United Nations which is not a member of the Security Council or any state which is not a Member of the United Nations, if it is a party to a dispute under consideration by the Security Council, shall be invited to participate, without vote, in the discussion relating to the dispute. The Security Council shall lay down such conditions as it deems just for the participation of a state which is not a Member of the United Nations.

CHAPTER VI

PACIFIC SETTLEMENT OF DISPUTES

Article 33

1. The parties to any disputes, the continuance of which is likely to endanger the maintenance of international peace and security, shall, first of all, seek a solution by negotiation, enquiry, mediation, conciliation, arbitration, judicial settlement, resort to regional agencies or arrangements, or other peaceful means of their own choice.

2. The Security Council shall, when it deems necessary, call upon the parties to settle their dispute by such means.

Article 34

The Security Council may investigate any dispute, or any situation which might lead to international friction or give rise to a dispute, in order to determine whether the continuance of the dispute or situation is likely to endanger the maintenance of international peace and security.

Article 35

1. Any Member of the United Nations may bring any dispute, or any situation of the nature referred to in Article 34, to the attention of the Security Council or of the General Assembly.

2. A state which is not a Member of the United Nations may bring to the attention of the Security Council or of the General Assembly any dispute to which it is a party if it accepts in advance, for the purposes of the dispute, the obligations of pacific settlement provided in the present Charter.

3. The proceedings of the General Assembly in respect of matters brought to its attention under this Article will be subject to the provisions of Articles 11 and 12.

Article 36

1. The Security Council may, at any stage of a dispute of the nature referred to in Article 33 or of a situation of like nature, recommend appropriate procedures or methods of adjustment.

2. The Security Council should take into consideration any procedures for the settlement of the dispute which have already been adopted by the parties.

3. In making recommendations under this Article the Security Council should also take into consideration that legal disputes should as a general rule be referred by the parties to the International Court of Justice in accordance with the provisions of the Statute of the Court.

Article 37

1. Should the parties to a dispute of the nature referred to in Article 33 fail to settle it by the means indicated in that Article, they shall refer it to the Security Council.

2. If the Security Council deems that the continuance of the dispute is in fact likely to endanger the maintenance of international peace and security, it shall

decide whether to take action under Article 36 or to recommend such terms of settlement as it may consider appropriate.

Article 38

Without prejudice to the provisions of Articles 33 to 37, the Security Council may, if all the parties to any dispute so request, make recommendations to the parties with a view to a pacific settlement of the dispute.

CHAPTER VII

ACTION WITH RESPECT TO THREATS TO THE PEACE, BREACHES OF THE PEACE, AND ACTS OF AGGRESSION

Article 39

The Security Council shall determine the existence of any threat to the peace, breach of the peace, or act of aggression and shall make recommendations, or decide what measures shall be taken in accordance with Articles 41 and 42, to maintain or restore international peace and security.

Article 40

In order to prevent an aggravation of the situation, the Security Council may, before making the recommendations or deciding upon the measures provided for in Article 39, call upon the parties concerned to comply with such provisional measures as it deems necessary or desirable. Such provisional measures shall be without prejudice to the rights, claims, or position of the parties concerned. The Security Council shall duly take account of failure to comply with such provisional measures.

Article 41

The Security Council may decide what measures not involving the use of armed force are to be employed to give effect to its decisions, and it may call upon the Members of the United Nations to apply such measures. These may include complete or partial interruption of economic relations and of rail, sea, air, postal, telegraphic, radio, and other means of communication, and the severance of diplomatic relations.

Article 42

Should the Security Council consider that measures provided for in Article 41 would be inadequate or have proved to be inadequate, it may take such action by air, sea, or land forces as may be necessary to maintain or restore international peace and security. Such action may include demonstrations, blockade, and other operations by air, sea, or land forces of Members of the United Nations.

Article 43

1. All Members of the United Nations, in order to contribute to the maintenance of international peace and security, undertake to make available to the Security Council, on its call and in accordance with a special agreement or agreements, armed forces, assistance, and facilities, including rights of passage, necessary for the purpose of maintaining international peace and security.

2. Such agreement or agreements shall govern the numbers and types of forces, their degree of readiness and general location, and the nature of the facilities and assistance to be provided.

3. The agreement or agreements shall be negotiated as soon as possible on the initiative of the Security Council. They shall be concluded between the Security Council and Members or between the Security Council and groups of Members and shall be subject to ratification by the signatory states in accordance with their respective constitutional processes.

Article 44

When the Security Council has decided to use force it shall, before calling upon a Member not represented on it to provide armed forces in fulfillment of the obligations assumed under Article 43, invite that Member, if the Member so desires, to participate in the decisions of the Security Council concerning the employment of contingents of that Member's armed forces.

Article 45

In order to enable the United Nations to take urgent military measures, Members shall hold immediately available national air-force contingents for combined international enforcement action. The strength and degree of readiness of these contingents and plans for their combined action shall be determined, within the limits laid down in the special agreement or agreements referred to in Article 43, by the Security Council with the assistance of the Military Staff Committee.

Article 46

Plans for the application of armed force shall be made by the Security Council with the assistance of the Military Staff Committee.

Article 47

1. There shall be established a Military Staff Committee to advise and assist the Security Council on all questions relating to the Security Council's military requirements for the maintenance of international peace and security, the employment and command of forces placed at its disposal, the regulation of armaments, and possible disarmament.

2. The Military Staff Committee shall consist of the Chiefs of Staff of the permanent members of the Security Council or their representatives. Any Member of the United Nations not permanently represented on the Committee shall be invited by the Committee to be associated with it when the efficient discharge of the Committee's responsibilities requires the participation of that Member in its work.

3. The Military Staff Committee shall be responsible under the Security Council for the strategic direction of any armed force placed at the disposal of the Security Council. Questions relating to the command of such forces shall be worked out subsequently.

4. The Military Staff Committee, with the authorization of the Security Council and after consultation with appropriate regional agencies, may establish regional subcommittees.

Article 48

1. The action required to carry out the decisions of the Security Council for the maintenance of international peace and security shall be taken by all the Members of the United Nations or by some of them, as the Security Council may determine.

2. Such decisions shall be carried out by the Members of the United Nations directly and through their action in the appropriate international agencies of which they are members.

Article 49

The Members of the United Nations shall join in affording mutual assistance in carrying out the measures decided upon by the Security Council.

Article 50

If preventive or enforcement measures against any state are taken by the Security Council, any other state, whether a Member of the United Nations or not, which finds itself confronted with special economic problems arising from the carrying out of those measures shall have the right to consult the Security Council with regard to a solution of those problems.

Article 51

Nothing in the present Charter shall impair the inherent right of individual or collective self-defense if an armed attack occurs against a Member of the United Nations, until the Security Council has taken the measures necessary to maintain international peace and security. Measures taken by Members in the exercise of this right of self-defense shall be immediately reported to the Security Council and shall not in any way affect the authority and responsibility of the Security Council under the present Charter to take at any time such action as it deems necessary in order to maintain or restore international peace and security.

CHAPTER VIII

REGIONAL ARRANGEMENTS

Article 52

1. Nothing in the present Charter precludes the existence of regional arrangements or agencies for dealing with such matters relating to the maintenance of international peace and security as are appropriate for regional action, provided that such arrangements or agencies and their activities are consistent with the Purposes and Principles of the United Nations.

2. The Members of the United Nations entering into such arrangements or constituting such agencies shall make every effort to achieve pacific settlement of local disputes through such regional arrangements or by such regional agencies before referring them to the Security Council.

3. The Security Council shall encourage the development of pacific settlement of local disputes through such regional arrangements or by such regional agencies either on the initiative of the states concerned or by reference from the Security Council.

4. This Article in no way impairs the application of Articles 34 and 35.

Article 53

1. The Security Council shall, where appropriate, utilize such regional arrangements or agencies for enforcement action under its authority. But no enforcement action shall be taken under regional arrangements or by regional agencies without the authorization of the Security Council, with the exception of measures against any enemy state, as defined in paragraph 2 of this Article, provided for pursuant to Article 107 or in regional arrangements directed against renewal of aggressive policy on the part of any such state, until such time as the Organization may, on request of the Governments concerned, be charged with the responsibility for preventing further aggression by such a state.

2. The term enemy state as used in paragraph 1 of this Article applies to any state which during the Second World War has been an enemy of any signatory of the present Charter.

Article 54

The Security Council shall at all times be kept fully informed of activities undertaken or in contemplation under regional arrangements or by regional agencies for the maintenance of international peace and security.

CHAPTER IX

INTERNATIONAL ECONOMIC AND SOCIAL COOPERATION

Article 55

With a view to the creation of conditions of stability and well-being which are necessary for peaceful and friendly relations among nations based on respect for the principles of equal rights and self-determination of peoples, the United Nations shall promote:

    a. higher standards of living, full employment, and conditions of economic and social progress and development;

    b. solutions of international economic, social, health, and related problems; and international cultural and educational cooperation; and

    c. universal respect for, and observance of, human rights and fundamental freedoms for all without distinction as to race, sex, language, or religion.

Article 56

All Members pledge themselves to take joint and separate action in cooperation with the Organization for the achievement of the purposes set forth in Article 55.

Article 57

1. The various specialized agencies, established by intergovernmental agreement and having wide international responsibilities, as defined in their basic instruments, in economic, social, cultural, educational, health, and related fields, shall be brought into relationship with the United Nations in accordance with the provisions of Article 63.

2. Such agencies thus brought into relationship with the United Nations are hereinafter referred to as specialized agencies.

Article 58

The Organization shall make recommendations for the coordination of the policies and activities of the specialized agencies.

Article 59

The Organization shall, where appropriate, initiate negotiations among the states concerned for the creation of any new specialized agencies required for the accomplishment of the purposes set forth in Article 55.

Article 60

Responsibility for the discharge of the functions of the Organization set forth in this Chapter shall be vested in the General Assembly and, under the authority of the

General Assembly, in the Economic and Social Council, which shall have for this purpose the powers set forth in Chapter X.

CHAPTER X

THE ECONOMIC AND SOCIAL COUNCIL

Composition

Article 61

1. The Economic and Social Council shall consist of eighteen Members of the United Nations elected by the General Assembly.

2. Subject to the provisions of paragraph 3, six members of the Economic and Social Council shall be elected each year for a term of three years. A retiring member shall be eligible for immediate re-election.

3. At the first election, eighteen members of the Economic and Social Council shall be chosen. The term of office of six members so chosen shall expire at the end of one year, and of six other members at the end of two years, in accordance with arrangements made by the General Assembly.

4. Each member of the Economic and Social Council shall have one representative.

Functions and Powers

Article 62

1. The Economic and Social Council may make or initiate studies and reports with respect to international economic, social, cultural, educational, health, and related matters to the General Assembly, to the Members of the United Nations, and to the specialized agencies concerned.

2. It may make recommendations for the purpose of promoting respect for, and observance of, human rights and fundamental freedoms for all.

3. It may prepare draft conventions for submission to the General Assembly, with respect to matters falling within its competence.

4. It may call, in accordance with the rules prescribed by the United Nations, international conferences on matters falling within its competence.

Article 63

1. The Economic and Social Council may enter into agreements with any of the agencies referred to in Article 57, defining the terms on which the agency concerned shall be brought into relationship with the United Nations. Such agreements shall be subject to approval by the General Assembly.

2. It may coordinate the activities of the specialized agencies through consultation with and recommendations to such agencies and through recommendations to the General Assembly and to the Members of the United Nations.

Article 64

1. The Economic and Social Council may take appropriate steps to obtain regular reports from the specialized agencies. It may make arrangements with the Members of the United Nations and with the specialized agencies to obtain reports on the steps taken to give effect to its own recommendations and to recommendations on matters falling within its competence made by the General Assembly.

2. It may communicate its observations on these reports to the General Assembly.

Article 65

The Economic and Social Council may furnish information to the Security Council and shall assist the Security Council upon its request.

Article 66

1. The Economic and Social Council shall perform such functions as fall within its competence in connection with the carrying out of the recommendations of the General Assembly.

2. It may, with the approval of the General Assembly, perform services at the request of Members of the United Nations and at the request of specialized agencies.

3. It shall perform such other functions as are specified elsewhere in the present Charter or as may be assigned to it by the General Assembly.

Voting

Article 67

1. Each member of the Economic and Social Council shall have one vote.

2. Decisions of the Economic and Social Council shall be made by a majority of the members present and voting.

Procedure

Article 68

The Economic and Social Council shall set up commissions in economic and social fields and for the promotion of human rights, and such other commissions as may be required for the performance of its functions.

Article 69

The Economic and Social Council shall invite any Member of the United Nations to participate, without vote, in its deliberations on any matter of particular concern to that Member.

Article 70

The Economic and Social Council may make arrangements for representatives of the specialized agencies to participate, without vote, in its deliberations and in those of the commissions established by it, and for its representatives to participate in the deliberations of the specialized agencies.

Article 71

The Economic and Social Council may make suitable arrangements for consultation with non-governmental organizations which are concerned with matters within its competence. Such arrangements may be made with international organizations and, where appropriate, with national organizations after consultation with the Member of the United Nations concerned.

Article 72

1. The Economic and Social Council shall adopt its own rules of procedure, including the method of selecting its President.

2. The Economic and Social Council shall meet as required in accordance with its

rules, which shall include provision for the convening of meetings on the request of a majority of its members.

CHAPTER XI

DECLARATION REGARDING NON-SELF-GOVERNING TERRITORIES

Article 73

Members of the United Nations which have or assume responsibilities for the administration of territories whose peoples have not yet attained a full measure of self-government recognize the principle that the interests of the inhabitants of these territories are paramount, and accept as a sacred trust the obligation to promote to the utmost, within the system of international peace and security established by the present Charter, the well-being of the inhabitants of these territories, and, to this end:

    a. to ensure, with due respect for the culture of the peoples concerned, their political, economic, social, and educational advancement, their just treatment, and their protection against abuses;

    b. to develop self-government, to take due account of the political aspirations of the peoples, and to assist them in the progressive development of their free political institutions, according to the particular circumstances of each territory and its peoples and their varying stages of advancement;

    c. to further international peace and security;

    d. to promote constructive measures of development, to encourage research, and to cooperate with one another and, when and where appropriate, with specialized international bodies with a view to the practical achievement of the social, economic, and scientific purposes set forth in this Article; and

    e. to transmit regularly to the Secretary-General for information purposes, subject to such limitations as security and constitutional considerations may require, statistical and other information of a technical nature relating to economic, social, and educational conditions in the territories for which they are respectively responsible other than those territories to which Chapters XII and XIII apply.

Article 74

Members of the United Nations also agree that their policy in respect of the territories to which this Chapter applies, no less than in respect of their metropolitan areas, must be based on the general principle of good-neighborliness, due account being taken of the interests and well-being of the rest of the world, in social, economic, and commercial matters.

CHAPTER XII

INTERNATIONAL TRUSTEESHIP SYSTEM

Article 75

The United Nations shall establish under its authority an international trusteeship system for the administration and supervision of such territories as may be placed thereunder by subsequent individual agreements. These territories are hereinafter referred to as trust territories.

Article 76

The basic objectives of the trusteeship system, in accordance with the Purposes of the United Nations laid down in Article 1 of the present Charter, shall be:

a. to further international peace and security;

b. to promote the political, economic, social, and educational advancement of the inhabitants of the trust territories, and their progressive development towards self-government or independence as may be appropriate to the particular circumstances of each territory and its peoples and the freely expressed wishes of the peoples concerned, and as may be provided by the terms of each trusteeship agreement;

c. to encourage respect for human rights and for fundamental freedoms for all without distinction as to race, sex, language, or religion, and to encourage recognition of the interdependence of the peoples of the world; and

d. to ensure equal treatment in social, economic, and commercial matters for all Members of the United Nations and their nationals, and also equal treatment for the latter in the administration of justice, without prejudice to the attainment of the foregoing objectives and subject to the provisions of Article 80.

Article 77

1. The trusteeship system shall apply to such territories in the following categories as may be placed thereunder by means of trusteeship agreements:

a. territories now held under mandate;

b. territories which may be detached from enemy states as a result of the Second World War; and

c. territories voluntarily placed under the system by states responsible for their administration.

2. It will be a matter for subsequent agreement as to which territories in the foregoing categories will be brought under the trusteeship system and upon what terms.

Article 78

The trusteeship system shall not apply to territories which have become Members of the United Nations, relationship among which shall be based on respect for the principle of sovereign equality.

Article 79

The terms of trusteeship for each territory to be placed under the trusteeship system, including any alteration or amendment, shall be agreed upon by the states directly concerned, including the mandatory power in the case of territories held under mandate by a Member of the United Nations, and shall be approved as provided for in Articles 83 and 85.

Article 80

1. Except as may be agreed upon in individual trusteeship agreements, made under Articles 77, 79, and 81, placing each territory under the trusteeship system, and until such agreements have been concluded, nothing in this Chapter shall be construed in or of itself to alter in any manner the rights whatsoever of any states or any peoples or the terms of existing international instruments to which Members of the United Nations may respectively be parties.

2. Paragraph 1 of this Article shall not be interpreted as giving grounds for delay or postponement of the negotiation and conclusion of agreements for placing mandated and other territories under the trusteeship system as provided for in Article 77.

Article 81

The trusteeship agreement shall in each case include the terms under which the trust territory will be administered and designate the authority which will exercise the administration of the trust territory. Such authority, hereinafter called the administering authority, may be one or more states or the Organization itself.

Article 82

There may be designated, in any trusteeship agreement, a strategic area or areas which may include part or all of the trust territory to which the agreement applies, without prejudice to any special agreement or agreements made under Article 43.

Article 83

1. All functions of the United Nations relating to strategic areas, including the approval of the terms of the trusteeship agreements and of their alteration or amendment, shall be exercised by the Security Council.

2. The basic objectives set forth in Article 76 shall be applicable to the people of each strategic area.

3. The Security Council shall, subject to the provisions of the trusteeship agreements and without prejudice to security considerations, avail itself of the assistance of the Trusteeship Council to perform those functions of the United Nations under the trusteeship system relating to political, economic, social, and educational matters in the strategic areas.

Article 84

It shall be the duty of the administering authority to ensure that the trust territory shall play its part in the maintenance of international peace and security. To this end the administering authority may make use of volunteer forces, facilities, and assistance from the trust territory in carrying out the obligations towards the Security Council undertaken in this regard by the administering authority, as well as for local defense and the maintenance of law and order within the trust territory.

Article 85

1. The functions of the United Nations with regard to trusteeship agreements for all areas not designated as strategic, including the approval of the terms of the trusteeship agreements and of their alteration or amendment, shall be exercised by the General Assembly.

2. The Trusteeship Council, operating under the authority of the General Assembly, shall assist the General Assembly in carrying out these functions.

CHAPTER XIII

THE TRUSTEESHIP COUNCIL

Composition

Article 86

1. The Trusteeship Council shall consist of the following Members of the United Nations:

    a. those Members administering trust territories;

    b. such of those Members mentioned by name in Article 23 as are not administering trust territories; and

c. as many other Members elected for three-year terms by the General Assembly as may be necessary to ensure that the total number of members of the Trusteeship Council is equally divided between those Members of the United Nations which administer trust territories and those which do not.

2. Each member of the Trusteeship Council shall designate one specially qualified person to represent it therein.

Functions and Powers

Article 87

The General Assembly and, under its authority, the Trusteeship Council, in carrying out their functions, may:

a. consider reports submitted by the administering authority;
b. accept petitions and examine them in consultation with the administering authority;
c. provide for periodic visits to the respective trust territories at times agreed upon with the administering authority; and
d. take these and other actions in conformity with the terms of the trusteeship agreements.

Article 88

The Trusteeship Council shall formulate a questionnaire on the political, economic, social, and educational advancement of the inhabitants of each trust territory, and the administering authority for each trust territory within the competence of the General Assembly shall make an annual report to the General Assembly upon the basis of such questionnaire.

Voting

Article 89

1. Each member of the Trusteeship Council shall have one vote.
2. Decisions of the Trusteeship Council shall be made by a majority of the members present and voting.

Procedure

Article 90

1. The Trusteeship Council shall adopt its own rules of procedures, including the method of selecting its President.
2. The Trusteeship Council shall meet as required in accordance with its rules, which shall include provision for the convening of meetings on the request of a majority of its members.

Article 91

The Trusteeship Council shall, when appropriate, avail itself of the assistance of the Economic and Social Council and of the specialized agencies in regard to matters with which they are respectively concerned.

CHAPTER XIV

THE INTERNATIONAL COURT OF JUSTICE

Article 92

The International Court of Justice shall be the principal judicial organ of the United Nations. It shall function in accordance with the annexed Statute, which is based upon the Statute of the Permanent Court of International Justice and forms an integral part of the present Charter.

Article 93

1. All Members of the United Nations are *ipso facto* parties to the Statute of the International Court of Justice.

2. A state which is not a Member of the United Nations may become a party to the Statute of the International Court of Justice on conditions to be determined in each case by the General Assembly upon the recommendation of the Security Council.

Article 94

1. Each Member of the United Nations undertakes to comply with the decision of the International Court of Justice in any case to which it is a party.

2. If any party to a case fails to perform the obligations incumbent upon it under a judgment rendered by the Court, the other party may have recourse to the Security Council, which may, if it deems necessary, make recommendations or decide upon measures to be taken to give effect to the judgment.

Article 95

Nothing in the present Charter shall prevent Members of the United Nations from entrusting the solution of their differences to other tribunals by virtue of agreements already in existence or which may be concluded in the future.

Article 96

1. The General Assembly or the Security Council may request the International Court of Justice to give an advisory opinion on any legal question.

2. Other organs of the United Nations and specialized agencies, which may at any time be so authorized by the General Assembly, may also request advisory opinions of the Court on legal questions arising within the scope of their activities.

CHAPTER XV

THE SECRETARIAT

Article 97

The Secretariat shall comprise a Secretary-General and such staff as the Organization may require. The Secretary-General shall be appointed by the General Assembly upon the recommendation of the Security Council. He shall be the chief administrative officer of the Organization.

Article 98

The Secretary-General shall act in that capacity in all meetings of the General Assembly, of the Security Council, of the Economic and Social Council, and of the

Trusteeship Council, and shall perform such other functions as are entrusted to him
by these organs. The Secretary-General shall make an annual report to the General
Assembly on the work of the Organization.

Article 99

The Secretary-General may bring to the attention of the Security Council any
matter which in his opinion may threaten the maintenance of international peace
and security.

Article 100

1. In the performance of their duties the Secretary-General and the staff shall
not seek or receive instructions from any government or from any other authority
external to the Organization. They shall refrain from any action which might reflect
on their position as international officials responsible only to the Organization.

2. Each Member of the United Nations undertakes to respect the exclusively
international character of the responsibilities of the Secretary-General and the staff
and not to seek to influence them in the discharge of their responsibilities.

Article 101

1. The staff shall be appointed by the Secretary-General under regulations established by the General Assembly.

2. Appropriate staffs shall be permanently assigned to the Economic and Social
Council, the Trusteeship Council, and, as required, to other organs of the United
Nations. These staffs shall form a part of the Secretariat.

3. The paramount consideration in the employment of the staff and in the determination of the conditions of service shall be the necessity of securing the highest
standards of efficiency, competence, and integrity. Due regard shall be paid to the
importance of recruiting the staff on as wide a geographical basis as possible.

CHAPTER XVI

MISCELLANEOUS PROVISIONS

Article 102

1. Every treaty and every international agreement entered into by any Member
of the United Nations after the present Charter comes into force shall as soon as
possible be registered with the Secretariat and published by it.

2. No party to any such treaty or international agreement which has not been
registered in accordance with the provisions of paragraph 1 of this Article may invoke that treaty or agreement before any organ of the United Nations.

Article 103

In the event of a conflict between the obligations of the Members of the United
Nations under the present Charter and their obligations under any other international agreement, their obligations under the present Charter shall prevail.

Article 104

The Organization shall enjoy in the territory of each of its Members such legal
capacity as may be necessary for the exercise of its functions and the fulfillment of
its purposes.

Article 105

1. The Organization shall enjoy in the territory of each of its Members such privileges and immunities as are necessary for the fulfillment of its purposes.

2. Representatives of the Members of the United Nations and officials of the Organization shall similarly enjoy such privileges and immunities as are necessary for the independent exercise of their functions in connection with the Organization.

3. The General Assembly may make recommendations with a view to determining the details of the application of paragraphs 1 and 2 of this Article or may propose conventions to the Members of the United Nations for this purpose.

CHAPTER XVII

TRANSITIONAL SECURITY ARRANGEMENTS

Article 106

Pending the coming into force of such special agreements referred to in Article 43 as in the opinion of the Security Council enable it to begin the exercise of its responsibilities under Article 42, the parties to the Four-Nation Declaration, signed at Moscow, October 30, 1943, and France, shall, in accordance with the provisions of paragraph 5 of that Declaration, consult with one another and as occasion requires with other Members of the United Nations with a view to such joint action on behalf of the Organization as may be necessary for the purpose of maintaining international peace and security.

Article 107

Nothing in the present Charter shall invalidate or preclude action, in relation to any state which during the Second World War has been an enemy of any signatory to the present Charter, taken or authorized as a result of that war by the Governments having responsibility for such action.

CHAPTER XVIII

AMENDMENTS

Article 108

Amendments to the present Charter shall come into force for all Members of the United Nations when they have been adopted by a vote of two thirds of the members of the General Assembly and ratified in accordance with their respective constitutional processes by two thirds of the Members of the United Nations, including all the permanent members of the Security Council.

Article 109

1. A General Conference of the Members of the United Nations for the purpose of reviewing the present Charter may be held at a date and place to be fixed by a two-thirds vote of the members of the General Assembly and by a vote of any seven members of the Security Council. Each Member of the United Nations shall have one vote in the conference.

2. Any alteration of the present Charter recommended by a two-thirds vote of the conference shall take effect when ratified in accordance with their respective constitutional processes by two thirds of the Members of the United Nations including all the permanent members of the Security Council.

3. If such a conference has not been held before the tenth annual session of the General Assembly following the coming into force of the present Charter, the proposal to call such a conference shall be placed on the agenda of that session of the General Assembly, and the conference shall be held if so decided by a majority vote of the members of the General Assembly and by a vote of any seven members of the Security Council.

CHAPTER XIX

RATIFICATION AND SIGNATURE

Article 110

1. The present Charter shall be ratified by the signatory states in accordance with their respective constitutional processes.

2. The ratifications shall be deposited with the Government of the United States of America, which shall notify all the signatory states of each deposit as well as the Secretary-General of the Organization when he has been appointed.

3. The present Charter shall come into force upon the deposit of ratifications by the Republic of China, France, the Union of Soviet Socialist Republics, the United Kingdom of Great Britain and Northern Ireland, and the United States of America, and by a majority of the other signatory states. A protocol of the ratifications deposited shall thereupon be drawn up by the Government of the United States of America which shall communicate copies thereof to all the signatory states.

4. The states signatory to the present Charter which ratify it after it has come into force will become original Members of the United Nations on the date of the deposit of their respective ratifications.

Article 111

The present Charter, of which the Chinese, French, Russian, English, and Spanish texts are equally authentic, shall remain deposited in the archives of the Government of the United States of America. Duly certified copies thereof shall be transmitted by that Government to the Governments of the other signatory states.

IN FAITH WHEREOF the representatives of the Governments of the United Nations have signed the present Charter.

DONE at the city of San Francisco the twenty-sixth day of June, one thousand nine hundred and forty-five.

Appendix 2

STATUTE OF THE INTERNATIONAL
COURT OF JUSTICE

Article 1

The International Court of Justice established by the Charter of the United Nations as the principal judicial organ of the United Nations shall be constituted and shall function in accordance with the provisions of the present Statute.

CHAPTER I

ORGANIZATION OF THE COURT

Article 2

The Court shall be composed of a body of independent judges, elected regardless of their nationality from among persons of high moral character, who possess the qualifications required in their respective countries for appointment to the highest judicial offices, or are jurisconsults of recognized competence in international law.

Article 3

1. The Court shall consist of fifteen members, no two of whom may be nationals of the same state.

2. A person who for the purposes of membership in the Court could be regarded as a national of more than one state shall be deemed to be a national of the one in which he ordinarily exercises civil and political rights.

Article 4

1. The members of the Court shall be elected by the General Assembly and by the Security Council from a list of persons nominated by

the national groups in the Permanent Court of Arbitration, in accordance with the following provisions.

2. In the case of Members of the United Nations not represented in the Permanent Court of Arbitration, candidates shall be nominated by national groups appointed for this purpose by their governments under the same conditions as those prescribed for members of the Permanent Court of Arbitration by Article 44 of the Convention of The Hague of 1907 for the pacific settlement of international disputes.

3. The conditions under which a state which is a party to the present Statute but is not a Member of the United Nations may participate in electing the members of the Court shall, in the absence of a special agreement, be laid down by the General Assembly upon recommendation of the Security Council.

Article 5

1. At least three months before the date of the election, the Secretary-General of the United Nations shall address a written request to the members of the Permanent Court of Arbitration belonging to the states which are parties to the present Statute, and to the members of the national groups appointed under Article 4, paragraph 2, inviting them to undertake, within a given time, by national groups, the nomination of persons in a position to accept the duties of a member of the Court.

2. No group may nominate more than four persons, not more than two of whom shall be of their own nationality. In no case may the number of candidates nominated by a group be more than double the number of seats to be filled.

Article 6

Before making these nominations, each national group is recommended to consult its highest court of justice, its legal faculties and schools of law, and its national academies and national sections of international academies devoted to the study of law.

Article 7

1. The Secretary-General shall prepare a list in alphabetical order of all the persons thus nominated. Save as provided in Article 12, paragraph 2, these shall be the only persons eligible.

2. The Secretary-General shall submit this list to the General Assembly and to the Security Council.

Article 8

The General Assembly and the Security Council shall proceed independently of one another to elect the members of the Court.

Article 9

At every election, the electors shall bear in mind not only that the persons to be elected should individually possess the qualifications required, but also that in the body as a whole the representation of the main forms of civilization and of the principal legal systems of the world should be assured.

Article 10

1. Those candidates who obtain an absolute majority of votes in the General Assembly and in the Security Council shall be considered as elected.

2. Any vote of the Security Council, whether for the election of judges or for the appointment of members of the conference envisaged in Article 12, shall be taken without any distinction between permanent and non-permanent members of the Security Council.

3. In the event of more than one national of the same state obtaining an absolute majority of the votes both of the General Assembly and of the Security Council, the eldest of these only shall be considered as elected.

Article 11

If, after the first meeting held for the purpose of the election, one or more seats remain to be filled, a second and, if necessary, a third meeting shall take place.

Article 12

1. If, after the third meeting, one or more seats still remain unfilled, a joint conference consisting of six members, three appointed by the General Assembly and three by the Security Council, may be formed at any time at the request of either the General Assembly or the Security Council, for the purpose of choosing by the vote of an absolute

majority one name for each seat still vacant, to submit to the General Assembly and the Security Council for their respective acceptance.

2. If the joint conference is unanimously agreed upon any person who fulfils the required conditions, he may be included in its list, even though he was not included in the list of nominations referred to in Article 7.

3. If the joint conference is satisfied that it will not be successful in procuring an election, those members of the Court who have already been elected shall, within a period to be fixed by the Security Council, proceed to fill the vacant seats by selection from among those candidates who have obtained votes either in the General Assembly or in the Security Council.

4. In the event of an equality of votes among the judges, the eldest judge shall have a casting vote.

Article 13

1. The members of the Court shall be elected for nine years and may be re-elected; provided, however, that of the judges elected at the first election, the terms of five judges shall expire at the end of three years and the terms of five more judges shall expire at the end of six years.

2. The judges whose terms are to expire at the end of the above-mentioned initial periods of three and six years shall be chosen by lot to be drawn by the Secretary-General immediately after the first election has been completed.

3. The members of the Court shall continue to discharge their duties until their places have been filled. Though replaced, they shall finish any cases which they may have begun.

4. In the case of the resignation of a member of the Court, the resignation shall be addressed to the President of the Court for transmission to the Secretary-General. This last notification makes the place vacant.

Article 14

Vacancies shall be filled by the same method as that laid down for the first election, subject to the following provision: the Secretary-General shall, within one month of the occurrence of the vacancy, proceed to issue the invitations provided for in Article 5, and the date of the election shall be fixed by the Security Council.

Article 15

A member of the Court elected to replace a member whose term of office has not expired shall hold office for the remainder of his predecessor's term.

Article 16

1. No member of the Court may exercise any political or administrative function, or engage in any other occupation of a professional nature.

2. Any doubt on this point shall be settled by the decision of the Court.

Article 17

1. No member of the Court may act as agent, counsel, or advocate in any case.

2. No member may participate in the decision of any case in which he has previously taken part as agent, counsel, or advocate for one of the parties, or as a member of a national or international court, or of a commission of enquiry, or in any other capacity.

3. Any doubt on this point shall be settled by the decision of the Court.

Article 18

1. No member of the Court can be dismissed unless, in the unanimous opinion of the other members, he has ceased to fulfil the required conditions.

2. Formal notification thereof shall be made to the Secretary-General by the Registrar.

3. This notification makes the place vacant.

Article 19

The members of the Court, when engaged on the business of the Court, shall enjoy diplomatic privileges and immunities.

Article 20

Every member of the Court shall, before taking up his duties, make a solemn declaration in open court that he will exercise his powers impartially and conscientiously.

Article 21

1. The Court shall elect its President and Vice-President for three years; they may be re-elected.

2. The Court shall appoint its Registrar and may provide for the appointment of such other officers as may be necessary.

Article 22

1. The seat of the Court shall be established at The Hague. This, however, shall not prevent the Court from sitting and exercising its functions elsewhere whenever the Court considers it desirable.

2. The President and the Registrar shall reside at the seat of the Court.

Article 23

1. The Court shall remain permanently in session, except during the judicial vacations, the dates and duration of which shall be fixed by the Court.

2. Members of the Court are entitled to periodic leave, the dates and duration of which shall be fixed by the Court, having in mind the distance between The Hague and the home of each judge.

3. Members of the Court shall be bound, unless they are on leave or prevented from attending by illness or other serious reasons duly explained to the President, to hold themselves permanently at the disposal of the Court.

Article 24

1. If, for some special reason, a member of the Court considers that he should not take part in the decision of a particular case, he shall so inform the President.

2. If the President considers that for some special reason one of the members of the Court should not sit in a particular case, he shall give him notice accordingly.

3. If in any such case the member of the Court and the President disagree, the matter shall be settled by the decision of the Court.

Article 25

1. The full Court shall sit except when it is expressly provided otherwise in the present Statute.

2. Subject to the condition that the number of judges available to constitute the Court is not thereby reduced below eleven, the Rules of the Court may provide for allowing one or more judges, according to circumstances and in rotation, to be dispensed from sitting.

3. A quorum of nine judges shall suffice to constitute the Court.

Article 26

1. The Court may from time to time form one or more chambers, composed of three or more judges as the Court may determine, for dealing with particular categories of cases; for example, labor cases and cases relating to transit and communications.

2. The Court may at any time form a chamber for dealing with a particular case. The number of judges to constitute such a chamber shall be determined by the Court with the approval of the parties.

3. Cases shall be heard and determined by the chambers provided for in this Article if the parties so request.

Article 27

A judgment given by any of the chambers provided for in Articles 26 and 29 shall be considered as rendered by the Court.

Article 28

The chambers provided for in Articles 26 and 29 may, with the consent of the parties, sit and exercise their functions elsewhere than at The Hague.

Article 29

With a view to the speedy despatch of business, the Court shall form annually a chamber composed of five judges which, at the request of the parties, may hear and determine cases by summary procedure. In addition, two judges shall be selected for the purpose of replacing judges who find it impossible to sit.

Article 30

1. The Court shall frame rules for carrying out its functions. In particular, it shall lay down rules of procedure.

2. The Rules of the Court may provide for assessors to sit with the Court or with any of its chambers, without the right to vote.

Article 31

1. Judges of the nationality of each of the parties shall retain their right to sit in the case before the Court.

2. If the Court includes upon the Bench a judge of the nationality of one of the parties, any other party may choose a person to sit as judge. Such person shall be chosen preferably from among those persons who have been nominated as candidates as provided in Articles 4 and 5.

3. If the Court includes upon the Bench no judge of the nationality of the parties, each of these parties may proceed to choose a judge as provided in paragraph 2 of this Article.

4. The provisions of this Article shall apply to the case of Articles 26 and 29. In such cases, the President shall request one or, if necessary, two of the members of the Court forming the chamber to give place to the members of the Court of the nationality of the parties concerned, and, failing such, or if they are unable to be present, to the judges specially chosen by the parties.

5. Should there be several parties in the same interest, they shall, for the purpose of the preceding provisions, be reckoned as one party only. Any doubt upon this point shall be settled by the decision of the Court.

6. Judges chosen as laid down in paragraphs 2, 3, and 4 of this Article shall fulfil the conditions required by Articles 2, 17 (paragraph 2), 20, and 24 of the present Statute. They shall take part in the decision on terms of complete equality with their colleagues.

Article 32

1. Each member of the Court shall receive an annual salary.

2. The President shall receive a special annual allowance.

3. The Vice-President shall receive a special allowance for every day on which he acts as President.

4. The judges chosen under Article 31, other than members of the Court, shall receive compensation for each day on which they exercise their functions.

5. These salaries, allowances, and compensation shall be fixed by the General Assembly. They may not be decreased during the term of office.

6. The salary of the Registrar shall be fixed by the General Assembly on the proposal of the Court.

7. Regulations made by the General Assembly shall fix the conditions under which retirement pensions may be given to members of the Court and to the Registrar, and the conditions under which members of the Court and the Registrar shall have their traveling expenses refunded.

8. The above salaries, allowances, and compensation shall be free of all taxation.

Article 33

The expenses of the Court shall be borne by the United Nations in such a manner as shall be decided by the General Assembly.

CHAPTER II

COMPETENCE OF THE COURT

Article 34

1. Only states may be parties in cases before the Court.

2. The Court, subject to and in conformity with its Rules, may request of public international organizations information relevant to cases before it, and shall receive such information presented by such organizations on their own initiative.

3. Whenever the construction of the constituent instrument of a public international organization or of an international convention adopted thereunder is in question in a case before the Court, the Registrar shall so notify the public international organization concerned and shall communicate to it copies of all the written proceedings.

Article 35

1. The Court shall be open to the states parties to the present Statute.

2. The conditions under which the Court shall be open to other states shall, subject to the special provisions contained in treaties in force, be laid down by the Security Council, but in no case shall such conditions place the parties in a position of inequality before the Court.

3. When a state which is not a Member of the United Nations is a party to a case, the Court shall fix the amount which that party is to contribute towards the expenses of the Court. This provision shall not apply if such state is bearing a share of the expenses of the Court.

Article 36

1. The jurisdiction of the Court comprises all cases which the parties refer to it and all matters specially provided for in the Charter of the United Nations or in treaties and conventions in force.

2. The states parties to the present Statute may at any time declare that they recognize as compulsory *ipso facto* and without special agreement, in relation to any other state accepting the same obligation, the jurisdiction of the Court in all legal disputes concerning:

    a. the interpretation of a treaty;

    b. any question of international law;

    c. the existence of any fact which, if established, would constitute a breach of an international obligation;

    d. the nature or extent of the reparation to be made for the breach of an international obligation.

3. The declarations referred to above may be made unconditionally or on condition of reciprocity on the part of several or certain states, or for a certain time.

4. Such declarations shall be deposited with the Secretary-General of the United Nations, who shall transmit copies thereof to the parties to the Statute and to the Registrar of the Court.

5. Declarations made under Article 36 of the Statute of the Permanent Court of International Justice and which are still in force shall be deemed, as between the parties to the present Statute, to be acceptances of the compulsory jurisdiction of the International Court of Justice for the period which they still have to run and in accordance with their terms.

6. In the event of a dispute as to whether the Court has jurisdiction, the matter shall be settled by the decision of the Court.

Article 37

Whenever a treaty or convention in force provides for reference of a matter to a tribunal to have been instituted by the League of Nations, or to the Permanent Court of International Justice, the matter shall, as between the parties to the present Statute, be referred to the International Court of Justice.

Article 38

1. The Court, whose function is to decide in accordance with international law such disputes as are submitted to it, shall apply:

a. international conventions, whether general or particular, establishing rules expressly recognized by the contesting states;

b. international custom, as evidence of a general practice accepted as law;

c. the general principles of law recognized by civilized nations;

d. subject to the provisions of Article 59, judicial decisions and the teachings of the most highly qualified publicists of the various nations, as subsidiary means for the determination of rules of law.

2. This provision shall not prejudice the power of the Court to decide a case *ex aequo et bono*, if the parties agree thereto.

CHAPTER III

PROCEDURE

Article 39

1. The official languages of the Court shall be French and English. If the parties agree that the case shall be conducted in French, the judgment shall be delivered in French. If the parties agree that the case shall be conducted in English, the judgment shall be delivered in English.

2. In the absence of an agreement as to which language shall be employed, each party may, in the pleadings, use the language which it prefers; the decision of the Court shall be given in French and English. In this case the Court shall at the same time determine which of the two texts shall be considered as authoritative.

3. The Court shall, at the request of any party, authorize a language other than French or English to be used by that party.

Article 40

1. Cases are brought before the Court, as the case may be, either by the notification of the special agreement or by a written application addressed to the Registrar. In either case the subject of the dispute and the parties shall be indicated.

2. The Registrar shall forthwith communicate the application to all concerned.

3. He shall also notify the Members of the United Nations through the Secretary-General, and also any other states entitled to appear before the Court.

Article 41

1. The Court shall have the power to indicate, if it considers that circumstances so require, any provisional measures which ought to be taken to preserve the respective rights of either party.

2. Pending the final decision, notice of the measures suggested shall forthwith be given to the parties and to the Security Council.

Article 42

1. The parties shall be represented by agents.

2. They may have the assistance of counsel or advocates before the Court.

3. The agents, counsel, and advocates of parties before the Court shall enjoy the privileges and immunities necessary to the independent exercise of their duties.

Article 43

1. The procedure shall consist of two parts: written and oral.

2. The written proceedings shall consist of the communication to the Court and to the parties of memorials, counter-memorials and, if necessary, replies; also all papers and documents in support.

3. These communications shall be made through the Registrar, in the order and within the time fixed by the Court.

4. A certified copy of every document produced by one party shall be communicated to the other party.

5. The oral proceedings shall consist of the hearing by the Court of witnesses, experts, agents, counsel, and advocates.

Article 44

1. For the service of all notices upon persons other than the agents, counsel, and advocates, the Court shall apply direct to the government of the state upon whose territory the notice has to be served.

2. The same provision shall apply whenever steps are to be taken to procure evidence on the spot.

Article 45

The hearing shall be under the control of the President or, if he is unable to preside, of the Vice-President; if neither is able to preside, the senior judge present shall preside.

Article 46

The hearing in Court shall be public, unless the Court shall decide otherwise, or unless the parties demand that the public be not admitted.

Article 47

1. Minutes shall be made at each hearing and signed by the Registrar and the President.
2. These minutes alone shall be authentic.

Article 48

The Court shall make orders for the conduct of the case, shall decide the form and time in which each party must conclude its arguments, and make all arrangements connected with the taking of evidence.

Article 49

The Court may, even before the hearing begins, call upon the agents to produce any document or to supply any explanations. Formal note shall be taken of any refusal.

Article 50

The Court may, at any time, entrust any individual, body, bureau, commission, or other organization that it may select, with the task of carrying out an enquiry or giving an expert opinion.

Article 51

During the hearing any relevant questions are to be put to the witnesses and experts under the conditions laid down by the Court in the rules of procedure referred to in Article 30.

Article 52

After the Court has received the proofs and evidence within the time specified for the purpose, it may refuse to accept any further oral or written evidence that one party may desire to present unless the other side consents.

Article 53

1. Whenever one of the parties does not appear before the Court, or fails to defend its case, the other party may call upon the Court to decide in favor of its claim.

2. The Court must, before doing so, satisfy itself, not only that it has jurisdiction in accordance with Articles 36 and 37, but also that the claim is well founded in fact and law.

Article 54

1. When, subject to the control of the Court, the agents, counsel, and advocates have completed their presentation of the case, the President shall declare the hearing closed.
2. The Court shall withdraw to consider the judgment.
3. The deliberations of the Court shall take place in private and remain secret.

Article 55

1. All questions shall be decided by a majority of the judges present.
2. In the event of an equality of votes, the President or the judge who acts in his place shall have a casting vote.

Article 56

1. The judgment shall state the reasons on which it is based.
2. It shall contain the names of the judges who have taken part in the decision.

Article 57

If the judgment does not represent in whole or in part the unanimous opinion of the judges, any judge shall be entitled to deliver a separate opinion.

Article 58

The judgment shall be signed by the President and by the Registrar. It shall be read in open court, due notice having been given to the agents.

Article 59

The decision of the Court has no binding force except between the parties and in respect of that particular case.

Article 60

The judgment is final and without appeal. In the event of dispute as to the meaning or scope of the judgment. the Court shall construe it upon the request of any party.

Article 61

1. An application for revision of a judgment may be made only when it is based upon the discovery of some fact of such a nature as to be a decisive factor, which fact was, when the judgment was given, unknown to the Court and also to the party claiming revision, always provided that such ignorance was not due to negligence.

2. The proceedings for revision shall be opened by a judgment of the Court expressly recording the existence of the new fact, recognizing that it has such a character as to lay the case open to revision, and declaring the application admissible on this ground.

3. The Court may require previous compliance with the terms of the judgment before it admits proceedings in revision.

4. The application for revision must be made at latest within six months of the discovery of the new fact.

5. No application for revision may be made after the lapse of ten years from the date of the judgment.

Article 62

1. Should a state consider that it has an interest of a legal nature which may be affected by the decision in the case, it may submit a request to the Court to be permitted to intervene.

2. It shall be for the Court to decide upon this request.

Article 63

1. Whenever the construction of a convention to which states other than those concerned in the case are parties is in question, the Registrar shall notify all such states forthwith.

2. Every state so notified has the right to intervene in the proceedings; but if it uses this right, the construction given by the judgment will be equally binding upon it.

Article 64

Unless otherwise decided by the Court, each party shall bear its own costs.

CHAPTER IV

ADVISORY OPINIONS

Article 65

1. The Court may give an advisory opinion on any legal question at the request of whatever body may be authorized by or in accordance with the Charter of the United Nations to make such a request.

2. Questions upon which the advisory opinion of the Court is asked shall be laid before the Court by means of a written request containing an exact statement of the question upon which an opinion is required, and accompanied by all documents likely to throw light upon the question.

Article 66

1. The Registrar shall forthwith give notice of the request for an advisory opinion to all states entitled to appear before the Court.

2. The Registrar shall also, by means of a special and direct communication, notify any state entitled to appear before the Court or international organization considered by the Court, or, should it not be sitting, by the President, as likely to be able to furnish information on the question, that the Court will be prepared to receive, within a time limit to be fixed by the President, written statements, or to hear, at a public sitting to be held for the purpose, oral statements relating to the question.

3. Should any such state entitled to appear before the Court have failed to receive the special communication referred to in paragraph 2 of this Article, such state may express a desire to submit a written statement or to be heard; and the Court will decide.

4. States and organizations having presented written or oral statements or both shall be permitted to comment on the statements made by other states or organizations in the form, to the extent, and within the time limits which the Court, or, should it not be sitting, the President, shall decide in each particular case. Accordingly, the Registrar shall in due time communicate any such written statements to states and organizations having submitted similar statements.

Article 67

The Court shall deliver its advisory opinions in open court, notice having been given to the Secretary-General and to the representatives of Members of the United Nations, of other states and of international organizations immediately concerned.

Article 68

In the exercise of its advisory functions the Court shall further be guided by the provisions of the present Statute which apply in contentious cases to the extent to which it recognizes them to be applicable.

CHAPTER V

AMENDMENT

Article 69

Amendments to the present Statute shall be effected by the same procedure as is provided by the Charter of the United Nations for amendments to that Charter, subject however to any provisions which the General Assembly upon recommendation of the Security Council may adopt concerning the participation of states which are parties to the present Statute but are not Members of the United Nations.

Article 70

The Court shall have power to propose such amendments to the present Statute as it may deem necessary, through written communications to the Secretary-General, for consideration in conformity with the provisions of Article 69.

Appendix 3

THE FOURTEEN POINTS OF
PRESIDENT WOODROW WILSON [1]

I. Open covenants of peace, openly arrived at, after which there shall be no private international understandings of any kind but diplomacy shall proceed always frankly and in the public view.

II. Absolute freedom of navigation upon the seas, outside territorial waters, alike in peace and in war, except as the seas may be closed in whole or in part by international action for the enforcement of international covenants.

III. The removal, so far as possible, of all economic barriers and the establishment of an equality of trade conditions among all the nations consenting to the peace and associating themselves for its maintenance.

IV. Adequate guarantees given and taken that national armaments will be reduced to the lowest point consistent with domestic safety.

V. A free, open-minded, and absolutely impartial adjustment of all colonial claims, based upon a strict observance of the principle that in determining all such questions of sovereignty the interests of the populations concerned must have equal weight with the equitable claims of the government whose title is to be determined.

. . . .

XIV. A general association of nations must be formed under specific covenants for the purpose of affording mutual guarantees of political independence and territorial integrity to great and small states alike.

[1] Address delivered at a joint session of the two houses of Congress, Jan. 8, 1918 (*Excerpt*), Ray Stannard Baker and William E. Dodd, *The Public Papers of Woodrow Wilson, War and Peace*, Vol. I, Harper, New York, 1926, pp. 159–161.

Appendix 4

COVENANT OF THE LEAGUE OF NATIONS
(Selected Provisions)

Article 2

The action of the League under this Covenant shall be effected through the instrumentality of an Assembly and of a Council, with a permanent Secretariat.

Article 4

4. The Council may deal at its meetings with any matter within the sphere of action of the League or affecting the peace of the world.

Article 8

1. The Members of the League recognize that the maintenance of peace requires the reduction of national armaments to the lowest point consistent with national safety and the enforcement by common action of international obligations.

2. The Council, taking account of the geographical situation and circumstances of each State, shall formulate plans for such reduction for the consideration and action of the several Governments.

3. Such plans shall be subject to reconsideration and revision at least every ten years.

4. After these plans shall have been adopted by the several Governments, the limits of armaments therein fixed shall not be exceeded without the concurrence of the Council.

5. The Members of the League agree that the manufacture by private enterprise of munitions and implements of war is open to grave objections. The Council shall advise how the evil effects attendant upon such manufacture can be prevented, due regard being had to the necessities of those Members of the League which are not able to manufacture the munitions and implements of war necessary for their safety.

6. The Members of the League undertake to interchange full and frank information as to the scale of their armaments, their military, naval and air programs and the condition of such of their industries as are adaptable to warlike purposes.

Article 9

A permanent Commission shall be constituted to advise the Council on the execution of the provisions of Articles 1 and 8 and on military, naval and air questions generally.

Article 10

The Members of the League undertake to respect and preserve as against external aggression the territorial integrity and existing political independence of all Members of the League. In case of any such aggression or in case of any threat or danger of such aggression the Council shall advise upon the means by which this obligation shall be fulfilled.

Article 11

1. Any war or threat of war, whether immediately affecting any of the Members of the League or not, is hereby declared a matter of concern to the whole League, and the League shall take any action that may be deemed wise and effectual to safeguard the peace of nations. In case any such emergency should arise the Secretary-General shall on the request of any Member of the League forthwith summon a meeting of the Council.

2. It is also declared to be the friendly right of each Member of the League to bring to the attention of the Assembly or of the Council any circumstance whatever affecting international relations which threatens to disturb international peace or the good understanding between nations upon which peace depends.

Article 12

1. The Members of the League agree that, if there should arise between them any dispute likely to lead to a rupture, they will submit the matter either to arbitration *or judicial settlement* or to inquiry by the Council, and they agree in no case to resort to war until three months after the award by the arbitrators *or the judicial decision,* or the report by the Council.

2. In any case under this Article the award of the arbitrators *or the judicial decision* shall be made within a reasonable time, and the report of the Council shall be made within six months after the submission of the dispute.

Article 13

1. The Members of the League agree that, whenever any dispute shall arise between them which they recognize to be suitable for submission to arbitration *or judicial settlement,* and which can not be satisfactorily settled by diplomacy, they will submit the whole subject-matter to arbitration *or judicial settlement.*

2. Disputes as to the interpretation of a treaty, as to any question of international law, as to the existence of any fact which, if established, would constitute a breach of any international obligation, or as to the extent and nature of the reparation to be made for any such breach, are declared to be among those which are generally suitable for submission to arbitration *or judicial settlement.*

3. *For the consideration of any such dispute, the court to which the case is referred shall be the Permanent Court of International Justice, established in accordance with Article 14, or any tribunal agreed on by the parties to the dispute or stipulated in any convention existing between them.*

4. The Members of the League agree that they will carry out in full good faith any award *or decision* that may be rendered, and that they will not resort to war against a Member of the League which complies therewith. In the event of any failure to carry out such an award *or decision,* the Council shall propose what steps should be taken to give effect thereto.

Article 14

The Council shall formulate and submit to the Members of the League for adoption plans for the establishment of a Permanent Court of International Justice. The Court shall be competent to hear and determine any dispute of an international character which the parties thereto submit to it. The Court may also give an advisory opinion upon any dispute or question referred to it by the Council or by the Assembly.

Article 15

1. If there should arise between Members of the League any dispute likely to lead to a rupture, which is not submitted to arbitration *or judicial settlement* in accordance with Article 13, the Members of the League agree that they will submit the matter to the Council. Any party to the dispute may effect such submission by giving notice of the existence of the dispute to the Secretary-General, who will make all necessary arrangements for a full investigation and consideration thereof.

2. For this purpose the parties to the dispute will communicate to the Secretary-General, as promptly as possible, statements of their case with all the relevant facts and papers, and the Council may forthwith direct the publication thereof.

3. The Council shall endeavor to effect a settlement of the dispute, and, if such efforts are successful, a statement shall be made public giving such facts and explanations regarding the dispute and the terms of settlement thereof as the Council may deem appropriate.

4. If the dispute is not thus settled, the Council either unanimously or by a majority vote shall make and publish a report containing a statement of the facts of the dispute and the recommendations which are deemed just and proper in regard thereto.

5. Any member of the League represented on the Council may make a public statement of the facts of the dispute and of its conclusions regarding the same.

6. If a report by the Council is unanimously agreed to by the Members thereof other than the Representatives of one or more of the parties to the dispute, the Members of the League agree that they will not go to war with any party to the dispute which complies with the recommendation of the report.

7. If the Council fails to reach a report which is unanimously agreed to by the members thereof, other than the Representatives of one or more of the parties to the dispute, the Members of the League reserve to themselves the right to take such action as they shall consider necessary for the maintenance of right and justice.

8. If the dispute between the parties is claimed by one of them, and is found by the Council, to arise out of a matter which by international law is solely within the domestic jurisdiction of that party, the Council shall so report, and shall make no recommendation as to its settlement.

9. The Council may in any case under this Article refer the dispute to the Assembly. The dispute shall be so referred at the request of either party to the dispute, provided that such request be made within fourteen days after the submission of the dispute to the Council.

10. In any case referred to the Assembly, all the provisions of this Article and of Article 12 relating to the action and powers of the Council shall apply to the action and powers of the Assembly, provided that a report made by the Assembly, if concurred in by the Representatives of those Members of the League represented on the Council and of a majority of the other Members of the League, exclusive in each

case of the Representatives of the parties to the dispute, shall have the same force as a report by the Council concurred in by all the members thereof other than the Representatives of one or more of the parties to the dispute.

Article 16

1. Should any Member of the League resort to war in disregard of its covenants under Articles 12, 13 or 15, it shall *ipso facto* be deemed to have committed an act of war against all other Members of the League, which hereby undertake immediately to subject it to the severance of all trade or financial relations, the prohibition of all intercourse between their nationals and the nationals of the covenant-breaking State, and the prevention of all financial, commercial or personal intercourse between the nationals of the covenant-breaking State and the nationals of any other State, whether a Member of the League or not.

2. It shall be the duty of the Council in such case to recommend to the several Governments concerned what effective military, naval or air force the Members of the League shall severally contribute to the armed forces to be used to protect the covenants of the League.

3. The Members of the League agree, further, that they will mutually support one another in the financial and economic measures which are taken under this Article, in order to minimize the loss and inconvenience resulting from the above measures, and that they will mutually support one another in resisting any special measures aimed at one of their number by the covenant-breaking State, and that they will take the necessary steps to afford passage through their territory to the forces of any of the Members of the League which are cooperating to protect the covenants of the League.

4. Any Member of the League which has violated any covenant of the League may be declared to be no longer a Member of the League by a vote of the Council concurred in by the Representatives of all the other members of the League represented thereon.

Article 22

1. To those colonies and territories which as a consequence of the late war have ceased to be under the sovereignty of the States which formerly governed them and which are inhabited by peoples not yet able to stand by themselves under the strenuous conditions of the modern world, there should be applied the principle that the well-being and development of such peoples form a sacred trust of civilization and that securities for the performance of this trust should be embodied in this Covenant.

2. The best method of giving practical effect to this principle is that the tutelage of such peoples should be intrusted to advanced nations who by reason of their resources, their experience or their geographical position can best undertake this responsibility, and who are willing to accept it, and that this tutelage should be exercised by them as Mandatories on behalf of the League.

3. The character of the mandate must differ according to the stage of the development of the people, the geographical situation of the territory, its economic conditions and other similar circumstances.

4. Certain communities formerly belonging to the Turkish Empire have reached a stage of development where their existence as independent nations can be provisionally recognized subject to the rendering of administrative advice and assistance by a Mandatory until such time as they are able to stand alone. The wishes of these communities must be a principal consideration in the selection of the Mandatory.

5. Other peoples, especially those of Central Africa, are at such a stage that the Mandatory must be responsible for the administration of the territory under conditions which will guarantee freedom of conscience and religion, subject only to the maintenance of public order and morals, the prohibition of abuses such as the slave trade, the arms traffic and the liquor traffic, and the prevention of the establishment of fortifications of military and naval bases and of military training of the natives for other than police purposes and the defense of territory, and will also secure equal opportunities for the trade and commerce of other Members of the League.

6. There are territories, such as Southwest Africa and certain of the South Pacific islands, which, owing to the sparseness of their population, or their small size, or their remoteness from the centers of civilization, or their geographical contiguity to the territory of the Mandatory, and other circumstances, can be best administered under the laws of the Mandatory as integral portions of its territory, subject to the safeguards above mentioned in the interests of the indigenous population.

7. In every case of mandate, the Mandatory shall render to the Council an annual report in reference to the territory committed to its charge.

8. The degree of authority, control or administration to be exercised by the Mandatory shall, if not previously agreed upon by the Members of the League, be explicitly defined in each case by the Council.

9. A permanent Commission shall be constituted to receive and examine the annual reports of the Mandatories and to advise the Council on all matters relating to the observance of the mandates.

Article 23

Subject to and in accordance with the provisions of international conventions existing or hereafter to be agreed upon, the Members of the League:

a. will endeavor to secure and maintain fair and humane conditions of labor for men, women and children, both in their own countries and in all countries to which their commercial and industrial relations extend, and for that purpose will establish and maintain the necessary international organizations;

b. undertake to secure just treatment of the native inhabitants of territories under their control;

c. will entrust the League with the general supervision over the execution of agreements with regard to traffic in women and children, and the traffic in opium and other dangerous drugs;

d. will entrust the League with the general supervision of the trade in arms and ammunition with the countries in which the control of this traffic is necessary in the common interest;

e. will make provision to secure and maintain freedom of communications and of transit and equitable treatment for the commerce of all Members of the League. In this connection, the special necessities of the regions devastated during the war of 1914–1918 shall be borne in mind;

f. will endeavor to take steps in matters of international concern for the prevention and control of disease.

Appendix 5

THE FOUR FREEDOMS [1]

In the future days, which we seek to make secure, we look forward to a world founded upon four essential human freedoms.

The first is freedom of speech and expression—everywhere in the world.

The second is freedom of every person to worship God in his way—everywhere in the world.

The third is freedom from want—which, translated into world terms, means economic understandings which will secure to every nation a healthy peacetime life for its inhabitants—everywhere in the world.

The fourth is freedom from fear—which translated into world terms, means a world-wide reduction of armaments to such a point and in such a thorough fashion that no nation will be in a position to commit an act of physical aggression against any neighbor—everywhere in the world.

[1] *Annual Message of the President to the Congress,* Jan. 6, 1941 (*Excerpt*), Senate Document No. 188, 77th Congress, 2d Session, pp. 86–87.

Appendix 6

THE ATLANTIC CHARTER, AUGUST 14, 1941 [1]

Joint Declaration of the President of the United States of America and the Prime Minister, Mr. Churchill, representing His Majesty's Government in the United Kingdom, being met together, deem it right to make known certain common principles in the national policies of their respective countries on which they base their hopes for a better future for the world.

First, their countries seek no aggrandizement, territorial or other;

Second, they desire to see no territorial changes that do not accord with the freely expressed wishes of the peoples concerned;

Third, they respect the right of all peoples to choose the form of government under which they will live; and they wish to see sovereign rights and self-government restored to those who have been forcibly deprived of them;

Fourth, they will endeavor, with due respect for their existing obligations, to further the enjoyment by all States, great or small, victor or vanquished, of access, on equal terms, to the trade and to the raw materials of the world which are needed for their economic prosperity;

Fifth, they desire to bring about the fullest collaboration between all nations in the economic field with the object of securing, for all, improved labor standards, economic advancement and social security;

Sixth, after the final destruction of the Nazi tyranny, they hope to see established a peace which will afford to all nations the means of dwelling in safety within their own boundaries, and which will afford assurance that all the men in all the lands may live out their lives in freedom from fear and want;

Seventh, such a peace should enable all men to traverse the high seas and oceans without hindrance;

Eighth, they believe that all of the nations of the world, for realistic as well as spiritual reasons must come to the abandonment of the use of force. Since no future peace can be maintained if land, sea or air armaments continue to be employed by nations which threaten, or may threaten, aggression outside of their frontiers, they believe, pending the establishment of a wider and permanent system of general security, that the disarmament of such nations is essential. They will likewise aid and encourage all other practicable measures which will lighten for peace-loving peoples the crushing burden of armaments.

Franklin D. Roosevelt

Winston S. Churchill

[1] U.S. Department of State Publication 1732, United States Executive Agreement Series 236, Washington, D.C., 1942.

Appendix 7

THE UNITED NATIONS DECLARATION, JANUARY 1, 1942 [1]

A joint declaration by the United States of America, the United Kingdom of Great Britain and Northern Ireland, the Union of Soviet Socialist Republics, China, Australia, Belgium, Canada, Costa Rica, Cuba, Czechoslovakia, Dominican Republic, El Salvador, Greece, Guatemala, Haiti, Honduras, India, Luxembourg, Netherlands, New Zealand, Nicaragua, Norway, Panama, Poland, South Africa, Yugoslavia.

The Governments signatory hereto,

Having subscribed to a common program of purposes and principles embodied in the Joint Declaration of the President of the United States of America and the Prime Minister of the United Kingdom of Great Britain and Northern Ireland dated August 14, 1941, known as the Atlantic Charter,

Being convinced that complete victory over their enemies is essential to defend life, liberty, independence and religious freedom, and to preserve human rights and justice in their own lands as well as in other lands, and that they are now engaged in a common struggle against savage and brutal forces seeking to subjugate the world, declare:

(1) Each Government pledges itself to employ its full resources, military or economic, against those members of the Tripartite Pact and its adherents with which such government is at war.

(2) Each Government pledges itself to cooperate with the Governments signatory hereto and not to make a separate armistice or peace with the enemies.

The foregoing declaration may be adhered to by other nations which are, or which may be, rendering material assistance and contributions in the struggle for victory over Hitlerism.

[1] U.S. Department of State Publication 1732, United States Executive Agreement Series 236, Washington, D.C., 1942.

Appendix 8

THE MOSCOW DECLARATION ON GENERAL SECURITY, NOVEMBER 1, 1943 [1]

The Governments of the United States of America, the United Kingdom, the Soviet Union and China: united in their determination, in accordance with the Declaration by the United Nations of January 1, 1942, and subsequent declarations, to continue hostilities against those Axis powers with which they respectively are at war until such powers have laid down their arms on the basis of unconditional surrender; conscious of their responsibility to secure the liberation of themselves and the peoples allied with them from the menace of aggression; recognizing the necessity of ensuring a rapid and orderly transition from war to peace and of establishing and maintaining international peace and security with the least diversion of the world's human and economic resources for armaments; jointly declare:

1. That their united action, pledged for the prosecution of the war against their respective enemies, will be continued for the organization and maintenance of peace and security.

2. That those of them at war with a common enemy will act together in all matters relating to the surrender and disarmament of that enemy.

3. That they will take all measures deemed by them to be necessary to provide against any violation of the terms imposed upon the enemy.

4. That they recognize the necessity of establishing at the earliest practicable date a general international organization, based on the principle of the sovereign equality of all peace-loving states, and open to membership by all such states, large and small, for the maintenance of international peace and security.

5. That for the purpose of maintaining international peace and security pending the reestablishment of law and order and the inauguration of a system of general security, they will consult with one another and as occasion requires with other members of the United Nations with a view to joint action on behalf of the community of nations.

6. That after the termination of hostilities they will not employ their military forces within the territories of other states except for the purposes envisaged in this declaration and after joint consultation.

7. That they will confer and co-operate with one another and with other members of the United Nations to bring about a practicable general agreement with respect to the regulation of armaments in the post-war period.

[1] *Department of State Bulletin,* Vol. IX, pp. 307*ff.*

Appendix 9

THE TEHRAN DECLARATION OF THE THREE POWERS, DECEMBER 1, 1943 [1]

We—the President of the United States, the Prime Minister of Great Britain, and the Premier of the Soviet Union, have met these four days past, in this, the Capital of our Ally, Iran, and have shaped and confirmed our common policy.

We express our determination that our nations shall work together in war and in the peace that will follow.

As to war—our military staffs have joined in our round table discussions, and we have concerted our plans for the destruction of the German forces. We have reached complete agreement as to the scope and timing of the operations to be undertaken from the east, west and south.

The common understanding which we have here reached guarantees that victory will be ours.

And as to peace—we are sure that our concord will win an enduring Peace. We recognize fully the supreme responsibility resting upon us and all the United Nations to make a peace which will command the goodwill of the overwhelming mass of the peoples of the world and banish the scourge and terror of war for many generations.

With our Diplomatic advisors we have surveyed the problems of the future. We shall seek the cooperation and active participation of all nations, large and small, whose peoples in heart and mind are dedicated, as are our own peoples, to the elimination of tyranny and slavery, oppression and intolerance. We will welcome them, as they may choose to come, into a world family of Democratic Nations.

No power on earth can prevent our destroying the German armies by land, their U Boats by sea, and their war plants from the air.

Our attack will be relentless and increasing.

Emerging from these cordial conferences we look with confidence to the day when all peoples of the world may live free lives, untouched by tyranny, and according to their varying desires and their own consciences.

We came here with hope and determination. We leave here, friends in fact, in spirit and in purpose.

ROOSEVELT, CHURCHILL AND STALIN

[1] *Toward the Peace—Documents,* U.S. Department of State Publication 2298, pp. 15–16.

Appendix 10

(DUMBARTON OAKS) PROPOSALS FOR THE ESTABLISHMENT OF A GENERAL INTERNATIONAL ORGANIZATION [1]

There should be established an international organization under the title of The United Nations, the Charter of which should contain provisions necessary to give effect to the proposals which follow.

CHAPTER I. PURPOSES

The purpose of the Organization should be:

1. To maintain international peace and security; and to that end to take effective collective measures for the prevention and removal of threats to the peace and the suppression of acts of aggression or other breaches of the peace, and to bring about by peaceful means adjustment or settlement of international disputes which may lead to a breach of the peace;

2. To develop friendly relations among nations and to take other appropriate measures to strengthen universal peace;

3. To achieve international cooperation in the solution of international economic, social and other humanitarian problems; and

4. To afford a center for harmonizing the actions of nations in the achievement of these common ends.

CHAPTER II. PRINCIPLES

In pursuit of the purposes mentioned in Chapter I the Organization and its members should act in accordance with the following principles:

1. The Organization is based on the principle of the sovereign equality of all peace-loving states.

2. All members of the Organization undertake, in order to ensure to all of them the rights and benefits resulting from membership in the Organization, to fulfill the obligations assumed by them in accordance with the Charter.

3. All members of the Organization shall settle their disputes by peaceful means in such a manner that international peace and security are not endangered.

4. All members of the Organization shall refrain in their international relations

[1] The United Nations Conference on International Organization. *Selected Documents*, U.S. Department of State Publication 2490, Conference Series, 83, pp. 87*ff*.

from the threat or use of force in any manner inconsistent with the purposes of the Organization.

5. All members of the Organization shall give every assistance to the Organization in any action undertaken by it in accordance with the provisions of the Charter.

6. All members of the Organization shall refrain from giving assistance to any state against which preventive or enforcement action is being undertaken by the Organization.

The Organization should ensure that states not members of the Organization act in accordance with these principles so far as may be necessary for the maintenance of international peace and security.

CHAPTER III. MEMBERSHIP

1. Membership of the Organization should be open to all peace-loving states.

CHAPTER IV. PRINCIPAL ORGANS

1. The Organization should have as its principal organs:
   a. A General Assembly;
   b. A Security Council;
   c. An international court of justice; and
   d. A Secretariat

2. The Organization should have such subsidiary agencies as may be found necessary.

CHAPTER V. THE GENERAL ASSEMBLY

Section A. Composition

All members of the Organization should be members of the General Assembly and should have a number of representatives to be specified in the Charter.

Section B. Functions and Powers

1. The General Assembly should have the right to consider the general principles of cooperation in the maintenance of international peace and security, including the principles governing disarmament and the regulation of armaments; to discuss any questions relating to the maintenance of international peace and security brought before it by any member or members of the Organization or by the Security Council; and to make recommendations with regard to any such principles or questions. Any such questions on which action is necessary should be referred to the Security Council by the General Assembly either before or after discussion. The General Assembly should not on its own initiative make recommendations on any matter relating to the maintenance of international peace and security which is being dealt with by the Security Council.

2. The General Assembly should be empowered to admit new members to the organization upon recommendation of the Security Council.

3. The General Assembly should, upon recommendation of the Security Council, be empowered to suspend from the exercise of any rights or privileges of membership any member of the Organization against which preventive or enforcement action shall have been taken by the Security Council. The exercise of the rights and

privileges thus suspended may be restored by decision of the Security Council. The General Assembly should be empowered, upon recommendation of the Security Council, to expel from the Organization any member of the Organization which persistently violates the principles contained in the Charter.

4. The General Assembly should elect the non-permanent members of the Security Council and the members of the Economic and Social Council provided for in Chapter IX. It should be empowered to elect, upon recommendation of the Security Council, the Secretary-General of the Organization. It should perform such functions in relation to the election of the judges of the international court of justice as may be conferred upon it by the statute of the court.

5. The General Assembly should apportion the expenses among the members of the Organization and should be empowered to approve the budgets of the Organization.

6. The General Assembly should initiate studies and make recommendations for the purpose of promoting international cooperation in political, economic and social fields and of adjusting situations likely to impair the general welfare.

7. The General Assembly should make recommendations for the coordination of the policies of international economic, social and other specialized agencies brought into relation with the Organization in accordance with agreements between such agencies and the Organization.

8. The General Assembly should receive and consider annual and special reports from the Security Council and reports from other bodies of the Organization.

Section C. Voting

1. Each member of the Organization should have one vote in the General Assembly.

2. Important decisions of the General Assembly, including recommendations with respect to the maintenance of international peace and security; election of members of the Security Council; election of members of the Economic and Social Council; admission of members, suspension of the exercise of the rights and privileges of members, and expulsion of members; and budgetary questions, should be made by a two-thirds majority of those present and voting. On other questions, including the determination of additional categories of questions to be decided by a two-thirds majority, the decisions of the General Assembly should be made by a simple majority vote.

Section D. Procedure

1. The General Assembly should meet in regular annual sessions and in such special sessions as occasion may require.

2. The General Assembly should adopt its own rules of procedure and elect its President for each session.

3. The General Assembly should be empowered to set up such bodies and agencies as it may deem necessary for the performance of its functions.

CHAPTER VI. THE SECURITY COUNCIL

Section A. Composition

The Security Council should consist of one representative of each of eleven members of the Organization. Representatives of the United States of America, the

United Kingdom of Great Britain and Northern Ireland, the Union of Soviet Socialist Republics, the Republic of China, and, in due course, France, should have permanent seats. The General Assembly should elect six states to fill the non-permanent seats. These six states should be elected for a term of two years, three retiring each year. They should not be immediately eligible for reelection. In the first election of the non-permanent members three should be chosen by the General Assembly for one-year terms and three for two-year terms.

Section B. *Principal Functions and Powers*

1. In order to ensure prompt and effective action by the Organization, members of the Organization should by the Charter confer on the Security Council primary responsibility for the maintenance of international peace and security and should agree that in carrying out these duties under this responsibility it should act on their behalf.

2. In discharging these duties the Security Council should act in accordance with the purposes and principles of the Organization.

3. The specific powers conferred on the Security Council in order to carry out these duties are laid down in Chapter VIII.

4. All members of the Organization should obligate themselves to accept the decisions of the Security Council and to carry them out in accordance with the provisions of the Charter.

5. In order to promote the establishment and maintenance of international peace and security with the least diversion of the world's human and economic resources for armaments, the Security Council, with the assistance of the Military Staff Committee referred to in Chapter VIII, Section B, paragraph 9, should have the responsibility for formulating plans for the establishment of a system of regulation of armaments for submission to the members of the Organization.

Section C. *Voting*

(Note.—The question of voting procedure in the Security Council is still under consideration.) [Agreed upon at the Yalta Conference. See Appendix 11 for text.]

Section D. *Procedure*

1. The Security Council should be so organized as to be able to function continuously and each state member of the Security Council should be permanently represented at the headquarters of the Organization. It may hold meetings at such other places as in its judgment may best facilitate its work. There should be periodic meetings at which each state member of the Security Council could if it so desired be represented by a member of the government or some other special representative.

2. The Security Council should be empowered to set up such bodies or agencies as it may deem necessary for the performance of its functions including regional subcommittees of the Military Staff Committee.

3. The Security Council should adopt its own rules of procedure, including the method of selecting its President.

4. Any member of the Organization should participate in the discussion of any question brought before the Security Council whenever the Security Council considers that the interests of that member of the Organization are specially affected.

5. Any member of the Organization not having a seat on the Security Council and any state not a member of the Organization, if it is a party to a dispute under con-

sideration by the Security Council, should be invited to participate in the discussion relating to the dispute.

Chapter VII. An International Court of Justice

1. There should be an international court of justice which should constitute the principal judicial organ of the Organization.

2. The court should be constituted and should function in accordance with a statute which should be annexed to and be a part of the Charter of the Organization.

3. The statute of the court of international justice should be either (a) the Statute of the Permanent Court of International Justice, continued in force with such modifications as may be desirable or (b) a new statute in the preparation of which the Statute of the Permanent Court of International Justice should be used as a basis.

4. All members of the Organization should *ipso facto* be parties to the statute of the international court of justice.

5. Conditions under which states not members of the Organization may become parties to the statute of the international court of justice should be determined in each case by the General Assembly upon recommendation of the Security Council.

Chapter VIII. Arrangements for the Maintenance of International Peace and Security Including Prevention and Suppression of Aggression

Section A. Pacific Settlement of Disputes

1. The Security Council should be empowered to investigate any dispute, or any situation which may lead to international friction or give rise to a dispute, in order to determine whether its continuance is likely to endanger the maintenance of international peace and security.

2. Any state, whether member of the Organization or not, may bring any such dispute or situation to the attention of the General Assembly or of the Security Council

3. The parties to any dispute the continuance of which is likely to endanger the maintenance of international peace and security should obligate themselves, first of all, to seek a solution by negotiation, mediation, conciliation, arbitration, or judicial settlement, or other peaceful means of their own choice. The Security Council should call upon the parties to settle their dispute by such means.

4. If, nevertheless, parties to a dispute of the nature referred to in paragraph 3 above fail to settle it by the means indicated in that paragraph, they should obligate themselves to refer it to the Security Council. The Security Council should in each case decide whether or not the continuance of the particular dispute is in fact likely to endanger the maintenance of international peace and security, and, accordingly, whether the Security Council should deal with the dispute, and, if so, whether it should take action under paragraph 5.

5. The Security Council should be empowered, at any stage of a dispute of the nature referred to in paragraph 3 above, to recommend appropriate procedures or methods of adjustment.

6. Justiciable disputes should normally be referred to the international court of justice. The Security Council should be empowered to refer to the court, for advice, legal questions connected with other disputes.

7. The provisions of paragraphs 1 to 6 of Section A should not apply to situations

or disputes arising out of matters which by international law are solely within the domestic jurisdiction of the state concerned.

Section B. Determination of Threats to the Peace or Acts of Aggression and Action with Respect Thereto

1. Should the Security Council deem that a failure to settle a dispute in accordance with procedures indicated in paragraph 3 of Section A, or in accordance with its recommendations made under paragraph 5 of Section A, constitutes a threat to the maintenance of international peace and security, it should take any measures necessary for the maintenance of international peace and security in accordance with the purposes and principles of the Organization.

2. In general the Security Council should determine the existence of any threat to the peace, breach of the peace or act of aggression and should make recommendations or decide upon the measures to be taken to maintain or restore peace and security.

3. The Security Council should be empowered to determine what diplomatic, economic, or other measures not involving the use of armed force should be employed to give effect to its decisions, and to call upon members of the Organization to apply such measures. Such measures may include complete or partial interruption of rail, sea, air, postal, telegraphic, radio and other means of communication and the severance of diplomatic and economic relations.

4. Should the Security Council consider such measures to be inadequate, it should be empowered to take such action by air, naval or land forces as may be necessary to maintain or restore international peace and security. Such action may include demonstrations, blockade and other operations by air, sea or land forces of members of the Organization.

5. In order that all members of the Organization should contribute to the maintenance of international peace and security, they should undertake to make available to the Security Council, on its call and in accordance with a special agreement or agreements concluded among themselves, armed forces, facilities and assistance necessary for the purpose of maintaining international peace and security. Such agreement or agreements should govern the numbers and types of forces and the nature of the facilities and assistance to be provided. The special agreement or agreements should be negotiated as soon as possible and should in each case be subject to approval by the Security Council and to ratification by the signatory states in accordance with their constitutional processes.

6. In order to enable urgent military measures to be taken by the Organization there should be held immediately available by the members of the Organization national air force contingents for combined international enforcement action. The strength and degree of readiness of these contingents and plans for their combined action should be determined by the Security Council with the assistance of the Military Staff Committee within the limits laid down in the special agreement or agreements referred to in paragraph 5 above.

7. The action required to carry out the decisions of the Security Council for the maintenance of international peace and security should be taken by all the members of the Organization in cooperation or by some of them as the Security Council may determine. This undertaking should be carried out by the members of the Or-

ganization by their own action and through action of the appropriate specialized organizations and agencies of which they are members.

8. Plans for the application of armed force should be made by the Security Council with the assistance of the Military Staff Committee referred to in paragraph 9 below.

9. There should be established a Military Staff Committee the functions of which should be to advise and assist the Security Council on all questions relating to the Security Council's military requirements for the maintenance of international peace and security, to the employment and command of forces placed at its disposal, to the regulation of armaments, and to possible disarmament. It should be responsible under the Security Council for the strategic direction of any armed forces placed at the disposal of the Security Council. The Committee should be composed of the Chiefs of Staff of the permanent members of the Security Council or their representatives. Any member of the Organization not permanently represented on the Committee should be invited by the Committee to be associated with it when the efficient discharge of the Committee's responsibilities requires that such a state should participate in its work. Questions of command of forces should be worked out subsequently.

10. The members of the Organization should join in affording mutual assistance in carrying out the measures decided upon by the Security Council.

11. Any state, whether a member of the Organization or not, which finds itself confronted with special economic problems arising from the carrying out of measures which have been decided upon by the Security Council should have the right to consult the Security Council in regard to a solution of those problems.

Section C. Regional Arrangements

1. Nothing in the Charter should preclude the existence of regional arrangements or agencies for dealing with such matters relating to the maintenance of international peace and security as are appropriate for regional action, provided such arrangements or agencies and their activities are consistent with the purposes and principles of the Organization. The Security Council should encourage settlement of local disputes through such regional arrangements or by such regional agencies, either on the initiative of the states concerned or by reference from the Security Council.

2. The Security Council should, where appropriate, utilize such arrangements or agencies for enforcement action under its authority, but no enforcement action should be taken under regional arrangements or by regional agencies without the authorization of the Security Council.

3. The Security Council should at all times be kept fully informed of activities undertaken or in contemplation under regional arrangements or by regional agencies for the maintenance of international peace and security.

Chapter IX. Arrangements for International Economic and Social Cooperation

Section A. Purpose and Relationships

1. With a view to the creation of conditions of stability and well-being which are necessary for peaceful and friendly relations among nations, the Organization should facilitate solutions of international economic, social and other humanitarian problems and promote respect for human rights and fundamental freedoms. Responsi-

bility for the discharge of this function should be vested in the General Assembly, and, under the authority of the General Assembly, in an Economic and Social Council.

2. The various specialized economic, social and other organizations and agencies would have responsibilities in their respective fields as defined in their statutes. Each such organization or agency should be brought into relationship with the Organization on terms to be determined by agreement between the Economic and Social Council and the appropriate authorities of the specialized organization or agency, subject to approval by the General Assembly.

Section B. Composition and Voting

The Economic and Social Council should consist of representatives of eighteen members of the Organization. The states to be represented for this purpose should be elected by the General Assembly for terms of three years. Each such state should have one representative, who should have one vote. Decisions of the Economic and Social Council should be taken by simple majority vote of those present and voting.

Section C. Functions and Powers of the Economic and Social Council

1. The Economic and Social Council should be empowered:
   a. to carry out, within the scope of its functions, recommendations of the General Assembly;
   b. to make recommendations, on its own initiative, with respect to international economic, social and other humanitarian matters;
   c. to receive and consider reports from the economic, social and other organizations or agencies brought into relationship with the Organization, and to coordinate their activities through consultations with, and recommendations to, such organizations or agencies;
   d. to examine the administrative budgets of such specialized organizations or agencies with a view to making recommendations to the organizations or agencies concerned;
   e. to enable the Secretary-General to provide information to the Security Council;
   f. to assist the Security Council upon its request; and
   g. to perform such other functions within the general scope of its competence as may be assigned to it by the General Assembly.

Section D. Organization and Procedure

1. The Economic and Social Council should set up an economic commission, a social commission, and such other commissions as may be required. These commissions should consist of experts. There should be a permanent staff which should constitute a part of the Secretariat of the Organization.

2. The Economic and Social Council should make suitable arrangements for representatives of the specialized organizations or agencies to participate without vote in its deliberations and in those of the commissions established by it.

3. The Economic and Social Council should adopt its own rules of procedure and the method of selecting its President.

Chapter X.   The Secretariat

1. There should be a Secretariat comprising a Secretary-General and such staff as may be required. The Secretary-General should be the chief administrative officer of the Organization. He should be elected by the General Assembly, on recommendation of the Security Council, for such term and under such conditions as are specified in the Charter.

2. The Secretary-General should act in that capacity in all meetings of the General Assembly, of the Security Council, and of the Economic and Social Council and should make an annual report to the General Assembly on the work of the Organization.

3. The Secretary-General should have the right to bring to the attention of the Security Council any matter which in his opinion may threaten international peace and security.

Chapter XI.   Amendments

Amendments should come into force for all members of the Organization, when they have been adopted by a vote of two-thirds of the members of the General Assembly and ratified in accordance with their respective constitutional processes by the members of the Organization having permanent membership on the Security Council and by a majority of the other members of the Organization.

Chapter XII.   Transitional Arrangements

1. Pending the coming into force of the special agreement or agreements referred to in Chapter VIII, Section B, paragraph 5, and in accordance with the provisions of paragraph 5 of the Four-Nation Declaration, signed at Moscow, October 30, 1943, the states parties to that Declaration should consult with one another and as occasion arises with other members of the Organization with a view to such joint action on behalf of the Organization as may be necessary for the purpose of maintaining international peace and security.

2. No provision of the Charter should preclude action taken or authorized in relation to enemy states as a result of the present war by the Governments having responsibility for such action.

Note

In addition to the question of voting procedure in the Security Council referred to in Chapter VI, several other questions are still under consideration.

Washington, D.C.
October 7, 1944

Appendix 11

YALTA AGREEMENTS ON WORLD ORGANIZATION, FEBRUARY 11, 1945 [1]

The Crimea Conference of the Heads of the Governments of the United States of America, the United Kingdom, and the Union of Soviet Socialist Republics which took place from February 4th to 11th came to the following conclusions:

I. WORLD ORGANISATION

It was decided:

(1) that a United Nations Conference on the proposed world organisation should be summoned for Wednesday, 25th April, 1945, and should be held in the United States of America.

(2) the Nations to be invited to this Conference should be:

(a) the United Nations as they existed on the 8th February, 1945; and

(b) such of the Associated Nations as have declared war on the common enemy by 1st March, 1945. (For this purpose by the term "Associated Nation" was meant the eight Associated Nations and Turkey). When the Conference on World Organization is held, the delegates of the United Kingdom and United States of America will support a proposal to admit to original membership two Soviet Socialist Republics, i.e. the Ukraine and White Russia.

(3) that the United States Government on behalf of the Three Powers should consult the Government of China and the French Provisional Government in regard to decisions taken at the present Conference concerning the proposed World Organisation.

(4) that the text of the invitation to be issued to all the nations which would take part in the United Nations Conference should be as follows:

INVITATION

"The Government of the United States of America, on behalf of itself and of the Governments of the United Kingdom, the Union of Soviet Socialist Republics, and the Republic of China and of the Provisional Government of the French Republic, invite the Government of —— to send representatives to a Conference of the United Nations to be held on 25th April, 1945, or soon thereafter, at San Francisco in the United States of America to prepare a Charter for a General International Organisation for the maintenance of international peace and security.

[1] U.S. Department of State Press Release 239, Mar. 24, 1947.

"The above named governments suggest that the Conference consider as affording a basis for such a Charter the Proposals for the Establishment of a General International Organisation, which were made public last October as a result of the Dumbarton Oaks Conference, and which have now been supplemented by the following provisions for Section C of Chapter VI:

" 'C. Voting

" '1. Each member of the Security Council should have one vote.

" '2. Decisions of the Security Council on procedural matters should be made by an affirmative vote of seven members.

" '3. Decisions of the Security Council on all other matters should be made by an affirmative vote of seven members including the concurring votes of the permanent members; provided that, in decisions under Chapter VIII, Section A and under the second sentence of paragraph 1 of Chapter VIII, Section C, a party to a dispute should abstain from voting.'

"Further information as to arrangements will be transmitted subsequently.

"In the event that the Government of —— desires in advance of the Conference to present views or comments concerning the proposals, the Government of the United States of America will be pleased to transmit such views and comments to the other participating Governments."

TERRITORIAL TRUSTEESHIP

It was agreed that the five Nations which will have permanent seats on the Security Council should consult each other prior to the United Nations Conference on the question of territorial trusteeship.

The acceptance of this recommendation is subject to its being made clear that territorial trusteeship will only apply to (a) existing mandates of the League of Nations; (b) territories detached from the enemy as a result of the present war; (c) any other territory which might voluntarily be placed under trusteeship; and (d) no discussion of actual territories is contemplated at the forthcoming United Nations Conference or in the preliminary consultations, and it will be a matter for subsequent agreement which territories within the above categories will be placed under trusteeship.

Appendix 12

STATEMENT BY THE DELEGATIONS OF THE FOUR SPONSORING GOVERNMENTS ON VOTING PROCEDURE IN THE SECURITY COUNCIL, JUNE 7, 1945 [1]

Specific questions covering the voting procedure in the Security Council have been submitted by a Sub-Committee of the Conference Committee on Structure and Procedures of the Security Council to the Delegations of the four Governments sponsoring the Conference—the United States of America, the United Kingdom of Great Britain and Northern Ireland, the Union of Soviet Socialist Republics, and the Republic of China. In dealing with these questions, the four Delegations desire to make the following statement of their general attitude towards the whole question of unanimity of permanent members in the decisions of the Security Council.

PART I

1. The Yalta voting formula recognizes that the Security Council, in discharging its responsibilities for the maintenance of international peace and security, will have two broad groups of functions. Under Chapter VIII, the Council will have to make decisions which involve its taking direct measures in connection with settlement of disputes, adjustment of situations likely to lead to disputes, determination of threats to the peace, removal of threats to the peace, and suppression of breaches of the peace. It will also have to make decisions which do not involve the taking of such measures. The Yalta formula provides that the second of these two groups of decisions will be governed by a procedural vote—that is, the vote of any seven members. The first group of decisions will be governed by a qualified vote—that is, the vote of seven members, including the concurring votes of the five permanent members, subject to the proviso that in decisions under Section A and a part of Section C of Chapter VIII parties to a dispute shall abstain from voting.

2. For example, under the Yalta formula a procedural vote will govern the decisions made under the entire Section D of Chapter VI. This means that the Council will, by a vote of any seven of its members, adopt or alter its rules of procedure;

[1] *A Decade of American Foreign Policy,* Senate Document No. 123, 81st Congress, 1st Session, pp. 1057–1060.

determine the method of selecting its President; organize itself in such a way as to be able to function continuously; select the times and places of its regular and special meetings; establish such bodies or agencies as it may deem necessary for the performance of its functions; invite a member of the Organization not represented on the Council to participate in its discussions when that member's interests are specially affected; and invite any state when it is a party to a dispute being considered by the Council to participate in the discussion relating to that dispute.

3. Further, no individual member of the Council can alone prevent consideration and discussion by the Council of a dispute or situation brought to its attention under paragraph 2, Section A, Chapter VIII. Nor can parties to such dispute be prevented by these means from being heard by the Council. Likewise, the requirement for unanimity of the permanent members cannot prevent any member of the Council from reminding the members of the Organization of their general obligations assumed under the Charter as regards peaceful settlement of international disputes.

4. Beyond this point, decisions and actions by the Security Council may well have major political consequences and may even initiate a chain of events which might, in the end, require the Council under its responsibilities to invoke measures of enforcement under Section B, Chapter VIII. This chain of events begins when the Council decides to make an investigation, or determines that the time has come to call upon states to settle their differences, or makes recommendations to the parties. It is to such decisions and actions that unanimity of the permanent members applies, with the important proviso, referred to above, for abstention from voting by parties to a dispute.

5. To illustrate: in ordering an investigation, the Council has to consider whether the investigation—which may involve calling for reports, hearing witnesses, dispatching a commission of inquiry, or other means—might not further aggravate the situation. After investigation, the Council must determine whether the continuance of the situation or dispute would be likely to endanger international peace and security. If it so determines, the Council would be under obligation to take further steps. Similarly, the decision to make recommendations, even when all parties request it to do so, or to call upon parties to a dispute to fulfill their obligations under the Charter, might be the first step on a course of action from which the Security Council could withdraw only at the risk of failing to discharge its responsibilities.

6. In appraising the significance of the vote required to take such decisions or actions, it is useful to make comparison with the requirements of the League Covenant with reference to decisions of the League Council. Substantive decisions of the League of Nations Council could be taken only by the unanimous vote of all its members, whether permanent or not, with the exception of parties to a dispute under Article XV of the League Covenant. Under Article XI, under which most of the disputes brought before the League were dealt with and decisions to make investigations taken, the unanimity rule was invariably interpreted to include even the votes of the parties to a dispute.

7. The Yalta voting formula substitutes for the rule of complete unanimity of the League Council a system of qualified majority voting in the Security Council. Under this system nonpermanent members of the Security Council individually would have no veto. As regards the permanent members, there is no question

under the Yalta formula of investing them with a new right, namely, the right to veto, a right which the permanent members of the League Council always had. The formula proposed for the taking of action in the Security Council by a majority of seven would make the operation of the Council less subject to obstruction than was the case under the League of Nations rule of complete unanimity.

8. It should also be remembered that under the Yalta formula the five major powers could not act by themselves, since even under the unanimity requirement any decisions of the Council would have to include the concurring votes of at least two of the non-permanent members. In other words, it would be possible for five non-permanent members as a group to exercise a "veto." It is not to be assumed, however, that the permanent members, any more than the non-permanent members, would use their veto power willfully to obstruct the operation of the Council.

9. In view of the primary responsibilities of the permanent members, they could not be expected, in the present condition of the world, to assume the obligation to act in so serious a matter as the maintenance of international peace and security in consequence of a decision in which they had not concurred. Therefore, if a majority voting in the Security Council is to be made possible, the only practicable method is to provide, in respect of non-procedural decisions, for unanimity of the permanent members plus the concurring votes of at least two of the non-permanent members.

10. For all these reasons, the four Sponsoring Governments agreed on the Yalta formula and have presented it to this Conference as essential if an international organization is to be created through which all peace-loving nations can effectively discharge their common responsibilities for the maintenance of international peace and security.

Part II

In the light of the considerations set forth in Part I of this statement, it is clear what the answers to the questions submitted by the Sub-committee should be, with the exception of Question 19. The answer to that question is as follows:

1. In the opinion of the Delegations of the Sponsoring Governments, the Draft Charter itself contains an indication of the application of the voting procedures to the various functions of the Council.

2. In this case, it will be unlikely that there will arise in the future any matters of great importance on which a decision will have to be made as to whether a procedural vote would apply. Should, however, such a matter arise, the decision regarding the preliminary question as to whether or not such a matter is procedural must be taken by a vote of seven members of the Security Council, including the concurring votes of the permanent members.

Appendix 13

CONVENTION ON THE PRIVILEGES AND IMMUNITIES OF THE UNITED NATIONS, APPROVED BY GENERAL ASSEMBLY, FEBRUARY 13, 1946 [1]

Whereas Article 104 of the Charter of the United Nations provides that the Organization shall enjoy in the territory of each of its Members such legal capacity as may be necessary for the exercise of its functions and the fulfillment of its purposes and

Whereas Article 105 of the Charter of the United Nations provides that the Organization shall enjoy in the territory of each of its Members such privileges and immunities as are necessary for the fulfillment of its purposes and that representatives of the Members of the United Nations and officials of the Organization shall similarly enjoy such privileges and immunities as are necessary for the independent exercise of the functions in connection with the Organization:

Consequently the General Assembly by a resolution adopted on 13 February 1946, approved the following convention and proposes it for accession by each Member of the United Nations.

ARTICLE I. JURIDICAL PERSONALITY

Section 1. The United Nations shall possess juridical personality. It shall have the capacity:

(a) to contract;
(b) to acquire and dispose of immovable and movable property;
(c) to institute legal proceedings.

ARTICLE II. PROPERTY, FUNDS AND ASSETS

Section 2. The United Nations, its property and assets wherever located and by whomsoever held, shall enjoy immunity from every form of legal process except in so far as in any particular case it has expressly waived its immunity. It is, however, understood that no waiver of immunity shall extend to any measure of execution.

Section 3. The premises of the United Nations shall be inviolable. The property and assets of the United Nations, wherever located and by whomsoever held, shall be immune from search, requisition, confiscation, expropriation and any other form of interference, whether by executive, administrative, judicial or legislative action.

[1] UN Doc. A/64, pp. 25–27.

Section 4.   The archives of the United Nations, and in general all documents belonging to it or held by it, shall be inviolable wherever located.

Section 5.   Without being restricted by financial controls, regulations or moratoria of any kind,

(a) The United Nations may hold funds, gold or currency of any kind and operate accounts in any currency;

(b) The United Nations shall be free to transfer its funds, gold or currency from one country to another or within any country and to convert any currency held by it into any other currency.

Section 6.   In exercising its rights under section 5 above, the United Nations shall pay due regard to any representations made by the Government of any Member in so far as it is considered that effect can be given to such representations without detriment to the interests of the United Nations.

Section 7.   The United Nations, its assets, income and other property shall be:

(a) exempt from all direct taxes; it is understood, however, that the United Nations will not claim exemption from taxes which are, in fact, no more than charges for public utility services;

(b) exempt from customs duties and prohibitions and restrictions on imports and exports in respect of articles imported or exported by the United Nations for its official use.   It is understood, however, that articles imported under such exemption will not be sold in the country into which they were imported except under conditions agreed with the Government of that country;

(c) exempt from customs duties and prohibitions and restrictions on imports and exports in respect of its publications.

Section 8.   While the United Nations will not, as a general rule, claim exemption from excise duties and from taxes on the sale of movable and immovable property which form part of the price to be paid, nevertheless when the United Nations is making important purchases for official use of property on which such duties and taxes have been charged or are chargeable, Members will, whenever possible, make appropriate administrative arrangements for the remission or return of the amount of duty or tax.

ARTICLE III.   FACILITIES IN RESPECT OF COMMUNICATIONS

Section 9.   The United Nations shall enjoy in the territory of each Member for its official communications treatment not less favourable than that accorded by the Government of that Member to any other Government, including its diplomatic mission, including the matter of priorities, rates and taxes on mails, cables, telegrams, radiograms, telephotos, telephone and other communications; and press rates for information to the press and radio.   No censorship shall be applied to the official correspondence and other official communications of the United Nations.

Section 10.   The United Nations shall have the right to use codes and to dispatch and receive its correspondence by courier or in bags, which shall have the same immunities and privileges as diplomatic couriers and bags.

ARTICLE IV.   THE REPRESENTATIVES OF MEMBERS

Section 11.   Representatives of Members to the principal and subsidiary organs of the United Nations and to conferences convened by the United Nations, shall, while exercising their functions and during their journey to and from the place of meeting, enjoy the following privileges and immunities:

(a) immunity from personal arrest or detention and from seizure of their personal baggage, and, in respect of words spoken or written and all acts done by them in their capacity as representatives, immunity from legal process of every kind;

(b) inviolability for all papers and documents;

(c) the right to use codes and to receive papers or correspondence by courier or in sealed bags;

(d) exemption in respect of themselves and their spouses from immigration restrictions, alien registration or national service obligations in the State they are visiting or through which they are passing in the exercise of their functions;

(e) the same facilities in respect of currency or exchange restrictions as are accorded to representatives of foreign governments on temporary official missions;

(f) the same immunities and facilities in respect of their personal baggage as are accorded to diplomatic envoys, and also;

(g) such other privileges, immunities and facilities, not inconsistent with the foregoing, as diplomatic envoys enjoy, except that they shall have no right to claim exemption from customs duties on goods imported (otherwise than as part of their personal baggage) or from excise duties or sales taxes.

Section 12.   In order to secure, for the representatives of Members to the principal and subsidiary organs of the United Nations and to conferences convened by the United Nations, complete freedom of speech and independence in the discharge of their duties, the immunity from legal process in respect of words spoken or written and all acts done by them in discharging their duties shall continue to be accorded, notwithstanding that the persons concerned are no longer the representatives of Members.

Section 13.   Where the incidence of any form of taxation depends upon residence, periods during which the representatives of Members to the principal and subsidiary organs of the United Nations and to conferences convened by the United Nations are present in a State for the discharge of their duties shall not be considered as periods of residence.

Section 14. Privileges and immunities are accorded to the representatives of Members not for the personal benefit of the individuals themselves, but in order to safeguard the independent exercise of their functions in connection with the United Nations.   Consequently a Member not only has the right but is under a duty to waive the immunity of its representative in any case where in the opinion of the Member the immunity would impede the course of justice, and it can be waived without prejudice to the purpose for which the immunity is accorded.

Section 15.   The provisions of sections 11, 12 and 13 are not applicable as between a representative and the authorities of the State of which he is a national or of which he is or has been the representative.

Section 16.   In this article the expression "representatives" shall be deemed to include all delegates, deputy delegates, advisers, technical experts and secretaries of delegations.

ARTICLE V.   OFFICIALS

Section 17.   The Secretary-General will specify the categories of officials to which the provisions of this article and article VII shall apply.   He shall submit these categories to the General Assembly. Thereafter these categories shall be communicated to the Governments of all Members. The names of the officials included in these categories shall from time to time be made known to the Governments of Members.

Section 18. Officials of the United Nations shall:

(a) be immune from legal process in respect of words spoken or written and all acts performed by them in their official capacity;

(b) be exempt from taxation on the salaries and emoluments paid to them by the United Nations;

(c) be immune from national service obligations;

(d) be immune, together with their spouses and relatives dependent on them, from immigration restrictions and alien registration;

(e) be accorded the same privileges in respect of exchange facilities as are accorded to the officials of comparable ranks forming part of diplomatic missions to the government concerned;

(f) be given, together with their spouses and relatives dependent on them, the same repatriation facilities in time of international crisis as diplomatic envoys;

(g) have the right to import free of duty their furniture and effects at the time of first taking up their post in the country in question.

Section 19. In addition to the immunities and privileges specified in section 18, the Secretary-General and all Assistant Secretaries-General shall be accorded in respect of themselves, their spouses and minor children, the privileges and immunities, exemptions and facilities accorded to diplomatic envoys, in accordance with international law.

Section 20. Privileges and immunities are granted to officials in the interests of the United Nations and not for the personal benefit of the individuals themselves. The Secretary-General shall have the right and the duty to waive the immunity of any official in any case where, in his opinion, the immunity would impede the course of justice and can be waived without prejudice to the interests of the United Nations. In the case of the Secretary-General, the Security Council shall have the right to waive immunity.

Section 21. The United Nations shall co-operate at all times with the appropriate authorities of Members to facilitate the proper administration of justice, secure the observance of police regulations, and prevent the occurrence of any abuse in connection with the privileges, immunities and facilities mentioned in this article.

ARTICLE VI. EXPERTS ON MISSIONS FOR THE UNITED NATIONS

Section 22. Experts (other than officials coming within the scope of article V) performing missions for the United Nations shall be accorded such privileges and immunities as are necessary for the independent exercise of their functions during the period of their missions, including the time spent on journeys in connection with their missions. In particular they shall be accorded:

(a) immunity from personal arrest or detention and from seizure of their personal baggage;

(b) in respect of words spoken or written and acts done by them in the course of the performance of their mission, immunity from legal process of every kind. This immunity from legal process shall continue to be accorded notwithstanding that the persons concerned are no longer employed on missions for the United Nations.

(c) inviolability for all papers and documents;

(d) for the purpose of their communications with the United Nations, the right to use codes and to receive papers or correspondence by courier or in sealed bags;

(e) the same facilities in respect of currency or exchange restrictions as are accorded to representatives of foreign governments on temporary official missions;

(f) the same immunities and facilities in respect of their personal baggage as are accorded to diplomatic envoys.

Section 23.   Privileges and immunities are granted to experts in the interests of the United Nations and not for the personal benefit of the individuals themselves.   The Secretary-General shall have the right and the duty to waive the immunity of any expert in any case where, in his opinion, the immunity would impede the course of justice and it can be waived without prejudice to the interests of the United Nations.

ARTICLE VII.   UNITED NATIONS LAISSEZ-PASSER

Section 24.   The United Nations may issue United Nations *laissez-passer* to its officials.   These *laissez-passer* shall be recognized and accepted as valid travel documents, by the authorities of Members, taking into account the provisions of section 25.

Section 25.   Applications for visas (where required) from the holders of United Nations *laissez-passer,* when accompanied by a certificate that they are travelling on the business of the United Nations, shall be dealt with as speedily as possible. In addition, such persons shall be granted facilities for speedy travel.

Section 26.   Similar facilities to those specified in section 25 shall be accorded to experts and other persons who, though not holders of United Nations *laissez-passer,* have a certificate that they are travelling on the business of the United Nations.

Section 27.   The Secretary-General, Assistant Secretaries-General and Directors travelling on United Nations *laissez-passer* on the business of the United Nations shall be granted the same facilities as are accorded to diplomatic envoys.

Section 28.   The provisions of this article may be applied to the comparable officials of specialized agencies if the agreements for relationship made under Article 63 of the Charter so provide.

ARTICLE VIII.   SETTLEMENT OF DISPUTES

Section 29.   The United Nations shall make provisions for appropriate modes of settlement of:

(a) disputes arising out of contracts or other disputes of a private law character, to which the United Nations is a party;

(b) disputes involving any official of the United Nations who by reason of his official position enjoys immunity, if immunity has not been waived by the Secretary-General.

Section 30.   All differences arising out of the interpretation or application of the present convention shall be referred to the International Court of Justice, unless in any case it is agreed by the parties to have recourse to another mode of settlement. If a difference arises between the United Nations on the one hand and a Member on the other hand, a request shall be made for an advisory opinion on any legal question involved in accordance with Article 96 of the Charter and Article 65 of the Statute of the Court. The opinion given by the Court shall be accepted as decisive by the parties.

FINAL ARTICLE

Section 31.   This convention is submitted to every Member of the United Nations for accession.

Section 32.   Accession shall be effected by deposit of an instrument with the Secretary-General of the United Nations and the convention shall come into force as regards each Member on the date of deposit of each instrument of accession.

Section 33.   The Secretary-General shall inform all Members of the United Nations of the deposit of each accession.

Section 34.   It is understood that, when an instrument of accession is deposited on behalf of any Member, the Member will be in a position under its own law to give effect to the terms of this convention.

Section 35.   This convention shall continue in force as between the United Nations and every Member which has deposited an instrument of accession for so long as that Member remains a Member of the United Nations, or until a revised general convention has been approved by the General Assembly and that Member has become a party to this revised convention.

Section 36.   The Secretary-General may conclude with any Member or Members supplementary agreements adjusting the provisions of this convention so far as that Member or those Members are concerned. These supplementary agreements shall in each case be subject to the approval of the General Assembly.

Appendix 14

TRUSTEESHIP AGREEMENT FOR THE FORMER JAPANESE MANDATED ISLANDS— RESOLUTION OF THE SECURITY COUNCIL, APRIL 2, 1947 [1]

PREAMBLE

Whereas Article 75 of the Charter of the United Nations provides for the establishment of an international trusteeship system for the administration and supervision of such territories as may be placed thereunder by subsequent agreements; and

Whereas under Article 77 of the said Charter the trusteeship system may be applied to territories now held under mandate; and

Whereas on 17 December 1920 the Council of the League of Nations confirmed a mandate for the former German islands north of the equator to Japan, to be administered in accordance with Article 22 of the Covenant of the League of Nations; and

Whereas Japan, as a result of the Second World War, has ceased to exercise any authority in these islands;

Now, therefore, the Security Council of the United Nations, having satisfied itself that the relevant articles of the Charter have been complied with, hereby resolves to approve the following terms of trusteeship for the Pacific Islands formerly under mandate to Japan.

ARTICLE 1

The Territory of the Pacific Islands, consisting of the islands formerly held by Japan under mandate in accordance with Article 22 of the Covenant of the League of Nations, is hereby designated as a strategic area and placed under the trusteeship system established in the Charter of the United Nations. The Territory of the Pacific Islands is hereinafter referred to as the trust territory.

ARTICLE 2

The United States of America is designated as the administering authority of the trust territory.

[1] U.S. Deparment of State Publication 2992, Treaties and Other International Acts Series 1665.

ARTICLE 3

The administering authority shall have full powers of administration, legislation, and jurisdiction over the territory subject to the provisions of this agreement, and may apply to the trust territory, subject to any modifications which the administering authority may consider desirable, such of the laws of the United States as it may deem appropriate to local conditions and requirements.

ARTICLE 4

The administering authority, in discharging the obligations of trusteeship in the trust territory, shall act in accordance with the Charter of the United Nations, and the provisions of this agreement, and shall, as specified in Article 83(2) of the Charter, apply the objectives of the international trusteeship system, as set forth in Article 76 of the Charter, to the people of the trust territory.

ARTICLE 5

In discharging its obligations under Article 76(a) and Article 84, of the Charter, the administering authority shall ensure that the trust territory shall play its part, in accordance with the Charter of the United Nations, in the maintenance of international peace and security. To this end the administering authority shall be entitled:

1. to establish naval, military and air bases and to erect fortifications in the trust territory;

2. to station and employ armed forces in the territory; and

3. to make use of volunteer forces, facilities and assistance from the trust territory in carrying out the obligations toward the Security Council undertaken in this regard by the administering authority, as well as for the local defense and the maintenance of law and order within the trust territory.

ARTICLE 6

In discharging its obligations under Article 76(b) of the Charter, the administering authority shall:

1. foster the development of such political institutions as are suited to the trust territory and shall promote the development of the inhabitants of the trust territory toward self-government or independence, as may be appropriate to the particular circumstances of the trust territory and its peoples and the freely expressed wishes of the peoples concerned; and to this end shall give to the inhabitants of the trust territory a progressively increasing share in the administrative services in the territory; shall develop their participation in government; shall give due recognition to the customs of the inhabitants in providing a system of law for the territory; and shall take other appropriate measures toward these ends;

2. promote the economic advancement and self-sufficiency of the inhabitants, and to this end shall regulate the use of natural resources; encourage the development of fisheries, agriculture, and industries; protect the inhabitants against the loss of their lands and resources; and improve the means of transportation and communication;

3. promote the social advancement of the inhabitants, and to this end shall protect the rights and fundamental freedoms of all elements of the population without discrimination; protect the health of the inhabitants; control the traffic in arms and ammunition, opium and other dangerous drugs, and alcohol and other spirituous beverages; and institute such other regulations as may be necessary to protect the inhabitants against social abuses; and

4. promote the educational advancement of the inhabitants, and to this end shall take steps toward the establishment of a general system of elementary education; facilitate the vocational and cultural advancement of the population; and shall encourage qualified students to pursue higher education, including training on the professional level.

ARTICLE 7

In discharging its obligations under Article 76(c), of the Charter, the administering authority shall guarantee to the inhabitants of the trust territory freedom of conscience, and, subject only to the requirements of public order and security, freedom of speech, of the press, and of assembly; freedom of worship, and of religious teaching; and freedom of migration and movement.

ARTICLE 8

1. In discharging its obligations under Article 76(d) of the Charter, as defined by Article 83(2) of the Charter, the administering authority, subject to the requirements of security, and the obligation to promote the advancement of the inhabitants, shall accord to nationals of each Member of the United Nations and to companies and associations organized in conformity with the laws of such Member, treatment in the trust territory no less favorable than that accorded therein to nationals, companies and associations of any other United Nation except the administering authority.

2. The administering authority shall ensure equal treatment to the Members of the United Nations and their nationals in the administration of justice.

3. Nothing in this Article shall be so construed as to accord traffic rights to aircraft flying into and out of the trust territory. Such rights shall be subject to agreement between the administering authority and the state whose nationality such aircraft possesses.

4. The administering authority may negotiate and conclude commercial and other treaties and agreements with Members of the United Nations and other states, designed to attain for the inhabitants of the trust territory treament by the Members of the United Nations and other states no less favorable than that granted by them to the nationals of other states. The Security Council may recommend, or invite other organs of the United Nations to consider and recommend, what rights the inhabitants of the trust territory should acquire in consideration of the rights obtained by Members of the United Nations in the trust territory.

ARTICLE 9

The administering authority shall be entitled to constitute the trust territory into a customs, fiscal, or administrative union or federation with other territories under United States jurisdiction and to establish common services between such territories and the trust territory where such measures are not inconsistent with the basic objectives of the International Trusteeship System and with the terms of this agreement.

ARTICLE 10

The administering authority, acting under the provisions of Article 3 of this agreement, may accept membership in any regional advisory commission, regional authority, or technical organization, or other voluntary association of states, may cooperate with specialized international bodies, public or private, and may engage in other forms of international co-operation.

ARTICLE 11

1. The administering authority shall take the necessary steps to provide the status of citizenship of the trust territory for the inhabitants of the trust territory.

2. The administering authority shall afford diplomatic and consular protection to inhabitants of the trust territory when outside the territorial limits of the trust territory or of the territory of the administering authority.

ARTICLE 12

The administering authority shall enact such legislation as may be necessary to place the provisions of this agreement in effect in the trust territory.

ARTICLE 13

The provisions of Articles 87 and 88 of the Charter shall be applicable to the trust territory, provided that the administering authority may determine the extent of their applicability to any areas which may from time to time be specified by it as closed for security reasons.

ARTICLE 14

The administering authority undertakes to apply in the trust territory the provisions of any international conventions and recommendations which may be appropriate to the particular circumstances of the trust territory and which would be conducive to the achievement of the basic objectives of Article 6 of this agreement.

ARTICLE 15

The terms of the present agreement shall not be altered, amended or terminated without the consent of the administering authority.

ARTICLE 16

The present agreement shall come into force when approved by the Security Council of the United Nations and by the Government of the United States after due constitutional process.

Appendix 15

AGREEMENT BETWEEN THE UNITED NATIONS AND THE UNITED STATES OF AMERICA REGARDING THE HEADQUARTERS OF THE UNITED NATIONS, SIGNED JUNE 26, 1947 [1]

THE UNITED NATIONS AND THE UNITED STATES OF AMERICA:

Desiring to conclude an agreement for the purpose of carrying out the resolution adopted by the General Assembly on 14 December 1946 to establish the seat of the United Nations in the City of New York and to regulate questions arising as a result thereof;

Have appointed as their representatives for this purpose:

The United Nations:

Trygve Lie, Secretary-General, and

The United States of America:

George C. Marshall, Secretary of State,

Who have agreed as follows:

ARTICLE I. DEFINITIONS

Section 1

In this agreement:

(a) The expression "headquarters district" means:

(1) the area defined as such in Annex 1;

(2) any other lands or buildings which from time to time may be included therein by supplemental agreement with the appropriate American authorities;

(b) the expression "appropriate American authorities" means such federal, state, or local authorities in the United States as may be appropriate in the context and in accordance with the laws and customs of the United States, including the laws and customs of the state and local government involved;

(c) the expression "General Convention" means the Convention on the Privileges and Immunities of the United Nations approved by the General Assembly of the United Nations on 13 February 1946, as acceded to by the United States;

[1] UN Doc. A/427, Oct. 27, 1947, p. 9–18.

(d) the expression "United Nations" means the international organization established by the Charter of the United Nations, hereinafter referred to as the "Charter";

(e) the expression "Secretary-General" means the Secretary-General of the United Nations.

ARTICLE II. THE HEADQUARTERS DISTRICT

Section 2

The seat of the United Nations shall be the headquarters district.

Section 3

The appropriate American authorities shall take whatever action may be necessary to assure that the United Nations shall not be dispossessed of its property in the headquarters district, except as provided in Section 22 in the event that the United Nations ceases to use the same, provided that the United Nations shall reimburse the appropriate American authorities for any costs incurred, after consultation with the United Nations, in liquidating by eminent domain proceedings or otherwise any adverse claims.

Section 4

(a) The United Nations may establish and operate in the headquarters district:

(1) its own short-wave sending and receiving radio broadcasting facilities, including emergency link equipment, which may be used on the same frequencies (within the tolerances prescribed for the broadcasting service by applicable United States regulations) for radio-telegraph, radio-teletype, radio-telephone, radio-telephoto, and similar services;

(2) one point-to-point circuit between the headquarters district and the office of the United Nations in Geneva (using single side-band equipment) to be used exclusively for the exchange of broadcasting programmes and inter-office communications;

(3) low power, micro wave, low or medium frequencies, facilities for communication within headquarters buildings only, or such other buildings as may temporarily be used by the United Nations;

(4) facilities for point-to-point communications to the same extent and subject to the same conditions as committed under applicable rules and regulations for amateur operation in the United States, except that such rules and regulations shall not be applied in a manner inconsistent with the inviolability of the headquarters district provided by Section 9(a);

(5) such other radio facilities as may be specified by supplemental agreement between the United Nations and the appropriate American authorities.

(b) The United Nations shall make arrangements for the operation of the services referred to in this section with the International Telecommunication Union, the appropriate agencies of the Government of the United States and the appropriate agencies of other affected Governments with regard to all frequencies and similar matters.

(c) The facilities provided for in this section may, to the extent necessary for efficient operation, be established and operated outside the headquarters district. The appropriate American authorities will, on request of the United Nations, make arrangements, on such terms and in such manner as may be agreed upon by supplemental agreement, for the acquisition or use by the United Nations of appropriate premises for such purposes and the inclusion of such premises in the headquarters district.

Section 5

In the event that the United Nations should find it necessary and desirable to establish and operate an aerodrome, the conditions for the location, use and operation of such an aerodrome and the conditions under which there shall be entry into and exit therefrom shall be the subject of a supplemental agreement.

Section 6

In the event that the United Nations should propose to organize its own postal service, the conditions under which such service shall be set up shall be the subject of a supplemental agreement.

ARTICLE III. LAW AND AUTHORITY IN THE HEADQUARTERS DISTRICT

Section 7

(a) The headquarters district shall be under the control and authority of the United Nations as provided in this agreement.

(b) Except as otherwise provided in this agreement or in the General Convention, the federal, state and local law of the United States shall apply within the headquarters district.

(c) Except as otherwise provided in this agreement or in the General Convention, the federal, state and local courts of the United States shall have jurisdiction over acts done and transactions taking place in the headquarters district as provided in applicable federal, state and local laws.

(d) The federal, state and local courts of the United States, when dealing with cases arising out of or relating to acts done or transactions taking place in the headquarters district, shall take into account the regulations enacted by the United Nations under Section 8.

Section 8

The United Nations shall have the power to make regulations, operative within the headquarters district, for the purpose of establishing therein conditions in all respects necessary for the full execution of its functions. No federal, state or local law or regulation of the United States which is inconsistent with a regulation of the United Nations authorized by this section shall, to the extent of such inconsistency, be applicable within the headquarters district. Any dispute, between the United Nations and the United States, as to whether a regulation of the United Nations is authorized by this section or as to whether a federal, state or local law or regulation is inconsistent with any regulation of the United Nations authorized by this section, shall be promptly settled as provided in Section 21. Pending such settlement, the regulation of the United Nations shall apply, and the federal, state or local law or regulation shall be inapplicable in the headquarters district to the extent that the United Nations claims it to be inconsistent with the regulation of the United Nations. This section shall not prevent the reasonable application of fire protection regulations of the appropriate American authorities.

Section 9

(a) The headquarters district shall be inviolable. Federal, state or local officers or officials of the United States, whether administrative, judicial, military or police, shall not enter the headquarters district to perform any official duties therein except with the consent of and under conditions agreed to by the Secretary-General. The service of legal process, including the seizure of private property, may take place within the headquarters district only with the consent of and under conditions approved by the Secretary-General.

(b) Without prejudice to the provisions of the General Convention or Article IV of this agreement, the United Nations shall prevent the headquarters district from becoming a refuge either for persons who are avoiding arrest under the federal, state, or local law of the United States or are required by the Government of the United States for extradition to another country, or for persons who are endeavoring to avoid service of legal process.

Section 10

The United Nations may expel or exclude persons from the headquarters district for violation of its regulations adopted under Section 8 or for other cause. Persons who violate such regulations shall be subject to other penalties or to detention under arrest only in accordance with the provisions of such laws or regulations as may be adopted by the appropriate American authorities.

ARTICLE IV. COMMUNICATIONS AND TRANSIT

Section 11

The federal, state or local authorities of the United States shall not impose any impediments to transit to or from the headquarters district of (1) representatives of Members of officials of the United Nations, or of specialized agencies as defined in Article 57, paragraph 2, of the Charter, of the families of such representatives or officials; (2) experts performing missions for the United Nations or for such specialized agencies; (3) representatives of the press, or of radio, film, or other information agencies, who have been accredited by the United Nations (or by such a specialized agency) in its discretion after consultation with the United States; (4) representatives of non-governmental organizations recognized by the United Nations for the purpose of consultation under Article 71 of the Charter; or (5) other persons invited to the headquarters district by the United Nations or by such specialized agency on official business. The appropriate American authorities shall afford any necessary protection to such persons while in transit to or from the headquarters district. This section does not apply to general interruptions of transportation which are to be dealt with as provided in Section 17, and does not impair the effectiveness of generally applicable laws and regulations as to the operation of means of transportation.

Section 12

The provisions of Section 11 shall be applicable irrespective of the relations existing between the Governments of the persons referred to in that section and the Government of the United States.

Section 13

(a) Laws and regulations in force in the United States regarding the entry of aliens shall not be applied in such manner as to interfere with the privileges referred to in Section 11. When visas are required for persons referred to in that Section, they shall be granted without charge and as promptly as possible.

(b) Laws and regulations in force in the United States regarding the residence of aliens shall not be applied in such manner as to interfere with the privileges referred to in Section 11 and, specifically, shall not be applied in such manner as to require any such person to leave the United States on account of any activities performed by him in his official capacity. In case of abuse of such privileges of residence by any such person in activities in the United States outside his official capacity, it is understood that the privileges referred to in Section 11 shall not be construed to grant him exemption from the laws and regulations of the United States regarding the continued residence of aliens, provided that:

(1) No proceedings shall be instituted under such laws or regulations to require any such person to leave the United States except with the prior approval of the Secretary of State of the United States. Such approval shall be given only after consultation with the appropriate Member in the case of a representative of a Member (or a member of his family) or with the Secretary-General or the principal executive officer of the appropriate specialized agency in the case of any other person referred to in Section 11;

(2) A representative of the Member concerned, the Secretary-General or the principal Executive Officer of the appropriate specialized agency, as the case may be, shall have the right to appear in any such proceedings on behalf of the person against whom they are instituted;

(3) Persons who are entitled to diplomatic privileges and immunities under Section 15 or under the General Convention shall not be required to leave the United States otherwise than in accordance with the customary procedure applicable to diplomatic envoys accredited to the United States.

(c) This section does not prevent the requirement of reasonable evidence to establish that persons claiming the rights granted by Section 11 come within the classes described in that section, or the reasonable application of quarantine and health regulations.

(d) Except as provided above in this section and in the General Convention, the United States retains full control and authority over the entry of persons or property into the territory of the United States and the conditions under which persons may remain or reside there.

(e) The Secretary-General shall, at the request of the appropriate American authorities, enter into discussions with such authorities, with a view to making arrangements for registering the arrival and departure of persons who have been granted visas valid only for transit to and from the headquarters district and sojourn therein and in its immediate vicinity.

(f) The United Nations shall, subject to the foregoing provisions of this section, have the exclusive right to authorize or prohibit entry of persons or property into the headquarters district and to prescribe the conditions under which persons may remain or reside there.

Section 14

The Secretary-General and the appropriate American authorities shall, at the request of either of them, consult as to methods of facilitating entrance into the

United States, and the use of available means of transportation, by persons coming from abroad who wish to visit the headquarters district and do not enjoy the rights referred to in this Article.

ARTICLE V. RESIDENT REPRESENTATIVES TO THE UNITED NATIONS

Section 15

(1) Every person designated by a Member as the principal resident representative to the United Nations of such Member or as a resident representative with the rank of ambassador or minister plenipotentiary,

(2) Such resident members of their staffs as may be agreed upon between the Secretary-General, the Government of the United States and the Government of the Member concerned,

(3) Every person designated by a Member of a specialized agency, as defined in Article 57, paragraph 2, of the Charter, as its principal resident representative, with the rank of ambassador or minister plenipotentiary at the headquarters of such agency in the United States, and

(4) Such other principal resident representatives of members of a specialized agency and such resident members of the staffs of representatives of a specialized agency as may be agreed upon between the principal executive officer of the specialized agency, the Government of the United States and the Government of the Member concerned, shall whether residing inside or outside the headquarters district, be entitled in the territory of the United States to the same privileges and immunities, subject to corresponding conditions and obligations, as it accords to diplomatic envoys accredited to it.   In the case of Members whose governments are not recognized by the United States, such privileges and immunities need be extended to such representatives, or persons on the staffs of such representatives, only within the headquarters district, at their residences and offices outside the district, in transit between the district and such residences and offices, and in transit on official business to or from foreign countries.

ARTICLE VI. POLICE PROTECTION OF THE HEADQUARTERS DISTRICT

Section 16

(a) The appropriate American authorities shall exercise due diligence to ensure that the tranquility of the headquarters district is not disturbed by the unauthorized entry of groups of persons from outside or by disturbances in its immediate vicinity and shall cause to be provided on the boundaries of the headquarters district such police protection as is required for these purposes.

(b) If so requested by the Secretary-General, the appropriate American authorities shall provide a sufficient number of police for the preservation of law and order in the headquarters district, and for the removal therefrom of persons requested under the authority of the United Nations.   The United Nations shall, if requested, enter into arrangements with the appropriate American authorities to reimburse them for the reasonable cost of such services.

ARTICLE VII. PUBLIC SERVICES AND PROTECTION OF THE HEADQUARTERS DISTRICT

Section 17

(a) The appropriate American authorities will exercise to the extent requested by the Secretary-General the powers which they possess with respect to the supplying of public services to ensure that the headquarters district shall be supplied on equitable terms with the necessary public services, including electricity, water, gas, post, telephone, telegraph, transportation, drainage, collection of refuse, fire protection, snow removal, et cetera. In case of any interruption or threatened interruption of any such services, the appropriate American authorities will consider the needs of the United Nations as being of equal importance with the similar needs of essential agencies of the Government of the United States, and will take steps accordingly, to ensure that the work of the United Nations is not prejudiced.

(b) Special provisions with reference to maintenance of utilities and underground construction are contained in Annex 2.

Section 18

The appropriate American authorities shall take all reasonable steps to ensure that the amenities of the headquarters district are not prejudiced and the purposes for which the district is required are not obstructed by any use made of the land in the vicinity of the district. The United Nations shall on its part take all reasonable steps to ensure that the amenities of the land in the vicinity of the headquarters district are not prejudiced by any use made of the land in the headquarters district by the United Nations.

Section 19

It is agreed that no form of racial or religious discrimination shall be permitted within the headquarters district.

ARTICLE VIII. MATTERS RELATING TO THE OPERATION OF THIS AGREEMENT

Section 20

The Secretary-General and the appropriate American authorities shall settle by agreement the channels through which they will communicate regarding the application of the provisions of this agreement and other questions affecting the headquarters district, and may enter into such supplemental agreements as may be necessary to fulfill the purposes of this agreement. In making supplemental agreements with the Secretary-General, the United States shall consult with the appropriate state and local authorities. If the Secretary-General so requests, the Secretary of State of the United States shall appoint a special representative for the purpose of liaison with the Secretary-General.

Section 21

(a) Any dispute between the United Nations and the United States concerning the interpretation or application of this agreement or of any supplemental agreement, which is not settled by negotiation or other agreed mode of settlement, shall be referred for final decision to a tribunal of three arbitrators, one to be named by the Secretary-General, one to be named by the Secretary of State of the United States, and the third to be chosen by the two, or, if they should fail to agree upon a third, then by the President of the International Court of Justice.

(b) The Secretary-General or the United States may ask the General Assembly to request of the International Court of Justice an advisory opinion on any legal question arising in the course of such proceedings. Pending the receipt of the opinion of the Court, an interim decision of the arbitral tribunal shall be observed by both parties.   Thereafter, the arbitral tribunal shall render a final decision, having regard to the opinion of the Court.

Article IX.   Miscellaneous Provisions

Section 22

(a) The United Nations shall not dispose of all or any part of the land owned by it in the headquarters district without the consent of the United States.   If the United States is unwilling to consent to a disposition which the United Nations wishes to make of all or any part of such land, the United States shall buy the same from the United Nations at a price to be determined as provided in paragraph (d) of this section.

(b) If the seat of the United Nations is removed from the headquarters district, all right, title and interest of the United Nations in and to real property in the headquarters district or any part of it shall, on request of either the United Nations or the United States be assigned and conveyed to the sub-division of a state in which it is located or, if such sub-division shall not desire it, then to the state in which it is located.   If none of the foregoing desire the same, it may be disposed of as provided in paragraph (a) of this Section.

(c) If the United Nations disposes of all or any part of the headquarters district, the provisions of other sections of this agreement which apply to the headquarters district shall immediately cease to apply to the land and buildings so disposed of.

(d) The price to be paid for any conveyance under this section shall, in default of agreement, be the then fair value of the land, buildings and installations, to be determined under the procedure provided in Section 21.

Section 23

The seat of the United Nations shall not be removed from the headquarters district unless the United Nations should so decide.

Section 24

This agreement shall cease to be in force if the seat of the United Nations is removed from the territory of the United States, except for such provisions as may be applicable in connection with the orderly termination of the operations of the United Nations at its seat in the United States and the disposition of its property therein.

Section 25

Wherever this agreement imposes obligations on the appropriate American authorities, the Government of the United States shall have the ultimate responsibility for the fulfillment of such obligations by the appropriate American authorities.

Section 26

The provisions of this agreement shall be complementary to the provisions of the General Convention.   In so far as any provision of this agreement and any provisions of the General Convention relate to the same subject matter, the two provisions shall, wherever possible, be treated as complementary, so that both provisions shall be applicable and neither shall narrow the effect of the other; but in any case of absolute conflict, the provisions of this agreement shall prevail.

Section 27

This agreement shall be construed in the light of its primary purpose to enable the United Nations at its headquarters in the United States, fully and efficiently to discharge its responsibilities and fulfill its purposes.

Section 28

This agreement shall be brought into effect by an exchange of notes between the Secretary-General, duly authorized pursuant to a resolution of the General Assembly of the United Nations, and the appropriate executive officer of the United States, duly authorized pursuant to appropriate action of the Congress.

In witness thereof the respective representatives have signed this Agreement and have affixed their seals hereto.

Done in duplicate, in the English and French languages, both authentic, at Lake Success, this twenty-sixth day of June, 1947.

ANNEX 1

The area referred to in Section 1(a)(1) consists of:

(a) the premises bounded on the East by the westerly side of Franklin D. Roosevelt Drive, on the West by the easterly side of First Avenue, on the North by the southerly side of East Forty-Eighth Street, and on the South by the northerly side of East Forty-Second Street, all as proposed to be widened, in the Borough of Manhattan, City and State of New York, and

(b) an easement over Franklin D. Roosevelt Drive, above a lower limiting plane to be fixed for the construction and maintenance of an esplanade, together with the structures thereon and the foundations and columns to support the same in locations below such limiting plane, the entire area to be more definitely defined by supplemental agreement between the United Nations and the United States of America.

ANNEX 2.   MAINTENANCE OF UTILITIES AND UNDERGROUND CONSTRUCTION

Section 1

The Secretary-General agrees to provide passes to duly authorized employees of the City of New York, the State of New York, or any of their agencies or sub-divisions, for the purpose of enabling them to inspect, repair, maintain, reconstruct and relocate utilities, conduits, mains and sewers within the headquarters district.

Section 2

Underground constructions may be undertaken by the City of New York, or the State of New York, or any of their agencies or sub-divisions, within the headquarters district only after consultation with the Secretary-General, and under conditions which shall not disturb the carrying out of the functions of the United Nations.

Appendix 16

RESOLUTION OF THE GENERAL ASSEMBLY ESTABLISHING AN INTERIM COMMITTEE, NOVEMBER 13, 1947 [1]

THE GENERAL ASSEMBLY,

Conscious of the responsibility specifically conferred upon it by the Charter in relation to matters concerning the maintenance of international peace and security (Articles 11 and 35), the promotion of international co-operation in the political field (Article 13) and the peaceful adjustment of any situations likely to impair the general welfare or friendly relations among nations (Article 14);

Deeming it necessary for the effective performance of these duties to establish an interim committee to consider such matters during the period between the closing of the present session and the opening of the next regular session of the General Assembly, and report with its conclusions to the General Assembly;

Recognizing fully the primary responsibility of the Security Council for prompt and effective action for the maintenance of international peace and security (Article 24),

Resolves, that

1. There shall be established, for the period between the closing of the present session and the opening of the next regular session of the General Assembly, an Interim Committee on which each Member of the General Assembly shall have the right to appoint one representative;

2. The Interim Committee, as a subsidiary organ of the General Assembly established in accordance with Article 22 of the Charter, shall assist the General Assembly in the performance of its functions by discharging the following duties:

   (a) To consider and report, with its conclusions, to the General Assembly on such matters as have been referred to it by the General Assembly;

   (b) To consider and report with its conclusions to the General Assembly on any dispute or any situation which, in virtue of Articles 11 (paragraph 2), 14 or 35 of the Charter, has been proposed for inclusion in the agenda of the General Assembly by any Member of the United Nations or brought before the General Assembly by the Security Council, provided the Committee previously determines the matter to be both important and requiring preliminary study. Such determina-

[1] *The United States and the United Nations: Report by the President to the Congress for the Year* 1947, U.S. Department of State Publication 3024, International Organization and Conference Series III, 1, pp. 159–162.

tion shall be made by a majority of two-thirds of the members present and voting, unless the matter is one referred by the Security Council under Article 11 (paragraph 2), in which case a simple majority will suffice;

(c) To consider, as it deems useful and advisable, and report with its conclusions to the General Assembly on methods to be adopted to give effect to that part of Article 11 (paragraph 1), which deals with the general principles of co-operation in the maintenance of international peace and security, and to that part of Article 13 (paragraph 1a), which deals with the promotion of international co-operation in the political field;

(d) To consider, in connexion with any matter under discussion by the Interim Committee, whether occasion may require the summoning of a special session of the General Assembly and, if it deems that such session is required, so to advise the Secretary-General in order that he may obtain the views of the Members of the United Nations thereon;

(e) To conduct investigations and appoint commissions of enquiry within the scope of its duties, as it may deem useful and necessary, provided that decisions to conduct such investigations or enquiries shall be made by a two-thirds majority of the members present and voting. An investigation or enquiry elsewhere than at the headquarters of the United Nations shall not be conducted without the consent of the State or States in whose territory it is to take place;

(f) To report to the next regular session of the General Assembly on the advisability of establishing a permanent committee of the General Assembly to perform the duties of the Interim Committee as stated above with any changes considered desirable in the light of experience;

3. In discharging its duties the Interim Committee shall at all times take into account the responsibilities of the Security Council under the Charter for the maintenance of international peace and security as well as the duties assigned by the Charter or by the General Assembly or by the Security Council to other Councils or to any committee or commission. The Interim Committee shall not consider any matter of which the Security Council is seized;

4. Subject to paragraphs 2(b) and 2(e) above, the rules of procedure of the General Assembly shall, so far as they are applicable, govern the proceedings of the Interim Committee and such sub-committees and commissions as it may set up. The Interim Committee shall, however, have authority to adopt such additional rules as it may deem necessary provided that they are not inconsistent with any of the rules of procedure of the General Assembly. The Interim Committee shall be convened by the Secretary-General not later than six weeks following the close of the second regular session of the General Assembly. It shall meet as and when it deems necessary for the conduct of its business;

5. The Secretary-General shall provide the necessary facilities and assign appropriate staff as required for the work of the Interim Committee, its sub-committees and commissions.

Appendix 17

ADVISORY OPINION OF THE INTERNATIONAL COURT OF JUSTICE ON CONDITIONS OF ADMISSION OF A STATE TO MEMBERSHIP IN THE UNITED NATIONS, MAY 28, 1948 [1]

On November 17th, 1947, the General Assembly of the United Nations adopted the following Resolution:

THE GENERAL ASSEMBLY,

"Considering Article 4 of the Charter of the United Nations,

"Considering the exchange of views which has taken place in the Security Council at its Two hundred and fourth, Two hundred and fifth, and Two hundred and sixth Meetings, relating to the admission of certain States to membership in the United Nations,

"Considering Article 96 of the Charter,

"Requests the International Court of Justice to give an advisory opinion on the following question:

"'Is a Member of the United Nations which is called upon, in virtue of Article 4 of the Charter, to pronounce itself by its vote, either in the Security Council or in the General Assembly, on the admission of a State to membership in the United Nations, juridically entitled to make its consent to the admission dependent on conditions not expressly provided by paragraph 1 of the said Article? In particular, can such a Member, while it recognizes the conditions set forth in that provision to be fulfilled by the State concerned, subject its affirmative vote to the additional condition that other States be admitted to membership in the United Nations together with that State?' . . ."

   .   .   .   .

Before examining the request for an opinion, the Court considers it necessary to make the following preliminary remarks:

The question put to the Court is divided into two parts, of which the second begins with the words "In particular," and is presented as an application of a more general idea implicit in the first.

[1] Advisory Opinion of the International Court of Justice, May 28, 1948. *I.C.J. Reports of Judgments, Advisory Opinions and Orders,* 1948, pp. 57–115.

The request for an opinion does not refer to the actual vote. Although the Members are bound to conform to the requirements of Article 4 in giving their votes, the General Assembly can hardly be supposed to have intended to ask the Court's opinion as to the reasons which, in the mind of a Member, may prompt its vote. Such reasons, which enter into a mental process, are obviously subject to no control. Nor does the request concern a Member's freedom of expressing its opinion. Since it concerns a condition or conditions on which a Member "makes its consent dependent," the question can only relate to the statements made by a Member concerning the vote it proposes to give.

It is clear from the General Assembly's Resolution of November 17th, 1947, that the Court is not called upon either to define the meaning and scope of the conditions on which admission is made dependent, or to specify the elements which may serve in a concrete case to verify the existence of the requisite conditions.

The clause of the General Assembly's Resolution, referring to "the exchange of views which has taken place . . . ," is not understood as an invitation to the Court to say whether the views thus referred to are well founded or otherwise. The abstract form in which the question is stated precludes such an interpretation.

The question put is in effect confined to the following point only: are the conditions stated in paragraph 1 of Article 4 exhaustive in character in the sense that an affirmative reply would lead to the conclusion that a Member is not legally entitled to make admission dependent on conditions not expressly provided for in that Article, while a negative reply would, on the contrary, authorize a Member to make admission dependent also on other conditions.

*   *   *

Understood in this light, the question, in its two parts, is and can only be a purely legal one. To determine the meaning of a treaty provision—to determine, as in this case, the character (exhaustive or otherwise) of the conditions for admission stated therein—is a problem of interpretation and consequently a legal question.

It has nevertheless been contended that the question put must be regarded as a political one and that, for this reason, it falls outside the jurisdiction of the Court. The Court cannot attribute a political character to a request which, framed in abstract terms, invites it to undertake an essentially judicial task, the interpretation of a treaty provision. It is not concerned with the motives which may have inspired this request, nor with the considerations which, in the concrete cases submitted for examination to the Security Council, formed the subject of the exchange of views which took place in that body. It is the duty of the Court to envisage the question submitted to it only in the abstract form which has been given to it; nothing which is said in the present opinion refers, either directly or indirectly, to concrete cases or to particular circumstances.

It has also been contended that the Court should not deal with a question couched in abstract terms. That is a mere affirmation devoid of any justification. According to Article 96 of the Charter and Article 65 of the Statute, the Court may give an advisory opinion on any legal question, abstract or otherwise.

Lastly, it has also been maintained that the Court cannot reply to the question put because it involves an interpretation of the Charter. Nowhere is any provision to be found forbidding the Court, "the principal judicial organ of the United Nations," to exercise in regard to Article 4 of the Charter, a multilateral treaty, an interpretative function which falls within the normal exercise of its judicial powers.

Accordingly, the Court holds that it is competent, on the basis of Article 96 of the Charter and Article 65 of the Statute, and considers that there are no reasons why it should decline to answer the question put to it.

In framing this answer, it is necessary first to recall the "conditions" required, under paragraph 1 of Article 4, of an applicant for admission. This provision reads as follows:

"Membership in the United Nations is open to all other peace-loving States which accept the obligations contained in the present Charter and, in the judgment of the Organisation, are able and willing to carry out these obligations." The requisite conditions are five in number: to be admitted to membership in the United Nations, an applicant must (1) be a State; (2) be peace-loving; (3) accept the obligations of the Charter; (4) be able to carry out these obligations; and (5) be willing to do so.

All these conditions are subject to the judgment of the Organization. The judgment of the Organization means the judgment of the two organs mentioned in paragraph 2 of Article 4, and, in the last analysis, that of its Members. The question put is concerned with the individual attitude of each Member called upon to pronounce itself on the question of admission.

Having been asked to determine the character, exhaustive or otherwise, of the conditions stated in Article 4, the Court must in the first place consider the text of that Article. The English and French texts of paragraph 1 of Article 4 have the same meaning, and it is impossible to find any conflict between them. The text of this paragraph, by the enumeration which it contains and the choice of its terms, clearly demonstrates the intention of its authors to establish a legal rule which, while it fixes the conditions of admission, determines also the reasons for which admission may be refused; for the text does not differentiate between these two cases and any attempt to restrict it to one of them would be purely arbitrary.

The terms "Membership in the United Nations is open to all other peace-loving States which . . ." and *"Peuvent devenir Membres des Nations unies tous autres États pacifiques,"* indicate that States which fulfil the conditions stated have the qualifications requisite for admission. The natural meaning of the words used leads to the conclusion that these conditions constitute an exhaustive enumeration and are not merely stated by way of guidance or example. The provision would lose its significance and weight, if other conditions, unconnected with those laid down, could be demanded. The conditions stated in paragraph 1 of Article 4 must therefore be regarded not merely as the necessary conditions, but also as the conditions which suffice.

Nor can it be argued that the conditions enumerated represent only an indispensable minimum, in the sense that political considerations could be superimposed upon them, and prevent the admission of an applicant which fulfils them. Such an interpretation would be inconsistent with the terms of paragraph 2 of Article 4, which provide for the admission of *"tout État* remplissant ces conditions"—"any *such* State." It would lead to conferring upon Members an indefinite and practically unlimited power of discretion in the imposition of new conditions. Such a power would be inconsistent with the very character of paragraph 1 of Article 4 which, by reason of the close connexion which it establishes between membership and the observance of the principles and obligations of the Charter, clearly constitutes a legal regulation of the question of the admission of new States. To warrant an interpretation other than that which ensues from the natural meaning of the words, a decisive reason would be required which has not been established.

Moreover, the spirit as well as the terms of the paragraph preclude the idea that considerations extraneous to these principles and obligations can prevent the admission of a State which complies with them. If the authors of the Charter had meant to leave Members free to import into the application of this provision considerations extraneous to the conditions laid down therein, they would undoubtedly have adopted a different wording.

The Court considers that the text is sufficiently clear; consequently, it does not feel that it should deviate from the consistent practice of the Permanent Court of International Justice, according to which there is no occasion to resort to preparatory work if the text of a convention is sufficiently clear in itself.

The Court furthermore observes that Rule 60 of the Provisional Rules of Procedure of the Security Council is based on this interpretation. The first paragraph of this Rule reads as follows:

"The Security Council shall decide whether in its judgment the applicant is a peace-loving State and is able and willing to carry out the obligations contained in the Charter, and accordingly whether to recommend the applicant State for membership."

It does not, however, follow from the exhaustive character of paragraph 1 of Article 4 that an appreciation is precluded of such circumstances of fact as would enable the existence of the requisite conditions to be verified.

Article 4 does not forbid the taking into account of any factor which it is possible reasonably and in good faith to connect with the conditions laid down in that Article. The taking into account of such factors is implied in the very wide and very elastic nature of the prescribed conditions; no relevant political factor—that is to say, none connected with the conditions of admission—is excluded.

It has been sought to deduce either from the second paragraph of Article 4, or from the political character of the organ recommending or deciding upon admission, arguments in favor of an interpretation of paragraph 1 of Article 4, to the effect that the fulfilment of the conditions provided for in that Article is necessary before the admission of a State can be recommended or decided upon, but that it does not preclude the Members of the Organization from advancing considerations of political expediency, extraneous to the conditions of Article 4.

But paragraph 2 is concerned only with the procedure for admission, while the preceding paragraph lays down the substantive law. This procedural character is clearly indicated by the words "will be effected," which, by linking admission to the decision, point clearly to the fact that the paragraph is solely concerned with the manner in which admission is effected, and not with the subject of the judgment of the Organization, nor with the nature of the appreciation involved in that judgment, these two questions being dealt with in the preceding paragraph. Moreover, this paragraph, in referring to the "recommendation" of the Security Council and the "decision" of the General Assembly, is designed only to determine the respective functions of these two organs which consist in pronouncing upon the question whether or not the applicant State shall be admitted to membership after having established whether or not the prescribed conditions are fulfilled.

The political character of an organ cannot release it from the observance of the treaty provisions established by the Charter when they constitute limitations on its powers or criteria for its judgment. To ascertain whether an organ has freedom of choice for its decisions, reference must be made to the terms of its constitution. In this case, the limits of this freedom are fixed by Article 4 and allow for a wide liberty of appreciation. There is therefore no conflict between the functions of the political organs, on the one hand, and the exhaustive character of the prescribed conditions, on the other.

It has been sought to base on the political responsibilities assumed by the Security Council, in virtue of Article 24 of the Charter, an argument justifying the necessity for according to the Security Council as well as to the General Assembly complete freedom of appreciation in connexion with the admission of new Members. But Article 24, owing to the very general nature of its terms, cannot, in the absence of any provision, affect the special rules for admission which emerge from Article 4.

The foregoing considerations establish the exhaustive character of the conditions prescribed in Article 4.

* * *

The second part of the question concerns a demand on the part of a Member making its consent to the admission of an applicant dependent on the admission of other applicants.

Judged on the basis of the rule which the Court adopts in its interpretation of Article 4, such a demand clearly constitutes a new condition, since it is entirely unconnected with those prescribed in Article 4. It is also in an entirely different category from those conditions, since it makes admission dependent, not on the conditions required of applicants, qualifications which are supposed to be fulfilled, but on an extraneous consideration concerning States other than the applicant State.

The provisions of Article 4 necessarily imply that every application for admission should be examined and voted on separately and on its own merits; otherwise it would be impossible to determine whether a particular applicant fulfils the necessary conditions. To subject an affirmative vote for the admission of an applicant State to the condition that other States be admitted with that State would prevent Members from exercising their judgment in each case with complete liberty, within the scope of the prescribed conditions. Such a demand is incompatible with the letter and spirit of Article 4 of the Charter.

For these reasons,

THE COURT,

by nine votes to six,

is of opinion that a Member of the United Nations which is called upon, in virtue of Article 4 of the Charter, to pronounce itself by its vote, either in the Security Council or in the General Assembly, on the admission of a State to membership in the United Nations, is not juridically entitled to make its consent to the admission dependent on conditions not expressly provided by paragraph 1 of the said Article;

and that, in particular, a Member of the Organization cannot, while it recognizes the conditions set forth in that provision to be fulfilled by the State concerned, subject its affirmative vote to the additional condition that other States be admitted to membership in the United Nations together with that State.

The present opinion has been drawn up in French and in English, the French text being authoritative. . . .

Judges ALVAREZ and AZEVEDO, whilst concurring in the opinion of the Court, have availed themselves of the right conferred on them by Article 57 of the Statute and appended to the opinion a statement of their individual opinion.

JUDGES BASDEVANT, WINIARSKI, MCNAIR, READ, ZORICIC and KRYLOV, declaring that they are unable to concur in the opinion of the Court, have availed themselves of the right conferred on them by Article 57 of the Statute and appended to the opinion a statement of their dissenting opinion. . . .

Appendix 18

VANDENBERG RESOLUTION—THE POLICY OF THE UNITED STATES TO ACHIEVE PEACE AND SECURITY THROUGH THE UNITED NATIONS, JUNE 11, 1948 [1]

Whereas peace with justice and the defense of human rights and fundamental freedoms require international cooperation through more effective use of the United Nations: Therefore be it

Resolved, That the Senate reaffirm the policy of the United States to achieve international peace and security through the United Nations so that armed force shall not be used except in the common interest, and that the President be advised of the sense of the Senate that this Government, by constitutional process, should particularly pursue the following objectives within the United Nations Charter:

(1) Voluntary agreement to remove the veto from all questions involving pacific settlements of international disputes and situations, and from the admission of new members.

(2) Progressive development of regional and other collective arrangements for the individual and collective self-defense in accordance with the purposes, principles, and provisions of the Charter.

(3) Association of the United States, by constitutional process, with such regional and other collective arrangements as are based on continuous and effective self-help and mutual aid, and as affect its national security.

(4) Contributing to the maintenance of peace by making clear its determination to exercise the right of individual or collective self-defense under article 51 should any armed attack occur affecting its national security.

(5) Maximum efforts to obtain agreements to provide the United Nations with armed forces as provided by the Charter, and to obtain agreement among member nations upon universal regulation and reduction of armaments under adequate and dependable guaranty against violation.

(6) If necessary, after adequate effort toward strengthening the United Nations, review of the Charter at an appropriate time by a General Conference under article 109 or by the General Assembly.

[1] Senate Resolution 239, 80th Congress, 2d Session, June 11, 1948.

Appendix 19

UNIVERSAL DECLARATION OF HUMAN RIGHTS, RESOLUTION OF GENERAL ASSEMBLY, DECEMBER 10, 1948 [1]

Whereas recognition of the inherent dignity and of the equal and inalienable rights of all members of the human family is the foundation of freedom, justice and peace in the world,

Whereas disregard and contempt for human rights have resulted in barbarous acts which have outraged the conscience of mankind, and the advent of a world in which human beings shall enjoy freedom of speech and belief and freedom from fear and want has been proclaimed as the highest aspiration of the common people,

Whereas it is essential, if man is not to be compelled to have recourse, as a last resort, to rebellion against tyranny and oppression, that human rights should be protected by the rule of law,

Whereas it is essential to promote the development of friendly relations between nations,

Whereas the peoples of the United Nations have in the Charter reaffirmed their faith in fundamental human rights, in the dignity and worth of the human person and in the equal rights of men and women and have determined to promote social progress and better standards of life in larger freedom,

Whereas Member States have pledged themselves to achieve, in co-operation with the United Nations, the promotion of universal respect for and observance of human rights and fundamental freedoms,

Whereas a common understanding of these rights and freedoms is of the greatest importance for the full realization of this pledge,

Now therefore

The General Assembly,

Proclaims this Universal Declaration of Human Rights as a common standard of achievement for all peoples and all nations, to the end that every individual and every organ of society, keeping this Declaration constantly in mind, shall strive by teaching and education to promote respect for these rights and freedoms and by progressive measures, national and international, to secure their universal and effective recognition and observance, both among the peoples of Member States themselves and among the peoples of territories under their jurisdiction.

Article 1. All human beings are born free and equal in dignity and rights. They

[1] U.N. press release PGA/100, Pt. IV, pp. 11–16.

are endowed with reason and conscience and should act towards one another in a spirit of brotherhood.

Article 2.   Everyone is entitled to all the rights and freedoms set forth in this Declaration, without distinction of any kind, such as race, colour, sex, language, religion, political or other opinion, national or social origin, property, birth or other status.

Furthermore, no distinction shall be made on the basis of the political, jurisdictional or international status of the country or territory to which a person belongs, whether it be independent, trust, non-self-governing or under any other limitation of sovereignty.

Article 3.   Everyone has the right to life, liberty and the security of person.

Article 4.   No one shall be held in slavery or servitude; slavery and the slave trade shall be prohibited in all their forms.

Article 5.   No one shall be subjected to torture or to cruel, inhuman or degrading treatment or punishment.

Article 6.   Everyone has the right to recognition everywhere as a person before the law.

Article 7.   All are equal before the law and are entitled without any discrimination to equal protection of the law.   All are entitled to equal protection against any discrimination in violation of this Declaration and against any incitement to such discrimination.

Article 8.   Everyone has the right to an effective remedy by the competent national tribunals for acts violating the fundamental rights granted him by the constitution or by law.

Article 9.   No one shall be subjected to arbitrary arrest, detention or exile.

Article 10.   Everyone is entitled in full equality to a fair and public hearing by an independent and impartial tribunal, in the determination of his rights and obligations and of any criminal charge against him.

Article 11.   1. Everyone charged with a penal offence has the right to be presumed innocent until proved guilty according to law in a public trial at which he has had all the guarantees necessary for his defence.

2. No one shall be held guilty of any penal offence on account of any act or omission which did not constitute a penal offence, under national or international law, at the time when it was committed.   Nor shall a heavier penalty be imposed than the one that was applicable at the time the penal offence was committed.

Article 12.   No one shall be subjected to arbitrary interference with his privacy, family, home or correspondence, nor to attacks upon his honor and reputation. Everyone has the right to the protection of the law against such interference or attacks.

Article 13.   1. Everyone has the right to freedom of movement and residence within the borders of each state.

2. Everyone has the right to leave any country, including his own, and to return to his country.

Article 14.   1. Everyone has the right to seek and to enjoy in other countries asylum from persecution.

2. This right may not be invoked in the case of prosecutions genuinely arising

from non-political crimes or from acts contrary to the purposes and principles of the United Nations.

Article 15. 1. Everyone has the right to a nationality.

2. No one shall be arbitrarily deprived of his nationality nor denied the right to change his nationality.

Article 16. 1. Men and women of full age, without any limitation due to race, nationality or religion, have the right to marry and to found a family. They are entitled to equal rights as to marriage, during marriage and at its dissolution.

2. Marriage shall be entered into only with the free and full consent of the intending spouses.

3. The family is the natural and fundamental group unit of society and is entitled to protection by society and the State.

Article 17. 1. Everyone has the right to own property alone as well as in association with others.

2. No one shall be arbitrarily deprived of his property.

Article 18. Everyone has the right to freedom of thought, conscience and religion; this right includes freedom to change his religion or belief, and freedom, either alone or in community with others and in public or private, to manifest his religion or belief in teaching, practice, worship and observance.

Article 19. Everyone has the right to freedom of opinion and expression; this right includes freedom to hold opinions without interference and to seek, receive and impart information and ideas through any media and regardless of frontiers.

Article 20. 1. Everyone has the right to freedom of peaceful assembly and association.

2. No one may be compelled to belong to an association.

Article 21. 1. Everyone has the right to take part in the Government of his country, directly or through freely chosen representatives.

2. Everyone has the right of equal access to public service in his country.

3. The will of the people shall be the basis of the authority of government; this will shall be expressed in periodic and genuine elections which shall be by universal and equal suffrage and shall be held by secret vote or by equivalent free voting procedures.

Article 22. Everyone, as a member of society, has the right to social security and is entitled to realization, throught national effort and international co-operation and in accordance with the organization and resources of each State, of the economic, social and cultural rights indispensable for his dignity and the free development of his personality.

Article 23. 1. Everyone has the right to work, to free choice of employment, to just and favorable conditions of work and to protection against unemployment.

2. Everyone, without any discrimination, has the right to equal pay for equal work.

3. Everyone who works has the right to just and favourable remuneration insuring for himself and his family an existence worthy of human dignity, and supplemented, if necessary, by other means of social protection.

4. Everyone has the right to form and to join trade unions for the protection of his interests.

Article 24. Everyone has the right to rest and leisure, including reasonable limitation of working hours and periodic holidays with pay.

Article 25. 1. Everyone has the right to a standard of living adequate for the health and well-being of himself and of his family, including food, clothing, housing and medical care and necessary social services, and the right to security in the event of unemployment, sickness, disability, widowhood, old age or other lack of livelihood in circumstances beyond his control.

2. Motherhood and childhood are entitled to special care and assistance. All children, whether born in or out of wedlock, shall enjoy the same social protection.

Article 26. 1. Everyone has the right to education. Education shall be free, at least in the elementary and fundamental stages. Elementary education shall be compulsory. Technical and professional education shall be made generally available and higher education shall be equally accessible to all on the basis of merit.

2. Education shall be directed to the full development of the human personality and to the strengthening of respect for human rights and fundamental freedoms. It shall promote understanding, tolerance and friendship among all nations, racial or religious groups, and shall further the activities of the United Nations for the maintenance of peace.

3. Parents have a prior right to choose the kind of education that shall be given to their children.

Article 27. 1. Everyone has the right freely to participate in the cultural life of the community, to enjoy the arts and to share in scientific advancement and its benefits.

2. Everyone has the right to the protection of the moral and material interests resulting from any scientific, literary or artistic production of which he is the author.

Article 28. Everyone is entitled to a social and international order in which the rights and freedoms set forth in this Declaration can be fully realized.

Article 29. 1. Everyone has duties to the community in which alone the free and full development of his personality is possible.

2. In the exercise of his rights and freedoms, everyone shall be subject only to such limitations as are determined by law solely for the purpose of securing due recognition and respect for the rights and freedoms of others and of meeting the just requirements of morality, public order and the general welfare in a democratic society.

3. These rights and freedoms may in no case be exercised contrary to the purposes and principles of the United Nations.

Article 30. Nothing in this Declaration may be interpreted as implying for any State, group or person any right to engage in any activity or to perform any act aimed at the destruction of any of the rights and freedoms set forth herein.

Appendix 20

THE ROAD TO PEACE—A TWENTY-YEAR UNITED NATIONS PROGRAM—MEMORANDUM BY SECRETARY-GENERAL TRYGVE LIE, JUNE 6, 1950 [1]

As Secretary-General, it is my firm belief that a new and great effort must be attempted to end the so-called "cold war" and to set the world once more on a road that will offer greater hope of lasting peace.

The atmosphere of deepening international mistrust can be dissipated and the threat of the universal disaster of another war averted by employing to the full the resources for conciliation and constructive peace-building present in the United Nations Charter. The employment of these resources can secure eventual peace if we accept, believe, and act upon the possibility of peaceful co-existence among all the Great Powers and the different economic and political systems they represent, and if the Great Powers evidence a readiness to undertake genuine negotiation—not in a spirit of appeasement—but with enlightened self-interest and common sense on all sides.

Measures for collective self-defence and regional remedies of other kinds are at best interim measures and cannot alone bring any reliable security from the prospect of war. The one common undertaking and universal instrument of the great majority of the human race is the United Nations. A patient, constructive, long-term use of its potentialities can bring a real and secure peace to the world. I am certain that such an effort will have the active interest and support of the smaller Member states, who have much to contribute in the conciliation of Big Power differences and in the development of constructive and mutually advantageous political and economic co-operation.

I therefore venture to suggest certain points for consideration in the formulation of a 20-year United Nations Peace Program. Certain of these points call for urgent action. Others are of a long-range nature, requiring continued effort over the next 20 years. I shall not discuss the problems of the peace settlements for Austria, Germany, and Japan—because the founders of the United Nations indicated that the peace settlements should be made separately from the United Nations. But I believe that the progress of a United Nations Peace Program such as is here suggested will help to bring these settlements far closer to attainment.

[1] *United Nations Bulletin*, Vol. VIII, No. 12, June 15, 1950, pp. 510–513, 540.

1. *Inauguration of periodic meetings of the Security Council, attended by foreign ministers, or heads or other members of governments, as provided by the United Nations Charter and the rules of procedure; together with further development and use of other United Nations machinery for negotiation, mediation, and conciliation of international disputes.*

The periodic meetings of the Security Council provided for in Article 28 of the Charter have never been held. Such periodic meetings should be held semi-annually, beginning with one in 1950. In my opinion, they should be used for a general review at a high level of outstanding issues in the United Nations, particularly those that divide the Great Powers. They should not be expected to produce great decisions every time; they should be used for consultation—much of it in private— for efforts to gain ground toward agreement on questions at issue, to clear up misunderstandings, to prepare for new initiatives that may improve the chances for definitive agreement at later meetings. They should be held away from Headquarters as a general rule, in Geneva, the capitals of the permanent members, and in other regions of the world.

Further development of the resources of the United Nations for mediation and conciliation should be undertaken, including re-establishment of the regular practice of private consultations by the representatives of the five Great Powers, and a renewed effort to secure agreement by all the Great Powers on limitations on the use of the veto power in the pacific settlement procedures of the Security Council.

2. *A new attempt to make progress toward establishing an international control system for atomic energy that will be effective in preventing its use for war and promoting its use for peaceful purposes.*

We cannot hope for any quick or easy solution of this most difficult problem of atomic energy control. The only way to find out what is possible is to resume negotiation in line with the directive of the General Assembly last fall "to explore all possible avenues and examine all concrete suggestions with a view to determining what might lead to an agreement." Various suggestions for finding a basis for a fresh approach have been put forward. One possibility would be for the Security Council to instruct the Secretary-General to call a conference of scientists whose discussions might provide a reservoir of new ideas on the control of weapons of mass destruction and the promotion of peaceful uses of atomic energy that could thereafter be explored in the United Nations Atomic Energy Commission. Or it may be that an interim agreement could be worked out that would at least be some improvement on the present situation of an unlimited atomic arms race, even though it did not afford full security. There are other possibilities for providing the basis for a new start; every possibility should be explored.

3. *A new approach to the problem of bringing the armaments race under control, not only in the field of atomic weapons, but in other weapons of mass destruction and in conventional armaments.*

Here is another area where it is necessary to re-activate negotiation and to make new efforts at finding some area of common ground. It must be recognized that up to now there has been virtually a complete failure here and that the immediate prospects seem poor indeed. Clearly disarmament requires an atmosphere of confidence in which political disputes are brought nearer to solution. But it is also true that any progress at all toward agreement on the regulation of armaments of any kind would help to reduce cold war tensions and thus assist in the adjustment of political disputes. Negotiation on this problem should not be deferred until the other great political problems are solved, but should go hand-in-hand with any effort to reach political settlements.

4. *A renewal of serious efforts to reach agreement on the armed forces to be made available under the Charter to the Security Council for the enforcement of its decisions.*

A new approach should be made toward resolving existing differences on the size, location, and composition of the forces to be pledged to the Security Council under Article 43 of the Charter. Basic political difficulties which may delay a final solution should not be permitted to stand in the way of some sort of an interim accord for a small force sufficient to prevent or stop localized outbreaks threatening international peace. The mere existence of such a force would greatly enhance the ability of the Security Council to bring about peaceful settlements in most of the cases which are likely to come before it.

5. *Acceptance and application of the principle that it is wise and right to proceed as rapidly as possible toward universality of Membership.*

Fourteen nations are now awaiting admission to the United Nations. In the interests of the people of these countries and of the United Nations, I believe they should all be admitted, as well as other countries which will attain their independence in the future. It should be made clear that Germany and Japan would also be admitted as soon as the peace treaties have been completed.

6. *A sound and active program of technical assistance for economic development and encouragement of broad-scale capital investment, using all appropriate private, governmental, and inter-governmental resources.*

A technical assistance program is in its beginnings, assisted by the strong support of the President of the United States. Its fundamental purpose is to enable the people of the under-developed countries to raise their standard of living peacefully by specific and practicable measures. It should be a continuing and expanding program for the next 20 years and beyond, carried forward with the co-operation of all Member governments, largely through the United Nations and the specialized agencies, with mutual beneficial programs planned and executed on a basis of equality rather than on a basis of charity. Through this means, the opportunities can be opened up for capital investment on a large and expanding scale. Here lies one of our best hopes for combating the dangers and costs of the cold war.

7. *More vigorous use by all Member governments of the specialized agencies of the United Nations to promote, in the words of the Charter, "higher standards of living, full employment, and conditions of economic and social progress."*

The great potentialities of the specialized agencies to participate in a long-range program aimed at drastically reducing the economic and social causes of war can be realized by more active support from all governments, including the membership of the Soviet Union in some or all of the agencies to which it does not now belong. The expansion of world trade which is vital to any long-range effort for world betterment requires the early ratification of the Charter of the International Trade Organization.

8. *Vigorous and continued development of the work of the United Nations for wider observance and respect for human rights and fundamental freedoms throughout the world.*

It is becoming evident that the Universal Declaration of Human Rights, adopted by the General Assembly in 1948 without a dissenting vote, is destined to become one of the great documents of history. The United Nations is now engaged on a program that will extend over the next 20 years—and beyond—to secure the extension and wider observance of the political, economic, and social rights there set down. Its success needs the active support of all governments.

9. *Use of the United Nations to promote, by peaceful means instead of by force, the advancement of dependent, colonial, or semi-colonial peoples toward a place of equality in the world.*

The great changes which have been taking place since the end of the war among the peoples of Asia and Africa must be kept within peaceful bounds by using the universal framework of the United Nations. The old relationships will have to be replaced with new ones of equality and fraternity. The United Nations is the instrument capable of bringing such a transition to pass without violent upheavals and with the best prospect of bringing long-run economic and political benefits to all nations of the world.

10. *Active and systematic use of all the powers of the Charter and all the machinery of the United Nations to speed up the development of international law toward an eventual enforceable world law for a universal world society.*

These three last points deal with programs already under way to carry out important principles of the United Nations Charter. They respond to basic human desires and aspirations, and co-ordinated efforts by all governments to further these programs are indispensable to the eventual peaceful stabilization of international relations. There are many specific steps which need to be taken: for example, under point 10, ratification of the Genocide Convention, greater use of the International Court of Justice, and systematic development and codification of international law. More important is that governments should give high priority in their national policies to the continued support and development of these ideals which are at the foundation of all striving of the peoples for a better world.

What is here suggested is only an outline of preliminary proposals for a program; much more development will be needed. It is self-evident that every step mentioned, every proposal made, will require careful and detailed, even laborious, preparation, negotiation, and administration. It is equally self-evident that the necessary measures of agreement will be hard to realize most of the time, and even impossible some of the time. Yet the world can never accept the thesis of despair—the thesis of irrevocable and irreconcilable conflict.

Appendix 21

UNITING FOR PEACE—GENERAL ASSEMBLY RECOMMENDATIONS TO SECURITY COUNCIL, RECOMMENDATIONS TO PERMANENT MEMBERS, NOVEMBER 2, 1950 [1]

RESOLUTION A

UNITING FOR PEACE

The General Assembly,

Recognizing that the first two stated Purposes of the United Nations are:

"To maintain international peace and security, and to that end: to take effective collective measures for the prevention and removal of threats to the peace, and for the suppression of acts of aggression or other breaches of the peace, and to bring about by peaceful means, and in conformity with the principles of justice and international law, adjustment or settlement of international disputes or situations which might lead to a breach of the peace," and

"To develop friendly relations among nations based on respect for the principle of equal rights and self-determination of peoples, and to take other appropriate measures to strengthen universal peace,"

Reaffirming that it remains the primary duty of all Members of the United Nations, when involved in an international dispute, to seek settlement of such a dispute by peaceful means through the procedures laid down in Chapter VI of the Charter, and recalling the successful achievements of the United Nations in this regard on a number of previous occasions,

Finding that international tension exists on a dangerous scale,

Recalling its resolution 290 (IV) entitled "Essentials of Peace," which states that disregard of the Principles of the Charter of the United Nations is primarily responsible for the continuance of international tension, and desiring to contribute further to the objectives of that resolution,

Reaffirming the importance of the exercise by the Security Council of its primary responsibility for the maintenance of international peace and security, and the duty of the permanent members to seek unanimity and to exercise restraint in the use of the veto,

---

[1] *United Nations Bulletin,* Vol. IX, No. 10, Nov. 15, 1950, pp. 508–509.

Reaffirming that the initiative in negotiating the agreements for armed forces provided for in Article 43 of the Charter belongs to the Security Council, and desiring to ensure that, pending the conclusion of such agreements, the United Nations has at its disposal means for maintaining international peace and security,

Conscious that failure of the Security Council to discharge its responsibilities on behalf of all the Member states, particularly those responsibilities referred to in the two preceding paragraphs, does not relieve Member states of their obligations or the United Nations of its responsibility under the Charter to maintain international peace and security,

Recognizing in particular that such failure does not deprive the General Assembly of its rights or relieve it of its responsibilities under the Charter in regard to the maintenance of international peace and security,

Recognizing that discharge by the General Assembly of its responsibilities in these respects calls for possibilities of observation which would ascertain the facts and expose aggressors; for the existence of armed forces which could be used collectively; and for the possibility of timely recommendation by the General Assembly to Members of the United Nations for collective action which, to be effective, should be prompt,

A.

1. *Resolves* that if the Security Council, because of lack of unanimity of the permanent members, fails to exercise its primary responsibility for the maintenance of international peace and security in any case where there appears to be a threat to the peace, breach of the peace, or act of aggression, the General Assembly shall consider the matter immediately with a view to making appropriate recommendations to Members for collective measures, including in the case of a breach of the peace or act of aggression the use of armed force when necessary, to maintain or restore international peace and security. If not in session at the time, the General Assembly may meet in emergency special session within 24 hours of the request therefor. Such emergency special session shall be called if requested by the Security Council on the vote of any seven members, or by a majority of the Members of the United Nations;

2. *Adopts* for this purpose the amendments to its rules of procedure set forth in the annex [2] to the present resolution;

B.

3. *Establishes* a Peace Observation Commission, which for the calendar years 1951 and 1952 shall be composed of fourteen Members, namely: China, Colombia, Czechoslovakia, France, India, Iraq, Israel, New Zealand, Pakistan, Sweden, the Union of Soviet Socialist Republics, the United Kingdom of Great Britain and Northern Ireland, the United States of America and Uruguay, and which could observe and report on the situation in any area where there exists international tension the continuance of which is likely to endanger the maintenance of international peace and security. Upon the invitation or with the consent of the state into whose territory the Commission would go, the General Assembly, or the Interim Committee when the Assembly is not in session, may utilize the Commission if the Security Council is not exercising the functions assigned to it by the Charter

[2] The text of the annex is omitted.

with respect to the matter in question. Decisions to utilize the Commission shall be made on the affirmative vote of two-thirds of the Members present and voting. The Security Council may also utilize the Commission in accordance with its authority under the Charter;

4. *The Commission shall have* authority in its discretion to appoint sub-commissions and to utilize the services of observers to assist it in the performance of its functions;

5. *Recommends* to all governments and authorities that they co-operate with the Commission and assist it in the performance of its functions;

6. *Requests* the Secretary-General to provide the necessary staff and facilities, utilizing, where directed by the Commission, the United Nations Panel of Field Observers envisaged in resolution 297 B (IV);

C.

7. *Invites* each Member of the United Nations to survey its resources in order to determine the nature and scope of the assistance it may be in a position to render in support of any recommendations of the Security Council or of the General Assembly for the restoration of international peace and security;

8. *Recommends* to the states Members of the United Nations that each Member maintain within its national armed forces elements so trained, organized, and equipped that they could promptly be made available, in accordance with its constitutional processes, for service as a United Nations unit or units, upon recommendation by the Security Council or General Assembly, without prejudice to the use of such elements in exercise of the right of individual or collective self-defence recognized in Article 51 of the Charter;

9. *Invites* the Members of the United Nations to inform the Collective Measures Committee, provided for in paragraph 11, as soon as possible of the measures taken in implementation of the preceding paragraph;

10. *Requests* the Secretary-General to appoint, with the approval of the Committee provided for in paragraph 11, a panel of military experts who could be made available, on request to Member states wishing to obtain technical advice regarding the organization, training, and equipment for prompt service as United Nations units of the elements referred to in paragraph 8;

D.

11. *Establishes* a Collective Measures Committee consisting of fourteen Members, namely: Australia, Belgium, Brazil, Burma, Canada, Egypt, France, Mexico, Philippines, Turkey, the United Kingdom of Great Britain and Northern Ireland, the United States of America, Venezuela, and Yugoslavia, and directs the Committee, in consultation with the Secretary-General and with such Member states as the Committee finds appropriate, to study and make a report to the Security Council and the General Assembly, not later than September 1, 1951, on methods, including those in Section C of present resolution, which might be used to maintain and strengthen international peace and security in accordance with the Purposes and Principles of the Charter, taking account of collective self-defence and regional arrangements (Articles 51 and 52 of the Charter);

12. *Recommends* to all Member states that they co-operate with the Committee and assist it in the performance of its functions;

13. *Requests* the Secretary-General to furnish the staff and facilities necessary for the effective accomplishment of the purposes set forth in Sections C and D of this resolution;

E.

14. *The General Assembly,* in adopting the proposals set forth above, is fully conscious that enduring peace will not be secured solely by collective security arrangements against breaches of international peace and acts of aggression, but that a genuine and lasting peace depends also upon the observance of all the Principles and Purposes established in the Charter of the United Nations, upon the implementation of the resolutions of the Security Council, the General Assembly, and other principal organs of the United Nations intended to achieve the maintenance of international peace and security, and especially upon respect for and observance of human rights and fundamental freedoms for all and on the establishment and maintenance of conditions of economic and social well-being in all countries; and accordingly

15. *Urges* Member states to respect fully, and to intensify, joint action, in co-operation with the United Nations, to develop and stimulate universal respect for and observance of human rights and fundamental freedoms, and to intensify individual and collective efforts to achieve conditions of economic stability and social progress, particularly through the development of under-developed countries and areas.

Resolution B

For the purpose of maintaining international peace and security, in accordance with the Charter of the United Nations and, in particular, with Chapters V, VI, and VII of the Charter,

The General Assembly

Recommends to the Security Council:

That it should take the necessary steps to ensure that the action provided for under the Charter is taken with respect to threats to the peace, breaches of the peace, or acts of aggression and with respect to the peaceful settlement of disputes or situations likely to endanger the maintenance of international peace and security;

That it should devise measures for the earliest application of Articles 43, 45, 46, and 47 of the Charter of the United Nations regarding the placing of armed forces at the disposal of the Security Council by the states Member of the United Nations and the effective functioning of the Military Staff Committee.

The above disposition should in no manner prevent the General Assembly from fulfilling its functions under resolution A.

Resolution C

The General Assembly

Recognizing that the primary function of the United Nations organization is to maintain and promote peace, security, and justice among all nations,

Recognizing the responsibility of all Member states in promoting the cause of international peace in accordance with their obligations as provided in the Charter,

Recognizing that the Charter charges the Security Council with the primary responsibility for maintaining international peace and security,

Reaffirming the importance of unanimity among the permanent members of the Security Council on all problems which are likely to threaten world peace,

Recalling General Assembly resolution 190 (III) entitled "Appeal to the Great Powers to Renew their Efforts to Compose their Differences and Establish a Lasting Peace,"

Recommends to the permanent members of the Security Council that:

(a) They meet and discuss, collectively or otherwise, and, if necessary, with other states concerned, all problems which are likely to threaten international peace and hamper the activities of the United Nations, with a view to their resolving fundamental differences and reaching agreement in accordance with the spirit and letter of the Charter;

(b) They advise the General Assembly and, when it is not in session, the Members of the United Nations, as soon as appropriate, of the results of their consultations.

INDEX

443